AMERICAN GLASS CUP PLATES

BOOKS BY RUTH WEBB LEE

EARLY AMERICAN PRESSED GLASS

HANDBOOK OF EARLY AMERICAN PRESSED GLASS PATTERNS

ANTIQUE FAKES & REPRODUCTIONS

SANDWICH GLASS

SANDWICH GLASS HANDBOOK

VICTORIAN GLASS

VICTORIAN GLASS HANDBOOK

PRICE GUIDE TO PATTERN GLASS

A HISTORY OF VALENTINES

NINETEENTH-CENTURY ART GLASS

CURRENT VALUES OF ANTIQUE GLASS

LEE AND ROSE

AMERICAN GLASS CUP PLATES

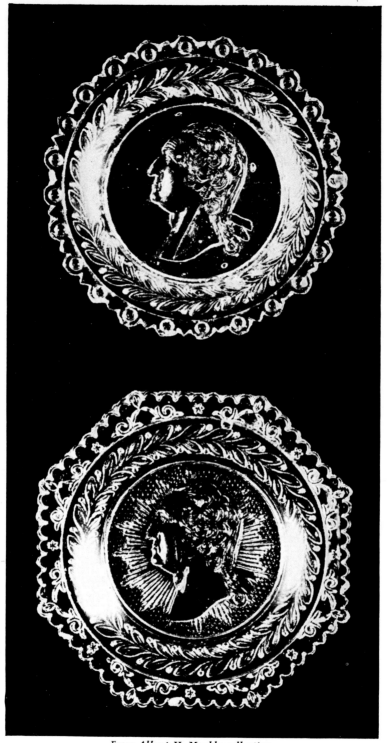

The only two known portraits of George Washington in
cup plates.

AMERICAN GLASS
CUP PLATES

The First Classified Check List and
Historical Treatise on the Subject

BY
RUTH WEBB LEE
AND
JAMES H. ROSE

LEE PUBLICATIONS

WELLESLEY HILLS   MASSACHUSETTS

FOURTH PRINTING

To Albert C. Marble

DEAN OF AMERICAN GLASS CUP PLATE COL-
LECTORS, THIS BOOK IS RESPECTFULLY AND
AFFECTIONATELY DEDICATED BY THE AUTHORS.

ACKNOWLEDGMENTS

While many collectors and dealers have lent valuable assistance in the preparation of this volume, two individuals must be given special mention for devotion "beyond the call of duty." They are Messrs. Albert C. Marble and George C. Cannon. It required Christian fortitude as well as patience and optimism for Mr. Albert C. Marble to allow us to rephotograph his collection, thereby supplying the backbone of this work. Every cup plate had to be handled several times during the process, and many of them are practically irreplaceable. He materially shortened our task by furnishing complete details concerning each plate in his, the key collection. We hope Mr. Marble may find his reward in seeing his collection perpetuated in this book, where it will be an inspiration to thousands of new collectors.

Mr. George C. Cannon also has his niche in our personal hall of fame. He not only supplied photographs and statistical data on the rarities in his collection, but spent many hours discussing with us the problems of early pressing. He has financed laboratory research into formulas and techniques and, with characteristic scholarly generosity, has permitted us to publish the results.

Mr. A. H. Heisey II, familiar through the Heisey Glassworks with the "hand shop" tradition, has patiently answered many questions about process.

Mr. George C. Cannon, Mr. Douglas Carapata, Mr. Paul Carson, Dr. Grace O. Doane, Mrs. Frederick L. Parker and Mr. Richard H. Wood have been especially faithful in reporting new discoveries in color as well as design. In many cases they have furnished photographs unobtainable elsewhere.

For cheerfully sharing their special knowledge of the New England glass field, we are indebted to Mr. George S. McKearin, Mr. George Tilden and Mrs. George W. Whichelow. Problems relating to the Philadelphia region were referred to Mrs. Harry S. High, Mr. James McGowan, Jr., Dr. A. J. Ruff and Mr. Richard H. Wood. We are grateful to them for the light cast on that local scene. In the Midwest our thanks are due to Mr. Neil C. Gest, Mr. Earl J. Knittle and Mr. J. E.

Nevil. Their combined experience in that area has been constantly at our disposal.

We are indebted to *The Magazine Antiques* and its editor, Miss Alice Winchester for permission to reprint the table of specific gravities and fluorescence observations.

It has been our earnest desire to formulate an accurate check list of cup plates against a background of abundant historical data. Without the assistance of collectors and dealers in various sections of the country a great deal of basic data would not have been available. It is impossible to name each one but we wish to thank them here for their suggestions and cooperation.

Last but by no means least, the co-authors are under great obligation to Mary Longfellow Rose for solving many a knotty problem. Her patience has been akin to Job's.

RUTH WEBB LEE
JAMES H. ROSE

EXPLANATION

Cup plate collecting is not the unexplored province that pattern glass was when *Early American Pressed Glass* appeared in 1931. Had it not been for the dean of cup plate collectors, Mr. Albert C. Marble, very little would be known about them today. Early in Mr. Marble's collecting career, he began to photograph and number his plates in order of acquisition. As time went on, he discovered more and more variants of plates already acquired until he had accumulated a staggering number of both plates and photographs. Though importuned at various times, Mr. Marble declined to undertake a book on this subject, and so we, with his endorsement and "blessings" have made this venture in recognition of its growing need. The authors of this volume not only hesitated to change his cup plate numbers, they felt it almost a sacrilege to do so. To our deep regret, this has been necessary in order to bring related plates together in their respective groups, for the benefit of thousands of new collectors.

It has been our desire to make this book as complete and easily workable as possible, both as a reference volume and check list. A copious amount of technical data will be found for those interested in the details of cup plate manufacture extending from the earliest days. The cup plates themselves are illustrated fully and are accompanied by all available information as confirmed by leading experts.

A practical system of numbering was necessarily devised in order to keep this book up to date whenever new finds appear. It is for this reason that the reader will frequently encounter notations such as "Nos. 5 to 7 left open for new discoveries." To shorten the wording, this finally resolved itself into "Nos. 5 to 7 left open." Supplements will be printed from time to time. When new plates or new colors are found, it would be greatly appreciated if the finder would notify Mr. James H. Rose.

The numbering system is simple, but some explanations are in order. First, a number indicates a design. Any change in a design die (for example, the addition of rays behind Washington's bust) means a new number. A following letter, A, B, C, etc., means a change in rim or serration pattern.

Other margin notations may read, "Nos. 5 and 6 described in text." This simply indicates that those numbers are so closely related and similar that photographs of the minor differences are unnecessary.

We wish to call to the attention of the reader the difficulty encountered in photographing so many cup plates with respect to their varying backgrounds, when shown on the same plate. We particularly realize the great value of showing related cup plates in their proper groupings. When plates with a stippled background are pictured with others having plain or faintly patterned backgrounds, each plate cannot be photographed with the best results in detail. Then again, when eight plates are in a certain group, as against perhaps three or four in another, the size may not appear in its proper proportion. We urge collectors to note the exact sizes as given in the check list. In a few instances we had to depend on photographs of plates which Mr. Marble does not own. These came in from owners who went to no end of trouble to send them to us, but usually the size of these pictures did not correspond with ours, and therefore had to be either reduced or enlarged. In several cases plates were deliberately enlarged for detail, when it seemed particularly necessary to do so. We earnestly hope the photographs and text will give full satisfaction.

RUTH WEBB LEE
JAMES H. ROSE

CONTENTS

xiii

ILLUSTRATIONS

CONVENTIONAL GROUPS

AMERICAN GLASS CUP PLATES

Chapter I

INTRODUCTION TO CUP PLATES

There are a host of enthusiastic collectors of American glass cup plates today, as well as established dealers who have specialized in them for years. Thus, in discussing these little plates, we assume that nearly everyone is aware that they were used over a century ago to hold the teacups after the very hot tea was poured into saucers to cool. It should be kept in mind that tea drinking originated with the Chinese, who took theirs quite hot, and that early cups were often handleless. When filled, they were much too warm to hold with comfort. Cup plates performed a multiple service—they not only served as coasters for teacups, but at the same time kept the table linen from being soiled, or a bare table from being marred. In addition, they provided a cooling medium. Our forefathers, one hundred and fifty years ago, did not consider it bad manners to drink tea from their saucers. The great Dr. Samuel Johnson absorbed his scalding hot, and the sound of his cautious intake was audible in the neighborhood. Students of our Colonial period will tell you that, before the Boston Tea Party, people asked for a *dish* of tea.

China or pottery cup plates preceded those in glass, but they were largely made in Europe and, therefore, do not have a place in this book. Pressed glass could be produced much more cheaply than china in this country; so, as machinery for pressing glass was perfected, it is not surprising that among the earliest items made were numerous cup plates. While we record a half dozen or so blown glass cup plates, or what have become known to collectors as cup plates because of their size, it is reasonable to assume that these were much too fragile to withstand everyday use, and so were not made in quantity. Our early pressed glass plates are indicative of mechanical development as it began to expand in this country. It is another typical instance of the American genius for replacing hand with machine technique.

While Bakewell & Company of Pittsburgh were granted a patent for a pressed glass knob in 1825, we believe the first examples of these pressed glass cup plates were made at Sandwich, because the first recorded pieces of pressed glass produced in the form of a tumbler or dish were made by the Boston and Sandwich Glass Company in this small village on Cape Cod, in 1826. That other nearby factories were quick to follow suit is evidenced by a sales sheet of the New England Glass Company, under date of May 2, 1829, listing three dozen 3 inch cup plates at $1.50 and three dozen 3½ inch cup plates at $1.87. On the same bill are listed a half-dozen cup plate "footed bulb lamps" at $1.12, proving that these early lamps were being made simultaneously with some of the earliest plates. Whale oil was utilized as a burning fluid for the lamps at this period.

A number of our earlier writers stressed the cheapness of pressed glass, seemingly forgetting that over one hundred years ago labor costs, not to mention living costs, were proportionately lower. Certainly those writers could not complain of the same pressed glass pieces being cheap today. Prices have kept in tune with our times!

As to what constitutes a cup plate, we believe this problem well nigh solves itself, since it is obvious that the glass would have to be of the period when cup plates were fashionable, and the center well of the plate of a size to accommodate a cup. We have set the proper size in diameter as being from 2⅝ inches up to, but not including, 4¼ inches. A smaller plate would fall into the miniature, or toy, size and the 4¼ inch into the so-called toddy plate. This is not to say that the larger plates, especially if the centers were small, could not have been intended as cup plates. We simply have no proof. The problem of what the user did with a spoon has always presented another interesting question which we have not solved to our satisfaction.

In studying the progress of patterns in cup plates, it will be found that they reflect, over their entirety, the best cross section obtainable in any American collection of the development of design from the geometric cut glass designs stemming from the late XVIII century, through the beginning of the Greek Revival to its end in the Gothic Revival, and thence on to our well-known pattern glass. Aside from the few blown glass specimens known, the earliest cup plates are those illustrated on Plates 2 and 3. They were thick and clumsy compared with those glistening jewels in lacy glass which followed within a comparatively short length of time.

The duration of popularity for cup plates would date from approximately 1826 or 1827 into the 1850's. Later there appeared a few small plates in the field of pattern glass of the type collectible in sets of table-ware, which were obviously meant for butter chips. Cup plates were no longer fashionable, but butter chips were; while a few of these are listed because Mr. Marble showed them, they have been placed in their proper period at the end of the check list.

There are many ways in which cup plates could be classified, but none of these is completely satisfactory. A system based solely on design simplifies the student's search through the check list for the illustration of a particular plate, but it does not show either the vital chronological progression of design and technique or the equally important relationship between plates whose designs may be as far apart as the poles. A system founded on a purely chronological basis has the same faults—no one but the expert could locate the cut of a specific plate. Division into factory groups, although it seems the most logical approach, would also require vast experience before a collector could find a certain design. When this book was first proposed, advanced collectors all over the country were consulted concerning their views on arrangement. Their replies were almost unanimously in favor of a classification based on origin. When it was pointed out, however, that under this plan such natural groups as the eagles, hearts and sunbursts would be scattered throughout the check list, the consensus of opinion was that the system should be modified so that these groups would be kept intact.

Accordingly, the classification used here is a compromise. We have tried to retain the virtues of all systems and, at the same time, to avoid their most obvious disadvantages. In the first place, the plates are divided into chronological periods. To do this, we have had to assume that there was a regular sequence of both designs and techniques all over the country. But who can prove that innovations at a factory under progressive management did not antedate by as much as five or even ten years the adoption of identical improvements by some ultra-conservative glassmaker? Nevertheless, where the evidence based on design and technique seems to show that a specific plate was made at a particular time, this has been accepted as final. All such dating, however, applies only to the birth of a mechanical improvement or a design. It is certain, for example, that certain commercially successful patterns conceived in an early period were still being pressed at a much later date. To a considerable degree, the temperament and background of the individual manufacturer were the deciding factors. In conservative, cautious New

England once an expensive design die was acquired, the tendency was to use it as long as possible. The men who went West, on the other hand, were likely to be of a more restless, impatient, adventurous sort. Patterns there seem to have been scrapped for reasons that would have seemed frivolous to New England.

The plates are divided, then, into the following main groups:

1. Cup plates made before the invention of the pressing machine. These are blown glass. Since no one seems to know just when the vogue for cup plates started, no date can be set for the beginning of the period; and since blowing continued as a technique side by side with pressing, it is also impossible to assign a date for the end of the period.
2. Plates whose molds were made after the invention of pressing, but prior to the invention of the cap-ring. From the fragmentary evidence available, the limits of the period may be set, roughly, at from 1826 or 1827 to 1828 or 1829. The designs of these plates are, on the whole, geometric and, as a rule, they do not have stippled backgrounds.
3. Plates made with a cap-ring, frequently the wide, experimental ring of Figures 3-E and 3-F, but sometimes a narrow ring, and mostly before the stippled and other forms of lacy background were used. The dates of the period are approximately 1827 or 1828 to 1830. As you see, there is some overlapping of the dates of this and the previous period. Even if we knew the exact date of the basic cap-ring patent, it would be impossible to say just when any particular factory started to use it.
4. Plates made during the lacy period. Usually, but not always, these have stippled, engine-turned, lined or other backgrounds, and the vast majority of them were pressed in cap-ring molds. The period extends from about 1829 or 1830 to possibly as late as 1840.
5. Plates that due to increased competition and other economic factors are more cheaply made. Less attention is paid to design. Stippling, when present, is likely to be the uneven, late type shown in the Ringgolds. The dates appear to be from about 1838 or 1840 to 1850 or later.
6. Plates that are purely commercial trash, made after 1850 without a trace of pride in workmanship. In this period cup plates are no longer fashionable. The market probably consisted of people of very limited means who could afford neither fine craftsmanship nor fine glass.

After these chronological groups come special groups based on design, as follows:

7. Hearts. These are cup plates where the heart motif is a major factor in the design. In a few instances where the heart is a minor factor, plates have been listed in one of the original main divisions. In the section devoted to hearts, we have tried to retain a chronological arrangement.
8. Sunbursts. A great many plates have the sunburst as a centering device. These are treated elsewhere. Here are grouped only those plates having the sunburst as their main ornamental feature. No chronological sequence is

possible but, for convenient reference, the plates are arranged according to the number of rays in the sunburst.

9. Historicals. The term, while inaccurate ("commemorative" would be better), is sanctioned by long use and is self-explanatory. The historicals are subdivided into:

    A. Busts
    B. Log cabins
    C. Ships
    D. Monuments, including the so-called "Maid of the Mist" which is primarily a bridge
    E. Eagles

10. Semi-historicals, so-called. Here, again, the heading is inaccurate. In our opinion, some of these plates should have been considered under "Historicals," while others should be relegated to their proper place among the "Conventionals." The category has been long established, however, and to break it up at this late date would be confusing to many collectors. It contains such plates as the Steam Coach, Harp and Star, the Plows, the Lyres, the Beehives, the Erin Go Bragh, the Wedding Day and the Hound. This group is a sort of catch-all.

These are followed by plates that are collected and valued by cup plate collectors but which, for various reasons, are not considered cup plates under the arbitrary limits set for this book. These are:

11. Pontil-marked plates, not cup plates because of use.
12. Toddy plates, not cup plates because of size.
13. Foreign plates, English, French and Belgian, eliminated because of origin.
14. Butter pats and children's toys.
15. Fakes and modern plates.

Within the framework provided by the six chronological groups and also in the nine other divisions, cup plates are classified in series. A series is usually, but not always, the result of combining one design die with two or more serration patterns. In other words, the design remains substantially the same, while the rim pattern varies. In the early days of cup plate collecting, design was everything and rim variations were considered to be of little importance. Gradually, it began to dawn on a few collectors that serrations and other rim treatments were a clue to origin and, therefore, are of more significance than the central design. The commercially successful patterns of one factory were sometimes copied by a competitor (in collectors' jargon this practice is called "pirating"); more often, a basic concept, the eagle, the log cabin, the Roman Rosette, was used by several factories. For this reason, central design is not a reliable guide to origin. Serration and rim patterns are another matter. The ultimate consumer might, and probably did, demand a pattern in which a particular motif predominated and may even have preferred a rope to a plain rim. We can be sure, however, that this hypothetical buyer did not insist that the desired pattern have 44 even serrations. Counting scallops is a pleasure reserved for the present-day collector. It is evident that no moldmaker in his right mind would go to the trouble of cutting a competitor's rim pattern into a surface die or cap-ring when the consumer was utterly indifferent to such things. These base-mold assemblies (surface die and cap-ring combinations), furthermore, were so constructed that they could be used with more than one design die. If, then, it can be established that a certain type of rim was used at a particular factory, it follows that all plates having this characteristic edge, no matter what their central pattern may be, originated at the same glass factory. Such a factory may be, and usually is, nameless, but its general location can frequently be determined with reasonable accuracy.

In spite of its simplicity, this method is not foolproof. The mere fact that two plates, otherwise dissimilar, have 44 even scallops and measure 3¼ inches in diameter is not enough to demonstrate a common source. The contours of the scallops must be identical and, since these range from approximately the half-circle to an arc that is nearly flat, comparisons must be made with great care. The only perfect way of doing this would be to use a low-power, comparative microscope, but the cost would be prohibitive. In the check list, although we have used reasonable care in determining relationships by comparing rim patterns, it is not impossible that errors have crept in where rim patterns seem the same but are not actually identical.

The measurements used in this book are, for the most part, taken from data generously furnished by Mr. Albert C. Marble from plates in his collection. Very few cup plates are exactly circular, so that a diameter taken in one direction may vary from another taken at right angles to it by as much as 1/16 of an inch. Consequently, all measurements are approximate. On rare occasions slight deviations from Mr. Marble's figures are noted in the text. In no case should these be considered as criticism of his accuracy. Such irregularities are important because they show either that two almost identical rings were in use, or that cleaning scale from a base-mold assembly had increased its inside diameter. In the latter circumstance, the larger of two plates was pressed subsequently to the other.

Attributions, when given, are based on density of distribution, characteristic rim pattern, design typical of given areas and, to a limited extent, on color. In the past, a few collectors have questioned attributions founded on distribution. This attitude seems to us unreasonable. In all other branches of collecting, such evidence is considered valid. It is challenged in the cup plate field only by those who, completely ignoring the probabilities, think that all cup plates were made at Sandwich. Ideally, the attribution is worked out somewhat as follows: if certain cup plates turn up much more frequently in, say, New England than elsewhere, there is a suspicion that they were made in that neighborhood. If, later, it is discovered that many of these designs have a rim pattern or show peculiarities of design or technique not commonly found in other areas, the suspicion becomes an assumption. Then, if other plates with these same characteristics, but with different designs, keep on turning up, and investigation shows that their distribution likewise is to all intents and purposes confined to New England, the theory comes pretty close to being a certainty. Finally, if one of this now large group of plates is found in emerald-green or yellow, or opaque turquoise-blue or "silver stain," colors not so far associated with the output of Philadelphia or Midwestern glassworks, there can be no doubt as to New England origin. Naturally, such complete data are seldom available for any given plate and, luckily, such an overwhelming mass of evidence is not necessary. Suppose that a clear glass cup plate of hitherto unknown design turns up in, of all places, Salt Lake City. Distribution, naturally, means nothing. But, if it has *exactly* the same serration pattern as some plates of known New England origin, the new find may be attributed to the same source with a good deal of confidence.

While attribution to an area in most cases is comparatively safe, assignment to a particular factory is not. In this book the country's glass-producing region of the cup plate period has been divided into three main glassfields: New England, the Philadelphia area and the Midwest. As you know, New England had two large factories pressing glass, The Boston & Sandwich Glass Company and the New England Glass Company (the latter hereafter referred to as NEG), and at least one other smaller factory, at Providence, concerning whose product nothing is known. Many cup plates in this book are assigned to either

Sandwich or NEG, but none to Providence. If, as seems possible, some were made there, and if New England techniques and styles were adhered to, they will be found assigned incorrectly to either NEG or Sandwich. In fact, all attributions to a specific factory, with the exception of those assigned to R. B. Curling & Sons, who marked one of its series, should be viewed with some skepticism. They are based on little more than tradition and are, therefore, tentative. Attributions to an area are much more reliable and are, to a considerable extent, confirmed by technical data. (See Table on pages 12 and 13.)

Just as New England had its Providence, so, too, the other glassfields had marginal factories. The Philadelphia area had such a glassworks near Jersey City which, judging by its marked salt, followed NEG practice. If Baltimore made cup plates they are probably attributed here to the Philadelphia region. Similarly, the Midwest with its largest factories in and around Pittsburgh had others, such as Ritchie and Wheat, in nearby Wheeling. While it is unlikely that we will ever be able to make truly accurate distinctions between the products of neighboring factories, it has seemed best to note in the check list any peculiarity of distribution, history of ownership, traditional attribution and other allied evidence that might otherwise be unavailable to future investigators.

Statements about the comparative rarity of anything that was produced mechanically can never be more than tentative. The rarities given in the check list are based on twenty-five years of personal experience, revised according to the particular knowledge of the leading specialists in the field. As a further check, the want lists of leading collectors were carefully searched. Thus, if a certain plate of, let us say, New England origin is extremely rare in the authors' opinion and inquiry shows that Mrs. Whichelow, Mr. Tilden and Mr. McKearin, whose combined knowledge of the New England glassfield is encyclopedic, also find the plate to be equally rare and, if the plate appears time after time on the want lists of leading collectors, there can be little doubt that an "extremely rare" classification is amply justified.

Seven categories have been set up and are given below in descending order of rarity:

1. Unique
2. Extremely rare
3. Very rare

4. Rare
5. Scarce
6. Plentiful
7. Common

In a few cases in the second bracket, the number of extant specimens known to the authors is given. This, of course, is a risky business. Obviously, there are many collections unknown to us, as well as many plates still undiscovered by dealers and collectors. Nevertheless, in this second bracket it seemed necessary to distinguish between the rarity of the round Washington, of which but two specimens are known, and another plate in the same category of which, like No. 612, seventeen examples are known.

For the most part, however, no one really knows just how many examples of a particular plate exist. And so, below the first two divisions, supply in relation to demand becomes a deciding factor. Who knows, and indeed who cares, whether there are 200 or 500 examples of the Barberry No. 417, in dealers' hands at the moment? As long as beginners, dealers as well as collectors, understand that it is a common plate and, consequently, worth very little money, the exact extent of a comparatively vast floating supply is unimportant. The Barberry is, of course, an extreme case. Perhaps a better illustration would be No. 285, of which there are many known specimens, but whose design is so universally attractive that all collectors want an example. It is evident that such a plate is going to be harder to find than another less engaging plate which, from the point of view of numbers extant, is actually scarcer, but which is in demand only by advanced collectors. The "plentiful" category suggested by Mrs. Whichelow was set up to cover this very situation. Plates in this classification, by actual count, would probably be found to exist in about the same number of specimens as other less desirable plates listed here as common. Availability, the relative ease of acquisition, is the standard, not the number of extant examples.

In point of fact, no cup plate is common. If several hundred new collectors were to start tomorrow, each having as his goal a complete collection, every cup plate in this book, even the Barberry, would become rare. On the other hand, there is no doubt that there are many plates still in private hands and in collections unknown to the writers, whose existence is not even suspected. We fully expect a flood of letters about these shortly after the publication of this book; it takes just one letter to change a "unique" listing to "extremely rare," and not too many letters to drop a plate from "extremely" rare to "very rare." Cup plates were sold in sets of dozens and half dozens and not infrequently turn up that way today.

No one recognizes the impermanent nature of these listings any better than we do. Nevertheless, however imperfect they may be, they represent the consensus of expert opinion as of the Fall of 1947.

One last word of warning. It is impossible to translate comparative rarity into terms of dollars and cents. A single example will suffice. Both the round Washington and the No. 490 sunburst are known by but two specimens. The first is worth at least fifty times as much as the second. Any dealer or collector who decides that one unique plate is as valuable as another is in for a sad awakening.

TABLE

Cup Plate Number	Specific Gravity	Visible Fluorescence		Attribution by experts
		Color	Intensity	
R-13-C	3.2091	Bluish	1	Eastern
R-39	2.8423	Yellowish Green	2	Eastern *
R-48	3.2212	Bluish (Green)	2	Eastern
R-101	3.1422	Green (Blue)	1	Eastern
R-106	3.1410	Bluish	1	Eastern
R-120	3.2222	Bluish	2	Western *
R-127-A	3.0890	Green (Blue)	2	Western
R-130	2.9646	Yellow Green	2	Western
R-136-A	2.9793	Yellowish Green	2	Western
R-157-B	2.9360	Yellow Green	1	Western
R-164-A	2.9794	Green (Blue)	1	Western
R-176	2.9018	Pale Salmon	1	Western
R-177	3.1861	Bluish	2	Eastern
R-178-B	2.5351	Yellow Green	3	Western
R-180	3.1359	Green (Blue)	1	Western *
R-184-B	2.9294	Yellowish Green	2	Western
R-197-A	2.8563	Salmon (Rose)	2	Western
R-203	3.0727	Greenish (Blue)	1	Western
R-216-B	3.0270	Yellow Green	1	Western
R-226-A	3.2200	Bluish (Green)	2	Eastern
R-229-B	3.1536	Bluish (Green)	1	Eastern
R-240	3.1649	Bluish	2	Eastern
R-242	3.2556	Bluish	1	Eastern

TABLE

Cup Plate Number	Specific Gravity	Visible Fluorescence		Attribution by experts
		Color	Intensity	
R-257-A	3.1049	Bluish	2	Eastern
R-260	3.2189	Blue	3	Eastern
R-267	2.8757	Yellowish Green	3	Eastern *
R-275	3.2461	Bluish	2	Eastern
R-564-B	3.1105	Bluish	1	Eastern
R-585-A	3.1172	Bluish	1	Eastern
R-610-A	3.2267	Bluish	2	Eastern
R-655	3.1777	Bluish	2	Western *
R-656	3.0322	Green (Blue)	1	Western
R-661	2.8433	Yellow Green	2	Eastern *
R-666-A	3.1797	Bluish (Green)	1	Eastern
R-670	3.0775	Yellowish Green	3	Western
R-676-B	3.1575	Bluish	1	Western *
R-677-G	2.8535	Yellowish Green	3	Western
R-694	2.9478	Yellowish Green	3	Western

These statistics were compiled by Penniman and Browne, research chemists, for Mr. George C. Cannon and are reprinted here through the courtesy of *The Magazine Antiques.* Fluorescence observations were made with a high-pressure mercury tube and a corex filter. The background for these tests is the hypothesis that Western glassmakers normally used less lead in their mixes than was customary in Eastern practice. If the theory was correct, the smaller lead content would show up in lower specific gravity and, possibly, in typical fluorescence. The sampling is too small to be conclusive, but seems to indicate that usually, but not always, plates having a specific gravity of over 3.100, and with a basic blue reaction under ultra-violet light, are of Eastern origin, while those whose specific gravity is below 3.0900 and show a greenish (typically of a yellow hue) or salmon colored reaction are Midwestern.

Of the 38 tests shown, 31, roughly 81%, agree with the conclusions of experts whose opinions were based on distribution and style. In the seven plates indicated by asterisks, the tests are in disagreement with expert opinion. Two of these Midwestern plates, however, R-120 and R-655, are among the earliest of Western pressings, so that it is safe to assume they were made before the characteristic Western low-lead mixes were developed. A third plate, R-676-B, was made by Curling's Fort Pitt Glassworks as an advertisement, and its abnormally high lead content may be due to the manufacturer's pride in the marked specimens of his factory's output. If these three explanations are valid, agreement between technical and expert opinion approaches 89%.

CHEMICAL ANALYSES OF FOUR GLASS CUP PLATES

PENNIMAN & BROWNE

CHEMICAL ENGINEERS

ANALYSTS

341 St. Paul Place

Baltimore, April 7, 1944.

CERTIFICATE OF ANALYSIS

No. 208839–41
Sample of Glass Cup Plates
From Mr. George C. Cannon
Marked A Henry Clay, B Eagle, C Bee Hive

Marked	A Henry Clay R-564-B	B Eagle R-670	C Bee Hive R-694
	Per Cent	*Per Cent*	*Per Cent*
Silica .... (SiO_2)	52.01	55.46	57.64
Iron Oxide .... (Fe_2O_3)	0.32	0.30	0.32
Alumina .... (Al_2O_3)	0.33	0.60	0.43
Titanium Oxide ...... (TiO_2)	0.07	0.20	0.09
Lead Oxide .... (PbO)	35.66	29.75	24.81
Calcium Oxide ...... (CaO)	0.00	0.00	0.00
Magnesium Oxide .... (MgO)	0.00	0.00	0.00
Boron Trioxide ...... (B_2O_3)	0.10	0.10	0.10
Sodium Oxide .... (Na_2O)	0.91	1.60	1.62
Potassium Oxide ..... (K_2O)	9.88	11.48	11.46
Fluorine .... (F)	0.04	0.02	0.02
Sulphuric Anhydride .. (SO_3)	0.05	0.05	0.05
Chlorine .... (Cl)	0.28	0.09	0.19
Manganese Oxide .... (Mn_2O_3)	0.03	0.03	0.02
Copper Oxide .... (CuO)	0.01	0.004	0.01
Loss @ 105° C.	0.05	0.12	0.05
Total	99.74	99.80	96.81

PENNIMAN & BROWNE

CHEMICAL ENGINEERS

ANALYSTS

341 St. Paul Place

Baltimore, April 7, 1944.

CERTIFICATE OF ANALYSIS

No. 208839–41
Sample of Glass Cup Plates
From Mr. George C. Cannon
Marked A, B, C (R-564-B, R-670, R-694)

QUALITATIVE SPECTROGRAPHIC ANALYSIS

The three glass samples A, B, C show spectroscopically essentially the same composition, except for small changes noted below (Sn, Mo). Lead is by far the predominant element. The following elements were found, or looked for and found absent. It is to be noted that the spectroscopic sensitivity is not always the same. In general, the sensitivity of the non-metals is less than for typical metals. The following elements cannot be found spectroscopically: S, F, Cl, O, N, etc.

Strong: Lead very strong
           Silicon
           Titanium
           Sodium
           Potassium

Medium: Iron
           Manganese
           Boron
           Aluminum

Weak: Magnesium
           Calcium
           Copper
           Tin much stronger in A than in B and C
           Molybdenum strongest in B, weakest in A
           Barium
           Silver

Very weak or doubtful:
           Zirconium
           Vanadium

Absent: Co, Ni, Zn, Sb, P, As.
No rare earths found in conspicuous amounts.

PENNIMAN & BROWNE

CHEMICAL ENGINEERS

ANALYSTS

341 St. Paul Place

Baltimore, June 20, 1944.

CERTIFICATE OF ANALYSIS

No. 209594
Sample of Glass Cup Plate
From Mr. George C. Cannon
Marked Ringgold Cup Plate—"D" (R-585-A)

QUALITATIVE SPECTROGRAPHIC ANALYSIS

The following elements were found spectroscopically with an indication of the strength of the lines which represent them:

Strong:	Lead
	Silicon
	Titanium
	Sodium
	Potassium
Medium:	Iron
	Manganese
	Boron
	Aluminum
	Lithium
Weak:	Magnesium
	Calcium
	Copper
	Tin
	Barium
	Silver

Very weak or doubtful: Molybdenum
Zirconium
Absent: Co, Ni, Zn, Sb, P, As, Mo, Au, V.
No rare earths found in conspicuous amounts.

The analysis of this sample is almost identical with the analysis of the three samples previously analyzed. There is indication that the amount of titanium is slightly less, that tin is less, and molybdenum considerably less, but these latter two elements vary considerably among the former three samples. No essential differences were noted. It may be added that glasses of different origin usually show very pronounced differences.

PENNIMAN & BROWNE

CHEMICAL ENGINEERS

ANALYSTS

341 St. Paul Place

Baltimore, June 20, 1944.

CERTIFICATE OF ANALYSIS

No. 209594

Sample of Glass Cup Plate

From Mr. George C. Cannon

Marked Ringgold Cup Plate—"D" (R-585-A)

		Per Cent
Silica	(SiO_2)	56.68
Iron Oxide	(Fe_2O_3)	0.76
Alumina	(Al_2O_3)	0.04
Titanium Oxide	(TiO_2)	0.10
Lead Oxide	(PbO)	31.64
Calcium Oxide	(CaO)	0.04
Magnesium Oxide	(MgO)	0.19
Boron Trioxide	(B_2O_2)	0.17
Sodium Oxide	(Na_2O)	1.89
Potassium Oxide	(K_2O)	8.48
Fluorine	(F)	0.03
Sulphuric Anhydride	(SO_3)	0.03
Chlorine	(Cl)	0.06
Manganese Oxide	(MnO)	0.04
Copper Oxide	(CuO)	0.01
Total		100.16

Chapter II

EARLY PROCESS OF MANUFACTURE

While a comprehensive knowledge of the formulas and methods used in making glass is desirable, it is not absolutely necessary in order to understand pressing and pressed glass. The process is one of very great complexity and its thorough discussion would add undue bulk to an already unwieldy book. Moreover, it seems reasonably safe to assume that the collector of, and the dealer in, antique glass has some knowledge of the procedure; so we propose to consider here only the glassmaker's failures, his blunders that resulted in plates which, to him at least, were regrettable accidents. Today such plates, freaks if you will, are highly regarded, not through perversity or oversophistication or even because of their relative rarity, but because they demonstrate the problems confronting a glassmaker in perfecting a new technique.

If, then, the sand used for a particular batch was improperly cleansed of impurities, especially iron, the finished product had a faint greenish tint. Most pressed glass is, in cross section, much thicker than blown glass, with a resulting increase in the depth and intensity of such tints. Consequently, glass used in pressed wares to be commercially acceptable had to be clearer than that commonly used in blown pieces of the period. This superior clarity, other factors being equal, could be and was achieved by the addition of a very small quantity of manganese to the batch as a decolorizer. But manganese is powerful stuff and a shade too much of it produced a glass with an amethyst tint, an effect from the point of view of the glassmaker every bit as undesirable as the green tint he was trying to overcome. The amounts of either iron or manganese sufficient to cause these tints are so small that the wonder is we do not find more of them. The only possible conclusion is that the early glass manufacturer was far more precise in measuring his ingredients than we have suspected. A good idea of the complexity of the glass formulas of the 1835–1847 period can be obtained by careful study of tables on pages 14, 15, 16 and 17, which give, respectively, quantitative and spectroscopic analyses of four clear glass cup plates.

The preceding paragraph should not be construed to mean that all green or amethyst tints are due to carelessness in washing sand or to too heavy a hand in adding manganese. There is considerable evidence that many such tints ensue from the too sketchy cleaning of pots that had been used previously for mixes of colored glasses. Thus, if a certain plate exists in a deep green or deep amethyst (or, for that matter, blue or opal), it frequently follows that examples showing faint tints of these colors are also known or will eventually be found. Used cautiously, evidence of this kind can lead to interesting conclusions. We know, for example, that one type of the Fort Pitt eagle occurs in blue, a deep amethyst and quite often in amethyst tints. The other two recorded varieties of this eagle, however, are not found in tints. The only explanation that comes to mind is that these light amethyst tints were pressed from a batch of glass made in the pot that had previously held the deep amethyst mix, and also that at this particular time the variant mold assemblies, the even-serration and plain rim types, either were not in use or, possibly, had not been made. Statistical data on tints are also of great help in supporting attributions. Let us suppose that a hypothetical glassworks, Factory X, can be assumed to have made certain rare plates in deep amethyst or deep green, and that variants of these plates are known in corresponding tints. Suppose further that, in the same area where these plates are found, other designs turn up vaguely similar to the first group in design or technique, or both. If the second group is known only in clear glass, an attribution may be made to Factory X, but this is at best no more than tentative. If, however, a few characteristic tints are found, the case for a common origin is strengthened and sometimes even clinched. Having leaned rather heavily on this method of making attributions, we feel obliged to point out its dangers. It is impossible to distinguish between an amethyst tint due to an overdose of manganese inserted into the basic mix, and an excess chargeable to careless cleaning of pots. In the absence of other supporting indications (distribution, design, technique, etc.), inferences drawn from tints are unreliable.

So much for tints. Not infrequently one sees cup plates with cloudy, "frosted" and even deeply pitted surfaces. Opinions differ as to the cause of this phenomenon, but the school of thought we follow here holds that it is due to an overabundance of soda in the mix. Soda in large quantities increases the solubility of glass in water, and heightens its vulnerability to attack by the carbonic acid gas in the atmosphere. These "sick" cup plates simply have too much soda in their composition, and are slowly disintegrating. Eventually, the plate will be completely dissolved, but this need not worry you. The process is a very slow one and, even though you may be collecting for posterity when you buy a sick plate, your grandchildren can count on inheriting it, looking little, if any, worse than it does today.

In accounting for this superfluity of soda, we must digress a bit. Although coal was used as a fuel in glass furnaces in England as early as the XVIII century, the change from wood to coal in this country occurred during the cup plate period. Unfortunately, it is impossible to assign any definite date for this transition. It varied from factory to factory, depending on the exhaustion of the local supply of wood, the availability of coal as a substitute, the costs not only of the fuel but of the covered or hooded pots necessary in coal-fired furnaces and, probably, on the conservatism of the individual plant owner. If we set the decade 1840–1850 as an artificial dividing line between wood-burning furnaces, on the one hand, and coal-burning furnaces on the other, we shall not be far out of line. However, it must be kept constantly in mind that some factories, through progressive management or fortunate location, used coal earlier than this, and that other factories clung to wood-burning until long after the Civil War. The highest temperature that can be attained using wood as fuel is about 2200° Fahrenheit. This is not enough, as you will see when you check the Fluid Points and Working Temperatures given at the foot of the Table on page 419. This maximum could be, and must have been, stepped up by the additions of resin to the fuel, by using forced draft or, possibly, by preheating the air. Or, and now we get to the point, the manufacturer could increase the amount of soda in the mix. Soda expedites the melting of glass and lowers the range of working temperatures. Unfortunately, as we have seen earlier, it also affects the quality. Since this deterioration seems to have been a delayed reaction and was not readily apparent for some time, possibly not for years, it speaks well for the conscience of the manufacturer of the period that he did not more often decide to cut costs (the cooking and "fining" of glass takes from 30 to 40 hours and consumes enormous quantities of fuel) at the expense of quality. Certain cup plates, notably Nos. 68, 435 and 678 are nearly always found sick; others, like No. 69, are frequently sick and, finally, almost any plate may turn up showing some degree of surface corrosion. In the first instance, the conclusion must be drawn either that the manufacturer intentionally made bad glass or that he was experimenting with new formulas and overdid it. Sporadic sickness, however, can be the result of a lone pot of bad glass, a thing which can very easily happen in the best-intentioned and best-managed glassworks. A collector should not object to sick examples of very rare plates, especially where sickness is characteristic of factory practice, as it seems to have been in that early factory in the Philadelphia area (the Union Glass Works) that made Nos. 68 and 69. The check list is a good guide to this. Where a plate is mentioned as commonly or always found sick, frosted and even pitted specimens are acceptable additions to any collection.

"Bubbly" glass is another result of this natural desire to conserve fuel. After a batch has been melted, the long, slow process of cooking out the impurities begins. These rise to the top, where they are skimmed off. Various gases form during the process and these too ascend. If they have not all escaped, if the cooking is interrupted or prematurely stopped, a bubbly glass results. Such glass seldom occurs in cup plates. Many plates have a few bubbles, but we are considering here only those containing a myriad of tiny bubbles. No. 154-A is the only plate that comes to mind that commonly turns up so, and even here the odds that all came from a single faulty pot of glass are great, since the rim variants are of satisfactory glass. Bubbly glass for the most part is from a bottle-glass factory.

Still another blemish that gets into the glass during melting and fining is the so-called "sand pit" or "lime spot." Once in a while these terms may be accurate, but usually the bit of foreign material is a piece of the pot, not sand or lime. In a very delicate lacy plate, such a flaw should probably be considered objectionable. In early or crude plates and in most Midwestern plates, they are usually of little consequence. When very large and unsightly, they sometimes add a sort of perverse attractiveness to a plate.

So far, all the phenomena considered came about before the plates were pressed. They were of accidental nature and so are the exception rather than the rule. Another set of surface manifestations was, so to speak, inherent in the then new process of pressing, resulting from the mechanical treatment of the glass; these persisted from the beginning until nearly the close of the lacy period, roughly the decade 1827–1837, when they were largely overcome. To understand them, some knowledge of the technique of pressing and its peculiar problems is required.

When the melted glass is ready to be worked, a pressing machine is brought up close to the furnace to facilitate handling. The machine illustrated in Fig. 1 is taken from a cut in Apsley Pellatt's book, *Curiosities of Glass Making*. It is primitive and, therefore, probably a

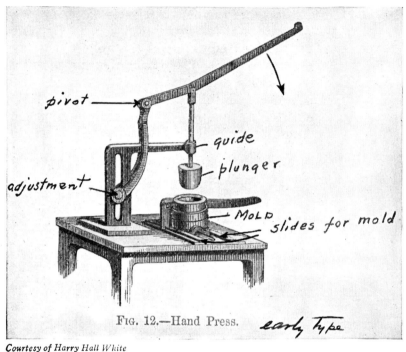

FIG. 12.—Hand Press.

Courtesy of Harry Hall White

Fig. 1

Early type of Hand Press for pressing glass.

fairly early English version of an American invention. Nevertheless, it seems likely that the first American pressings were made in a similar, but not necessarily identical, contrivance. The host of patents on the pressing process filed between 1826 and 1830 is sufficient evidence that this rudimentary mechanism was rapidly improved, so that perhaps as early as 1830 (though more likely several years later) something resembling the vastly improved press shown in Fig. 2 was in common use. Between the two extremes, there must have been a number of presses transitional in nature but each more efficient and possibly more complicated than the preceding one.

Once one of these pressing machines, of the type currently in use, has been rolled up to a convenient position near the furnace, it is ready for the actual pressing. A member of the pressing crew now inserts an iron rod into the pot of hot glass and, by rotating the rod rapidly, collects on it a gathering of glass somewhat larger than, but still approximately the size of, the piece to be pressed. Still twirling this rod, he carries the gather to the pressing machine and holds it over the open mold. The constant twirling is necessary, because the glass is still so plastic that, without such rotation, the gather would string out and drop off the rod in transit from the pot to the pressing machine. However, while the gather is still intensely hot and plastic, its surface has already begun to cool, and this brings us to a problem inherent in pressing. In blowing glass, such cooling is of little consequence, since the workman can take the partly finished piece back to the furnace and reheat it at any stage of the operation. Pressing, on the other hand, is a single operation and reheating is impossible. In making all pressed glass, but particularly in pressing cup plates, due to the smallness of the gather, this loss of heat is an important factor. By the time the gather is in position over the mold, the string of glass that, taffy-like, starts falling into the mold the instant the rotary motion of the rod is stopped has cooled to a temperature perilously close to the setting point. This phase of the process is very much misunderstood. Collectors have a tendency to picture the gather dropping into the mold as a pear-shaped or tadpole-like mass, in both instances with the small or tail end of the gather at the top. Precisely the opposite is true. The stringy tail end drops in first, and the gather drops as a mass only when the operator of the press shears off what he considers to be the proper amount of glass from the gather. Meanwhile, however, the comparatively cool string of glass that has already dropped into the mold has undergone further chilling as it comes into contact with the mold, which, although it has been preheated, is still at a temperature lower than that of the glass.

And so, before the plunger comes down to press and shape the glass, we have on the floor of the mold (most cup plates were pressed upside down so that this floor or base of the mold usually forms the top of the plate) a string of glass that is nearly if not altogether set.

On top of this string is a blob of relatively hot, plastic glass, and on the surface of this mass is a straight line of rough, chilled and set glass caused by the contact of the comparatively cool, and not infrequently dirty, shears when the workman cuts off the gather. Neither the string of glass on the bottom (later the top) nor the shear mark disappears in pressing. You can see them on the cup plates in your cabinets, the shear mark on the back of the plate and the string of glass on the front. Of course, marks of this kind are more in evidence in the early period when wood was the fuel and the glass was worked at a lower temperature. On later plates, when coal permitted higher furnace temperatures, they are much less apparent, although many fairly late plates, the Ringgolds are a good example, still retain them. Neither a surface string nor a shear mark should be considered detrimental. In fact, a pronounced surface string often adds to the value of a plate. Usually, though, these strings have been to some extent reincorporated into the plate, so that they show up as faint spiral coils or perhaps only as wavy surfaces. The elaborate designs, and particularly the stippled, engine-turned, lined and other backgrounds, are primarily an effort to mask these blemishes characteristic of early pressed glass.

Obviously, the thickness of a cup plate depended on the skill and judgment of the man who, using glassmaker's shears, cut off from the gather what in his opinion was the proper amount of glass. If he cut off too much, the plate would be too thick; if he cut off too little, the plate would be too thin. You must remember, too, that he was working against time, against the possibility that the glass would be too cool to press before he sheared it off into the mold. Of course, when the pressing process was new, no one had had a chance to develop these special skills and as a result most of the very early plates are thick and heavy. There are two reasons for this. Too little glass in the mold could mean that there was an insufficient amount to make a plate, and such a waste of glass was frowned upon. Then, also, too little glass, combined with too heavy a hand on the plunger or, rather, on the lever that actuated it, permitted the mold faces to meet to their possible injury. Faced with these undesirable consequences, it was natural for the workmen to overcorrect by shearing off too much glass. However, while most of the earliest plates are much thicker than those of the lacy and later periods, it does not necessarily follow that all thick plates are early. The best and most experienced workman could, and on occasion did, sheer off too much glass even in the late period. Undoubtedly, too, some of the late heavy plates may be the work of beginners or apprentices. There must have been many of these to staff the numerous glass factories that started up in the 1840's.

Seemingly, but probably not actually, allied to the size of the gather and the force of the plunger stroke is the phenomenon called under-filling. The tendency among collectors has been to attribute this to too small a gather. From what we have been able to learn from practical glassmen, this is not the case. The difficulty in modern prac-tice seems to be due to a fault in the mold, but modern molds are a far cry from those of the cup plate period. Many underfilled plates are thicker on one side than the other, and this means that the plunger, usually the design die, was insecurely or improperly attached, so that its face was not parallel to the receiving die. But this does not seem to be the whole story, because usually when one side of such a plate is underfilled, the opposite side shows an extensive fin. Horizontal fins develop where the cap-ring does not meet the receiving die. But why, or even whether, the slight lifting of a cap-ring on one side would cause underfilling at the opposite side, we do not profess to know. Some underfilling seems to have been caused by working the glass at too low a temperature, too close to its setting point, so that it did not readily flow to the edges of the mold. If to glass that is too cool there be added a plunger stroke that is too weak, underfilling would almost certainly result. In fact, the working temperature of glass and mold seem important factors. As we have said before, molds are preheated (in modern practice they are run red-hot), but the melting point of cast iron is below the average working temperature or, more precisely, the ideal working temperature of glass, so that molds are normally somewhat cooler than the gather. Theoretically, then, the molds with the early, experimental, wide cap-rings used, probably, at the New England Glass Company should have brought about premature setting or, in other words, underfilling, because the glass, in being forced out to the edge by plunger pressure, came into contact not only with the relatively cool receiving die, and the still cooler plunger, but also with the extremely wide overhang of the cap-ring. The theory is confirmed by the comparatively high incidence of underfilled specimens of such wide cap-ring plates as No. 89.

Underfilling should not be confused with fire polishing or flashing.

Flashed edges are continuously smooth all around the plate, while underfilling is, in our experience, never so extensive. In fact, it is seldom that one encounters a plate with more than a third of its rim unfilled. Fire polishing is characteristic of foreign pressing and, in American plates, is confined almost entirely to the Clay-type Victorias which were, of course, made for the European market. Flashing is not a defect; underfilling is, but is not considered a serious one unless it includes a loss of pattern, as well as loss of contour. Nevertheless, collectors should be on guard against the occasional plate whose damaged serrations have been ground and polished by some unscrupulous dealer in imitation of underfilling. Such partial grinding and polishing of serrations is rare; more commonly, all serrations are ground off so that the plate has a smooth rim. All old plates with smooth rims have sharp edges, while haggled plates never have them.

Misunderstanding about the way cup plates were removed from the molds is so widespread as to be practically universal. The method is indeed surprising. The base mold was simply inverted and the plate fell out onto the leer or lehr pan and was ready to be taken to the annealing furnace. In most cases, the plate dropped out of the mold freely but, in the event it stuck, the workman simply tapped the mold with a hammer, thus knocking the plate loose. Collectors, uncomfortably aware of the fragility of antique glass, will shudder at this picture of a potentially valuable plate's clattering out of the mold onto the pan. They must remember that glass is tremendously strong when it is first made. While cooling, particularly during the handling necessary in pressing, cuts this initial strength to a great degree, the plate is not nearly so brittle when it falls out of the mold as it would be a century or, for that matter, a few hours later. In this connection, it is interesting to note that the modern theory is that the comparative fragility of finished glass is due in great part to minute, almost microscopic, surface fractures and scratches. Fire polishing and similar treatments eliminate these and strengthen the glass. If you think back, you will find that seldom, if ever, have you seen a flashed Clay-type Victoria in bad condition.

As the cup plates now on the lehr pan cool, great strains are set up between the comparatively rapidly cooling exterior and the more slowly cooling interior. Then the plates must be taken to the annealing furnace where the cooling can be slowed down and controlled, so that

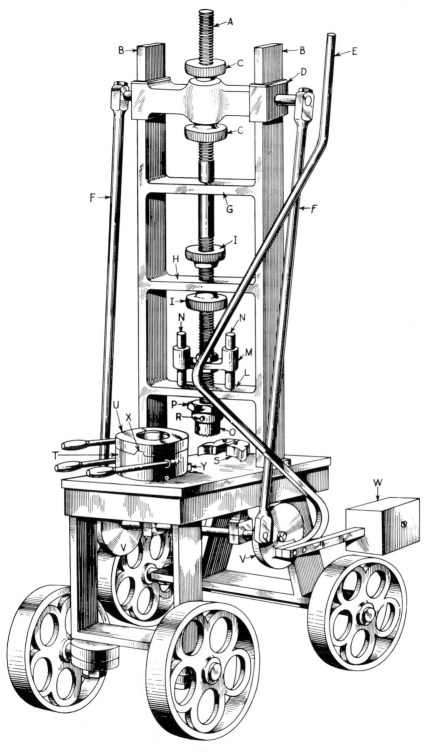

Fig. 2

Cup Plate Press of about 1835.

these strains are equalized and, to a considerable extent, removed. Annealing, today, is a complicated process and those of you who care to explore its theory further should read Phillips' book, *Glass, The Miracle Maker* (New York, 1941, p. 221 ff.). While it seems likely that many plates have been lost to us through bad annealing, and certainly an occasional extant specimen has crazed or crackled surfaces for the same reason, the hit-or-miss annealing of the cup plate period appears to have been quite successful as a whole.

For a thorough understanding of the pressing process, students should study Mr. Cannon's reconstruction of the lacy period press and the explanation that accompanies it (Fig. 2).

DETAILS AND WORKING OF A CUP PLATE PRESS
OF ABOUT 1835

The rectangular sectioned uprights, B and B, are solidly bolted to the worktable of the press. This table is, in turn, fastened to and supported by a heavy frame which rests on axles and four wheels. The front wheels are castered to facilitate moving the press. The rear wheels revolve freely on each end of a straight axle.

The crosshead, D, slides up and down to a limited extent on the uprights, B and B. D receives its movement from the connecting rods, F and F, which are fastened at their lower ends and receive their motion from the disk cranks, V and V. To one of these disk cranks, as shown in the drawing, is fastened the lever, E, an outward and downward movement of which actuates the press. The counterweight, W, is supported on a rod which is secured to the same disk crank, and at the same place, as the lever, E. The counterweight, W, can slide and then be locked in position so that it a little more than balances the lever, E, and the connecting rod assembly. It is so adjusted that it will normally hold the lever, E, in the upright position shown in the drawing.

The two disk cranks, V and V, are keyed to a cross shaft which runs transversely across and under the worktable, and is supported by suitable bearings hung from the worktable. Thus the disk cranks work together and impart an up-and-down motion to the crosshead, D, through the connecting rods, F and F, as the lever, E, is raised and lowered.

The central plunger shaft, A, is threaded for a certain distance on each end with a smooth portion between the threaded ends. This smooth section slides in the guide crossbrace, G. The plunger shaft, A, at its upper end goes through the crosshead, D, and two hand adjusting nuts, C and C, working on the upper, threaded portion of A, allow adjustment to the plunger shaft in relation to the crosshead, D. Thus, when the lever, E, is operated, the plunger shaft, A, will descend and rise the proper distance for the correct operation of the design die, O, which is fastened to the lower end of the plunger shaft.

The lower portion of the plunger shaft goes through the second crossbrace, H, and two hand adjusting nuts, I and I, allow adjustment on the lower threaded part to limit the vertical travel of the plunger shaft so that, in pressing the plate, it cannot go so far down as to injure the design die or, on the return stroke, so far up that it throws the connecting rods, F and F, on center of the disk cranks, V and V.

Farther down, the small crosshead, M, is locked very solidly to the plunger shaft by nuts, one above and one below M. This small crosshead slides on the vertical pins, N and N, and is designed to keep A perfectly steady and free from twisting so that the design die, O, will press the cup plate as correctly as possible. The plunger shaft slides freely through the lowest crossbrace, L. The three crossbraces insure rigidity of the uprights.

On the lower end of the plunger shaft is screwed the design die, O. R is a round hole in O in which a short rod is placed to hold O, the design die, in correct relationship with the main mold while the locking nut, P, is being tightened. This insures that the design die will be in the proper position when it enters the main mold.

The mold, seen on the front part of the press table, is composed of two parts. The upper section with one handle is the cap-ring, U. The lower part with two handles is the surface die, T. These upper and lower sections are held in approximately the proper relationship by the projection, X, which protrudes from the surface die and engages itself in a recess in the cap-ring as shown.

While the mold, T-U, is on the front part of the press table, the proper amount of hot glass is introduced into it through the hole where the design die enters. In practice, it is not always possible to shear from the gather into the mold exactly the amount of glass needed to produce a cup plate of ideal thickness. Within reasonable limits, too much or too little glass will not seriously affect the pressing of a plate. The travel of the design die can be somewhat more or less than normal and still produce a commercially acceptable plate and any abnormal thickness or thinness will be confined to the main body of the plate. Thickness at the edge is controlled by the cap-ring and remains constant.

The mold, T-U, after being filled with glass, is slid under the design die against the stop, S. The surface die, T, has a small nub, Y, on its rear part which engages the recess shown in the front center of the stop, S. This locates the mold in its proper position for the correct pressing of the cup plate. After the mold is slid against the stop and properly centered, an almost instantaneous operation, the lever, E, is brought forward and down and the plate is pressed. The lever is then returned to its upright position and is held there by the action of the counter-weight, W. The mold containing the pressed plate is then removed from the press; the cap-ring, U, is raised; the mold is inverted and the plate falls out.

It will be noted that if the design die is improperly set and locked into position on the plunger shaft, an error that is easy to make, then the main design of the plate which is formed by the design die will be at an abnormal angle to the plate's serrations or edge which are formed by either the surface die or the cap-ring as the case may be. It will also be noted that if there is any wear or looseness between the nub and its recess in the stop, S, the serration pattern could shift slightly in its relation to the design die, perhaps even from plate to plate. Furthermore, any looseness between the projection, X, and its corresponding recess in the cap-ring would, when the serration pattern is on the cap-ring, produce a similar shift. Finally, the stop, S, might be improperly adjusted and this would produce another slight clockwise or counterclockwise shift.

This press is not at all complicated or expensive to build. All its adjustments are simple and are easily made. On the other hand, there are several places where, through carelessness or wear, improper relationships of the various parts could occur, and these maladjustments account for many of the variations, shifting in particular, so frequently observed in cup plates. With reasonable care, however, such a press would produce thousands upon thousands of pressings of acceptable quality. Even so, it is doubtful that it could be adapted to the pressing of larger articles where a different style press with greater leverage and larger parts would probably be needed.

Chapter III

CUP PLATE MOLDS

Scrap metal was in just as great demand, comparatively speaking, during the Civil War as it was in 1942, with the result that no cup plate mold has come down to us. It may be that one is hidden away somewhere and will eventually turn up but, so far, all reported finds of molds have been errors, where the finder mistook an iron cup plate for a mold. An iron plate is illustrated on Plate 126 and need not be discussed here, except to say that it in no way resembles a mold and that it would be impossible to press a cup plate with such a contrivance. Since no student of cup plates has ever been lucky enough to see a mold, our knowledge of them is necessarily theoretical and is based on deductions drawn very largely from the cup plates themselves, on scraps of documentary evidence from contemporary sources and on the present-day molds in use in the so-called "hand shops," which, basically, seem to be much the same as they must have been a century or more ago. And so, while there can be no doubt that our present conceptions of the early molds are correct in principle, we are still in the dark on many things.

To begin with, who designed them? The making of a wooden model, usually carved from a mahogany block, is the first step in the making of a mold. These models are just that and nothing more. They were carved to show how the finished piece of glass would look and not, as was widely thought until recently, as matrices for castings. Who designed these models, no one really knows. It does not seem likely that the woodcarvers, the moldmakers, the glassworkers or the owners of the glass factories would have had the artistic background and training essential for designing many of the beautifully conceived lacy patterns. For these, a professional designer, a local architect or artist thoroughly grounded in the idiom of the Classic Revival must have been called in. In other cases, where the cruder or quainter designs were used, it is not impossible that the carver or someone else around the factory, not excluding the proprietor's wife, was responsible.

31

The question of who made the molds is also unanswered. We know that the Sandwich factory had moldmakers on its payroll. But, unless a glass factory is a large one, making many different items, a full-time moldmaker could hardly have been kept busy unless, as seems probable, most of his time was spent in cleaning scale from used molds. On the other hand, we know from the directories of the period that there were many independent firms of moldmakers. Their number implies that the glass factories gave them plenty of business. About all that can be said with any certainty today is that newly established or small factories must have bought their molds from outside sources, while large establishments, like Sandwich, the New England Glass Company, Bakewell, and Curling, probably made some or, just possibly, all of theirs. This last is not very likely if modern practice can be taken as a guide. Many large, present-day glassworks make some of their own molds and buy others outside, and the chances are this was true a hundred years ago too.

Mold material is less puzzling. Jarves mentions both brass and iron molds; but brass, while much easier to work than cast iron, has a lower melting point. Brass is an alloy and its melting point varies with its ingredients and their proportions, but if we assign 1900° Fahrenheit as the average melting point of the brass used in glass molds, we are not far off. Since glass was often worked at temperatures in excess of this, brass molds at first glance seem an impossibility, and indeed the low melting point was serious—but not quite fatal. The very large mass of the mold, in contrast to the very small mass of hot glass, coupled with the good heat conductivity of the brass, as compared with the poor conductivity of the hot glass, and, most important, the very short period of time (not over a few seconds) in which the hot glass was in contact with the mold materially changes the picture. There is no doubt that cup plates could have been, and very likely were, pressed in brass molds in the earliest period; but it must have been necessary to interrupt production at fairly frequent intervals to cool the molds a bit and, even then, the chances are that brass molds deteriorated rapidly. It is unlikely, therefore, that brass was much used as a mold material after the early days except, perhaps, under special circumstances. It may have been used later, for example, in making an article of limited appeal or in getting out small special orders where the life span of the mold was not a factor. By and large, most cup plates must have been made in cast iron molds. They were much more expensive because of the harder material, but were in the end more economical by reason of their superior durability.

Brass or iron, the method of manufacturing the mold was much the same. The moldmaker took a block of either one of these materials and laid out the pattern on its surface, perhaps in wax. Then, using such hand and machine techniques as die-sinking, engine-turning, engraving and so on, he cut the pattern into the metal. The other parts of the mold—the surface die and the cap-ring, when the latter was used—were made in the same way except that, in most cases, there was no design on the cap-ring and no hand techniques were necessary. Cutting these dies was time-consuming, expensive work, but the wage scales of the time were low; a great many cup plates, barring accident, could be made with one mold and the caliber of the workmanship was not as high as we are now inclined to think. In fact, if one of these old molds ever turns up its crudity will surprise many of us, even though it happens to be one of the most delicate lacy patterns. The glitter of glass masks many errors and irregularities in the pattern and, when slovenly moldmaking does show in the plate, it is quite properly regarded as being amusing or quaint. A seeming lack of symmetry may be explained in more than one way. For example, extra work would have been required to remove the turning center and, to cut costs, it was incorporated into the design. Most conventional plates have centering dots. In the Midwest one early moldmaker went so far as to leave turning dots on the surface die in such plates as Nos. 120, 121 and 655. A similar cutting of corners is responsible for the development of the bull's-eye serrations typical of Midwestern practice. For some unknown reason, the diemakers west of the mountains from the very beginning indented their serrations more deeply than was the custom in the East. As these scallops neared the half circle, the centering dot of the boring tool showed up on the plate as is seen in Nos. 204 and 206. Apparently this was considered too slipshod, because an attempt was made to correct it by enlarging and polishing the dots, until eventually they evolved into fully developed bull's eyes.

Occasionally, a design that had seemed satisfactory in the wooden model turned out to be signally short of the ideal when translated into glass. This was natural, since details that showed up plainly enough in wood would be rendered obscure by the refraction and reflection of glass. To check on such inadequacies, it may even have been customary to run trial proofs, after the manner of engravers and etchers. If a test plate proved that an element of the design lacked sufficient emphasis, the design die was recut. Thus, we have plates in first and second states—Washington with a plain background and then with rays behind the bust; the running-vine cabins where the vine is plain and weak followed by the variant where the vine is boldly stippled.

Our primary interest is not in the making of molds, but in the pressing of plates from these molds—or, to phrase it differently, in how the molds operated. Our knowledge of this phase, while based on deductions made from cup plates and hence theoretical, is on a much firmer foundation. The methods of determining how a mold worked are simple and, once a few basic principles are thoroughly understood, any layman should be able to apply them. The first of these principles is that the opening of a receiving die (this is the lower part of the mold into which the plunger descends) must be slightly larger than its bottom. In other words, the walls of the receiving die slope gradually inward, from the top to the bottom. This slight angle is called, variously, the rake or draw angle. Without it, removing a finished plate from the mold would be practically impossible. The first cup plate molds, however, were straight-sided (see Nos. 11 and 13), or so nearly so that plates made in them show no perceptible draw angle. Moreover, contrary to later practice, they were pressed right-side up. By this time you will be wondering how we know these things, and this brings us to the second basic principle. It was impossible to make a mold whose two or, later, three parts fitted so perfectly together that the hot, plastic glass, under the pressure exerted by the plunger, did not to some degree ooze out between the various mold parts and form what is known as a fin. By locating and studying these glass fins, it is possible to reconstruct the mold and see how it worked. It is axiomatic that the lower part of a mold, the receiving die, is cup-shaped. Otherwise, any glass that was too hot and runny would flow off and out of it. Also, the plunger must have something to press against. A flat mold without walls is plainly impossible. Moreover, it was mechanically impossible to make either the plunger or the hole in the receiving die perfectly round. At some place or another the fit between the two will be loose, and here a fin will develop. On the earliest plates, No. 13 for example, this fin is vertical and extends up from the rim of the surface of the plate. Obviously, a plate with a fin protruding above its surface had to be made right-side up. Fig. 3-A is a schematic cross section of such a mold.

As soon as this mold was put into operation, its faults began to show up. We have already speculated on the difficulties that were surely encountered in removing a plate from this straight-sided mold, once it was pressed. The presence of a fin on top, where it was plainly visible, was another unexpected and unwelcome defect. To overcome the first of these deficiencies, the sticking of the plate in the mold, the base mold or receiving die was made in two vertical parts and these were hinged so that the mold would open to release the plate. Figures 3-B and 3-C show this mold closed for pressing and opened for dumping, respectively. In practice, this device also proved unsatisfactory. The hinge was not strong enough to hold the two halves in good alignment, so that finished plates had, in addition to the original vertical fin, a new fin or mold mark bisecting them. Sometimes the alignment was so bad that one half of the plate has shifted laterally in relation to the other half. Only two designs made in this experimental mold, Nos. 10 and 12, have been recorded.

At about this time, some genius in the moldmaking shop discovered that if a plate were pressed upside down, the inevitable fin would be transferred to the back of the plate, where it was less noticeable; as a collateral reward for his efforts, he discovered that with the design die on top—on the plunger, that is—a much sharper impression of the pattern ensued. At nearly, if not exactly, the same time, someone thought of tapering the walls of the receiving die to facilitate the removal of the plate. Figure 3-D shows this type of mold; with its advent most of the serious defects of the early molds had been overcome.

Of the remaining shortcomings, one involved the human factor. Even the most experienced and proficient workman, acting at top speed, could not shear off the proper amount of glass into the mold. Consequently, the thickness of the plates was variable. Since contact between the faces of the design die and base mold—the natural result of having too little glass in the mold—could easily injure the design die beyond repair, the workman usually erred on the side of the too-heavy plate. The cap-ring solved this problem. Just when or where it was invented is not now known, but the available evidence, none of it documentary, hints at 1828 or 1829. Some factory in the New England

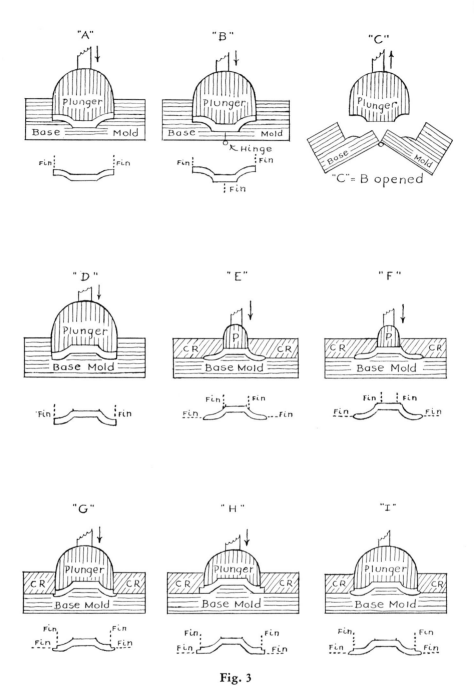

Fig. 3

Schematic cross sections of the main types of molds that were used to press cup plates. Underneath each type is shown a cross section of a cup plate from the mold with dotted lines indicating the fins developed in each kind of mold.

glassfield (probably the New England Glass Company, but possibly Sandwich) at about this time began to experiment with a broad cap-ring that reached from the rim of the plate to either just outside or immediately inside the table-ring. These are shown in Figures 3-E and 3-F. As you see, the whole shoulder pattern was formed by the cap-ring. For many reasons, this mold was not entirely satisfactory. While it solved the problem of thickness (plates pressed in it are uniform in that respect), it brought in its wake new problems hitherto unimportant. In Chapter II we discussed premature setting of glass and the allied phenomenon called underfilling. In this type of mold, where the glass comes into contact with a much greater expanse of metal and the plunger pressure is cut by a reduction in diameter, underfilling became very common. Patterns typical of those pressed in Figures 3-E and 3-F are Nos. 45, the 75 series, 78, 79, 82, 89 and 90.

It will be observed in the diagram that, with the coming of the cap-ring, plates have not only the old vertical fin that developed at the juncture of the plunger and base-mold assembly, but also a new, horizontal fin where the cap-ring meets the main receiving die. For some reason not now understood, these horizontal fins in plates pressed in the Figures 3-E and 3-F type molds are always vestigial and are never exaggerated, as they so frequently are in pressings from other cap-ring molds. Since an exaggerated vertical fin in plates of this type could easily extend beyond the table-ring and since, in this event, the fin would scratch the table and would thus constitute a fatal defect, it is just barely possible that a rigid system of inspection was set up through which any plate with an overgrown fin, horizontal as well as vertical, was discarded. On the other hand, such inspection should have eliminated or at least reduced the number of underfilled plates. Perhaps underfilling was considered a minor and finning a major defect.

At about the same time as, or maybe even earlier than, the invention of the wide cap-ring, a narrow one was developed. As we have said before, no one knows much about the chronological sequence of these early patents. All the record were destroyed in the famous Patent Office fire. In the absence of such records, it is impossible to decide which of the many types of cap-rings was the original and which was an attempt to utilize the principle of the ring without infringing on the basic patent. The narrow, flat cap-ring of Figure 3-G is the simplest of all cap-ring forms and was among the first to be made. Moreover, it was a satisfactory device. It not only kept the edge of the plate of uniform thickness, but it moved the objectionable vertical fin away from the table-ring. In its new location on the shoulder just inside the rim, even the most exaggerated of fins could not scratch the table top. Any horizontal fins that developed were at the back of the plate where they were relatively obscure, unless they were very extensive—as, indeed, they frequently were. In G type molds, the edge of the plate was shaped by the receiving die so that the draw angle is the same as it is on plates made in the simple two-part mold of Figure 3-D. In other words, the top diameter of a cup plate made in this mold is less than its diameter taken at the back of the edge.

The next variation on the cap-ring theme, type H, reversed this draw angle. Here, the cap-ring not only controlled the plate's thickness but formed its edge and its serrations, if the plate did not have a plain rim. Manifestly, the wall of the ring that shaped the edge of the plate must slant out, from top to bottom, or the mold could not be opened. Thus, the draw angle of plates made in Figure 3-H is exactly the opposite of those pressed in Figure 3-G. The top diameters of such plates exceed their back diameters. Since the horizontal fin was in plain view as an extension of the shoulder, Figure 3-H was not quite as satisfactory as Figure 3-G, though a great many patterns were made in it, nevertheless.

Plates that had a rope rim on both their top and bottom edges needed still another kind of mold. Here, half of the rope rim is cut on the cap-ring and the other half is on the base mold. This seems to have been one of the earliest inventions and is no more than a narrowing of the very wide ring of Figures 3-E and 3-F. The horizontal fins occur at the juncture of cap-ring and base mold, midway between the top and bottom of the edge. In New England, when used in making a scalloped rope rim, this mold caused a lot of trouble. Matching the top and bottom scallops was an unsolved problem, so that often the top scallop overlaps the bottom scallop. No. 45, made in the slightly earlier wide cap-ring mold, is a constant offender in this respect. Probably for this very reason, the East soon abandoned the scalloped rope as a decorative rim treatment, but Philadelphia and the Midwest took it up and, by adding a locking device to keep the cap-ring and base mold in proper alignment, perfected it. A cross section is shown in Fig. 3-I.

Molds of the sort shown in Fig. 3, A through I, account for about 99% of the known cup plates. In arriving at and perfecting these molds, it was inevitable that a few mechanical monstrosities were tried out. The fault in each case lay in trying to match surfaces. Thus, in No. 282-A the serration pattern is shaped by the base mold, but is also an integral part of the design which was formed by the plunger. Keeping a plunger in perfect relationship with any part of the base-mold assembly is practically impossible. Similarly, in No. 205 the design die had to line up perfectly with the base-mold assembly, in order that the shoulder rosettes would maintain their proper position in respect to the big scallops. The ultimate in these mechanical absurdities is seen in Nos. 190, 656-B and 690-A, which were pressed in a mold where the serrations were shaped by the base mold, while the bull's eyes, that were supposed to be centered in the serrations, were cut into the cap-ring. The locking device that solved a similar dilemma for the scalloped rope rim had, it seems, not yet been invented and, consequently, the cap-ring kept shifting, so that its bull's eyes are sometimes half on and half off the scallops. These defects brought about the early scrapping of such molds, and plates made in them are today very rare.

Chapter IV

HISTORICAL CUP PLATES

Over the years since collecting cup plates became a diverting hobby, it was natural that they should have become classified into two groups, known today as "historicals" and "conventionals." The historicals are, for the most part, those which commemorate famous persons or historical events. "Conventionals" present an evolution of design, from the simple geometrical patterns of the early days, through the beautiful but sophisticated lacy glass patterns onward to their end in the Gothic Revival.

Probably the most eagerly sought-after cup plate among the historicals is a round plate bearing a simple bust of George Washington in the center. This plate was unknown until recent years; even at this writing only two specimens have been discovered. The only other Washington cup plate is octagonal in shape, with rays forming a background for the bust. The latter plate is a splendid addition to any collection, but is in no way so rare as the former.

It seems quite likely that the Washington cup plates were brought out at the centennial of his birth—1832. Certainly moldmakers were inspired by important events of the day in an age when horsedrawn vehicles represented speed. As a result, events such as centennial celebrations, political campaigns or progress made in industry or shipping were such important topics that they were recorded in glass, china and prints, as well as in verse. Popular subjects meant larger profits in sales!

Henry Clay was the subject for ten different plates, all apparently of Eastern origin and all but one bearing his name. The latter is our No. 563, sometimes called the "No Name" Clay.

There are two Henry Clay portrait busts facing to the right which are not only rarer than any of the others, but also appear to be of an earlier date. These are our No. 562 and its companion, No. 562-A. We believe these earlier plates undoubtedly came out in 1832 during his political campaign for the presidency, when he was the Whig candidate opposing Andrew Jackson. The Henry Clay plates to the right are the only ones in the series having stippled backgrounds. They represent finer workmanship than the later Clays. These later plates bearing his name could have been to honor a public-spirited servant of his country, particularly when he ran for the presidency as the sole Whig candidate against Polk in 1844. The Henry Clay plates should have been popular for many years, for he was continuously in the public eye from 1803 (though this was prior to the date of cup plate manufacture) until his death in 1852.

There is no more colorful or interesting character in American history depicted in cup plates than William Henry Harrison. Born in Berkeley, Virginia in 1773, he was a lieutenant in the army at the age of eighteen and elected to Congress at twenty-six. In fact, there was not a time over a period of fifty years when his life was not highlighted with important events, culminating in his becoming the ninth president of the United States and ending in tragedy when he died thirty-one days after his inauguration, at the age of sixty-eight.

William Henry Harrison is recorded in two groups of plates, one of which bears his bust and the other comprises a most interesting series of fifteen plates known to collectors as "the log cabins."

The two cup plates bearing his bust are our Nos. 568 and 569. Apparently, they were made from the same mold, No. 568 with the plain panels, above and below the bust, being a presidential campaign plate; and No. 569 a recut mold with "president" appearing in the plain panel above the bust, and the date "1841" below. Since Maj. General Harrison was elected to office in 1840 and died so shortly thereafter in 1841, it is possible that this second plate commemorates his death. Both of these plates are thought to be of Sandwich origin.

Probably no presidential campaign in our history carried so many political slogans as the Harrison-Tyler campaign for the presidency. While the Democrats smeared Harrison as a "hard cider drinking," war-worn old man, poverty stricken and mentally unfit for the office of president, the Whigs delightedly pounced on these stories and capitalized on them to their own advantage by promoting a series of campaign slogans for their candidate. To name a few of them, he was "The Farmer of North Bend," "The Log Cabin and Hard Cider Candidate," "Tippecanoe and Tyler too," "The American Ticket," "Harrison and Reform," "The North Bend Farmer," etc. Gen. Harrison was a wealthy man and lived well, though for political expedience he adopted the log cabin and hard cider barrel. His military career was played up by Tippecanoe Clubs (referring to his having been hailed as the hero of the battle of Tippecanoe in 1811), and log cabins became Whig headquarters. His campaign was implemented further by Harrison banners, Harrison buttons, Harrison and Tippecanoe handkerchiefs, log cabin bottles marked "Tippecanoe" and "North Bend," Harrison cup plates and whisky flasks. The log cabin cup plates marked "Fort Meigs" (our No. 596) commemorates Harrison's defense of Fort Meigs and the battle of the Thames, October 5, 1813, though of course they were made at a later date. The Whigs overlooked nothing in behalf of their candidate.

Students will note the campaign emblems in the photographs. The American flag flies over some but not all of the cabins. The latchstring is out on some doors and missing on others. The hard cider barrel is prominently displayed by some cabin doors and not shown by others. The liberty pole and cap appears only on our No. 592. No. 596 is the only one that is lettered. Though Harrison was a hero of the Midwest, many of the cup plates are of Eastern origin. Collectors will find the log cabin group a never ending source of interest, with some extreme rarities to spur them toward their goal.

The peaceful and victorious reign of Queen Victoria of England is illustrated in a number of cup plates, some of which we made for export to England. Others were produced in England for their home consumption, as well as for export. In general style, the earliest ones to appear date from the time of her ascension to the throne in 1837, or possibly for her coronation which took place in Westminster Abbey on June 20, 1838. It was a tremendous event in England when this young girl ascended the throne of her vast empire, and there was every reason to commercialize on it. Souvenirs appeared then, even as they do in our day, and cup plates were small and easy to carry. The group of plates from No. 570 through No. 574 are not exactly so typical of our workmanship as those on Plate 91, Nos. 575 through 579. These are often referred to by collectors as "the Victorias with Henry Clay border," because the border of the plate corresponds at first glance with all the Henry Clay series, beginning with No. 563 through

No. 566-B. To be more exact, the Henry Clay No. 563 is most closely related by similarity in serrations.

At the time of Victoria's marriage to Prince Albert in 1840, other cup plates as well as the toddy size (4¼″) appeared, bearing the bust of each. The English cup plates in this series are extremely rare today.

Plate 91 displays the first known illustration, in any book in this country, of the Jenny Lind cup plate, which belonged to the late Mrs. Hutchins. We have not seen it, so cannot vouch for the color which has been described as both green and blue. We believe it is undoubtedly foreign, probably English, and late. The "Swedish Nightingale" rose to great heights of popularity in London during 1847–1848, when she made her first appearance there. It is curious that more of these plates have not appeared in this country, but this could be explained by the fact that there was no particular reason to export them to America, since Jenny Lind up to that time had never visited here. What is more puzzling is that she was not utilized as a popular subject for a cup plate when she did appear here in 1850. She was under contract to P. T. Barnum for 95 concerts in the United States during 1850–1851. Nevertheless, the cup plate is illustrated because the one specimen known at this time has aroused a certain amount of interest. The bust in the center of the plate is surrounded by stars, topped in the border with a rose, and bird singing, the latter prettily suggestive of a nightingale.

Any Major Ringgold plate is rare, some more so than others. None is beautiful in point of design, and they are usually found in poor condition.

It has come as a surprise to us to find so few people know anything about Major Ringgold, though he was enough of a hero in his day to be commemorated on cup plates, flasks and Currier & Ives prints. Research yielded nothing until we remembered an old article in the *Saturday Evening Post* of October, 1929, entitled, "Why I Collect Empty Bottles" by the late Edwin Lefèvre. Mr. Lefèvre once commented that one reason he collected historical flasks was because he learned more about our history. He, too, had difficulty in finding Major Ringgold's story, but he finally unearthed it in a volume by Powell, titled, *Life of Zachary Taylor*. We regret that space does not permit the entire quote as written by Edwin Lefèvre. Brief excerpts will suffice to cover the main events. Major Ringgold was born in Washington County, Maryland, in 1800. His mother was the daughter of Gen. John Cadwalader of Philadelphia. He was graduated from West Point with high honors in 1818 and entered the artillery as a lieutenant. He was a fine-looking man, witty, keen-minded, magnetic, and Gen. Winfield Scott selected him as one of his aides. In 1836 he was engaged in the Florida campaign, and for his valuable services he was brevetted major.

At the opening of the Mexican War, he commanded the corps of flying artillery which he organized, the first body of that kind in this country.

The story of the battle of Palo Alto, where Ringgold met his death, can be read in detail in "The Life of Zachary Taylor." Of Ringgold Mr. Lefèvre says, "In 1846 many Americans could remember with shame the surrender of Hull at Detroit, the disgraceful refusal of the cowardly militia to fight at Queenstown, the conviction of Smyth of cowardice, the daily reports of mutiny, desertion and riot during the War of 1812. But now in faraway Mexico, 2300 heroes under "Rough and Ready" licked 6800 desperate Mexicans. Only nine Americans were killed. Unfortunately, one of them was the hero "without fear and without reproach," Major Ringgold—that is, the first American officer killed in the first battle in the first foreign war waged by the United States. The circumstances of that death, the brilliancy of his maneuvers which did so much to win the victory of the American army, his behavior when wounded, inflamed the imagination of his countrymen. Wrong the war might be, but Ringgold was 100 percent right, for he was an American who did his duty efficiently and died gloriously."

According to Powell, "A cannon ball, passing from right to left, carried with it a large mass of muscle and integuments, and tore off the front of the saddle and the withers of the noble steed he rode. Ringgold fell slowly from his horse and had scarcely reached the ground when Lt. Slaven came to his assistance. While he supported Major Ringgold up in his arms, he called for a caisson to carry his commander to the rear. "Never mind me, Sir," said Ringgold. "You have work to do. Go ahead with your men. You are all needed at the front." Finally he was prevailed upon to consent to their carrying him from the field. As he was leaving he turned to his lieutenant and calmly remarked: "Be sure this is an empty caisson. You will require all your ammunition."

This was on May 8, 1846. On May 11 the hero died at Point Isabel,

Texas. His body later was taken to Baltimore and there buried "with grand civic and military honors" on December 22, 1846, at the age of forty-six.

The cup plates commemorating Ringgold doubtless appeared in 1847.

A series of ships of various types embellish a group of cup plates, but identification is difficult, if not well-nigh impossible, when they are un-lettered. Unfortunately, at present speculation is the only basis for identification of these unmarked boats. For instance, our Nos. 604 through 606 illustrate two round and three octagonal plates, picturing what is thought to be the U.S. Frigate *Constitution,* popularly called "Old Ironsides." A frigate was an old-style war vessel in use from 1650 to about 1840. It was smaller than a ship of the line and carried from 24 to 50 guns on the main deck. Paul Jones was placed in com-mand of our first frigate on the same day that Congress adopted the U.S. flag, June 14, 1777.

It is believed plausible that the ship in the series we mentioned is the *Constitution,* and that the storm of patriotic protest brought about by the attempt to dismantle and sell her after her colorful career in-spired the glassmakers to take advantage of the furore by memorializing the ship in glass.

The round *Constitutions* are more rare than the octagonal forms, both styles being of Midwestern origin.

The small ship which has become known as the *Cadmus* (our Nos. 610 through 610-D) may be the *Constitution,* but it definitely is not the *Cadmus.* There is no way to prove it is anything other than a frigate! The *Cadmus* used steam and sails. We believe the name Cadmus was originally given this plate by early collectors who knew the Clews Staffordshire plate by that name and to whom a ship was merely another ship. This particular series of ships dates around 1840, which would be rather late to be commemorating the protest over the scrapping of the *Constitution,* which began about 1830. The theory held by some that it is the *Constitution* may be true, but at this point, lacking any tangible proof whatsoever, we believe the boat was used because ships have always been a popular decorative motif.

The so-called *Fulton* side-wheel steamboat cup plate may be found both round and octagonal in form, the first-named being extremely rare. Both appear to be of Midwestern origin (our Nos. 612 and 612-A).

It seems entirely reasonable to assume that the design of these ships was inspired by Robert Fulton's early experiments in navigation. The original exclusive privilege of navigating the waters of the state of New York by steam had been granted by the Legislature to Robert Livingston in 1798, but later the time limit was extended and issued to Livingston and Fulton, jointly. Interest in improvements in navigation was going forward steadily, but it appears strange that the Midwest should have commemorated the *Fulton,* in particular, since Robert Fulton died in 1815. The cup plate is of the 1835–38 period. The boat as depicted on the plate bears no resemblance to the *Fulton,* but is a clumsy side-wheel model with heavy superstructure. Our guess is that this is an Ohio or Mississippi River steamboat, possibly intended to further popularize travel by water.

Our No. 614 is a particularly interesting plate because it not only shows an early side-wheel riverboat, but it is marked with the factory name, "Union Glass Works, Pittsburgh." It is also dated 1836 and, curiously, each of the octagonal sides is numbered on the shoulder, from one to eight. It was a product of Parke, Campbell and Hanna. This extremely rare plate and the two following, our Nos. 615 and 615-A, show what appear to be side-wheel river boats which are not identifiable, so far as we know.

The efforts of all research workers would be greatly facilitated if the old-time glassworkers had marked the ship plates, as was done in the case of the *Benjamin Franklin* and the *Chancellor Livingston.*

Our Nos. 617 through 619 show the ship *Benjamin Franklin,* so-marked. It was natural that a ship or even several ships should have been named to honor Franklin, for he was one of our most famous pioneer inventors. In "Steamboats Come True," James Thomas Flexner says: "It is by no means chance that Franklin . . . (was) the one American capable of visualizing the steamboat problem in its entirety."

We have been reliably informed that there was a ship *Franklin,* also known as *"Pride of Boston"* which was built in 1824 and destroyed in 1836. There is a record of a frigate *Franklin* which saw service during the Civil War. Our first ship of the line was the *Benjamin Franklin.* It was launched in Philadelphia in 1815 and was carried on the lists of the United States Navy for one hundred years until it was sold for junk in 1915. We cannot tell which particular ship *Franklin* was intended to be commemorated in this cup plate. All of the group appear to be of Sandwich origin and to date between 1835–38.

The last group of ship cup plates is the *Chancellor Livingston,* our Nos. 624 through 632-A. Robert R. Livingston was a friend of Robert Fulton's, and for some years they were jointly interested in promoting steam navigation of ships. Robert Fulton built the original steamboat *Clermont* in 1807, obtaining his first patent in 1809. In 1816, a larger steamboat was built to replace the *Clermont* and was named *Chancellor Livingston,* in honor of his late friend Robert Livingston. This ship was dismantled in 1834, and the cup plate commemorating it came out some time thereafter. The *Chancellor Livingston* brought the Committee of Welcome to greet Lafayette when he arrived outside New York Harbor August 24, 1824. This gave added importance to the ship and is probably one more reason why so many variants of this one boat appear on cup plates.

There has been considerable controversy over the series of cup plates known as "Maid of the Mist," as to whether the bridge actually represents the Suspension Bridge over the Niagara River at Niagara Falls, N. Y. (our Nos. 635 to 637). Some believe firmly that it does; others have equally firm convictions that it merely represents a conventional bridge back in the days when villages and towns quarreled bitterly about who was to have the bridge over their local stream or river, just as they did later concerning railroad location and now do over airports. The one point in favor of the latter reasoning is that these plates, in point of distribution and findings, are not found in central New York State, but they have been discovered frequently around Wheeling, West Va., Steubenville, Ohio, or farther east at Columbia, Pa. It has been said that many towns over the country claim this bridge for its own. One variation of this plate is fairly plentiful, but the other two are rare.

The completion and dedication of the Bunker Hill Monument June 17, 1843, brought about no less than twelve cup plates showing the monument. The dedication ceremony was a momentous occasion in Boston, and the exercises took place in the presence of the President of the United States and his cabinet, besides many other people of importance. Daniel Webster was the orator.

This series of plates appear to be of Sandwich origin and are commonly found today except for those in color. Undoubtedly they were sold as souvenirs before and after the completion of the monument.

A story was circulated at one time to the effect that the monument was financed by the sale of the Bunker Hill cup plates, but this seems to us too dubious for serious consideration.

The largest single decorative figure shown on any group of cup plates is the eagle. There are some 58 plates displaying the bird, and nearly all of these are variations of the design on the United States seal. The figure of the eagle, as the king of birds, is commonly used as an heraldic emblem. France used one under the Bonapartes. The eagle has also appeared on many of our coins, the first time being on the copper cent issued before the adoption of the United States Constitution by the various states during the period of the Confederacy. It is not surprising therefore that enterprising moldmakers utilized the eagle as a standard patriotic symbol and found it a best seller over a long period of years during the cup plate era.

The group of eagle plates begins with our No. 650 and continues through to No. 680. Probably every factory ever making cup plates produced at least one bearing an eagle. Even so, few come under the heading of "plentiful" today, and many varieties are extremely rare. For specialization on any one group, the eagles offer inducement to the discriminating and, be it said, persevering collector!

SEMI-HISTORICALS

The following seventeen plates appear to have a certain amount of historical interest but it is of a limited nature (our Nos. 685 through 699). The stories associated with some of them are plain guesswork, but collectors like to collect stories along with their specialties.

An interesting plate or dish may be found in the steam coach, our No. 685. The "New Patent Steam Coach," as it is marked, was introduced for a limited time on English highways. It reflected the popular interest of the period in every improvement in transportation. The design is a very early automobile item, and should be particularly valued for this reason.

The "Harp and Star," No. 686, may have been introduced to appeal to the large Scotch and Irish population. Little is known about the plate except that it is both early and rare.

The Plow, No. 687, was made in round and octagonal form, and it may have had some particular significance. Being of Midwestern origin, it could have been intended to denote agriculture. Again, these may have had some connection with the well-known John Deere plows. Possibly John Deere used these plates for advertising purposes, though the idea may be slightly farfetched. If not, then these cup plates probably preceded the appearance of the Deere plow which came out along about 1837–1838. The plates appear to be of the 1835 period. Then, again, the design may have been a sort of Farmers' Arms to sell to the predominantly agricultural population west of the mountains.

The lyre plates (Nos. 690 through 692) do not have any special import, so far as we know, beyond the fact that they seem to fit into the group.

The Anchor may have been designed to appeal to sailors and other seafaring people (No. 693).

Among the cup plates known as "the beehives," there are three variations, one style being plentiful and the other two scarce, and rare, respectively. These plates (No. 694–695) presumably were meant to be suggestive of industry. They are attractive and lacy.

An unusual cup plate is No. 696, inscribed "Repeal-Erin go Bragh" (Ireland Forever). The correct spelling of Bragh, according to Webster, is "Brath," an ancient war cry of the Irish. This plate was presumably made during agitation led by Daniel O'Connell, Irish patriot. He was a member of the House of Commons and champion of the Roman Catholics for the "Repeal of the Union" of Ireland and England and "Repeal of the Corn Laws." This plate appears to be of Sandwich origin, period 1841–1844. Queen Victoria brought about repeal of the Corn Laws in 1845.

The "Before and After Marriage" cup plate, No. 697, has no particular significance beyond bucolic humor. It is lettered "The Wedding Day" and "Three Weeks after." The Wedding Day shows two happy smiling people. Reversed, three weeks after is quite the opposite. Any of the old plates in this design are scarce today.

The last cup plate in this series is known as "the hound"—No. 699. The significance of this dog could be interpreted as a representation of man's best friend! Again, farmers were dependent on dogs to a large extent in the early days, both for hunting and as useful animals to herd sheep and cattle. Dogs have always had a place in the home, so perhaps some moldmaker was simply commemorating a faithful friend. Hound cup plates are very scarce, particularly in fine condition.

Chapter V

COLOR CHART

Many terms, some of them quite fanciful, are used in describing cup plate colors. In the check list the tabular arrangement made it advisable to use the shortest word possible. For example, "opalescent" has been shortened to the technically incorrect, but readily understandable, "opal." Except for the use of "dark," "medium" and "light" as qualifiers, little attempt has been made to modify general terms—although, where confusion might result, additional description has been used, sometimes in the tables, more often in the notes below. Since ordinary correspondence between dealers and collectors is not subject to these restrictions, a list of the most frequently used terms is included here.

AMBER

(1) Black-amber can occur in two ways, a deep opaque reddish-amber, as in the rare sunburst, No. 522, or an equally deep opaque olive-amber. This last color has not, so far, been found in cup plates, but examples may turn up at any time, since it was used in blown glass during the cup plate period.

(2) "Deep reddish-amber" is also called "blood-amber" and, although it is a dark color, is not opaque. Again, the No. 522 sunburst is the usual example. Minus the qualifying "deep," it is, of course, a lighter shade, but still retains its redness.

(3) "Amber," when used without a modifier, is the rich color found most frequently in the log cabin, No. 594. Occasionally, this cabin is found in a lighter shade of amber approaching, but not quite reaching, "honey-amber" which follows.

(4) "Honey-amber" is a light amber with no reddish lights and is frequently found in No. 323.

(5) "Silver stain" is about the same as ordinary amber but is made in a different way. It is a surface wash painted on the backs of plates already pressed. The color is then fixed by reheating (flashing) the plate. In silver stains some part of the plate is left clear. Usually this clear glass portion is the serrations, but occasionally the background is clear and the raised design is in color. The color range is from a medium to a honey-amber. Two of the Franklins, Nos. 619-A and 619-B, the heart,

No. 459-G and the late conventional, No. 380, are the only plates that have been recorded in this technique.

AMETHYST

(1) "Black-amethyst" is an opaque black whose amethyst nature becomes apparent only when it is held to a very strong light, whereupon the thinnest portion of the plate, usually the extreme edge, is revealed to be amethyst. It is known only in Nos. 46 and 242-A and is an Eastern color.

(2) "Deep amethyst" needs no explanation.

(3) "Medium amethyst" is also self-explanatory.

(4) "Light amethyst" should not be confused with either amethyst or pink tints. It is a deeper shade than "amethyst tint" and is not as reddish as pink tint. It occurs commonly in No. 324.

(5) "Pink tint" is an unsatisfactory term but is frequently seen. As used in the check list, it denotes a color much stronger than a tint but is redder than "light amethyst." Nos. 159-B, 668 and 677-A are the only examples that come to mind, and they are very rare.

(6) "Purple" is a very bluish-amethyst and must not be confused with the blues that frequently show amethyst lights. It is very rarely seen in cup plates; No. 297, which is unique in this color, is the only one we can think of at the moment.

(7) "Lilac" and "lavender" are synonyms for a very bluish light or medium amethyst. It is a Midwestern color and occurs in the No. 680 and 680-E eagles and their allied sunbursts. By some dealers and collectors, the lighter specimens of No. 324 are described as lavender. We do this, ourselves. This last, however, is a redder amethyst.

BLUE

(1) "Blackish-blue" is a very deep blue with no trace of amethyst or reddish lights. It has been recorded only in the rare Midwestern octagonal plate, No. 183-B.

(2) "Deep" or "dark" or "sapphire-blue" are all much the same. They should have none of the greenish lights of "peacock-blue," but often show reddish or amethyst shades, especially under artificial light. Keeping in mind the restrictions about greenish tinges, the common Clays and Cadmuses are the examples most easily found. In the check list where blue examples are listed without a qualifier, it is this dark blue or the following "cobalt-blue" that is referred to.

(3) "Cobalt-blue" is a rather dark color, although it is sometimes lighter than deep blue. It lacks the amethyst tinge of deep blue and is less brilliant. It is a Midwestern color and is found most often in the eagles, Nos. 670-A, 677-A and 680.

(4) "Medium blue" is much the same as deep blue but is lighter. It also

has no amethyst lights. The lighter Clays and Cadmuses are good examples, if they show no trace of green.

(5) "Light blue" is a color not found in many cup plates. It should not be confused with blue tints which are much lighter. The Harp toddy plate, No. 808, is the best example.

(6) "Peacock-blue" may be of either medium or dark intensity, but must show very greenish lights in reflected light. Often in transmitted light it loses its greens and appears to be a medium blue. It is an Eastern (New England) color and may be seen in the Clays, Cadmuses and Chancellors.

(7) "Violet-blue" is a soft color needing no further description. It was used only in New England, chiefly in hearts but also, rarely, in Franklins.

(8) "Gray-blue" is found in the late conventional, No. 333, and needs no further description. It is an Eastern color.

(9) "Electric-blue" is an extremely brilliant color of only medium density. It was made only in New England and, in its pure form, occurs only in the hearts, although some Chancellors in medium blue are nearly as brilliant.

(10) "Ice-blue" is a very light shade of "electric-blue," and also is a New England color.

Note: The opaque blues are listed under "Slags."

GREEN

(1) "Emerald-green" is a deep, rich, brilliant color. It is a very rare color in cup plates, appearing only in the hearts, the Monuments and the 1831 eagles. Its use is confined to New England.

(2) "Deep green" is as dark as "emerald-green," but lacks its richness and brilliancy. The very rare 227 series is the most notable example.

(3) "Bluish-green" is the color frequently seen in No. 253.

(4) "Yellow-green," when a deep color, is not often found, but in lighter shades is frequently seen in such plates as No. 563.

(5) "Olive-green" is seen in such plates as Nos. 196, 253, etc.

(6) "Dirty green" is not too nice a term, but is a good description of the dull color sometimes seen in the 227 series.

(7) "Light green," when properly used, is somewhat bluish or, at any rate, has no yellow tones. The "No Name" Clay and No. 636 are good examples.

(8) "Light yellow-green" needs no further description.

(9) "Aquamarine" is a term that is rarely used in cup plates and is simply a light, rather bluish-green.

Note: The opaque jade-green is listed under "Slags."

OPALESCENT AND
OPAQUE-WHITE

(1) "Opaque-white" seems to be an attempt to imitate china. It is a New

England color and the best examples are No. 88 or 89. Any plate that shows opalescence when held to the light should not be described as "opaque-white." These are "opal-opaques."

(2) "Opal-opaque" is, as the name implies, opaque but still shows strong opal lights. Frequently the center of the plate is opaque and the shoulder opal. In the check list, the technically correct "opalescent-opaque" has been shortened to "opal-opaque."

(3) "Opal" is used throughout the check list and is a short form of "opalescent." No distinction is made here between the fiery and blue and other forms, but in the case of No. 81 "greenish" and "reddish" opals are noted. These are nothing like other opals and occur, so far as we know, only in this one plate. The opals were made in two ways, by a pigment (probably tin) mixed in the batch and by the application of a wash to the back of the plate. Statistics on these are currently so meagre that it seemed best to make no mention in the check list as to which method was used on any particular plate.

(4) "Light opal" needs no explanation.

PUCE

(1) "Puce" is a dirty, reddish-brown amethyst. Usually the color is not uniform and runs in streaks through the plate. The chances are it is an accidental color. It seems to occur only in such Midwestern plates as Nos. 127-B and 178-B.

SLAGS

(1) "Turquoise-blue-opaque" is the term usually seen. In the check list, "light blue-opaque" has been substituted for it because the plates in this color often have a silvery sheen completely unlike the precious stone. The use of this color was confined to New England and the best example is No. 85.

(2) "Medium blue-opaque" is a darker manifestation of the preceding color. It, too, is found only in plates of New England origin and No. 82 is a typical example in its lighter specimens.

(3) "Dark blue-opaque" is a still deeper shade of this color. The description is unsatisfactory because there are almost always streaks of purplish-blue running through these plates. The darker specimens of No. 82 are typical examples of this New England color.

(4) "Jade-opaque" is a grayish-green color that occurs only in the No. 459-M heart. Its origin is New England.

(5) "Red and green slag" is opaque muddy brown in reflected light, but when held to a strong light it is translucent and the color is a mixture of ruby and brilliant green streaks. Only one example is known, No. 654-A.

YELLOW

(1) "Yellow" and "canary" are one and the same. Yellow is the term used here. It is a New England color and is seen in the monuments, hearts, etc.

(2) Vaseline is a shade of yellow which has a greenish tone to it. It is usually referred to as yellowish-green.

(3) "Olive-yellow" is a color that is not too uncommon in blown glass but is rarely seen in cup plates. The little No. 502 sunburst is the best example.

In the tabulation of colors, no mention has been made of such terms as "clam broth" or "grayish" or "alabaster." These indicate lack of color rather than true colors. "Clam broth" and "grayish" are one and the same. It can best be described as a translucent-white. The origin is New England. "Alabaster" is a word used to describe a white which best resembles Bennington Parian. It is a dense white with no opal tint.

It should be pointed out that the whole system of cup plate color terminology is an oversimplification and most unsatisfactory. There are literally hundreds of blues, gradations from one shade to another, and only about a dozen standard terms to cover them. A few extremely rare blue plates are mixed colors. That is, they have opal mixed in with the basic blue. The resulting color is very attractive and extremely rare. In dark blues with this opal bloom or overcast we have only Mrs. High's 1832 eagle and Mrs. Wells' Franklin. In medium blues mixed with opal there is a handful of examples of No. 240-A.

Discouraging as this confusion may be, it is unlikely to get any better because of the fallibility of human eyesight. One man's blue is another man's green and probably always will be.

Chapter VI

BLOWN GLASS CUP PLATES

Nos. 1 through 7

TYPES MADE PRIOR TO THE INVENTION OF THE PRESSING MACHINE

It seems most unlikely that the invention of the pressing machine and the vogue for using cup plates were simultaneous occurrences, so we must assume that whatever demand there was for glass cup plates before 1826 was satisfied by the production of blown types. However, since blowing continued to be a popular technique during the whole cup plate period, with little or no change in style, it is impossible to single out a particular specimen and say definitely that it was made before the pressing process was invented. All we can safely say of the examples illustrated is that they *might* have been made prior to the advent of pressing.

A kick-up appears in the center of many of these blown plates and not infrequently is so high that it would seem to rule them out as cup plates. Any tea cup of the period would have wobbled precariously on this bulge if, indeed, it would have remained in place at all. Nevertheless, since no one has been able to suggest another use of these plates, as well as because they are universally accepted as cup plates by collectors, it has seemed best to include them here.

Blown plates with few exceptions were not made in full-size molds. Consequently, their diameters vary with the skill or whim of the workman who made them. A determined collector could get together a variety of sizes, but here we have listed only the pattern varieties without emphasis on diameter variation, which is given in inches.

No. 1.	*Diam.*	*Origin*	*Colors*	*Rarity*
	Variable.	Made in many	Clear	Scarce
	The one shown	glass factories,	Light green	Rare
	is 3¾	East and West	Amber	Very rare

55

Examples with a folded rim, as shown are considered more desirable than those with a plain rim. A rough pontil mark is preferred to a ground pontil which, when coupled with clear glass, is popularly considered to be a sign of foreign origin. This is debatable, to say the least. It is not impossible that other colors encountered in blown glass, notably blue and amethyst, will eventually be discovered. Amber specimens with an oily surface-bloom should be purchased only when guaranteed. Some of these are modern Mexican glass.

No. 2.	*Diam.*	*Origin*	*Colors*	*Rarity*
	Variable.	Uncertain,	Medium green	Unique
	That shown	probably		
	is 3⅝	Midwestern		

This specimen in the collection of Mr. George C. Cannon is the only ribbed one we have seen, although it is likely that others exist. The 18-rib mold is unusual in blown glass but, since this particular plate was found in Ohio and is typical of Midwestern technique, it was probably made west of the mountains.

No. 3.	*Diam.*	*Origin*	*Colors*	*Rarity*
	Variable.	Probably	Clear	Rare
	That shown	Sandwich		
	is 4			

This seems to be the only blown three-mold pattern made in cup plate size. All we have seen have big kick-ups. So far no colored specimens have been found.

No. 4.	*Diam.*	*Origin*	*Colors*	*Rarity*
	Variable.	See note	See note	Rare
	This is 3⅞			

These latticinio plates are popularly credited to Sandwich, specifically to Nicholas Lutz. Since Lutz started working at Sandwich in 1869 long after the vogue for cup plates had subsided, two things are indicated—either he did not make these or they are not cup plates. Still another possibility is that early-looking, delicately-made examples are European, perhaps Venetian like the one shown here. For later, cruder types, see No. 4-A. All we have seen have big kick-ups and may not be cup plates. The illustration is from the collection of Mr. George C. Cannon. It is blue, gold and white on clear.

1

4-A

2

5

3

6

4

7

Nos.
8 and 9
left open

Plate 1

No. 4-A.	*Diam.*	*Origin*	*Colors*	*Rarity*
	3 15/16	See note	Red and white on clear	Rare

This is a cruder but later example and may very well be of American origin. If it is a cup plate, which is doubtful since it has a big kick-up, it antedates Lutz's era. As always, the ground color is clear glass.

No. 5.	*Diam.*	*Origin*	*Colors*	*Rarity*
	3¼	See note	See note	Unique

Opinions differ as to whether this attractive plate is Bristol, Continental (perhaps Bohemian) or, just possibly, American. The milk-white ground seems to us to be bluer than typical Bristol and more like that found in the common "Friendship" mugs, although it lacks their opalescence. While the center is flat, it is not certain that this is a cup plate.

No. 6.	*Diam.*	*Origin*	*Colors*	*Rarity*
	4	Uncertain	Clear	Unique

This is a most important plate. It is blown glass with a ground pontil and has a pattern of radial ribs cut on its shoulder. Thus it seems possible that this or a similar plate was the inspiration for the design of the earliest of the pressed patterns, Nos. 10, 11, 12 and 13. It has a flat center and was almost certainly a cup plate. It might conceivably be English or Irish, but its crudity and its resemblance to the earliest New England pressings favor an American origin. It is in Mr. Cannon's collection.

No. 7.	*Diam.*	*Origin*	*Colors*	*Rarity*
	4⅛	Uncertain	Clear	Unique

This is another very important plate and is the only other cut glass one known. It may or may not have preceded the first pressing, but is unquestionably very early. Note the strawberry diamond cutting on alternate shoulder panels, a decorative device frequently seen in early pressed glass. As in No. 6 the origin might be English or Irish but, since it is well established that Pittsburgh (Bakewell) cut similar patterns and since this plate was found in that area, an American origin is not impossible.

Nos. 8 and 9 are reserved for new discoveries.

Chapter VII

THE BEGINNING OF PRESSING

Nos. 10 through 72

The first attempts at pressing are discussed in the opening chapters and need not be gone into here. It will suffice to say that, since a cup plate mold was the simplest of all molds and a cup plate the easiest possible thing to press, it seems likely the first cup plates followed closely on the heels of the famous tumbler which is supposed to have been the first piece made by the new process. Moreover, the earliest, or what we now think are the earliest, cup plates are very crude, which probably indicates that they were made during the experimental period. The first documentary evidence is an entry in the Sandwich account book where cup plates are mentioned under the date of April 20, 1827.

When we say, however, that a particular plate is early, it should be understood that we refer not to the specific plate but to the mold which produced it. There is every indication that the first molds were used over a long period so that, while the patterns are undoubtedly early, a cup plate in the pattern may have been pressed a decade later.

The plates in this section, except for an occasional late adaptation of an early design, were all pressed in molds manufactured before the invention of the cap-ring; in other words, in molds of the A, B-C or D (see Figure 3) type in which there was no way to control edge thickness. The result is that plates of the period vary greatly in this respect, but are more often thick than thin. Their designs are based on cut glass patterns of the period and are mostly geometric.

Proof examples, if the word is interpreted strictly, are extremely difficult if not impossible to find for several reasons. The earliest molds had no perceptible draw angle, so that getting a plate out of the mold was a tricky operation. Probably many rims were chipped at this time. In the earliest designs, Nos. 10, 11 and 12, the radial ribbing on the

59

top of the shoulder was very vulnerable, especially when stacked where these ribs were crossed by the concentric rings on the bottom of the shoulder. Consequently, no collector should insist on perfection in this group.

The attribution is to New England and, probably, to Sandwich. It is not impossible, however, that some of the group was made at the New England Glass Works. There is vague evidence that Nos. 11, 13, 13-A, B and C could have been pressed in the Philadelphia area. The argument is that all of the extremely rare deep blue examples of these plates were found in that region. Furthermore, the tiny No. 11 turns up in very high concentration in eastern Pennsylvania. Our experience, however, is that it occurs in even greater numbers in New England. All in all, the evidence pointing to Philadelphia origin seems inconclusive and unsatisfactory so, while not ruling out the possibility, we have favored a New England attribution.

Rarity designations on these early plates are deceptive. They were produced over a long period, so that clear glass specimens cannot be ranked much higher than "Scarce." And yet good, not proof but good, examples are hard to find.

No. 10	*Diam.*	*Rim*	*Origin*	*Colors*	*Rarity*
	3⅜	Plain	New England, probably Sandwich	Clear	Scarce

This plate, along with No. 12, was made in the curious B-C mold with the hinged receiving die. Note the mold seam that bisects it. Such a two-piece die could not have been attached to a plunger, so these plates were pressed right-side up.

No. 11	*Diam.*	*Rim*	*Origin*	*Colors*	*Rarity*
	2 13/16	Plain	New England, probably Sandwich	Clear	Plentiful

This miniature version was pressed in the A-type mold and is inserted here because, like No. 10, it has no concentric circles in its center. It was pressed upright. The high density of distribution in eastern Pennsylvania has been noted elsewhere and, of course, the possibility of its having been made in that area cannot be entirely disregarded.

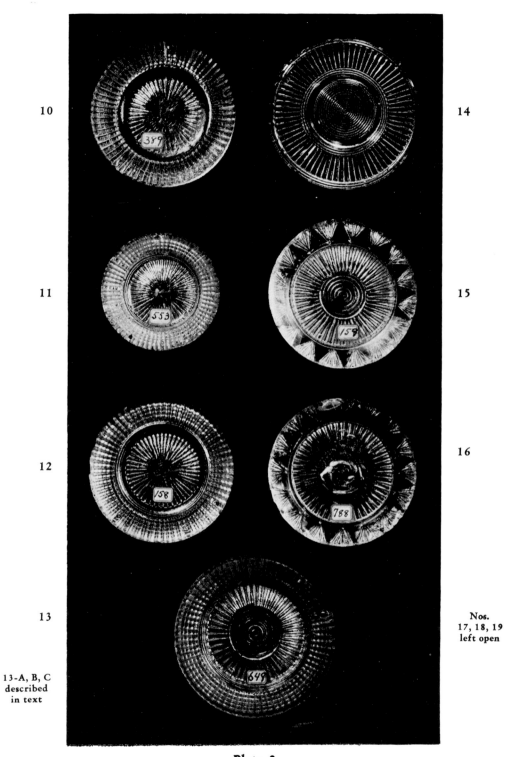

10

14

11

15

12

16

13

Nos.
17, 18, 19
left open

13-A, B, C
described
in text

Plate 2

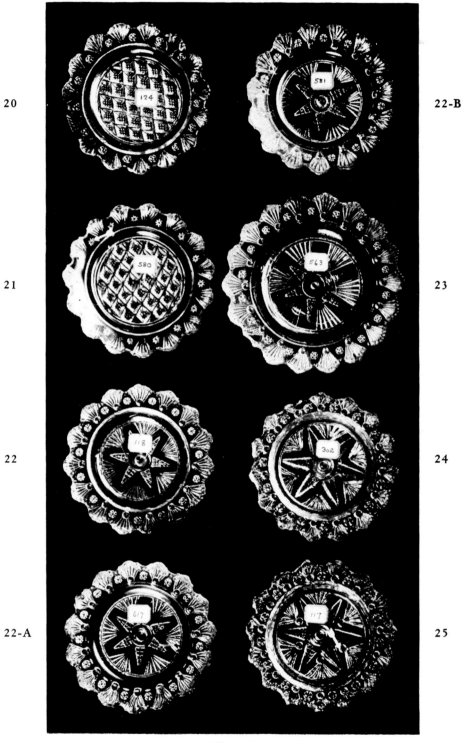

20

21

22

22-A

22-B

23

24

25

Plate 3

26

27

28

29

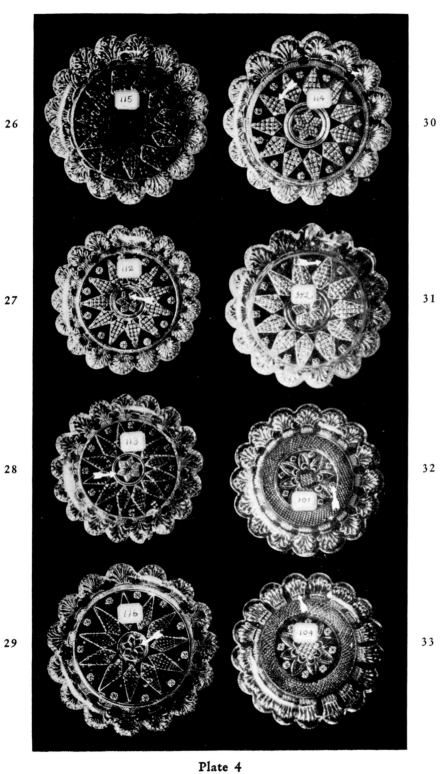

30

31

32

33

Plate 4

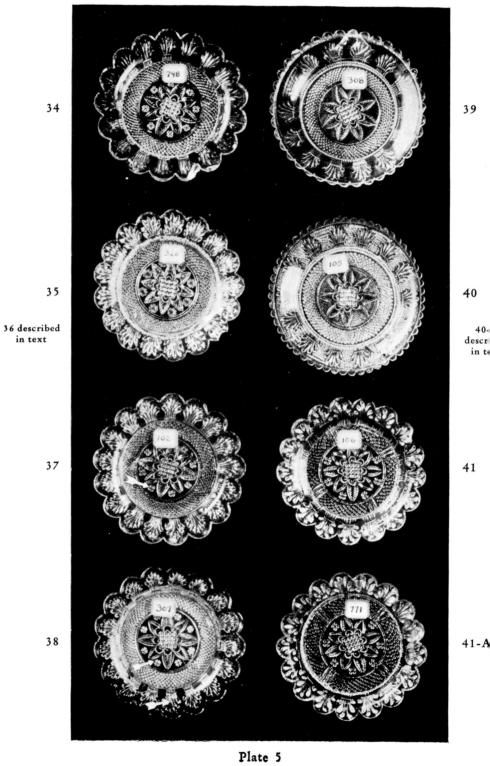

34

39

35

40

36 described
in text

40-
descr
in t

37

41

38

41-A

Plate 5

42

45

43

46

44

47

Plate 6

48

50

49

51

52

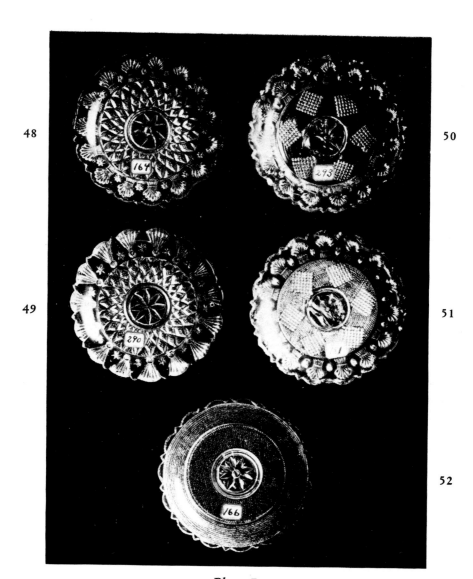

Plate 7

53

56

54

57

55

Plate 8

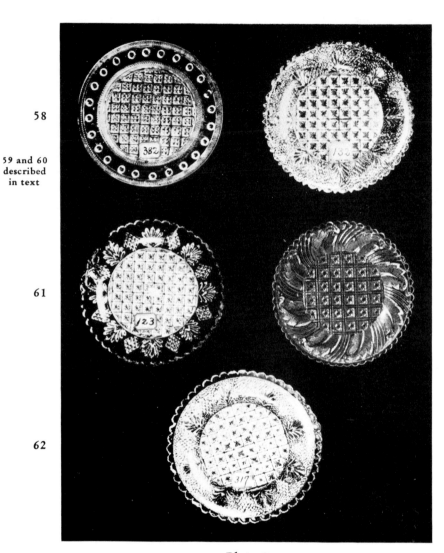

58

59 and 60
described
in text

61

62

62-A

63

No. 6
left ope

Plate 9

65

69

66

70

67

71

68

72

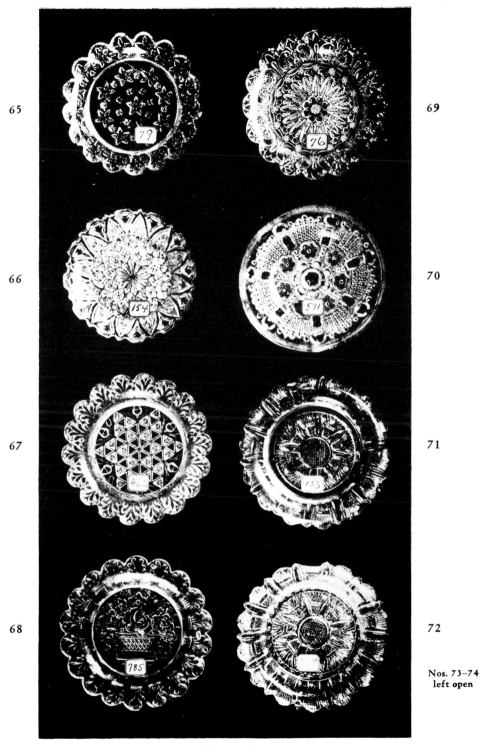

Nos. 73–74
left open

Plate 10

No. 12	*Diam.*	*Rim*	*Origin*	*Colors*	*Rarity*
	3⅜	Plain	New England, probably Sandwich	Clear	Scarce

Like No. 10, this was pressed in the B-C hinged mold and has the bisecting mold mark. It differs from No. 10 in having concentric circles in the center.

No. 13	*Diam.*	*Rim*	*Origin*	*Colors*	*Rarity*
	3¾	Plain	New England but see note	Clear Deep blue	Plentiful Extremely rare

This plate was pressed upright in the A-type mold. The rather dense distribution near Philadelphia, plus the fact that both of the known blue examples were found in that region, may possibly indicate origin in that area. Along with the following two plates, this is extremely difficult to number. We strongly suspect that all three were made in the same mold and vary only in quality of imprint, due to pressing the glass too near to its setting point. This variety has a raised dot in the center of the back of the plate surrounded by, seemingly, six concentric circles, but two outer circles are doubled, so actually there are eight circles. The doubled circles are not apparent to the eye and can be seen only in a rubbing.

No. 13-A	*Diam.*	*Rim*	*Origin*	*Colors*	*Rarity*
	3¾	Plain	As above	Deep blue	Unique

This is much like No. 13, only here the two inner concentric rings, those just outside the central dot, are the ones that are doubled. The only known specimen was found by Mr. Richard H. Wood in the vicinity of Frederick, Maryland, and is in Mr. Cannon's collection.

No. 13-B	*Diam.*	*Rim*	*Origin*	*Colors*	*Rarity*
	3¾	Plain	As above	Clear	Scarce

This lacks the raised central dot and has six concentric circles in its center. Mr. Marble says "five circles and a depressed dot," but this is the same thing, since our sixth circle is simply the outline of his depressed dot. We believe that this plate is no more than a bad impression of the previous mold, but there is always a possibility that two or more molds were used. Bad imprints of this early period are discussed in the chapter on Process and may be due to working the glass at too low a temperature. The plate was pressed in the A-type mold.

No 13-C	Diam.	Rim	Origin	Colors	Rarity
	3 7/16	Plain	As above	Clear	Plentiful
				Deep blue	Extremely rare

This is a slightly smaller plate and is usually much thinner than its variants. It has the raised center dot and five concentric rings on such specimens as we have checked, but we have little doubt that examples with a doubling of rings will eventually be discovered. The few blue specimens were found in the Philadelphia area. A pontil-marked example is known.

No. 14	Diam.	Rim	Origin	Colors	Rarity
	4	Plain	Unknown	Clear	Unique

For convenient reference, we here insert an astonishingly late revival of the design. It must have been made three decades or more after the preceding patterns. Its tone is dull and it contains little, if any, lead. Beyond the fact that it turned up in Ohio, nothing is known of its source. It is in Mr. Cannon's collection.

No. 15	Diam.	Rim	Origin	Colors	Rarity
	3 7/16	Plain	New England, probably Sandwich	Clear Pink tint	Scarce Rare

It is impossible to say whether this is a shade later or a bit earlier than Nos. 12 and 13. We have placed it later because the fan motif on the shoulder is characteristic of slightly later plates. The pinkish specimens are probably accidental, due to a slight excess of manganese in the mix.

No. 16	Diam.	Rim	Origin	Colors	Rarity
	3 7/16	Plain	As above	Clear	Rare

This has a dot added to the base of each of the shoulder fans. While the specimen shown has a pontil mark, examples lacking this scar are known.

Nos. 17, 18 and 19 are reserved for new discoveries.

The Second Phase of the Earliest Period

The cap-ring is not yet used. English, Irish and American geometrically cut glass still furnishes much of the inspiration for designs, but on a more delicate and complicated scale. The fan on the shoulder continues to appear; the strawberry diamond and waffle show up for the first time in pressed ware. Probably, however, the most characteristic feature of this group is the development of the scalloped rim which, although this is not generally understood, is also traceable to cut glass practice. Naturalistic ornament, the star, heart, sheaf of wheat—each treated in highly stylized form typical of the Classic Revival—begins to creep in. Individual specimens are still usually thick, and colored specimens are rarely seen.

All of these plates are of eastern origin, most of them from New England. Until very recent years, it was quite generally believed that all of the cup plates discussed in this section were made at NEG. This theory still has some adherents, and indeed it is entirely possible that some of them *were* made at Cambridge. The chances, with but few exceptions, are that most of them were pressed at Sandwich, although toward the end of the period we meet a few plates that can be assigned with reasonable confidence to Philadelphia.

Several series in this section do not lend themselves to chronological treatment because their designs proved so popular that their manufacture was continued over a long period. To facilitate reference, these are listed with their earlier prototypes.

No. 20	Diam.	Rim	Origin	Color	Rarity
	3 7/16	15 scallops with shelves	New England, Sandwich or NEG	Clear	Plentiful

Note the circles divided into quadrants between the fans of the shoulders—the distinguishing mark of this plate. As indicated by the strawberry diamond center, the fan border and the stepped or shelved serrations, all stemming from cut glass of English or Irish origin, this is a very early plate.

No. 21	Diam.	Rim	Origin	Color	Rarity
	3 7/16	15 scallops with shelves	New England, Sandwich or NEG	Clear	Scarce

The only difference between this and the preceding plate is that a star replaces the circular motif between the shoulder fans. This star variant seems to be considerably rarer.

No. 22	Diam.	Rim	Origin	Color	Rarity
	3⅜	15 scallops with shelves	New England, Sandwich or NEG	Clear Bluish tint	Plentiful Rare

Note the elongated dots on the top of the rim. These and a slightly smaller center distinguish it from the next plate.

No. 22-A	Diam.	Rim	Origin	Color	Rarity
	3 7/16	15 scallops with shelves	New England, Sandwich or NEG	Clear	Plentiful

This has round, not elongated, dots on the top of its rim, and its center is slightly larger and deeper. The increase in size of the center by changing the angle of refraction appears to cut off the bases of the shoulder fans.

No. 22-B	Diam.	Rim	Origin	Color	Rarity
	3 7/16	15 scallops with shelves	New England, Sandwich or NEG	Clear	Plentiful

Precisely like No. 22-A, except that it has no dots on top of the plate.

No. 23	Diam.	Rim	Origin	Color	Rarity
	4⅛	18 scallops with shelves	New England, Sandwich or NEG	Clear	Plentiful

This large version of the pattern has elongated dots on the top of the rim. It seems to be more difficult to find than the preceding members of the series and might almost be classed as scarce.

No. 24	Diam.	Rim	Origin	Color	Rarity
	3⅜	15 scallops with shelves	New England, Sandwich or NEG	Clear	Plentiful

The central 6-pointed star becomes much larger in this plate, and its points reach to the outer edge of the center. The dots on the top of the rim are round. The plate is much flatter than any we have heretofore encountered.

No. 25	Diam.	Rim	Origin	Color	Rarity
	3 7/16	15 scallops with shelves	New England, Sandwich or NEG	Clear	Plentiful

There are several differences, but the easiest to check is the bull's eye at the base of each center fan. These appear only in this plate. A pontil-marked specimen is known. Like No. 24, No. 25 is also a flat plate.

Other plates with stepped or shelved scallops will be found in the No. 53, 54 and 55 group.

Here in the next group the scallops lose their steps or shelves and become simple curves, although they are still large and characteristic of early practice. Long experience shows that beginners find these plates difficult to number. Disregarding No. 26, which is readily identified by its blank center, the method of determining is to count first the number of scallops, either 15 or 17. Then, examine the plate carefully to see if the big lance-like leaves of the center number 11 or 12. Following this, check the precise center for the tiny dot that appears in about half of the group. Next, see if the ring surrounding the small 6-pointed central star is single or double. Finally, compare the sheaf of wheat in the scallops.

No. 26	Diam.	Rim	Origin	Colors	Rarity
	3 9/16	15 even scallops	New England, Sandwich or NEG	Clear	Very rare

This is a curious and interesting plate. All specimens we have seen show a sort of over- or double-printing in the center as if a faint impression had been pressed, the plunger lifted and shifted a bit and a good impression made. It has been suggested that the blank center indicates that the plate was intended for use as a candlestick or lamp base. If this were the case, we should find examples with pontil marks but, so far as we know, none has been found.

No. 27	Diam.	Rim	Origin	Colors	Rarity
	3¼	17 even scallops	New England, Sandwich or NEG	Clear	Plentiful

There are 11 lance points in the big center figure. The plate has the tiny central dot and has a double ring surrounding the small central star. There are other variations, but these are sufficient for identification. A pontil-marked specimen is known.

No. 28	Diam.	Rim	Origin	Colors	Rarity
	3¼	17 even scallops	New England, Sandwich or NEG	Clear	Plentiful

Unlike No. 27, this has 12 lance points. It lacks the central dot and has a single ring surrounding the central star. The "bricking" in the lance points also differs.

No. 29	Diam.	Rim	Origin	Colors	Rarity
	3 11/16	15 even scallops	New England, Sandwich or NEG	Clear	Plentiful

This has 11 lance points with bricking, similar to that in No. 28. It lacks the central dot and has a single ring surrounding the central star. There are many other variations, but these above determine the variety.

No. 30	Diam.	Rim	Origin	Colors	Rarity
	3⅝	15 even scallops	New England, Sandwich or NEG	Clear Amber	Plentiful Extremely rare

This has 11 lance points, a central dot and a double ring surrounding its center. The occurrence of an amber specimen can, we feel, mean but one thing. The mold was in use over a long period and the colored specimen is a decade later. We say this because amber in cup plates is a relatively late color. Moreover, there is a considerable variation in the quality of the clear examples of this plate. Some, presumably those of the later period, are of vastly better quality.

No. 31	Diam.	Rim	Origin	Colors	Rarity
	3½	15 even scallops	New England, Sandwich or NEG	Clear	Rare

There are a number of variations, but the chief and determining one is that this is a much deeper plate, almost like a sauce dish. It may be that this deep shape was found impractical or inconvenient and that production was soon discontinued, thus accounting for the comparative rarity. See No. 42 for a similarly rare deep plate in another series.

Next comes a group guaranteed to perplex the beginner. Apparently, it was very popular and was made over a period of several decades, well into the cap-ring era. In fact, we suspect that some of the confusing variations encountered here are mold repairs, recutting of damaged design dies. The distinctions to watch for are changes in the sheaf of wheat, not only as to shape and the location of the binder, but also as to the number of individual stalks forming the sheaf. Another determining factor is the type of ornament in the spandrels between the center leaves.

No. 32	*Diam.*	*Rim*	*Origin*	*Colors*	*Rarity*
	3¼	16 even scallops	New England, Sandwich or NEG	Clear	Plentiful

This is the *only* plate of the type to have *16 serrations*. Pontil-marked specimens are known.

No. 33	*Diam.*	*Rim*	*Origin*	*Colors*	*Rarity*
	3¼	17 even scallops	New England, Sandwich or NEG	Clear	Plentiful

This is the *only* one of the type to have but *5 stalks* in its sheaf of wheat.

No. 34	*Diam.*	*Rim*	*Origin*	*Colors*	*Rarity*
	3¼	17 even scallops	As above	Clear	Possibly rare

The only one in the group to have a 6-stalk sheaf.

No. 35	*Diam.*	*Rim*	*Origin*	*Colors*	*Rarity*
	3¼	17 even scallops	New England, Sandwich or NEG	Clear	Rare

This has *7 pointed* stalks in its sheaves and is easily confused with the following plate. Up until recently most dealers, including ourselves, have listed this plate in opal. Now we understand it exists in clear glass only and that opal specimens are more likely to be the following plate.

Note that both this and the next plate have rosettes, instead of block-squares or Maltese crosses, in the spandrels between the central leaves.

No. 36	*Diam.*	*Rim*	*Origin*	*Colors*	*Rarity*
	3¼	17 even	As above	Clear	Rare
		scallops		Opal	Rare

Like the preceding in all respects except that the stalks of its sheaves are *rounded,* not pointed. Since the difference between this and the previous plate is a new discovery to us, we are not too confident about the rarity of either.

No. 37	*Diam.*	*Rim*	*Origin*	*Colors*	*Rarity*
	3¼	17 even	As above	Clear	Plentiful
		scallops		Opal	Very rare
				Green tint	Very rare

This has the 7-stalk sheaf with rounded points, but the spandrel ornament resembles a Maltese Cross.

No. 38	*Diam.*	*Rim*	*Origin*	*Colors*	*Rarity*
	3¼	17 even	As above	Clear	Plentiful
		scallops		Opal	Rare
				Amethyst	Unique

This resembles the previous plate but can be identified by the variation in the shape and style of its 7-stalk sheaf. The amethyst specimen is in Mr. Cannon's collection.

No. 39	*Diam.*	*Rim*	*Origin*	*Colors*	*Rarity*
	3⅜	38 even	As above	Clear	Plentiful
		scallops			

This is a much later plate than the previous members of the series. It is a revival or an adaptation of the earlier pattern and was made after the invention of the cap-ring. It may date from as late as 1840.

No. 40	*Diam.*	*Rim*	*Origin*	*Colors*	*Rarity*
	3⅜	55 even	New England,	Clear	Plentiful
		scallops	Sandwich or	Blue	Rare
			NEG	Peacock-blue	Rare

This differs from the preceding plate not only in the number of serrations, for it also has a stippled background both in the center and on the shoulders. It too is fairly late, in the 1835–1840 period.

No. 40-A	*Diam.*	*Rim*	*Origin*	*Colors*	*Rarity*
	3⅜	38 even scallops	New England, Sandwich or NEG	Clear	Plentiful

The only difference between this and the preceding plate is the number of serrations.

No. 41	*Diam.*	*Rim*	*Origin*	*Colors*	*Rarity*
	3 3/16	17 even scallops	New England, Sandwich or NEG	Clear Opal	Scarce Very rare

Except for the peculiar sheaf of wheat with its 6 stalks which are much coarser than those found on Nos. 26 to 38, and, most especially, for the radial lines which divide the cross-hatched band into quarters, this resembles the earlier plates. Since this was also made without a cap-ring, it probably antedates 1830.

No. 41-A	*Diam.*	*Rim*	*Origin*	*Colors*	*Rarity*
	3 3/16	17 even scallops	New England, Sandwich or NEG	Clear	See note

The contour of the top is different from that found on the preceding plate. The angle of the shoulder is much closer to the rim. The diameter on the two specimens we have seen is very slightly less than 3 3/16 but is nearer that figure than it is to 3⅛. With so easily overlooked a variation, we feel that many may exist improperly numbered, so that no attempt at estimating the comparative rarity is possible.

No. 42	*Diam.*	*Rim*	*Origin*	*Colors*	*Rarity*
	3½	15 even scallops	New England, Sandwich or NEG	Clear	Rare

This is a rather deep plate. The geometric shoulder pattern probably indicates a very early date.

No. 43	*Diam.*	*Rim*	*Origin*	*Colors*	*Rarity*
	3½	15 even scallops	New England, Sandwich or NEG	Clear Blue Amethyst tint	Scarce Very rare Rare

The rope on the shoulder probably indicates a slightly later date, but the plate was pressed without a cap-ring well before 1830. Pontil-marked specimens are known.

No. 44	*Diam.*	*Rim*	*Origin*	*Colors*	*Rarity*
	3¼	17 even scallops	New England, Sandwich or NEG	Clear	Very rare

This is the earliest instance of the use of naturalistic ornament in the center of a plate. It is also a very early use of stippling.

No. 45	*Diam.*	*Rim*	*Origin*	*Colors*	*Rarity*
	3 9/16	19 even scallops, rope top and bottom	New England, Sandwich or NEG	Clear Opal	Scarce Very rare

This plate was made with a wide, experimental cap-ring which carried the back half of the rope scallops and extended to just inside the table-ring. The surface die carried the top half of the rope scallops. This mold assembly had two serious faults. It was impossible at this early date to keep the surface die properly aligned with the cap-ring; thus the rope of the top seldom coincides with the rope on the bottom. In addition, a fin frequently developed where the plunger met the cap-ring at the table-ring, a perfect location for a fin to ruin a table top. These wide cap-rings are discussed later in Nos. 75, 78, 79, 82, 89, 90, etc.

No. 46	*Diam.*	*Rim*	*Origin*	*Colors*	*Rarity*
	3½	15 even scallops	Eastern	Clear	Plentiful
				Lavender	Rare
				Amethyst	Rare
				Black-amethyst	Extremely rare

This was made without a cap-ring and this, coupled with the geometric shoulder design and the strawberry diamond pattern, indicates a very early date. It is most likely of New England origin, but the colors are not characteristic of that region and, so far as we know, seem to be found mostly in eastern Pennsylvania. The black-amethyst specimens are so dark that their amethyst nature can only be seen with a very powerful light, and then only at the extreme edge. Pontil-marked examples are known.

No. 47	*Diam.*	*Rim*	*Origin*	*Colors*	*Rarity*
	3½	15 even scallops	Eastern	Clear	Plentiful

The design is so nearly like that of the preceding plate that a common origin is indicated. This is probably New England but might possibly be eastern Pennsylvania or New Jersey.

No. 48	*Diam.*	*Rim*	*Origin*	*Colors*	*Rarity*
	3 11/16	15 scallops, points between	Eastern	Clear	Plentiful

Made without a cap-ring. Style points to a New England origin, but distribution indicates the possibility of eastern Pennsylvania pressing.

No. 49	*Diam.*	*Rim*	*Origin*	*Colors*	*Rarity*
	3¾	15 scallops, points between	Eastern, probably New England	Clear	Plentiful

This was almost certainly made in the same factory as No. 48. In style it belongs to New England, but its densest distribution seems to be in eastern Pennsylvania.

No. 50	*Diam.*	*Rim*	*Origin*	*Colors*	*Rarity*
	3¾	15 scallops, points between	Eastern, probably New England	Clear	Rare

Here both style and distribution point to an origin in New England. With but one specimen known without the pontil mark (in the Essex Institute), it may be that these were made as a base for lamps or candlesticks. We have seen, however, two sets (one of four, the other of six plates) with pontils which seems to prove they were used as cup plates.

No. 51	*Diam.*	*Rim*	*Origin*	*Colors*	*Rarity*
	3¾	15 scallops, points between	Eastern, probably New England	Clear	Extremely rare

This differs from the preceding plate in that its background is stippled in the center. No examples are known without a pontil mark. The distribution is entirely New England.

No. 52	Diam.	Rim	Origin	Colors	Rarity
	3¾	15 scallops, points between	Eastern, probably New England	Clear Opal	Scarce Extremely rare

Judging by the stippling, this properly belongs to the lacy period and is a slightly later development from the same factory that made 48, 49, 50 and 51. Distribution, however, reaches its height in Pennsylvania, not in New England.

No. 53	Diam.	Rim	Origin	Colors	Rarity
	3⅜	15 scallops with shelves	New England, Sandwich or NEG	Clear	Plentiful

The geometric, so-called waffle, centers of this series are copied from cut glass and are undoubtedly very early. For allied serration patterns, see Nos. 20, 21, 22, 23, etc. In the present plate note that there is no bull's eye at the base of the shoulder fans.

No. 54	Diam.	Rim	Origin	Colors	Rarity
	3⅜	15 scallops with shelves	New England, Sandwich or NEG	Clear Blue	Plentiful Unique

This has a bull's eye at the base of each shoulder fan. No precise comparison has been made, but this seems to be from the same mold that was used in pressing the cameo plates. The blue example is a recent discovery of Mr. Wood's from the Philadelphia area and is now in Mr. Marble's collection.

No. 55	Diam.	Rim	Origin	Colors	Rarity
	3⅜	15 scallops with shelves	New England, Sandwich or NEG	Clear	Uncertain

This has a smaller bull's eye, one better fitted to the fans, than that found at the base of the shoulder fans on the preceding plate. The outer block of waffles on any side of the center is here composed of 4 full and

2 half-waffles while on No. 54 there are but 3 full waffles on each side and even these are slightly cut by the table-ring. We know of but this single example, which is in Mr. Marble's collection, but it is most likely others exist misnumbered.

No. 56	Diam.	Rim	Origin	Colors	Rarity
	3 1/16	15 plain scallops	New England, Sandwich or NEG	Clear	Scarce

The stepped or shelved scallops are replaced by plain ones, and stars take the place of the shoulder fans. This little plate is not related to the so-called "States" plate, No. 65, which has 17 plain scallops.

No. 57	Diam.	Rim	Origin	Colors	Rarity
	3 7/16	Plain	Uncertain but Eastern	Clear	Scarce

This plate is inserted here because of its waffling. It is not quite as thick as Nos. 53, 54, 55 and 56, and is probably not as early. It is not a late plate by any means.

No. 58	Diam.	Rim	Origin	Colors	Rarity
	3⅜	Plain rope on top	Eastern, see note	Clear Blue	Scarce Unique

This series is not properly appreciated by most collectors. Its members are all thick and heavy; it was made before the invention of the cap-ring and thus antedates 1830. Variations are confined to the bottom of the shoulder. In this particular type, there is a band of radial lines on both the inner and outer edge of the *underside* of the shoulder, leaving a plain band between, holding the bull's eyes. The blue specimen came from the vicinity of York, Pa., and is in the collection of Mrs. Harry S. High. Distribution seems a little higher in Pennsylvania than New England, but not enough so to warrant definite attribution. All three members of the series often have spalls and are hard to find in proof condition.

No. 59	Diam.	Rim	Origin	Colors	Rarity
	3⅜	Plain rope on top	Eastern, see note above	Clear	Rare

This has the band of fine radial lines only on the outer edge of the underside of the shoulder. The inner edge is plain.

No. 60	*Diam.*	*Rim*	*Origin*	*Colors*	*Rarity*
	3⅜	Plain rope on top	Eastern, see note on No. 58	Clear	Rare

The background of the underside of the shoulder consists of cross hatching, instead of the radial lines and plain bands of the two other members of the series. This seems the rarest of the three.

No. 61	*Diam.*	*Rim*	*Origin*	*Colors*	*Rarity*
	3⅜	48 even scallops	Eastern, probably New England	Clear	Scarce
				Dark blue	Extremely rare
				Medium blue	Extremely rare
				Opal	Extremely rare

This is the only member of the following group that is thick and that was made prior to the invention of the cap-ring. The blue specimens are soft, rather cloudy, not clear, crisp colors. Attribution is based on distribution and style.

No. 62	*Diam.*	*Rim*	*Origin*	*Colors*	*Rarity*
	3 9/16	46 even scallops	Eastern, probably New England	Clear	Rare

The design is that of No. 61, with coarse stippling added as a background on the shoulders. This is a thinner, later plate made after the invention of the cap-ring and properly belongs in the lacy period. Note the domed shoulder typical of some unidentified factory, possibly NEG. Proof examples are extremely rare.

No. 62-A	*Diam.*	*Rim*	*Origin*	*Colors*	*Rarity*
	3 7/16	29 scallops, points between	Eastern, probably New England	Clear	Scarce

Precisely like No. 62, except for the change in the serration pattern. Note that the serrations are stippled, a purely Eastern and probably New England device. For series related to this see Nos. 256 and 256-A.

No. 63	Diam.	Rim	Origin	Colors	Rarity
	3 13/16	56 even scallops	Uncertain	Clear	Extremely rare

Shown here because of the resemblance to the central pattern of the preceding series, this plate belongs within the lacy period. The two known examples are owned by Mr. Paul Carson and Mr. George Ertell. Distribution, therefore, is no guide whatsoever to origin. No precise comparison has been made but, statistically, the serrations seem much the same as those on the Jenny Lind and on one of the Victoria and Alberts. There is a distinct possibility that these two historicals are foreign pressing, so this plate may be, too, and this, of course, would account to some extent for its great rarity in this country. We have not examined the plate to see if it has the glassiness characteristic of European plates but, judging by the photograph, the plate looks to be American.

Other examples of later waffle-center plates will be found under Nos. 140, 141, 142 and 145.

No. 64 is reserved for a new discovery.

MISCELLANEOUS EARLY PLATES
Nos. 65 through 72

No. 65	Diam.	Rim	Origin	Colors	Rarity
	3¼	17 even scallops	Eastern, probably New England	Clear	Scarce

Stylistically this is a New England plate, but distribution is about as dense in eastern and central Pennsylvania as in New England. This is not necessarily related to No. 56, as is so commonly believed. No. 56 has 15 serrations. Most specimens of No. 65 are thick and heavy.

No. 66	Diam.	Rim	Origin	Colors	Rarity
	3 3/16	12 flats, points between	New England	Clear	Rare

A thick, heavy and very early plate whose pattern is based wholly on cut glass designs. It is never in our experience found outside New England. Ordinarily, it is in bad condition having severe top spalls. The contour is much the same as that of a piecrust table.

No. 67	*Diam.*	*Rim*	*Origin*	*Colors*	*Rarity*
	3 9/16	18 even scallops	Eastern, probably Philadelphia region	Clear	Extremely rare

All specimens we have been able to trace (they are very few) were found in eastern Pennsylvania, except for a broken one that came from Tennessee. Several of the known examples are cloudy or even sick, and this is typical of early Philadelphia pressing. Superficially, of course, the plate looks like New England, with its large scallops and sheaf of wheat shoulder pattern, but note that both the diameter and the number of scallops vary from established New England practice.

No. 68	*Diam.*	*Rim*	*Origin*	*Colors*	*Rarity*
	3 11/16	18 even scallops	Probably Philadelphia as above	Clear	Extremely rare

The two known specimens are in the cloudy, sick glass so characteristic of early Philadelphia production and, so far as we have been able to trace them, were found in that area. Here, again, there is the New England sheaf of wheat, but these are combined with the 18-scallop rim. We cannot explain the larger diameter of this plate as compared with No. 67.

No. 69	*Diam.*	*Rim*	*Origin*	*Colors*	*Rarity*
	3 7/16	16 even scallops	Philadelphia area	Clear	Very rare

We have traced about 20 specimens, all to the Philadelphia area. The uncertainty about the exact number is due to the fact that several examples may have been checked twice. The plate is very rare and 20 is a high percentage of the known copies. Of these, over half were typically cloudy or sick. We consider such distribution proof of local origin.

No. 70	*Diam.*	*Rim*	*Origin*	*Colors*	*Rarity*
	3 7/16	Plain rope	Midwestern, probably Bakewell	Clear	Extremely rare

No photograph does justice to this early, heavy plate. All specimens we have been able to locate came from Ohio, except two, possibly three, found in Pennslyvania. This, of course, does not mean they were made in Ohio. No factory pressed glass west of the Pittsburgh-Wheeling area before 1830 when these plates were made. The design seems to be an adaptation of one found on a very early glass furniture knob which bears on its shank the words "Bakewell's Patent." Consequently, on the basis of distribution and on the similarity of its design to a marked piece, a Bakewell attribution has been made. If this is correct, the chances are that this was one of the earliest, perhaps the first, of the cup plates made west of the mountains. It is also the only plate of Midwestern origin, so far identified, that was made before the use of the cap-ring.

No. 71	Diam.	Rim	Origin	Colors	Rarity
	3⅝	14 scallops, points between	Philadelphia area	Clear	Rare

This is almost certainly early Philadelphia pressing, since nearly all specimens can be traced to that region. These plates are lighter and thinner than those usually associated with this early period, but the design seems to antedate 1830 and the plates were pressed without a cap-ring. In this variety the table-ring is plain.

No. 72	Diam.	Rim	Origin	Colors	Rarity
	3 9/16	14 scallops, points between	Philadelphia area	Clear	Rare

There are a number of points of difference between this and No. 71, but the chief variation and the one easiest to spot is that here 33 hobnail table rests replace the plain table-ring of No. 71. Again, the distribution strongly favors an origin in eastern Pennsylvania. Both of these plates are normally found in rather bad condition.

Nos. 73 and 74 are reserved for new discoveries.

Chapter VIII

THE TRANSITION PERIOD IN THE EAST
Nos. 75 through 109

"Transition," as we use it here, refers to style as well as technique, but not necessarily to dates. Both distribution and design indicate two sources, and it is almost certain that one area would lag behind the other in the stream of technical development. Mr. Marble has in his collection a No. 90 bearing a label stating that it was purchased in 1829 and changed hands as a golden wedding present in 1879. An average date for the plates in this section would be about 1829–1830.

Some of them were pressed in the old, two-piece mold. Others were made with what seems to have been an experimental cap-ring. This cap-ring was, in New England at least, very wide and carried the whole shoulder pattern, sometimes including even the table-ring. Such a mold had one and probably two serious defects. For one thing, a vertical fin nicely located to scratch polished tables tended to appear near the table-ring where the cap-ring joined the plunger. Moreover, unless the glass were worked at a very high temperature (unlikely at so early a date when wood must have been the fuel), there must have been a possibility that the gather would set prematurely before completely filling the mold.

Designs for the most part remain geometric but become more complicated and more delicate in scale. The plates are thinner, especially where the crude, early cap-ring was used. Rim treatment changes, the rope rim becoming the order of the day. Where scalloped rims are retained, they differ greatly from the standard types of the earliest period.

Judging by distribution as well as design, two sources are indicated, a factory in eastern Pennsylvania or New Jersey and one, maybe two, in New England. It is interesting to speculate on the precise origin of the New England group. Lura Woodside Watkins, writing in *Antiques* for October, 1935, credits plates similar to Nos. 77 through 80 to the New

England Glass Company. We understand that Mrs. Watkins later decided that the evidence was not conclusive but, in view of the peculiar, archaic and apparently localized wide cap-ring and because of the high percentage of opal and opaque-white specimens (NEG is said to have been famous for its opal and opaque-white) in this group, we still favor this attribution. It is not, however, a certainty; a Sandwich origin is still a possibility.

No. 75	*Diam.*	*Rim*	*Origin*	*Colors*	*Rarity*
	3 11/16	12 even scallops	New England, possibly NEG	Clear	Very rare

The occurrence here of the strawberry diamond between the border sheaves may indicate a date considerably earlier than 1830. The rest of the design, however, seems later. The cap-ring extended from the rim to just outside the table-ring.

No. 75-A	*Diam.*	*Rim*	*Origin*	*Colors*	*Rarity*
	3 13/16	Rope, top and bottom	New England, possibly NEG	Clear	Rare

This differs from No. 75 only in rim and seems to have been a much more popular design. At least, it is found more often.

No. 76	*Diam.*	*Rim*	*Origin*	*Colors*	*Rarity*
	3 13/16	Rope, top and bottom	New England, possibly NEG	Clear	Scarce

The strawberry diamond on the shoulder of No. 75 is here changed to a diamond-shaped lozenge, and little quartered circles in pairs are added above these lozenges.

No. 77	*Diam.*	*Rim*	*Origin*	*Colors*	*Rarity*
	3¾	Rope, top and bottom	New England, possibly NEG	Clear	Extremely rare

The attribution is based entirely on style and resemblance to the four plates immediately following, which are unquestionably of New

75

75-A

76

77

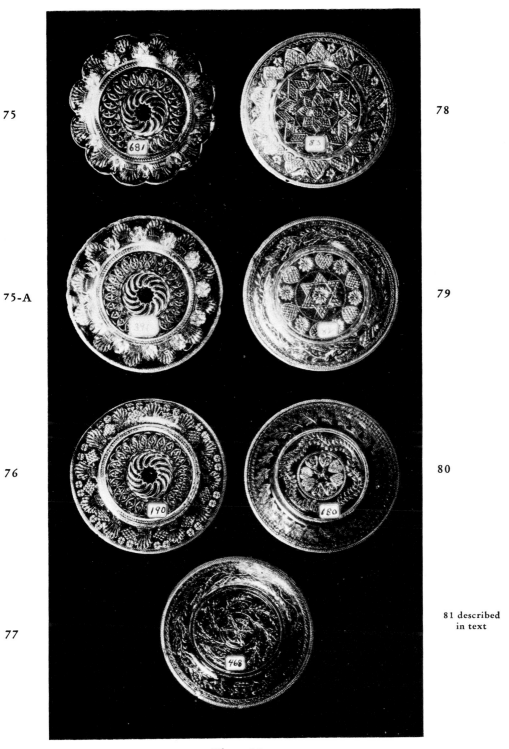

78

79

80

81 described
in text

Plate 11

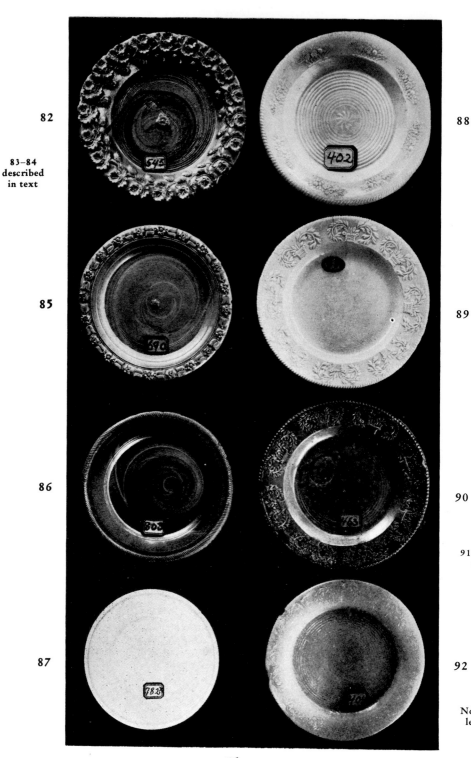

82

83–84
described
in text

85

86

87

88

89

90

91 desc
in te

92

Nos. 93
left op

Plate 12

95

98

96

99

97

100

100-A

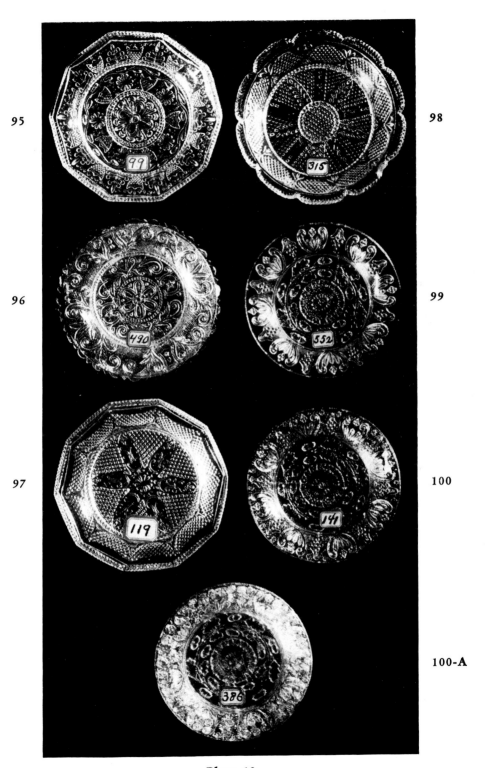

Plate 13

101

102

103

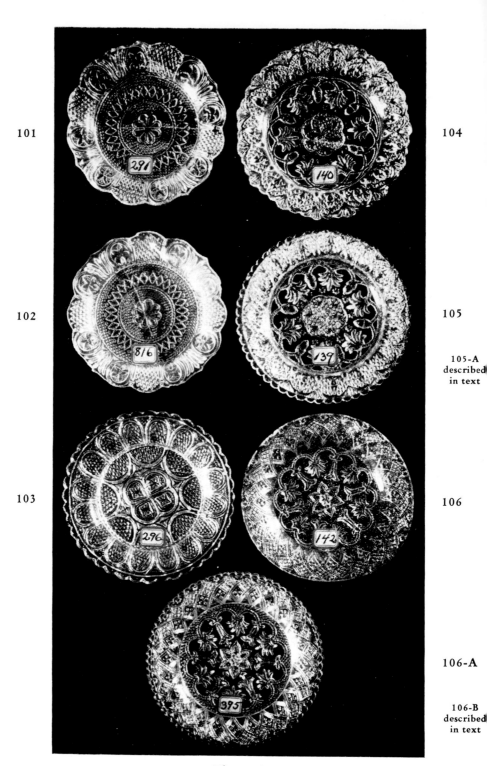

104

105

105-A
described
in text

106

106-A

106-B
described
in text

Plate 14

107

107-A

107-B
described
in text

108

109

Nos. 110
through
119
left open

Plate 15
Reduced in Size

England origin. So few of No. 77 are known (we can locate only two specimens) that distribution means nothing.

No. 78	Diam.	Rim	Origin	Colors	Rarity
	3 11/16	Rope, top and bottom	New England, possibly NEG	Clear Pink tint	Scarce Rare

The diameter given above is that of Mr. Marble's example. Others we have measured are 3¾″, and still others are in between these two extremes. The chances are the mold was 3¾″, as in the rest of the similar plates, Nos. 77, 79 and 80. The cap-ring used in making this plate extended from the rim to just outside the table-ring. We cannot account for the pink or lavender tints found occasionally in this and frequently in the following plate. Such tints are not characteristic of New England at this period. This plate has a rope table-ring with tiny feet.

No. 79	Diam.	Rim	Origin	Colors	Rarity
	3¾	Rope, top and bottom	New England, possibly NEG	Clear Greenish Grayish Pink tint Lavender tint	Plentiful Rare Scarce Plentiful Plentiful

This too has a rope table-ring with tiny feet. Like No. 78 it was made with a wide cap-ring. It is the most frequently found of the group.

No. 80	Diam.	Rim	Origin	Colors	Rarity
	3¾	Rope, top and bottom	New England, possibly NEG	Clear Opal	Rare Extremely rare

Unlike Nos. 78 and 79, this has a plain table-ring.

No. 81	Diam.	Rim	Origin	Colors	Rarity
	3¾	Rope, top and bottom	New England, possibly NEG	Opal Reddish-opal Greenish-opal	Extremely rare Extremely rare Extremely rare

Precisely like No. 80, except that this plate has a rope table-ring with tiny feet. This plate has not been reported in clear glass. The "reddish" and "greenish" opals are very striking colors and are not at all like fiery opals so often found in other plates. The whole plate is reddish or greenish, as the case may be.

No. 82	*Diam.*	*Rim*	*Origin*	*Colors*	*Rarity*
	3⅝	Plain	New England, possibly NEG	Opal Opaque-blue	Extremely rare Extremely rare

This has a 5-pointed star in the center. The opaque-blues defy description. They range from a light, near turquoise, to a deep purplish-blue. Usually they also have a silvery sheen. Once in a while a specimen turns up showing traces of gilt on the shoulder leaves. It is impossible to tell whether this gilding was done at the factory or not. The plate was made in a mold with a wide cap-ring extending from the rim to the center. Since the bottom of the plate has no table-ring, the fin that developed here would scratch the table very badly. All those we have examined show tool marks where the inner fin was removed while the plate was still hot. No clear glass specimens are known.

No. 83	*Diam.*	*Rim*	*Origin*	*Colors*	*Rarity*
	3 15/16	Plain	New England, possibly NEG	Opaque-blue	See note

This larger size has the star in the center but has 23 instead of 20 leaves on the shoulder. We can locate but two examples, those in the collections of Mrs. Harry S. High and Mr. George C. Cannon. It is likely that others exist, confused with the preceding plate. Both known examples are in a medium blue-opaque.

No. 84	*Diam.*	*Rim*	*Origin*	*Colors*	*Rarity*
	3⅝	Plain	New England, possibly NEG	Opaque-blue	See note

This lacks the central star. The concentric rings of the center terminate in a depressed dot. This variant is a recent discovery, and its degree of rarity is uncertain. It may be unique or, on the other hand, other specimens may exist where the missing star was not noticed. The color is an opaque light turquoise-blue.

No. 85	*Diam.*	*Rim*	*Origin*	*Colors*	*Rarity*
	3⅜	Plain	New England, Sandwich or NEG	Opaque-blue	Extremely rare

This is related to Nos. 82, 83 and 84 in color only and even in this respect 85 occurs only in a turquoise-blue-opaque which usually has a silvery sheen. The blue more often than not has much lighter, often nearly opaque-white, streaks running through it. The design appears to have been made to match the rare pedestal salts that turn up in the same color. These salts are popularly credited to Sandwich but may have been made at NEG.

No. 86	Diam.	Rim	Origin	Colors	Rarity
	3 5/16	Rope	Unknown	Opaque-blue	Extremely rare

Again, color is the only reason for placing this plate here. The rim pattern superficially resembles that on the Midwestern hearts, Nos. 442 and 443, and is unlike anything we associate with New England. The concentric circle center, however, follows New England practice of this period, as does the color. Distribution means nothing. We have been able to locate but seven specimens and six of these were found in, of all places, Iowa, by Mrs. John Anderson. Note that this plate is much larger than the Midwestern hearts. If, by some chance, the origin does prove to be the West, this will be the only known instance of the use of turquoise-opaque outside New England.

No. 87	Diam.	Rim	Origin	Colors	Rarity
	3⅜	Plain	Unknown	Opaque-white	Unique

Listed here because, quite frankly, we know of no other place to put it. We have never seen this plate; it is listed by Mr. Marble but is not in his collection. His photograph is from a plate in another collection. From the photograph and from Mr. Marble's description, we judge that the plate is perfectly plain and thus in a sense is similar to No. 889, which is not a cup plate. This, however, appears to be an earlier plate and may very well be one. According to Mr. Marble, the color is an opaque-white with traces of opal around the extreme edge.

No. 88	Diam.	Rim	Origin	Colors	Rarity
	3 11/16	Rope, top only	New England, Sandwich or NEG	Clear	Extremely rare
				Opal	Very rare
				Opal-opaque	Very rare
				White-opaque	Very rare
				Light cloudy blue	Unique

This plate was pressed in the old-fashioned two-piece mold, but must have been made on the very threshold of the cap-ring period. In many specimens there is a curious and, so far as we are concerned, inexplicable double impression of the center pattern. The basket in this plate lacks the frond-like leaves that depend from each side of the baskets in the rest of the group. The center has a pinwheel with stars.

No. 89	*Diam.*	*Rim*	*Origin*	*Colors*	*Rarity*
	3¾	Rope,	New England,	Clear	Rare
		top and	Sandwich or	Opal	Scarce
		bottom	NEG	Opal-opaque	Scarce
				White-opaque	Rare

The shoulder baskets have long pendant leaves at either side and there is no centering pinwheel or rosette. This is probably one of the earliest plates made with the wide cap-ring which forms the rope rim on the bottom of the plate and extends over the shoulder and includes the table-ring. The only part of the design on the plunger was the concentric ring pattern of the bottom of the plate. As in No. 88, double impressions are often seen.

No. 90	*Diam.*	*Rim*	*Origin*	*Colors*	*Rarity*
	3¾	Rope,	New England,	Opal	Rare
		top and	Sandwich or	Opal-opaque	Rare
		bottom	NEG	Opaque-blue	Unique

The shoulder baskets have the long, pendant leaves, but there is a small, swirled rosette in the center of the plate. So far as we know, no clear glass examples have been found, but specimens with opal centers and clear glass shoulders are known. The opaque-blue specimen is in Mr. Marble's collection and has a lavenderish sheen somewhat like that found on No. 82. The cap-ring on these plates was slightly narrower than that used on No. 89, and its inner rim was just outside, not inside, the table-ring.

No. 91	*Diam.*	*Rim*	*Origin*	*Colors*	*Rarity*
	3¾	Rope,	New England,	Opal	Unique
		top and	Sandwich or		
		bottom	NEG		

We have not seen this plate which is in the collection of Mr. Douglas Carapata. According to his description, it has a plain, instead of a rope, table-ring and the top center lacks the concentric rings of the rest of the series.

No. 92	*Diam.*	*Rim*	*Origin*	*Colors*	*Rarity*
	3½	Plain,	New England,	Opal	Unique
		no rope	Sandwich or	Opal-opaque	Unique
			NEG		

This lacks the rope rim of the rest of the series and is a smaller plate. The edge in cross section is a half-round with no fin and could not have been made in a mold. In fact, these plates, both of which are in Mr. Marble's collection, seem to us to be underfilled examples of No. 89, but we have never seen underfilling that extends the full circumference of a plate. The tendency to underfill or, better, to set prematurely, in these wide cap-ring plates is discussed in Chapter II. If the present plates are simply underfilled No. 89's, they are not true variants by our definition and should not be listed. However, in the absence of any trace of a rope rim, it is not certain that they are from the same mold and, conversely, they just may be true variants.

Nos. 93 and 94 are reserved for new discoveries.

No. 95	*Diam.*	*Rim*	*Origin*	*Colors*	*Rarity*
	3⅝	10-sided	New England,	Clear	Plentiful
		rope, top	possibly	Opal	Rare
		and bottom	NEG	Opaque-white	Rare

The complicated design probably indicates a date slightly later than that of the plates previously shown. For a related plate, see No. 97. Opaque-white specimens are a good deal rarer than opal ones.

No. 96	*Diam.*	*Rim*	*Origin*	*Colors*	*Rarity*
	3 7/16	25 scallops,	New England,	Clear	Plentiful
		points	Sandwich or		
		between	NEG		

Shown here only because it has for many years been popularly considered a variant of No. 95, which it most definitely is not. It is a considerably later plate, made well into the lacy period, and resembles No. 95 only in the central rosette.

No. 97	*Diam.*	*Rim*	*Origin*	*Colors*	*Rarity*
	3⅝	10-sided	Eastern,	Clear	Scarce
		rope, top	see note		
		and bottom			

This plate seems to have been pressed with the same surface die as No. 95, and thereby poses a problem. While the distribution of No. 95 is most dense in New England, No. 97 is fairly well concentrated in Pennsylvania. If microscopic comparisons show that the surface dies were the same, both plates must have been made in the same factory— but whether the factory was in New England or Pennsylvania, we do not know. For many years, persistent reports have reached us concerning both opal and opal-opaque examples of this plate, but we have never seen one in color and do not list any. They may, however, exist.

No. 98	Diam.	Rim	Origin	Colors	Rarity
	3⅝	10-scallop rope, top and bottom	Eastern, see note	Clear	Rare

The comparative incidence of this attractive plate in Pennsylvania is even higher than that of No. 97. Moreover, there is a marked resemblance in the character of the stippling and the treatment of the design as a whole. The evidence seems to point to a Pennsylvania origin for 97 and 98, but we are unable to fit the distribution of 95 into this picture. A pontil-marked example of No. 98 is known.

No. 99	Diam.	Rim	Origin	Colors	Rarity
	3¼	Plain	Philadelphia area, perhaps Union Glass Works	Clear	Rare
				Amethyst	Extremely rare
				Blue	Extremely rare
				Light green	Extremely rare

This interesting series was pressed in the early two-piece mold, but the design points to a date close to 1830. The colors are considered typical of early Philadelphia-region glassmaking. For some unknown reason, this plain variety usually has spalls off either the top or, more often, the bottom.

No. 100	Diam.	Rim	Origin	Colors	Rarity
	3¼	Plain	Philadelphia area, perhaps Union Glass Works	Clear	Rare

Like the preceding plate, except that here the background is stippled. This plate is much rarer than No. 99, but is not quite rare enough to be classed "very rare." Condition is usually better than in the plain variety. So far, no colored examples have been reported.

No. 100-A	Diam.	Rim	Origin	Colors	Rarity
	3¼	Plain	Philadelphia	Clear	Plentiful
			area, perhaps	Green tint	Plentiful
			Union Glass	Pink tint	Plentiful
			Works		

This has the stippled background of No. 100, but has a so-called "hop vine" pattern on the surface die. Of course the surface pattern obscures the one on the back, producing a very unsatisfactory result. It is difficult to understand why this was the most popular of the series. The green and pink tints are probably pressings from improperly cleaned pots previously used for the deep colors of No. 99. Note the acorn pattern. This motif constantly crops up in plates from eastern Pennsylvania. For allied historical plates, see the No. 651 eagles.

No. 101	Diam.	Rim	Origin	Colors	Rarity
	3¼	Ogee and scallop	Philadelphia area	Clear	Scarce

Made in a two-piece mold and, judging by its dependence on early cut glass for design, this is probably a very early plate, almost certainly antedating 1830. Very faint tints, too faint to list, in green, pink and blue are found. A high proportion of the specimens that turn up are underfilled. Diamond diapering on the shoulder extends to the rim.

No. 102	Diam.	Rim	Origin	Colors	Rarity
	3¼	Ogee and scallop	Philadelphia area	Clear	Uncertain

Here the diamond diapering does not extend to the rim of the plate. This is a recent discovery and, since the variation is so slight, misnumbered examples are probably the rule. At the moment it seems somewhat harder to find than No. 101. No tinted specimens have been reported.

No. 103	Diam.	Rim	Origin	Colors	Rarity
	3 7/16	40 even scallops	Philadelphia area	Clear	Rare

For many years this has been popularly considered a sort of companion plate to Nos. 101 and 102. Technically, however, it is later, since it was made in a three-part, cap-ring mold. The geometric design, on the other hand, is very early. Tints in a queer gray and in a blue, both too faint to list, are known.

No. 104	*Diam.*	*Rim*	*Origin*	*Colors*	*Rarity*
	3½	15 large scallops with two smaller between	Philadelphia area	Clear	Plentiful

This was made in a two-piece mold and, if thickness is a guide, is a very early plate. Note the recurrence of the Philadelphia acorn.

No. 105	*Diam.*	*Rim*	*Origin*	*Colors*	*Rarity*
	3½	57 even scallops	Philadelphia area	Clear	Plentiful

A later version of No. 104, made during the early lacy period in a cap-ring mold.

No. 105-A	*Diam.*	*Rim*	*Origin*	*Colors*	*Rarity*
	3½	58 even scallops	Philadelphia area	Clear	Uncertain

The one extra serration is easily overlooked so that many misnumbered specimens may exist.

No. 106	*Diam.*	*Rim*	*Origin*	*Colors*	*Rarity*
	3 7/16 approx.	Plain	Philadelphia area	Clear	Rare

The design is related to the 105 series, but is a more refined version and is probably a year or two later. This plate is always out of round in our experience, so that its diameter is impossible to measure accurately. The plate was pressed in a two-piece mold.

No. 106-A	*Diam.*	*Rim*	*Origin*	*Colors*	*Rarity*
	3½	71 even scallops	Philadelphia area	Clear	Rare

Like the previous plate, except it was made in a cap-ring mold and has serrations. It is not as rare as the plain rim type.

No. 106-B	Diam.	Rim	Origin	Colors	Rarity
	3½	77 even scallops	Philadelphia area	Clear	Uncertain

This has six serrations more than 106-A. It is a relatively recent discovery and there has not been time to decide its degree of rarity. At the moment it seems rare.

No. 107	Diam.	Rim	Origin	Colors	Rarity
	3⅜ approx.	Plain	Philadelphia area	Clear	Rare

Like No. 106 this plain rim type is always out of round, so that the diameter varies. This is a much more elaborate pattern and may have been made after 1830, but is included here because of its relation to the 106 series.

No. 107-A	Diam.	Rim	Origin	Colors	Rarity
	3½	71 even scallops	Philadelphia area	Clear	Scarce

This plate takes the same position in the 107 series as 106-A does in that series.

No. 107-B	Diam.	Rim	Origin	Colors	Rarity
	3½	68 even scallops	Philadelphia area	Clear	Scarce

It is astonishing to have a plate with 68 serrations turn up in this series where, by analogy with the 106 series, one would expect to find a 77-scallop variant. Collectors should be on the lookout for a 68-serration variant in the preceding series, as well as the 77-scallop type in this series. Both may exist.

No. 108	Diam.	Rim	Origin	Colors	Rarity
	3 7/16 across	Octagonal	Eastern	Clear	Scarce

This and No. 109 are a puzzling pair of plates. Those examined have no definite fins, although there is a line on the back of the shoulder that looks like the juncture of a cap-ring with a design die. Probably this fin-like line is simply a part of the design, and in this case the plates were pressed in the early two-piece mold. Everything about them, in fact, the design and the crudity of execution, looks early. Both members of the series turn up only east of the mountains, and attribution is based on this alone, since no similar plates exist for comparison.

No. 109	*Diam.*	*Rim*	*Origin*	*Colors*	*Rarity*
	3 7/16 across	Octagonal	Eastern	Clear	Scarce
				Opal	Very rare
				Opal tint	Very rare

A rope ring has been added on the bottom of the plate just inside the rim in an effort, it seems, to disguise the fin-like line mentioned under No. 108. Distribution is the same as in No. 108. If these plates are as early as they look, and we see no reason to doubt it, they are the first of the octagonal plates.

Nos. 110 through 119 are left open for new discoveries.

Chapter IX

THE LACY PERIOD. 1830–1845

THE BEGINNING IN THE WEST, WITH EASTERN ADDITIONS TO CLOSE SERIES
Nos. 120 through 196

The Lacy period is generally conceded to be the peak of cup plate design and technique. In design, although many geometric motifs persist, they are simply geometric and are not based on cut glass sources. There is an ever-increasing emphasis on classic motifs. Above all, there is the tendency to cover the background of the plates with some device like stippling, engine-turning, diagonal lines and so forth. Such background work seems to have been originally intended to conceal imperfections inherent in pressing, e.g., the unsightly scars caused by the shearing of the gather. Plates become thinner, more delicate and lighter, due to the almost universal use of a narrow cap-ring.

The color range is wide, wider in the East than in the Midwest. In New England, particularly, there was much experiment with color, and characteristic colors like violet-blue, peacock-blue and canary-yellow appear.

Except for an occasional discussion of the progression of design within a specific series, all attempts at chronological treatment are dropped. The period extends from about 1830 to 1840 (perhaps as late as 1845) and is treated as a whole.

Sources range from New England down through New York City (Gilliland), through New Jersey to Philadelphia and on to the Pittsburgh region.

THE BEGINNING IN THE MIDWEST

Although there is indisputable evidence (the Bakewell patent of September, 1825) that pressing began early in the Midwest, we know of but one cup plate, No. 70, that was pressed there before the invention of the cap-ring. If, as we believe, the cap-ring was in universal use by 1829 or 1830, there is a four-year period in which but one cup plate pattern was made in the West. This seems most unlikely. Perhaps certain pre-cap-ring plates now credited to Eastern, probably Philadelphia, sources are actually Midwestern pressings. It may be that the early Western plates are so rare that, so far, no examples have been recorded. Another possibility is that 1829 is too late a date to set for the Western adoption of cap-ring molds. Western manufacturers seem to have been a more adventurous and less cautious breed than their Eastern colleagues, so it would have been in character for them to seize upon the new invention while the New Englanders were no more than carefully testing it out. At any rate, always excluding No. 70, the first recognizable Midwestern plates were made with a cap-ring, had 30 large, deeply indented serrations and a turning or lathe center on the top of the plate in the form of a raised dot in the center. Mr. Cannon's careful laboratory research has shown that these, of all Midwestern plates, most nearly approach Eastern formulae in their high lead content. The Western tendency to reduce the percentage of lead seems to have begun very soon after 1830 and to have continued progressively, so that further research may give us a much better idea of dates.

Note that these early Western pressings all have geometric designs. They show the peculiar, cloth-like stippling characteristic of some Midwestern, probably Pittsburgh, moldmaker. Classic motives, notably the lunette, trefoil and cinquefoil, soon appear.

No. 120	*Diam.*	*Rim*	*Origin*	*Colors*	*Rarity*
	3 1/16	30 even scallops	Midwestern, probably Pittsburgh	Clear	Scarce

All we have seen show the lathe center on the top of the plate with one exception, and this was probably just a bad impression. These plates usually have pronounced fins and rough, pebbly surfaces. Note the cloth-like stippling and the relationship to the No. 655 eagle.

No. 121	*Diam.*	*Rim*	*Origin*	*Colors*	*Rarity*
	3 1/16	30 even scallops	Midwestern, probably Pittsburgh	Clear	Extremely rare

The porthole shoulder pattern is typical of Midwestern practice.

120

122-A

121

122-B

122

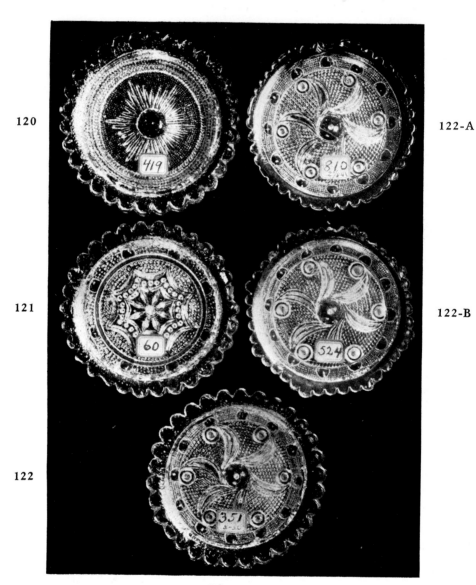

Plate 16
Enlarged

123

124-A

123-A

124-B

124

124-C

125

Plate 17

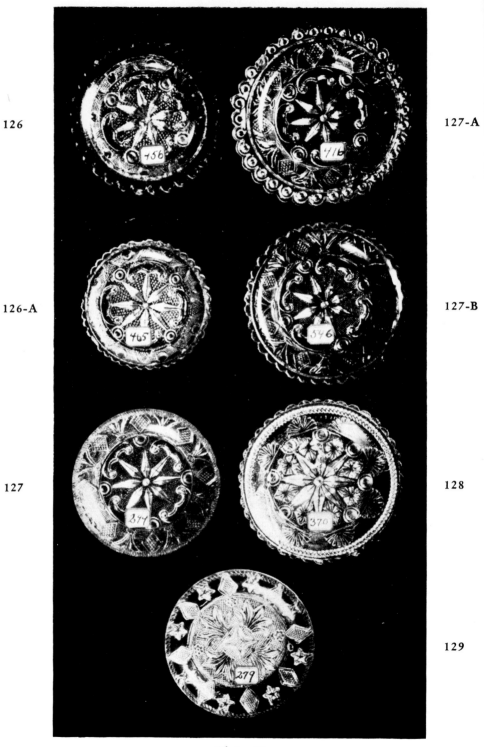

126

126-A

127

127-A

127-B

128

129

Plate 18

This has the turning center on top of the plate, but the stippling is much less regular. The plate is so rare that even badly damaged specimens are considered acceptable.

No. 122	*Diam.*	*Rim*	*Origin*	*Colors*	*Rarity*
	3 1/16	30 even scallops	Midwestern, probably Pittsburgh	Clear	Rare

The turning center is present. The stippling, while cloth-like, varies from the norm and may be a crude imitation of engine-turning.

No. 122-A	*Diam.*	*Rim*	*Origin*	*Colors*	*Rarity*
	2⅞	41 even scallops	Midwestern, probably Pittsburgh	Clear	Unique

The existence of this 41-scallop surface die is a great surprise. We can locate but one copy of this plate which was formerly in the collection of Mr. Jerome Strauss but now belongs to Mr. Marble. Others may exist and collectors should be alert to the possibility that 41-serration variants of other plates from the same factory may turn up.

No. 122-B	*Diam.*	*Rim*	*Origin*	*Colors*	*Rarity*
	2⅞ across	Octagonal	Midwestern, probably Pittsburgh	Clear	Extremely rare

Note that seven of the eight sides have 4 scallops between the corners while the eighth side has 5. Knowledge of the possession of this octagonal surface die by the unknown factory made possible the prediction that octagonal-footed eagles would some day be found. See No. 656-A.

No. 123	*Diam.*	*Rim*	*Origin*	*Colors*	*Rarity*
	3 1/16	30 even scallops	Midwestern, probably Pittsburgh	Clear	Rare

This lacks the turning center on the top of the plate and has a lower specific gravity (less lead in the glass), hence is probably of a slightly later date. See No. 656 eagle for a related plate. Notwithstanding these differences, it is from the same factory as the preceding series, since a variant has the same asymetrical octagonal surface die. No. 123 is rarer than No. 120 and commoner than No. 122.

No. 123-A	*Diam.*	*Rim*	*Origin*	*Colors*	*Rarity*
	2⅞ across	Octagonal	Midwestern, probably Pittsburgh	Clear	Extremely rare

The same octagonal surface die was used here that we find in No. 122-B. No comparable octagonal-footed eagle has so far been reported.

No. 124	*Diam.*	*Rim*	*Origin*	*Colors*	*Rarity*
	2⅞	16 scallops, points between	Midwestern, probably Pittsburgh	Clear	Rare

The wide scallop and point serration pattern is a later development. It is found on many Midwestern plates. See the Rose and Pansy and Open Rose, Nos. 148-B and 147-B for cognate examples. It should also be noted that by this time the early cloth-like stippling has disappeared. We have never seen this plate in good condition.

No. 124-A	*Diam.*	*Rim*	*Origin*	*Colors*	*Rarity*
	3	30 bull's eyes	Midwestern, probably Pittsburgh	Clear	Plentiful

It is very important to notice that, viewed from the back of the plate, these bull's-eye serrations meet in a sharp point, in contradistinction to the following plate with which it is easily confused.

No. 124-B	*Diam.*	*Rim*	*Origin*	*Colors*	*Rarity*
	2 15/16	30 bull's eyes	Midwestern, probably Pittsburgh	Clear	Plentiful

The bull's-eye scallops viewed from the back meet in a U-shaped juncture. There are many Midwestern plates having both the pointed and U-shaped meetings of their scallops and, in general, the U-shape seems slightly the rarer. This plate and its predecessor in the check list are relatively late and are probably closer to 1840 than to 1830.

No. 124-C	*Diam.*	*Rim*	*Origin*	*Colors*	*Rarity*
	3	Rope, top and bottom	Midwestern, probably Pittsburgh	Clear	Rare

For some unknown reason, this plate is usually found in bad condition. Proof specimens are extremely rare, if not unobtainable. Through its rim pattern this is related to the following plate and to the No. 442 and 443 hearts. It seems to be the latest of the 124 series.

No. 125	*Diam.*	*Rim*	*Origin*	*Colors*	*Rarity*
	3	Rope, top and bottom	Midwestern, probably Pittsburgh	Clear	Very rare

Related to the preceding plate and the hearts noted there, through the use of a single surface die on all four. It has been suggested that the mosaic design was inspired by a paperweight, but this seems a bit fanciful, although it may be true.

No. 126	*Diam.*	*Rim*	*Origin*	*Colors*	*Rarity*
	3 1/16	30 even scallops	Midwestern, probably Pittsburgh	Clear	Rare

With this plate we return to the early serration pattern of Nos. 120, 121, 122 and 123 and to the curious stippling on No. 122. The lunettes at the ends of alternating central rays are the first use of a device that soon became very popular in the West.

No. 126-A	*Diam.*	*Rim*	*Origin*	*Colors*	*Rarity*
	2⅝	42 even scallops	Midwestern, probably Pittsburgh	Clear	Rare

This little plate is exactly like the preceding one, except for the serration pattern. It is the smallest plate covered in this check list. For some reason or other, its rim is particularly sensitive and proof examples are unobtainable. Rough examples are plentiful.

No. 127	*Diam.*	*Rim*	*Origin*	*Colors*	*Rarity*
	3	Plain rope, top only	Midwestern, probably Pittsburgh	Clear Amethyst	Rare Extremely rare

The pattern is no more than similar to that of No. 126. The shoulder is wider, permitting completion of the diamond and the addition of a trefoil, and the stippling, while cloth-like, is more delicate in scale. So far as we know, this is the first appearance of color in a Midwestern plate. Judging by the extreme rarity of colored examples, all of them may have been pressed from a single pot of amethyst glass. But see the aftermath in the tints of No. 127-B. The surface die may be that found on No. 129.

No. 127-A	Diam.	Rim	Origin	Colors	Rarity
	3 9/16	34 bull's eyes	Midwestern, probably Pittsburgh	Clear Amethyst	Scarce Extremely rare

This is like the preceding plate except for the serrations. The 34-bull's-eye rim was widely used in the Midwest on other patterns. See Nos. 157, 158, 159, etc. As in the preceding plate, amethyst specimens are so rare that a single pot of glass, the same pot, would easily account for them.

No. 127-B	Diam.	Rim	Origin	Colors	Rarity
	3 3/16	36 even scallops	Midwestern, probably Pittsburgh	Faint pink Puce Red-amethyst	Very rare Very rare Very rare

Like Nos. 127 and 127-A, except for the serration pattern. The quality of the glass in this plate is bad. None we have seen ring. Moreover, No. 178-B also occurs only in inferior metal and, rarely, in puce. It seems to be related to this plate through its serration pattern. If proof examples of No. 127-B exist, we have not seen them. No clear examples are known.

No. 128	Diam.	Rim	Origin	Colors	Rarity
	3 5/16	39 even scallops	Midwestern, probably Pittsburgh	Clear Amethyst Lavender Blue	Very rare Extremely rare Extremely rare Extremely rare

While this strongly resembles the series just shown, it differs in many respects and there is no assurance that it was pressed in the same factory. The color range is uniformly more bluish and the similarity may be due to a common moldmaker rather than a common factory. It is an early plate. Note the cloth-like stippling, and it is thick and heavy.

No. 129	Diam.	Rim	Origin	Colors	Rarity
	3	Rope, top only	Pittsburgh	Clear	Plentiful

This little plate, with its modified cloth-like stippling and characteristically Midwestern cinquefoil, can, for once, be definitely assigned to Pittsburgh. It can also be dated, although the date is not necessarily that when the mold was first used. Mr. Albert Hise of the Massillon (Ohio) Museum has unearthed the following story. In May, 1833, Hugh Creighton married Jean McPherson in Pittsburgh. Shortly afterward, they met a friend, a local glassworker, who insisted that his wedding present to them should be a dozen cup plates of the bride's choice and his pressing. One of this dozen is now in the Massillon Museum. The rim pattern seems to be the one found on No. 127, which is a less elaborate and probably slightly earlier design.

THE LARGE BULL'S-EYE AND POINT PLATES AND THEIR VARIANTS

This group is most perplexing and, to even begin to understand it, we must include related historicals, semi-historicals and hearts. Take, first, the evidence of color.

Known in blue $\begin{cases} 134\text{-A} \\ 135\text{-A} \\ 670\text{-A} \\ 686 \end{cases}$ With one exception (686) all have bull's-eye and point and 36 bull's-eye variants.

Known in opal $\begin{cases} 605\text{-A} \\ 671 \\ 672 \end{cases}$ All are historicals and none has any bull's-eye serration variants.

In considering the historicals we meet an octagonal variety as follows:

Octagonal Constitution
Octagonal so-called Fulton
Octagonal Washington
Octagonal Plow

These have in common the fact that all have bull's-eye and point variants. None, to date, has a 36- or 40-bull's-eye variant.

This adds up to the conclusion that either two factories are involved:

Factory A owning a bull's-eye and point cap-ring
owning a 36-bull's-eye cap-ring
owning a 40-bull's-eye cap-ring
addicted to blue and blue only for color
more prone to make conventionals than historicals

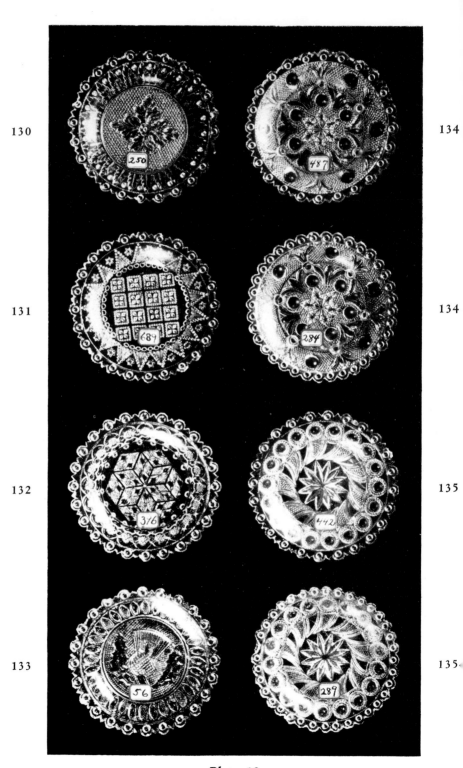

130

134

131

134

132

135

133

135

Plate 19

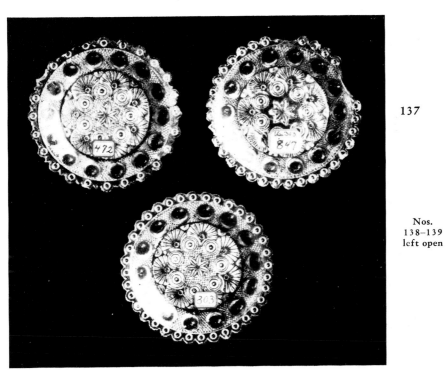

Plate 20

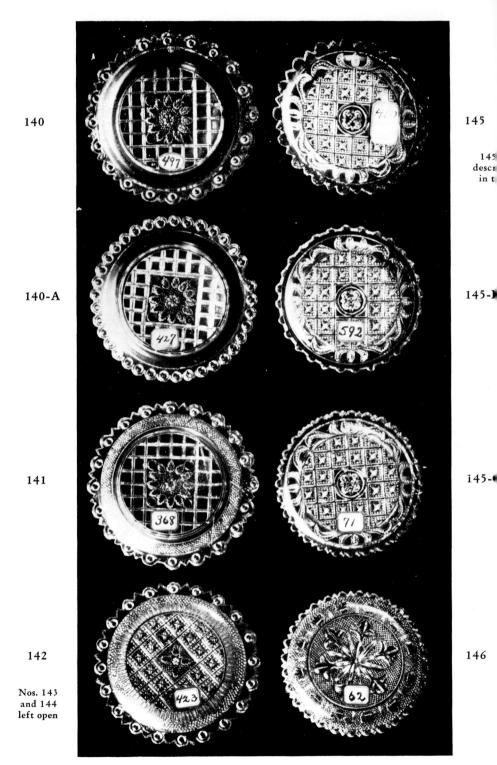

140

140-A

141

142

Nos. 143
and 144
left open

145

145
descr
in t

145-

145-

146

Plate 21

147

147-A

147-B

147-C

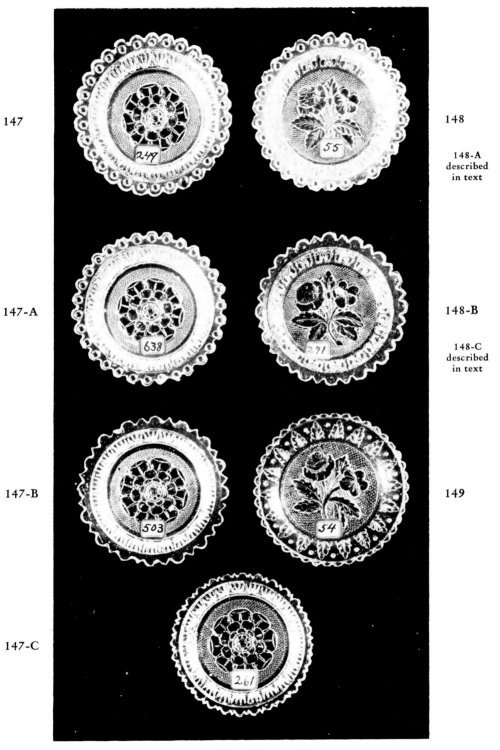

148

148-A
described
in text

148-B

148-C
described
in text

149

Plate 22

150

151

150-A

151-A

150-B

Nos. 152
and 153
left open

Plate 23

Factory B owning a bull's-eye and point cap-ring
owning an octagonal cap-ring (actually there were
two of these)
addicted to opal and opal only for color
and favoring historicals over conventionals

This means that there were two of the bull's-eye and point cap-rings. If the plates are carefully examined, we find that the historicals (always excluding the rayed eagle) have a cap-ring that shows a lathe mark at the base of the points and nearly at the base of the bull's-eyes, while most of the historicals show no such ring. This lathe mark or ring in no case appears on any of the plates having 36-bull's-eye or 40-bull's-eye variants.

Unfortunately, another peculiarity of the factory or factories is that there is a marked propensity shown for recutting design dies. Thus the Constitutions show several combinations of plain and stippled rigging; the Washington occurs with and without rays behind the bust; the Plows turn up with and without extra leafage and with and without the lined singletree, and the conventional No. 137 is found lacking stippling in its center. As nearly as we have been able to determine, this cuts across factory lines as outlined above and seems to show that but *one* factory is involved.

The only explanation that occurs to us is that the cap-ring with the lathe mark and the octagonal cap-rings were in use at a time when the factory was, rarely, using opal, while the cap-ring without the lathe mark was in use when they were occasionally making blue glass. On this basis, it can be predicted that possibly we *may* find opal Washingtons, Plows, Fultons and so on. And that we *may* find octagonal variants of the eagles, 671 and 672. Obviously, there is a chance of the blue and opal periods overlapping in the case of an individual transition plate, but this is unpredictable, since we have no idea as to which these transition plates may be.

The problem of precise origin is equally confusing. In our experience, the types found in opal and having octagonal variants are normally met with south of Pittsburgh, hence, perhaps, hinting at a Wheeling or Monongahela River origin. The types allied to the blue examples and lacking octagonal variants are more likely to be encountered north and west of Pittsburgh, thus nullifying the more southerly attribution. There is, in the case of the Plows, vague evidence of specific origin. The only known specimens of the octagonal Plows were found in north-central Ohio, just below Mansfield, and are said to have been purchased from a family whose grandfather or great-grandfather was an official at the Bakewell factory.

No. 130	*Diam.*	*Rim*	*Origin*	*Colors*	*Rarity*
	3 7/16	24 bull's eyes, point between	Midwest, probably Pittsburgh	Clear	Extremely rare

We see no reason why blue specimens should not eventually turn up. Nor why 36- or 40-bull's-eye variants should not be found.

No. 131	*Diam.*	*Rim*	*Origin*	*Colors*	*Rarity*
	3 7/16	24 bull's eyes, point between	Midwest, probably Pittsburgh	Clear	Extremely rare

Remarks here simply duplicate those on the previous plate except that, in our experience, this is even rarer.

No. 132	*Diam.*	*Rim*	*Origin*	*Colors*	*Rarity*
	3½	24 bull's eyes, point between	Midwest, probably Pittsburgh	Clear	Very rare

The cap-ring on this plate is, as you see, slightly larger and is, consequently, related to the eagles, Nos. 671 and 672, and the Washington. Thus, there is a possibility of an opal example eventually turning up. In this plate we have what seems to be the first use of the Roman Rosette band, a device later pirated and popularized in the East.

No. 133	*Diam.*	*Rim*	*Origin*	*Colors*	*Rarity*
	3 7/16	24 bull's eyes, point between	Midwest, probably Pittsburgh	Clear	Rare

Hitherto, this plate has been classified as semi-historical. Just why, we don't know. We see no commemorative significance in the thistle and suspect it was made to appeal to the Scotch-Irish elements of the early West.

No. 134	*Diam.*	*Rim*	*Origin*	*Colors*	*Rarity*
	3 7/16	24 bull's eyes, point between	Midwest, probably Pittsburgh	Clear	Scarce

The design shows just about as high a concentration of the char-acteristic Western trefoil as one can imagine. Blue specimens seem likely to turn up.

No. 134-A	Diam.	Rim	Origin	Colors	Rarity
	3 7/16	36 bull's eyes	Midwest, probably Pittsburgh	Clear Blue	Scarce Very rare

The blues found throughout this group are comparatively dull in tone and in no way resemble the deep brilliant blues of New England provenance.

No. 135	Diam.	Rim	Origin	Colors	Rarity
	3 7/16	24 bull's eyes, point between	Midwest, probably Pittsburgh	Clear See note	Scarce

Blue specimens have been reported. In fact, our own records as of 1925 show that we bought a pair in blue from Grace Black of Wil-loughby, Ohio, and sold them to George McKearin. All trace of these has been lost, and it is entirely possible that we misnumbered them. If they exist, they are certainly extremely rare.

No. 135-A	Diam.	Rim	Origin	Colors	Rarity
	3⅜	36 bull's eyes	Midwest, probably Pittsburgh	Clear Blue	Scarce Very rare

A very thin flat plate with peacock feather pattern, No. 284, is often classified with these plates. It is an eastern pressing (Philadelphia) and the resemblance is tenuous to say the least.

No. 136	Diam.	Rim	Origin	Colors	Rarity
	3 7/16	24 bull's eyes, point between	Midwest, probably Pittsburgh	Clear	Scarce

It seems not unlikely that a bull's-eye and point variant of the fol-lowing No. 137 series (lacking center stippling) will eventually turn up. Collectors should be on the lookout for it.

No. 136-A	Diam.	Rim	Origin	Colors	Rarity
	3⅜	36 bull's eyes	Midwest, probably Pittsburgh	Clear	Plentiful

So many of these exist that manufacture over a long period is indicated. If this is true, it may be that blue or even opal examples will be found, provided the "long period" included the time when these colors were being made at this factory.

No. 136-B	*Diam.*	*Rim*	*Origin*	*Colors*	*Rarity*
	3½	40 bull's eyes	Midwest, probably Pittsburgh	Clear	Rare

We are at a loss to explain why the factory, having this 40-bull's-eye pattern available, used it only so far as we can recall on this one design. Perhaps it was damaged in some way before it could be used in connection with another design die, but see Nos. 187 and 188 which have a similar ring.

No. 137	*Diam.*	*Rim*	*Origin*	*Colors*	*Rarity*
	3⅜	36 bull's eyes	Midwest, probably Pittsburgh	Clear	Extremely rare

This recent discovery seems to have been pressed with the design die in its initial state. We can locate only two copies, Mr. Cannon's and Mr. Marble's, but it is likely that others exist. Apparently, the factory found the design unsatisfactory and added stippling around the central rosette before many plates were pressed.

Nos. 138 and 139 are reserved for new discoveries.

THE SMALL BULL'S-EYE AND POINT PLATES AND THEIR VARIANTS

We do not know whether this group was made at the same factory as the preceding plates or not. There is evidence pro and con but nothing at all conclusive. On the negative side, there is the fact that the cap-rings used here were not used on any historical plates, nor do we find any colored specimens of the present series, except for one blue tint which is almost certainly accidental. On the positive side, we do see that this factory improved its design dies by recutting.

No. 140	*Diam.*	*Rim*	*Origin*	*Colors*	*Rarity*
	3⅛	20 bull's eyes, point between	Midwest	Clear	Rare

Note that one bull's eye extends beyond the proper boundary of the rim.

No. 140-A	*Diam.*	*Rim*	*Origin*	*Colors*	*Rarity*
	3⅛	37 bull's eyes	Midwest	Clear	Very rare

At this writing, we believe this is the only known use of this 37-bull's-eye cap-ring. The probability is that it was damaged before being long in service. Nevertheless, the possibility remains that it may have been employed in connection with some other design die, and collectors should be on the watch for such plates.

No. 141	*Diam.*	*Rim*	*Origin*	*Colors*	*Rarity*
	3⅛	20 bull's eyes,	Midwest	Clear	Scarce
		point between		Blue tint	Rare

The shoulder has been stippled in an attempt to improve the appearance of the plate, and so is unquestionably a bit later in date. The cap-ring is the same out-of-line one used on No. 140.

No. 142	*Diam.*	*Rim*	*Origin*	*Colors*	*Rarity*
	3⅛	20 bull's eyes,	Midwest	Clear	Rare
		point between			

At first glance, this seems to be a recutting of the design die used in the previous plates. Actually, it is not, since the central rosette is entirely different. We believe, too, that the cap-ring is different and does not have the protruding bull's eye. If this is correct this is the only use of this ring known to date.

Nos. 143 and 144 are reserved for new discoveries.

The following series has a vague resemblance to the preceding group and is usually considered with it. While the treatment of the waffling is much like that of No. 142, the central device is different and the shoulder pattern far more elaborate. One series may be a pirating of the other, or both series may have originated with the same mold-maker or even in the same factory. Again, there are no related historical plates, nor is there evidence of recutting. We do encounter one colored example but, since it is unique, it has little significance. The plain scallop and point serration pattern is ordinarily considered to be quite early and to follow directly after the large plain scallops of the earliest Midwestern plates.

No. 145	Diam.	Rim	Origin	Colors	Rarity
	2⅞	17 scallops, point between	Midwest	Clear	Very rare

In all plates with this plain scallop and point serration pattern it is imperative to count carefully the number of scallops since two varieties occur, one with 17, the other with 16 scallops.

No. 145-A	Diam.	Rim	Origin	Colors	Rarity
	2 15/16	16 scallops, point between	Midwest	Clear	Extremely rare

The difference in rarity is perhaps debatable, since collectors have been known to overlook the important point of counting scallops. So far as the major collections are concerned, this with 16 scallops is much the rarer of the two. Both are usually imperfect.

No. 145-B	Diam.	Rim	Origin	Colors	Rarity
	2¾	28 teeth, flats between	Midwest	Clear	Extremely rare

This is the only instance of the use of this gear-wheel type of serration. As usual, there is the possibility that these serrations will some day turn up on another design die. Judging by the very great rarity of this plate, this serration ring could hardly have been used for more than one day's production.

No. 145-C	Diam.	Rim	Origin	Colors	Rarity
	2¾	28 scallops, point between	Midwest	Clear	Plentiful
				Deep blue	Unique

By far the most common of the series. The deep blue specimen was discovered in the Howe collection and was probably found in the Midwest. Since one blue example is known, others will probably be found.

No. 146	Diam.	Rim	Origin	Colors	Rarity
	2¾	28 scallops, point between	See note	Clear	Scarce

To the casual glance, and even with face-to-face matching, this seems to be the same cap-ring that was used in No. 145-C, but closer inspection shows that this had a larger inside diameter, permitting the use of a larger design die. Thus, if it is the same ring, the center must have been reamed out. Since this plate has its greatest density of distribution in New Jersey and eastern Pennsylvania and rarely appears west of the mountains, we feel it was made in the East.

No. 147	*Diam.*	*Rim*	*Origin*	*Colors*	*Rarity*
	3	30 bull's eyes	Midwest	Clear	Scarce

Mr. Marble gives the diameter of this plate as 3 1/16. Specimens we have examined seem to be 3″ and the cap-ring seems to us to be that used on Nos. 148 and 150 where our measurement is also 3″. Serrations viewed from the back meet in a sharp point. Blue specimens may turn up.

No. 147-A	*Diam.*	*Rim*	*Origin*	*Colors*	*Rarity*
	2 15/16	30 bull's eyes	Midwest	Clear	Scarce

Here Mr. Marble gives the diameter as 3″, while those we have measured are as above and coincide with those with similar serration pattern, as shown below. This plate where, as viewed from the back, the serrations meet in a U rather than in a V is slightly rarer than No. 147. Blue specimens have been reported, but we have never seen one.

No. 147-B	*Diam.*	*Rim*	*Origin*	*Colors*	*Rarity*
	2 15/16	16 scallops, point between	Midwest	Clear	Rare

Proof specimens are almost impossible to obtain. A 17-scallop variant should turn up.

No. 147-C	*Diam.*	*Rim*	*Origin*	*Colors*	*Rarity*
	2¾	28 scallops, point between	Midwest	Clear	Scarce
				Blue	Very rare

The blue is the soft shade typical of the Midwest. Perfect specimens in either clear or blue are practically unheard of.

No. 148	*Diam.*	*Rim*	*Origin*	*Colors*	*Rarity*
	3	30 bull's eyes	Midwest	Clear	Plentiful

The bull's-eye serrations, as seen from the back, meet in a point. Blue specimens have frequently been reported and may exist, but we suspect these are the plate shown below.

No. 148-A	*Diam.*	*Rim*	*Origin*	*Colors*	*Rarity*
	2 15/16	30 bull's eyes	Midwest	Clear	Scarce
				Blue	Very rare

The scallops viewed from the back meet in a U. Again, the blue is the soft Midwestern shade.

No. 148-B	*Diam.*	*Rim*	*Origin*	*Colors*	*Rarity*
	2 15/16	16 scallops, point between	Midwest	Clear	Rare

This type serration seems to be very vulnerable so that perfect specimens are very difficult to find.

No. 148-C	*Diam.*	*Rim*	*Origin*	*Colors*	*Rarity*
	2⅞	17 scallops, point between	Midwest	Clear	Rare

Similar to No. 148-B except for the extra scallop. Proof specimens are virtually unobtainable.

No. 149	*Diam.*	*Rim*	*Origin*	*Colors*	*Rarity*
	3	42 scallops	Midwest	Clear	Plentiful

This is not, as is commonly supposed, the same design die as that of the four preceding plates. The leaves at the left, for example, differ markedly. Whether it was made in the same factory as the others is not known. It seems unlikely, however, that a specific factory would have two so similar dies. Distribution is country-wide, and the attribution is by analogy with the leaf pattern on the shoulders of other Midwestern plates. See Nos. 130, 181 and 191.

No. 150	*Diam.*	*Rim*	*Origin*	*Colors*	*Rarity*
	3	30 bull's eyes	Midwest	Clear	Plentiful

The bull's eyes meet in a V, but it seems not unlikely that a U-juncture variant will some day be found.

No. 150-A	*Diam.*	*Rim*	*Origin*	*Colors*	*Rarity*
	2⅞	17 scallops, point between	Midwest	Clear	Rare

By comparison, it would seem likely that a 16-scallop and point variant will turn up.

No. 150-B	*Diam.*	*Rim*	*Origin*	*Colors*	*Rarity*
	2 15/16	Plain, rope on bottom	Midwest	Clear	Very rare

This type rim is thought to be somewhat later in date than the bull's eye and scallop and point.

No. 151	*Diam.*	*Rim*	*Origin*	*Colors*	*Rarity*
	3	30 bull's eyes	Midwest	Clear	Plentiful

This and the following plate seem to us to be a little later in date than other plates with similar serrations. It is thus unlikely that the scallop and point serration patterns will appear with this design die.

No. 151-A	*Diam.*	*Rim*	*Origin*	*Colors*	*Rarity*
	2 15/16	Plain, rope on bottom	Midwest	Clear	Plentiful

Mr. Marble gives 3″ as the diameter of this plate. Those we have measured are closer to 2 15/16 and agree in size with other plates with similar rim.

For similar rims see hearts Nos. 441, 441-A, 442, 443 and 444.

Nos. 152 and 153 are reserved for new discoveries.

154

156

154-A

156-A

154-B

156-B

155

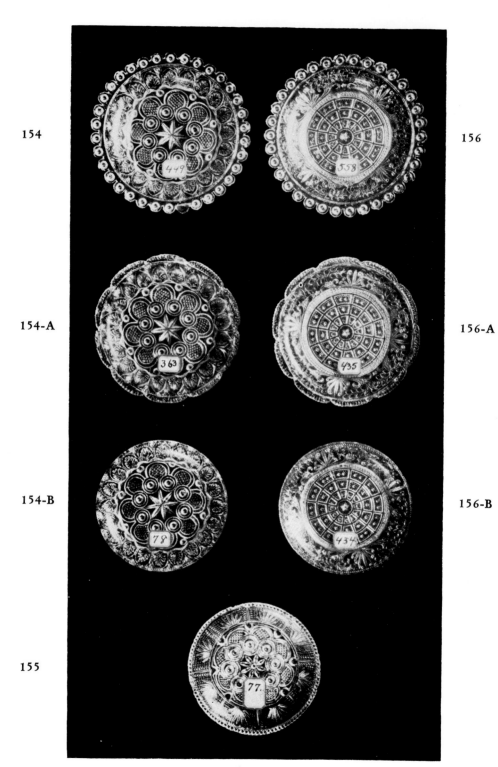

Plate 24

157 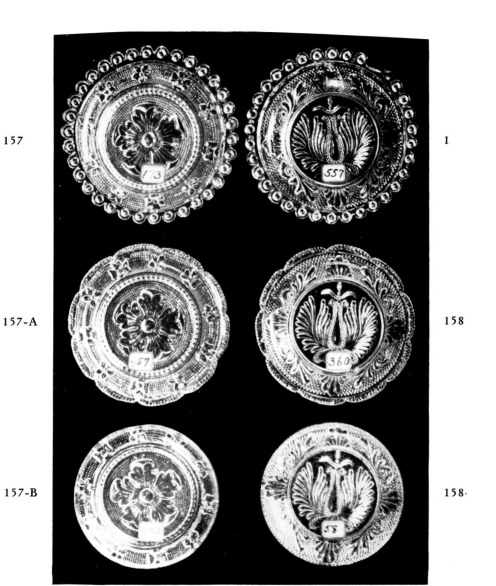 1

157-A 158

157-B 158·

Plate 25

159

159-A

159-B

161

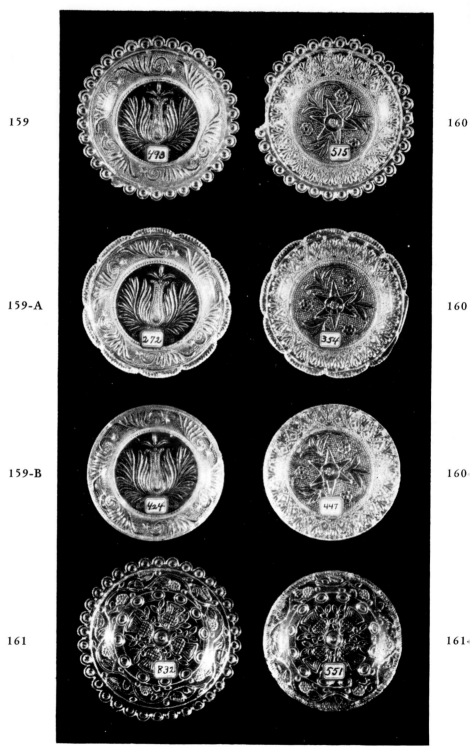

160

160

160

161

Plate 26

2

163

2-A

163-A

2-B

321

559

283

802

59

Plate 27

164

166

164-A

166-

164-B

166-

165

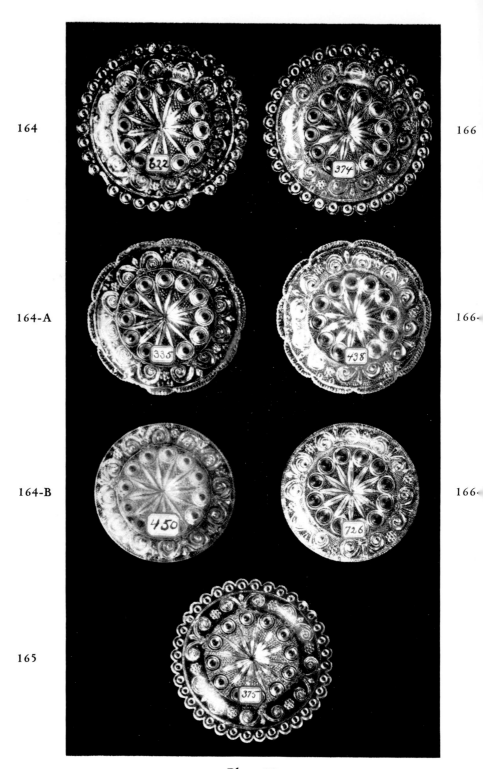

Plate 28

167

168

167-A

168-A

167-B

Plate 29

169

170

169-A

171

169-B

171-A

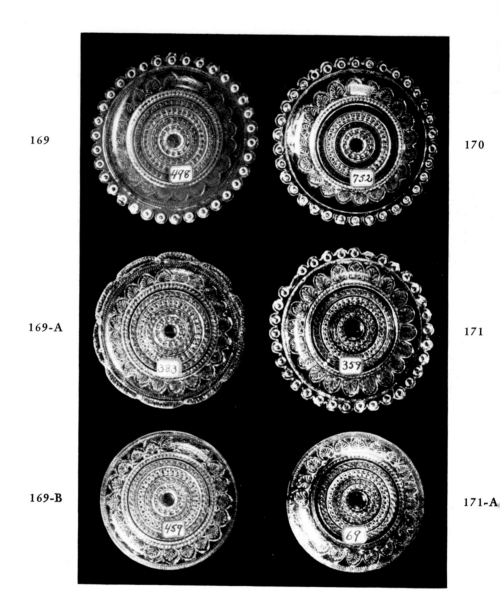

Plate 30

172

172-A

172-B

173

174

175

Plate 31

176

177

176-A

177-A

176-B

177-B

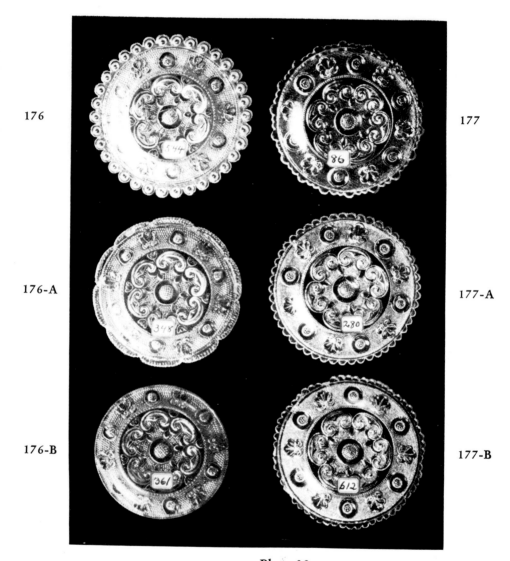

Plate 32

178

179

178-A

179-A

178-B

Plate 33

THE LARGE 34-BULL'S-EYE PLATES AND THEIR VARIANTS

With over fifty members the group makes up a high percentage of the total of Midwestern plates. The normal series in the group is:

(1) A 34-bull's-eye serration pattern with serrations formed by the cap-ring.

(2) A 10-scallop rope rim with the upper half of the scalloped rope formed by the surface die and the lower half by the cap-ring and, incidentally, it must have been a nice trick to match these two surfaces.

and (3) A plain rope rim (rope on top only) made without benefit of the cap-ring technique in a dam-type mold. We are at a loss to understand why, having developed the cap-ring and understanding its advantages, a manufacturer should deliberately discard it, but there can be no doubt it was done.

Several bull's-eye rings may have been used. The diameters, as given by Mr. Marble, range for the most part (there are a couple of exceptions) from 3 7/16" through 3½" to 3 9/16". The scalloped rope ring varies from 3¼" to 3 5/16" and, again, there are several exceptions. The plain rope rim formed by the surface die ranges from 2 15/16" to 3". These various mold parts, tools, so to speak, were expensive even by the standards of 1835. If all these plates, or most of them, were made in *one* factory, it must have been a large one to own such an inventory of molds. Probably the variation in size came from cleaning scale from the rings or surface dies.

Colors in the early period of the use of this type mold are very rarely found, but at a later date some bottle-glass factory, using inferior metal, made some light green specimens. In addition to the certain Midwestern source of most of these plates, it seems reasonably certain that one, perhaps two, Eastern factories used a similar but not identical 10-scallop rope rim. In the Eastern plates colors occur more frequently.

For a plate placed in an earlier series, but made with this 34-bull's-eye cap-ring, see No. 127-A.

No. 154	Diam.	Rim	Origin	Colors	Rarity
	3½	34 bull's eyes	Midwest	Clear	Rare

This design is related to the series with which we closed the previous group. Whether this means a common factory, a common moldmaker or designer or just plain piracy, we have no way of telling at this date.

No. 154-A	*Diam.*	*Rim*	*Origin*	*Colors*	*Rarity*
	3¼	10-scallop rope, top and bottom	Midwest	Clear	Plentiful

A large percentage of these turn up in a poor and very bubbly metal. Since other metal throughout the group is good, we assume that these bubbly examples were all pressed from one improperly cooked pot of glass. Judging by their number, it must have been a busy day at the factory.

No. 154-B	*Diam.*	*Rim*	*Origin*	*Colors*	*Rarity*
	3	Plain rope, top only	Midwest	Clear	Plentiful

This is often, perhaps usually, found underfilled.

No. 155	*Diam.*	*Rim*	*Origin*	*Colors*	*Rarity*
	3	108 dots on bottom	Midwest	Clear	Plentiful

This is an entirely different design die and is, we feel, a good bit later in date of manufacture. See also No. 199 and Lyre, 692, for similar rims.

No. 156	*Diam.*	*Rim*	*Origin*	*Colors*	*Rarity*
	3 9/16	34 bull's eyes	Midwest	Clear	Rare

Generally speaking, and with but few exceptions, the bull's-eye type throughout this group is rarer than its rope and scallop-rope companions.

No. 156-A	*Diam.*	*Rim*	*Origin*	*Colors*	*Rarity*
	3 5/16	10-scallop rope, top and bottom	Midwest	Clear	Scarce

No. 156-B	*Diam.*	*Rim*	*Origin*	*Colors*	*Rarity*
	2 15/16	Plain rope, top only	Midwest	Clear	Plentiful

No. 157	*Diam.*	*Rim*	*Origin*	*Colors*	*Rarity*
	3 9/16	34 bull's eyes	Midwest	Clear	Very rare

This series, as a whole, seems to be one of the rarest of the group.

No. 157-A	*Diam.* 3¼	*Rim* 10-scallop rope, top and bottom	*Origin* Midwest	*Colors* Clear	*Rarity* Rare
No. 157-B	*Diam.* 2 15/16	*Rim* Plain rope, top only	*Origin* Midwest	*Colors* Clear	*Rarity* Rare
No. 158	*Diam.* 3 9/16	*Rim* 34 bull's eyes	*Origin* Midwest	*Colors* Clear Blue	*Rarity* Very rare Extremely rare

The series shown here with its coarser stippling is somewhat rarer throughout than the fine-stippling series that follows. Blue specimens are in the soft blue so characteristic of the West. Proof examples are hard to find.

No. 158-A	*Diam.* 3 5/16	*Rim* 10-scallop rope, top and bottom	*Origin* Midwest	*Colors* Clear	*Rarity* Rare

This and the following series travel under the fanciful names of "Torch," "Liberty Torch" and "Victory Torch." We are unable to see such symbolism and confess that it looks to us like a stylized iris.

No. 158-B	*Diam.* 2 15/16	*Rim* Plain rope, top only	*Origin* Midwest	*Colors* Clear	*Rarity* Scarce
No. 159	*Diam.* 3 9/16	*Rim* 34 bull's eyes	*Origin* Midwest	*Colors* Clear	*Rarity* Very rare

The design die changes. It seems most unlikely that two so similar designs were the product of one factory. We should like to see precision methods used to determine whether or not the same cap-ring was used here as on No. 158. Blue specimens have been reported, but since we have never seen one and know no competent authority who has, we suspect they were No. 158's.

No. 159-A	*Diam.* 3¼	*Rim* 10-scallop rope, top and bottom	*Origin* Midwest	*Colors* Clear	*Rarity* Scarce

No. 159-B	*Diam.*	*Rim*	*Origin*	*Colors*	*Rarity*
	2 15/16	Plain rope, top only	Midwest	Clear Strong pink tint	Plentiful Unique

The pink-lavender tint is quite strong and is the color seen in several Midwestern eagles.

No. 160	*Diam.*	*Rim*	*Origin*	*Colors*	*Rarity*
	3½	34 bull's eyes	Midwest	Clear	Very rare

Perfect specimens are very difficult to secure.

No. 160-A	*Diam.*	*Rim*	*Origin*	*Colors*	*Rarity*
	3 5/16	10-scallop rope, top and bottom	Midwest	Clear	Plentiful

No. 160-B	*Diam.*	*Rim*	*Origin*	*Colors*	*Rarity*
	3	Plain rope, top only	Midwest	Clear	Plentiful

No. 161	*Diam.*	*Rim*	*Origin*	*Colors*	*Rarity*
	3 9/16	34 bull's eyes	Midwest	Clear	Extremely rare

This is one of the rarest plates known. We can locate but two specimens and one of these is badly damaged. The 10-scallop rope variant has not yet been found.

No. 161-A	*Diam.*	*Rim*	*Origin*	*Colors*	*Rarity*
	3	Plain rope, top only	Midwest	Clear	Extremely rare

Not nearly so rare as its bull's-eye serration mate but still in the first rank, since there are probably not over a dozen examples known.

No. 162	*Diam.*	*Rim*	*Origin*	*Colors*	*Rarity*
	3 9/16	34 bull's eyes	Midwest	Clear	Scarce

The rarity given refers to the average specimen. Proof examples are difficult to find.

No. 162-A	*Diam.*	*Rim*	*Origin*	*Colors*	*Rarity*
	3¼	10-scallop rope, top and bottom	Midwest	Clear	Plentiful

This is easily confused with No. 163-A, which is known only in light green and has some differences in shoulder pattern. This is a much smaller plate than No. 163-A and has its stippling in straight lines, while the stippling on No. 163-A is irregular.

No. 162-B	*Diam.*	*Rim*	*Origin*	*Colors*	*Rarity*
	2 15/16	Plain rope, top only	Midwest	Clear	Plentiful

No. 163	*Diam.*	*Rim*	*Origin*	*Colors*	*Rarity*
	3¼	34 scallops with radial lines beneath	Midwest	Light green	Very rare

This crude plate seems to be a pirating of the preceding series by some bottle-glass factory. No clear specimens are known; all are light green glass of very bad quality. The design die is crudely executed and the stippling is irregular.

No. 163-A	*Diam.*	*Rim*	*Origin*	*Colors*	*Rarity*
	3 7/16	10-scallop rope, top and bottom	Midwest	Light green	Extremely rare

A plate that is constantly mistaken for No. 162-A. This is much larger and exists only in light green. Note that there is a gap between the rope scallops and the design die.

No. 164	*Diam.*	*Rim*	*Origin*	*Colors*	*Rarity*
	3½	34 bull's eyes	Midwest	Clear	Scarce

In this series the center is stippled, but the shoulder is not. Note that here, as in the 166 series, there is a pair of disc-like dots over the rosettes on the shoulder. Proof examples of these bull's-eye plates are rare.

No. 164-A	*Diam.*	*Rim*	*Origin*	*Colors*	*Rarity*
	3¼	10-scallop rope, top and bottom	Midwest	Clear	Plentiful

This plain (not stippled) shoulder series is a bit more common than the 166 series which has stippled shoulders.

No. 164-B	*Diam.*	*Rim*	*Origin*	*Colors*	*Rarity*
	2 15/16	Plain rope, top only	Midwest	Clear	Plentiful

The plain-rope types throughout the group measure variously 3″, as well as 2 15/16″. The size does not constitute a variation, being due to either mold-cleaning or plate-warping.

No. 165	*Diam.*	*Rim*	*Origin*	*Colors*	*Rarity*
	3 7/16	36 bull's eyes	Midwest	Clear	Scarce

This has the plain shoulder of the 164 series, but lacks the pair of disc-like dots over the shoulder rosettes. The 36-bull's-eye rim is a surprise in this group and seems to establish this plate's relationship to similar plates of the 134-A category although this is 1/16″ larger.

No. 166	*Diam.*	*Rim*	*Origin*	*Colors*	*Rarity*
	3 9/16	34 bull's eyes	Midwest	Clear	Extremely rare

The stippling is much finer than that on No. 164 and No. 165 and covers the shoulder as well as the center. The disc-like dots of the 164 series are present on the shoulder.

No. 166-A	*Diam.*	*Rim*	*Origin*	*Colors*	*Rarity*
	3¼	10-scallop rope, top and bottom	Midwest	Clear	Plentiful

No. 166-B	*Diam.*	*Rim*	*Origin*	*Colors*	*Rarity*
	3	Plain rope, top only	Midwest	Clear	Scarce

When it was first discovered a few years ago, this plate was thought to be very rare but many have turned up since.

No. 167	*Diam.*	*Rim*	*Origin*	*Colors*	*Rarity*
	3 9/16	34 bull's eyes	Midwest	Clear	Extremely **rare**

Collectors have loosely assumed that this series, because of its plainness, is late and allied to the sunbursts. Nothing can be farther from the truth. These plates are unquestionably early and are among the rarest of plates. This is not to say they are the most desirable—their relatively uninteresting design prohibits that.

No. 167-A	*Diam.*	*Rim*	*Origin*	*Colors*	*Rarity*
	3¼	10-scallop rope, top and bottom	Midwest	Clear	Extremely rare

No. 167-B	*Diam.*	*Rim*	*Origin*	*Colors*	*Rarity*
	3	Plain rope, top only	Midwest	Clear	Extremely **rare**

This is a shade less rare than the two preceding plates but the difference is in the existence of only three or four more specimens and cannot be translated into broad rarity statements.

No. 168	*Diam.*	*Rim*	*Origin*	*Colors*	*Rarity*
	3¼	10-scallop rope, top and bottom	Midwest	Clear	Extremely rare

The 34-bull's-eye variant has not yet been reported. This type minus the center dot and concentric rings of the preceding series is even rarer. It is the first version of the design, and the series just discussed is from a recut design die.

No. 168-A	*Diam.*	*Rim*	*Origin*	*Colors*	*Rarity*
	3	Plain rope, top only	Midwest	Clear	Extremely rare

No. 169	*Diam.*	*Rim*	*Origin*	*Colors*	*Rarity*
	3½	34 bull's eyes	Midwest	Clear	Scarce

The porthole in the center of the plate measures ⅜″. Just inside the bull's-eye rim there is a rope band.

No. 169-A	*Diam.*	*Rim*	*Origin*	*Colors*	*Rarity*
	3¼	10-scallop rope, top and bottom	Midwest	Clear	Plentiful

This has the ⅜″ porthole and the rope band inside the serration line.

No. 169-B	*Diam.*	*Rim*	*Origin*	*Colors*	*Rarity*
	3	Plain rope, top only	Midwest	Clear	Plentiful

With the ⅜″ porthole and the rope band as above.

No. 170	*Diam.*	*Rim*	*Origin*	*Colors*	*Rarity*
	3 9/16	34 bull's eyes	Midwest	Clear	Extremely rare

This has the small porthole, but does not have the rope band just inside the serration line. The two center circles carrying the diamond or cross-hatch pattern are much fainter than in the preceding series.

No. 171	*Diam.*	*Rim*	*Origin*	*Colors*	*Rarity*
	3½	34 bull's eyes	Midwest	Clear	Plentiful
				Amethyst	Extremely rare

The center porthole is larger by 1/16″ and measures 7/16″ and it is amazing how much larger it seems. The conventionalized leaf-forms on the shoulder are more elongated than on the previous plates. There is no rope band next to the serrations. The six known deep amethyst plates were found in Oxford, Ohio. No 10-scallop rope variant has been reported.

No. 171-A	*Diam.*	*Rim*	*Origin*	*Colors*	*Rarity*
	3	Plain rope, top only	Midwest	Clear	Scarce

This has the larger 7/16″ porthole, no rope band next to the rim and has the longer shoulder leaves.

No. 172	*Diam.*	*Rim*	*Origin*	*Colors*	*Rarity*
	3 9/16	34 bull's eyes	Midwest	Clear	Rare

The triangular central figures are filled with tiny, elongated diamonds. The pattern was, in its day, one of the most popular the West produced. The bull's-eye type is astonishingly hard to find. The glass in this plate is usually cloudy.

No. 172-A	*Diam.*	*Rim*	*Origin*	*Colors*	*Rarity*
	3 5/16	10-scallop rope, top and bottom	Midwest	Clear	Plentiful

Like the preceding plate, except for the rim.

No. 172-B	*Diam.*	*Rim*	*Origin*	*Colors*	*Rarity*
	2 15/16	Plain rope, top only	Midwest	Clear	Plentiful

Like the two plates immediately preceding it, except for the rim.

No. 173	*Diam.*	*Rim*	*Origin*	*Colors*	*Rarity*
	3 5/16	10-scallop rope, top and bottom	Midwest	Clear	Plentiful

The center triangles are filled with tiny squares, instead of the little elongated diamonds of the preceding series. The lines dividing the triangles are badly drawn, leaving a gap between the outer edges of the triangles.

No. 174	*Diam.*	*Rim*	*Origin*	*Colors*	*Rarity*
	3⅝	10-scallop	Uncertain,	Clear	Plentiful
		rope, top	probably	Opal	Very rare
		and bottom	Eastern	Opaque-white	Very rare
				Opaque-blue	Extremely rare

Note that this is a much larger plate than Nos. 172-A and 173. The radial lines forming the central triangles taper toward the center. Both distribution and color range point to an Eastern, probably New England, origin. As to which area originated and which pirated the design, we have no idea.

No. 175	*Diam.*	*Rim*	*Origin*	*Colors*	*Rarity*
	3½	Plain rim,	Unknown	Clear	Plentiful
		rope on			
		bottom			

Note how much finer the tiny squares are that fill the central triangles. With no data available on distribution, we cannot even guess at the source.

No. 176	*Diam.*	*Rim*	*Origin*	*Colors*	*Rarity*
	3 9/16	34 bull's eyes	Midwest	Clear	Rare

The design has an Eastern counterpart. See No. 177. Proof or even good specimens of these bull's-eye rims are hard to find.

No. 176-A	*Diam.*	*Rim*	*Origin*	*Colors*	*Rarity*
	3 5/16	10-scallop	Midwest	Clear	Plentiful
		rope, top			
		and bottom			

Examples in a very faint bluish tint are often found.

No. 176-B	*Diam.*	*Rim*	*Origin*	*Colors*	*Rarity*
	3	Plain rope,	Midwest	Clear	Plentiful
		top only			

As above, faint blue tints, occasionally faint lavender, are frequently encountered.

No. 177	*Diam.*	*Rim*	*Origin*	*Colors*	*Rarity*
	3½	18 large	New England,	Clear	Plentiful
		scallops	probably		
		with 2 smaller	Sandwich		
		ones between			

This series by no means belongs in any bull's-eye group, but the design is so similar to the preceding series that placing it elsewhere might confuse collectors. As to whether the West pirated the design from the East or vice versa, we do not pretend to know.

No. 177-A	*Diam.*	*Rim*	*Origin*	*Colors*	*Rarity*
	3⅜	49 even scallops	New England, probably Sandwich	Clear	Plentiful

Note that in this series the stippling is much finer than in No. 176.

No. 177-B	*Diam.*	*Rim*	*Origin*	*Colors*	*Rarity*
	3 7/16	60 scallops, faintly 12-sided	New England, probably Sandwich	Clear	Scarce

While rarity is given as "scarce," this plate is very difficult to find in fine condition. There is a faint possibility that this series was made farther south than New England, around New York or Philadelphia.

For similar plates see Nos. 230, 230-A and 230-B and the 666 eagles.

No. 178	*Diam.*	*Rim*	*Origin*	*Colors*	*Rarity*
	3 7/16	10-scallop rope, top and bottom	Midwest	Clear	Very rare

Strictly speaking, this plate and its variants do not belong in this group at all, but collectors for many years have lumped them together. These are larger in diameter than other members of the group and are deeper plates. They are unquestionably Midwestern pressing but are, most likely, from another factory. We doubt if a bull's-eye variant will be found.

No. 178-A	*Diam.*	*Rim*	*Origin*	*Colors*	*Rarity*
	3⅛	Rope, top only	Midwest	Clear	Rare

For some unknown reason, this plate is often found with a spall off its surface.

No. 178-B	*Diam.*	*Rim*	*Origin*	*Colors*	*Rarity*
	3¼	36 even scallops	Midwest	Clear	Plentiful
				Light green	Plentiful
				Green tint	Plentiful
				Puce	Very rare
				Pinkish tint	Rare
				Blue	Unique

All specimens we have seen are in a very poor quality of metal. None ring properly when tapped. We believe this plate to be a late use of the original design die with a new serration ring.

No. 179	Diam.	Rim	Origin	Colors	Rarity
	3 7/16	10-scallop rope, top and bottom	Philadelphia area	Clear	Rare
				Lavender	Very rare
				Amethyst	Extremely rare

Like the preceding series, this does not properly belong in this group. This and its variant are larger than the norm and much deeper. The attribution is based on distribution and on similarity to No. 69.

No. 179-A	Diam.	Rim	Origin	Colors	Rarity
	3⅛	Plain rope, top only	Philadelphia area	Clear	Rare

THE SMALL 40-BULL'S-EYE PLATES AND THEIR EVEN-SERRATION VARIANTS

For other (larger) 40-bull's-eye plates see Nos. 187 and 188.

No. 180	Diam.	Rim	Origin	Colors	Rarity
	3¼	40 bull's eyes	Midwest	Clear	Plentiful

"Plentiful" is a deceptive term here. In both this and the following plate, proof examples are hard to find.

No. 180-A	Diam.	Rim	Origin	Colors	Rarity
	3⅛	48 even scallops	Midwest	Clear	Plentiful

No. 181	Diam.	Rim	Origin	Colors	Rarity
	3¼	40 bull's eyes	Midwest	Clear	Unique

Mr. Marble's badly battered specimen is the only one known to us. Others may exist in less well-known collections.

No. 181-A	Diam.	Rim	Origin	Colors	Rarity
	3⅛	48 even scallops	Midwest	Clear	Very rare

As usual throughout this group, proof specimens are next to impossible to obtain.

No. 182	*Diam.*	*Rim.*	*Origin*	*Colors*	*Rarity*
	3 3/16	40 bull's eyes	Midwest	Clear	Extremely rare

The measurement, which was made from Mr. Marble's copy, is, as you see, 1/16″ smaller than that of kindred plates. We are convinced that this is the same cap-ring, and assume that Mr. Marble's specimen is slightly out-of-round or warped. Probably the average example will measure 3¼″.

No. 182-A	*Diam.*	*Rim*	*Origin*	*Colors*	*Rarity*
	3⅛	48 even scallops	Midwest	Clear	Very rare

The difference in rarity between this and its bull's-eye variant is indeed tenuous. At this writing it seems to us that there are a few more, possibly four or five, of the 48-scallop type known. Probably both plates should be classed "extremely rare."

THE LARGE 36-BULL'S-EYE PLATES AND THEIR OCTAGONAL AND SCALLOP AND POINT VARIANTS

For other 36-bull's-eye plates see Nos. 134-A, 135-A, 136-A and 137.

No. 183	*Diam.*	*Rim*	*Origin*	*Colors*	*Rarity*
	3½	36 bull's eyes	Midwest	Clear	Extremely rare

The bull's-eye type seems slightly rarer than the octagonal and possibly a shade less rare than the scallop and point type. All members of the series are so rare that the distinction is meaningless.

No. 183-A	*Diam.*	*Rim*	*Origin*	*Colors*	*Rarity*
	3⅜	24 scallops, with points between	Midwest	Clear	Extremely rare

Practically all specimens are at best slightly rough.

180

180-A

181

181-A

182

182-A

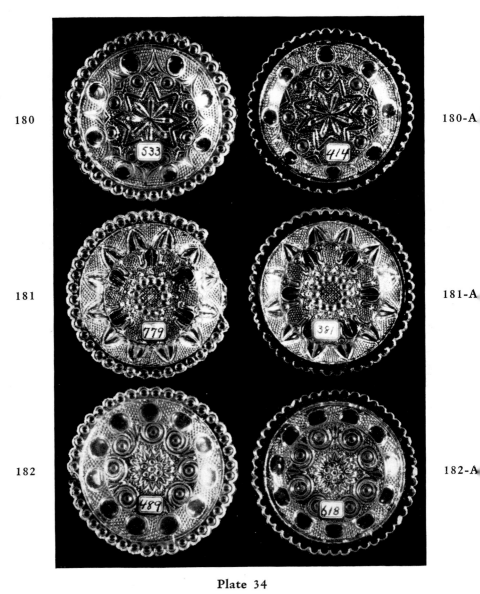

Plate 34

183

184

183-A

184-A

183-B

184-B

185

No. 186
left
open

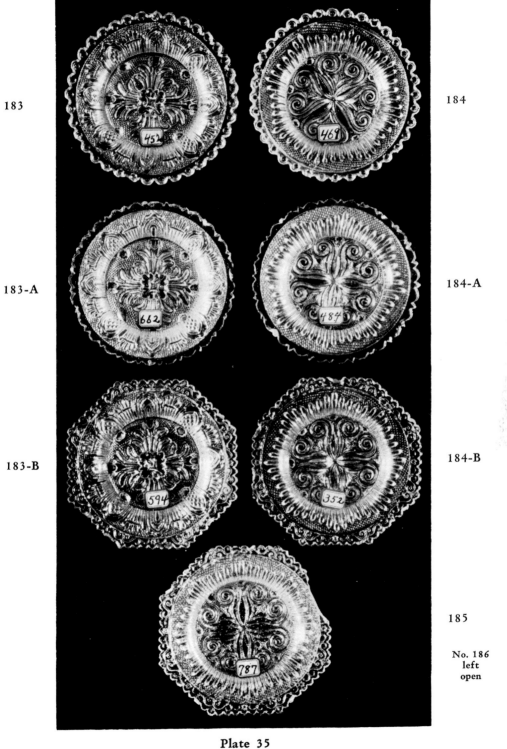

Plate 35

187

188

187-A

189

190

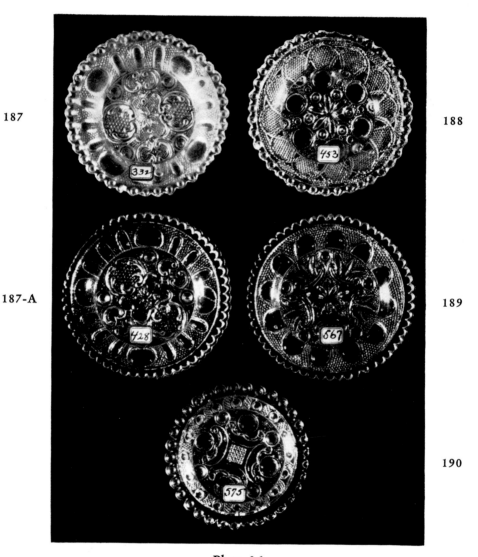

Plate 36

191

A, 191-C
D, 191-E
scribed
1 text

191-B

192

192-A

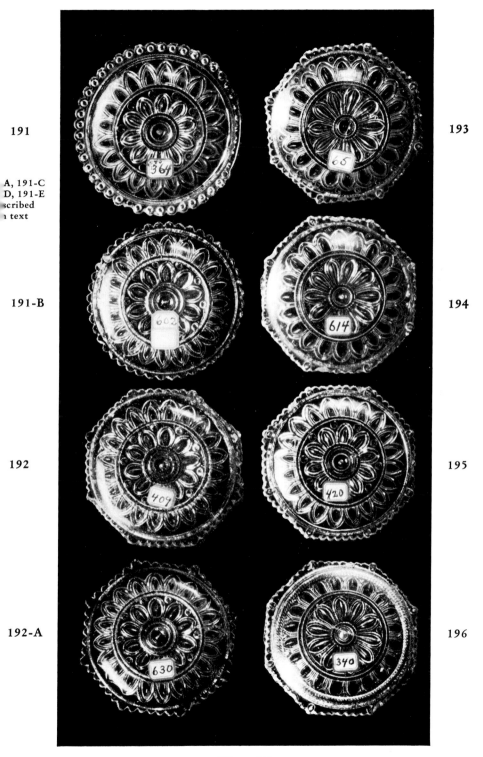

193

194

195

196

Plate 37

No. 183-B	*Diam.*	*Rim*	*Origin*	*Colors*	*Rarity*
	3½	Octagonal, 7 scallops	Midwest	Clear	Extremely rare
		between the corners		Deep blue	Extremely rare

The blue specimens are a very deep color, nearly an inky-black or blue-black. We know of no other plates in a similar color. A set of six (one broken into many pieces) constitutes all the known colored examples. They were found in Pittsburgh in 1941.

No. 184	*Diam.*	*Rim*	*Origin*	*Colors*	*Rarity*
	3½	36 bull's eyes	Midwest	Clear	Very rare

This design is slightly less rare than the preceding one.

No. 184-A	*Diam.*	*Rim*	*Origin*	*Colors*	*Rarity*
	3⅜	24 scallops with points between	Midwest	Clear	Very rare

Most specimens we have seen are a little rough.

No. 184-B	*Diam.*	*Rim*	*Origin*	*Colors*	*Rarity*
	3½	Octagonal, 7 scallops	Midwest	Clear	Rare
		between the corners		Light green	Unique

Some 25 years ago, one of the present writers and George McKearin saw a green specimen in the McIntyre Antique Shop at Jacksontown, Ohio. It was being held for a customer who took it and we have been unable to trace it. Amber specimens have been reported, but no reliable observer has seen one.

No. 185	*Diam.*	*Rim*	*Origin*	*Colors*	*Rarity*
	3 7/16	Octagonal, 7 scallops between the corners	Midwest	Clear	Unique

The differences between this and the preceding plate defy adequate description. The size is a shade less, but this might be peculiar to Mr. Marble's specimen through warping or other distortion, and is not conclusive. The speed of the curves of the center scrolls is here a bit more abrupt. These scrolls in the preceding plate in *cross section* are a wide bevel while in this plate in *cross section* the scrolls are formed by a narrow bevel. Needless to say, the light green and amber specimens credited to the preceding plate may be this one. The great rarity is most likely more apparent than real. We are convinced that others exist improperly numbered.

No. 186 is reserved for a new discovery.

THE 40-BULL'S-EYE PLATES AND THEIR VARIANTS

Only one of the three series or designs in this group is properly and logically filled out. It is possible that the missing members will eventually turn up, but the already known members are so rare that we have our doubts. While we have been unable to match surfaces, it seems likely that No. 136-B was made with this same bull's-eye cap-ring.

No. 187	*Diam.*	*Rim*	*Origin*	*Colors*	*Rarity*
	3 7/16	40 bull's eyes	Midwest	Clear See note	Rare

The design is reminiscent of the popular Eastern Shell pattern and was probably inspired by it or it may be an out-and-out pirating of that design. See Nos. 245, etc.

No. 187-A	*Diam.*	*Rim*	*Origin*	*Colors*	*Rarity*
	3 7/16	56 even scallops	Midwest	Clear	Rare

In our experience this is rarer than its bull's-eye variant and might even qualify as "very rare." This is especially true if only specimens in fine condition are considered.

No. 188	*Diam.*	*Rim*	*Origin*	*Colors*	*Rarity*
	3 7/16	40 bull's eyes	Midwest	Clear	Extremely rare

This is much rarer than No. 187. No even-serration variant has so far been found. Logically one should turn up.

No. 189	*Diam.*	*Rim*	*Origin*	*Colors*	*Rarity*
	3 7/16	56 even scallops	Midwest	Clear	Extremely rare

No bull's-eye serration variant of this plate has as yet been found, although it is logical to expect one.

THE 33-BULL'S-EYE PLATE

No. 190	Diam.	Rim	Origin	Colors	Rarity
	3	33 bull's eyes	Midwest	Clear	Extremely rare

Theoretically this *could* be the first of all bull's-eye plates. Mechanically, it is an absurdity, since the bull's eyes are on a cap-ring while the serrations are cut by a surface die. The difficulty of matching these two surfaces was tremendous, and probably accounts for the great rarity of this plate, the assumption being that the manufacturer became tired of trying to match them and scrapped the mold. Most, if not all, examples have their bull's eyes hanging half on and half off the scallops. The plate has no conventional counterpart but does have an eagle and a lyre, Nos. 656-B and 690-A.

THE 45- AND 48-BULL'S-EYE PLATES AND THEIR ROUND AND OCTAGONAL VARIANTS

There is a distinct possibility that this group properly belongs in a later (the second transition) period. Serration analogies with late eagles, the 680 series, and late sunbursts tend to confirm this. Gothic influences begin to replace Classic motives about 1840. Since the design is somewhat elaborate for the late transition period, we consider the group here. Nos. 191 through 191-E have large targets.

No. 191	Diam.	Rim	Origin	Colors	Rarity
	3¼	45 bull's eyes	Midwest	Clear	Scarce

We may have underestimated rarity. All specimens known to us have turned up in the Pittsburgh region and, since we are somewhat more familiar with that area than others, there is always a chance of our interpreting regional degrees of relative plenty as national in scope.

No. 191-A	Diam.	Rim	Origin	Colors	Rarity
	3⅛	48 bull's eyes	Midwest	Clear	Unique

This rarity appraisal should be accepted with great caution. Probably there are others whose serrations have not been counted and which are thus catalogued as the preceding plate.

No. 191-B	*Diam.*	*Rim*	*Origin*	*Colors*	*Rarity*
	3	44 even scallops	Probably Midwest	Clear Blue	Common Extremely rare

We can locate only seven specimens in blue. We think it likely that the plain-scallop variants are also from the Pittsburgh glassfield, but recognize the possibility of these plates having been made in several factories.

No. 191-C	*Diam.*	*Rim*	*Origin*	*Colors*	*Rarity*
	3	50 even scallops	Probably Midwest	Clear	Common

No. 191-D	*Diam.*	*Rim*	*Origin*	*Colors*	*Rarity*
	3	52 even scallops	Probably Midwest	Clear	Common

No. 191-E	*Diam.*	*Rim*	*Origin*	*Colors*	*Rarity*
	2 15/16	53 even scallops	As above	Clear Light green	Rare Unique

Probably frequently confused with one of the above and so not as rare as it seems. The green example is in the Morrill collection.

While the following octagonal plates seem to be closely allied to the previous series of circular plates, it should be noted that here we encounter design variations not found in the circular plates. It is thus possible that there is another source for these plates. Note also the close resemblance not only to the eagles, 680 series and sunbursts, 517 series, but to the 291 group.

No. 192	*Diam.*	*Rim*	*Origin*	*Colors*	*Rarity*
	3 across	Octagonal, 6 scallops each side between larger corners	Probably Midwest	Clear	Common

Dots in center spandrels. No dots in shoulder spandrels and no "eggs" in corner serrations. Large target in center.

No. 192-A	*Diam.*	*Rim*	*Origin*	*Colors*	*Rarity*
	2 15/16 across	Octagonal, 5 scallops each side between *very* bold corners	Probably Midwest	Clear	Scarce

Except for diameter and serrations, like the preceding plate.

No. 193	*Diam.*	*Rim*	*Origin*	*Colors*	*Rarity*
	3 across	Octagonal, 7 scallops each side with *eggs in corner scallops*	Probably Midwest	Clear Light green	Common Rare

Dots in center spandrels and also in shoulder spandrels. The center target is smaller than in No. 192.

No. 194	*Diam.*	*Rim*	*Origin*	*Colors*	*Rarity*
	3 across	Octagonal as above	Probably Midwest	Clear Light green	Common Common

Similar to the preceding in serrations and center pattern. The dots in the shoulder spandrels have prongs or rays. Small target.

No. 195	*Diam.*	*Rim*	*Origin*	*Colors*	*Rarity*
	3 across	Octagonal as above	Probably Midwest	Clear	Scarce

Similar to the two preceding plates in serrations and in center dots, but *no dots in shoulder spandrels.* Large target.

No. 196	*Diam.*	*Rim*	*Origin*	*Colors*	*Rarity*
	3 across	Octagonal as above	Probably Midwest	Clear Light green Olive-green	Common Rare Very rare

Similar to the preceding in center dots but with a rope band just inside the serration line. Small target.

197

197-C

197-A

197-D

197-B

197-E

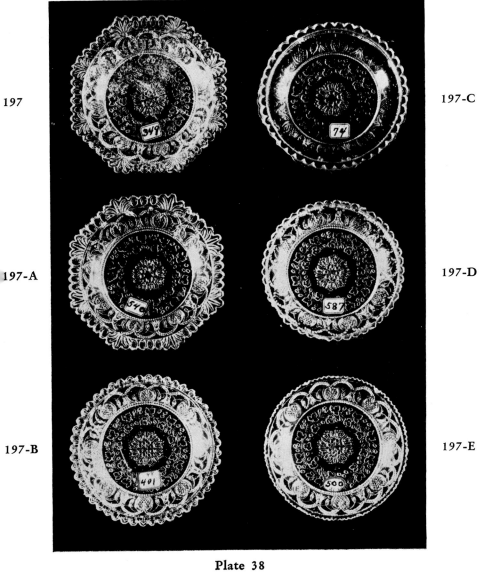

Plate 38

198

198-A
described
in text

199

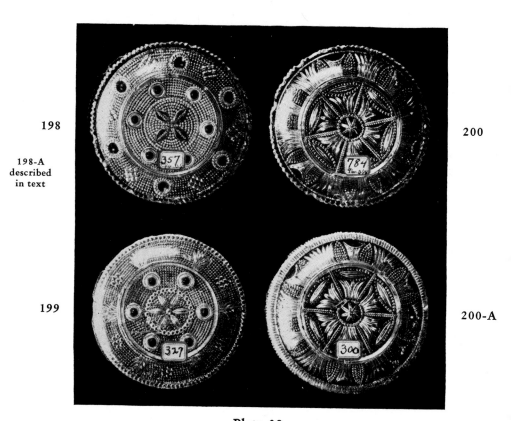

200

200-A

Plate 39

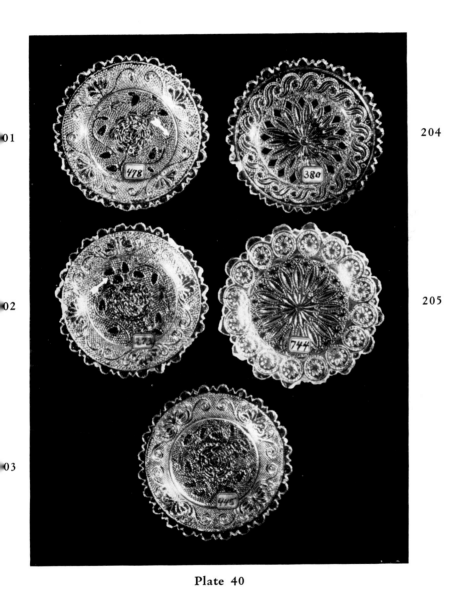

201

202

203

204

205

Plate 40

206

20

207

20

Plate 41

Chapter X

THE LACY PERIOD

MISCELLANEOUS PLATES, CHIEFLY MIDWESTERN

Nos. 197 through 227-C

No. 197	*Diam.*	*Rim*	*Origin*	*Colors*	*Rarity*
	3 7/16 across	Octagonal, 6 scallops each side	Midwest, probably Pittsburgh	Clear	Rare

The series is patently allied to the eagles (677 series). The plate shown here has 4 "eggs" on each of its eight sides and is somewhat rarer than the following one. As usual in octagonal plates, really proof specimens are almost impossible to find.

No. 197-A	*Diam.*	*Rim*	*Origin*	*Colors*	*Rarity*
	3 7/16 across	See note below	Midwest, probably Pittsburgh	Clear	Scarce

While six of the eight sides have 6 scallops between their corner points as in the preceding plate, the other two sides have but 5 scallops each. Moreover, two sides have but 3 "eggs" instead of 4. There is a similar eagle. Examples in proof condition are rare.

No. 197-B	*Diam.*	*Rim*	*Origin*	*Colors*	*Rarity*
	3 5/16	48 scallops alternating egg and dart	Midwest, probably Pittsburgh	Clear	Scarce

This and its companion eagle are the only plates known to date with these egg and dart scallops.

No. 197-C	*Diam.*	*Rim*	*Origin*	*Colors*	*Rarity*
	3¼	44 even scallops	Midwest, probably Pittsburgh	Clear Blue	Plentiful Rare

The blue in which this plate occurs is the soft shade characteristic of some Midwestern pressing. While we list the clear examples as "common," they seem somewhat rarer than the following plate. There is a similar eagle, No. 677-A.

No. 197-D	*Diam.*	*Rim*	*Origin*	*Colors*	*Rarity*
	3⅛	46 even scallops	Midwest, probably Pittsburgh	Clear Greenish tint	Plentiful Rare

Here, unlike the No. 677 eagles, the 46-scallop type seems to be the one most frequently found. This difference in rarity is not marked and may be illusory.

No. 197-E	*Diam.*	*Rim*	*Origin*	*Colors*	*Rarity*
	3⅛	98 saw-tooth scallops	Midwest, probably Pittsburgh	Clear	Scarce

The tiny serrations are especially vulnerable and proof specimens are virtually unknown.

No. 198	*Diam.*	*Rim*	*Origin*	*Colors*	*Rarity*
	3⅛	98 sawtooth scallops	Midwest, probably Pittsburgh	Clear	Plentiful

Related to the preceding plate through the common serration pattern. Proof specimens are unobtainable.

No. 198-A	*Diam.*	*Rim*	*Origin*	*Colors*	*Rarity*
	3 3/16	Tiny sawtooth	Midwest, probably Pittsburgh	Clear	Unique

This is exactly like the preceding plate, except that its rim is the same found on No. 200-A. We can locate but one specimen, that in Mr. Cannon's collection.

No. 199	*Diam.*	*Rim*	*Origin*	*Colors*	*Rarity*
	3	Plain, 108 dots on back	Midwest	Clear	Plentiful

The design is markedly like that seen in the preceding series, but seems to us to be a slightly later adaptation of the pattern. See No. 155 for another use of this rim.

No. 200	*Diam.*	*Rim*	*Origin*	*Colors*	*Rarity*
	3⅛	96 sawtooth scallops	Midwest	Clear	Very rare

We would have sworn this sawtooth rim was the same as that seen on No. 198, and are greatly indebted to Mr. Marble for pointing out that this has 2 less sawteeth.

No. 200-A	*Diam.*	*Rim*	*Origin*	*Colors*	*Rarity*
	3 3/16	Tiny sawtooth	Midwest	Clear	Plentiful

This has the tiny sawtooth rim found on only one other pattern, No. 198-A. The plate is not rare, but proof examples cannot be found.

No. 201	*Diam.*	*Rim*	*Origin*	*Colors*	*Rarity*
	3 7/16	24 scallops, points between	Midwest, probably Pittsburgh	Clear	Very rare

Superficially examined, this is difficult to distinguish from the two following plates. The center foliage is much sparser and the leaves have no veins. The anthemion on the shoulder is plainer, as are its accompanying scrolls.

No. 202	*Diam.*	*Rim*	*Origin*	*Colors*	*Rarity*
	3 7/16	24 scallops, points between	Midwest, probably Pittsburgh	Clear	Rare

The anthemia become more ornate, as do their accompanying scrolls. Leaves are added to the center foliage but do not become markedly veined, as in the following plate. It is interesting to note the resemblance to eagle No. 672 which points to the possible finding of specimens in opal.

No. 203	*Diam.*	*Rim*	*Origin*	*Colors*	*Rarity*
	3 7/16	24 scallops, points between	Midwest, probably Pittsburgh	Clear	Fairly rare

The center foliage varies from both the preceding plates and its leaves are plainly veined. Perfect examples are very difficult to obtain.

No. 204	*Diam.*	*Rim*	*Origin*	*Colors*	*Rarity*
	3 7/16	24 scallops, points between	Midwest, probably Pittsburgh	Clear	Rare

Related to the previous series through the use of a seemingly identical 24-scallop cap-ring and, hence, from the same source. Note that in all these plates there are tiny dots in the base of each scallop. These are the drill-centers.

No. 205	*Diam.*	*Rim*	*Origin*	*Colors*	*Rarity*
	3 11/16	16 large scallops with small scallops between	Uncertain	Clear	Extremely rare

Included here because of its vague resemblance to the preceding design. This is the only instance known to us of this peculiar rim. So far as we know, the only set so far discovered turned up in California, so distribution is no guide to origin. In addition to the similarity to No. 204, however, the plate has a turning pimple on its top center, and we believe this to be a purely Midwestern trait.

No. 206	*Diam.*	*Rim*	*Origin*	*Colors*	*Rarity*
	3½	38 even scallops	Probably Midwest	Clear	Rare

The attribution is based on distribution. Note the tiny dot in each scallop, a vestigial turning center. This plate is thicker than most plates of the lacy period and is probably quite early.

No. 207	*Diam.*	*Rim*	*Origin*	*Colors*	*Rarity*
	3	22 scallops, points between	Probably Midwest	Clear	Rare

The design seems the same as that of the preceding plate, but the shoulder baskets and the central target differ. This is a much smaller plate and, in our experience, is rarer than No. 206. Proof specimens are practically unobtainable. There is a tiny dot in each scallop.

No. 208	*Diam.*	*Rim*	*Origin*	*Colors*	*Rarity*
	3	22 scallops, points between	Probably Midwest	Clear	Scarce

Mr. Marble's specimen measures 1/16″ larger, but we have examined 5 that measure 3″ even and which match perfectly the serrations on both the preceding and following plates. Moreover, all have the tiny dots in the serrations. Mr. Marble's plate may be a variant, but it is more likely to have been slightly flattened or warped. Proof examples are rare.

No. 209	*Diam.*	*Rim*	*Origin*	*Colors*	*Rarity*
	3	22 scallops, points between	Probably Midwest	Clear	Plentiful

This plate was pressed with the same cap-ring as Nos. 207 and 208 and, while this is the pattern most often seen, proof examples are hard to find.

The following large group of plates seems certain to have been made by Curling at his Fort Pitt Glass Works. The definite attribution is made on the basis of a group of serration patterns used on or linked to those found on the Fort Pitt eagles. Not only are serration patterns alike, but all these plates have a peculiarly flat shoulder. The entire group is of extraordinary importance, because it is one of the few that can be assigned to a particular glass works with any degree of confidence. It should be studied with great care.

No. 210	*Diam.*	*Rim*	*Origin*	*Colors*	*Rarity*
	3 9/16	55 even scallops	Ft. Pitt Glass Works	Clear	Unique

Mr. Marble's battered specimen is the only one we can locate. Besides having fewer serrations than the following plate, it has a larger center dot.

No. 211	*Diam.*	*Rim*	*Origin*	*Colors*	*Rarity*
	3⅝	60 even scallops	Ft. Pitt Glass Works	Clear	Extremely rare

This has a smaller center dot than the preceding plate and 5 more serrations. Nos. 210, 211, 212 and 212-A represent just about the peak of Midwestern design and technique.

No. 212	*Diam.*	*Rim*	*Origin*	*Colors*	*Rarity*
	3⅝	60 even scallops	Ft. Pitt Glass Works	Clear	Extremely rare

Obviously, this plate is related to the preceding series through a common serration pattern and, most particularly, through its very flat shoulder, a feature of Nos. 210–217 and which reappears in the 535 sunburst series. Note the engine-turning of the design which here appears on the shoulder, instead of in the center as in Nos. 210–211.

No. 212-A	*Diam.*	*Rim*	*Origin*	*Colors*	*Rarity*
	3 9/16	56 even scallops	Ft. Pitt Glass Works	Clear	Unique

Exactly like the preceding plate, except for its serrations. The only specimen we can locate is the one in Mr. Cannon's collection. Similar rims are on Nos. 214-A and 215-A.

No. 213	*Diam.*	*Rim*	*Origin*	*Colors*	*Rarity*
	3⅝	59(?) even scallops	Ft. Pitt Glass Works	Clear	Unique

The serrations on this battered specimen defy accurate count, but number either 59 or 60 and the Fort Pitt Glass Works had both these cap-rings. The center pattern varies a great deal, of course, and the stippling is much coarser. This plate, the only example known, was discovered several years ago by Mr. J. Earl Kohler. It is in Mr. Marble's collection.

No. 214	*Diam.*	*Rim*	*Origin*	*Colors*	*Rarity*
	3⅝	60 even scallops	Ft. Pitt Glass Works	Clear	Very rare

The serration pattern matches Nos. 211, 212, 215 and 217. The characteristic flat shoulder persists throughout.

No. 214-A	*Diam.*	*Rim*	*Origin*	*Colors*	*Rarity*
	3⅝	56 even scallops	Ft. Pitt Glass Works	Clear	Extremely rare

The rarity may be overstated. While we have traced but three copies, others may exist confused with the preceding plate. None of those we have seen was proof.

No. 214-B	*Diam.*	*Rim*	*Origin*	*Colors*	*Rarity*
	3 11/16	20 scallops with smaller ones between	Ft. Pitt Glass Works	Clear	Rare

210

211

212

212-A
described
in text

213

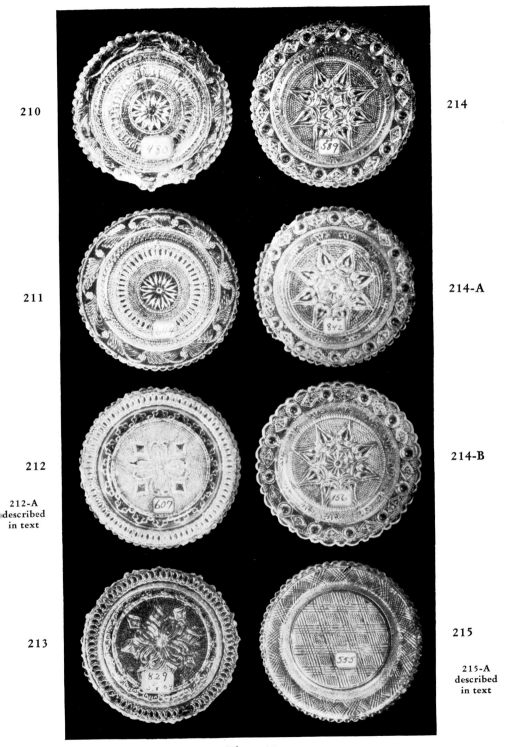

214

214-A

214-B

215

215-A
described
in text

Plate 42

216

217

216-A

217-A

216-B
described
in text

Nos. 218
and 219
left open

216-C

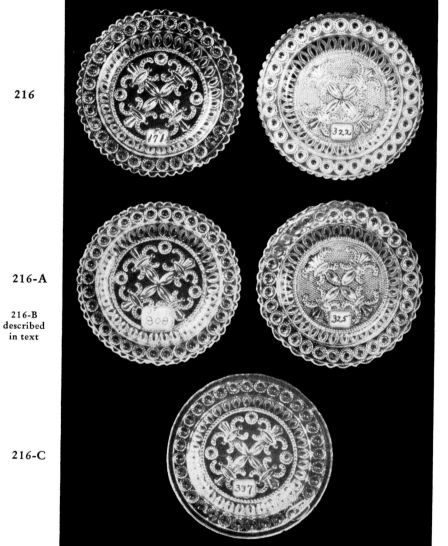

Plate 43

220

223

221

224

222

Plate 44

225

226

225-A

226-A

225-B

226-B

225-C

226-C

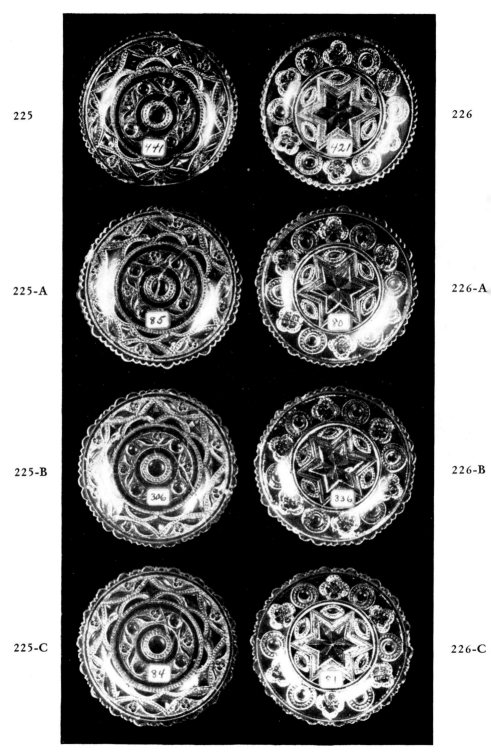

Plate 45

227

Photo-
raphed
om back

227-A

227-B

227-C
escribed
in text

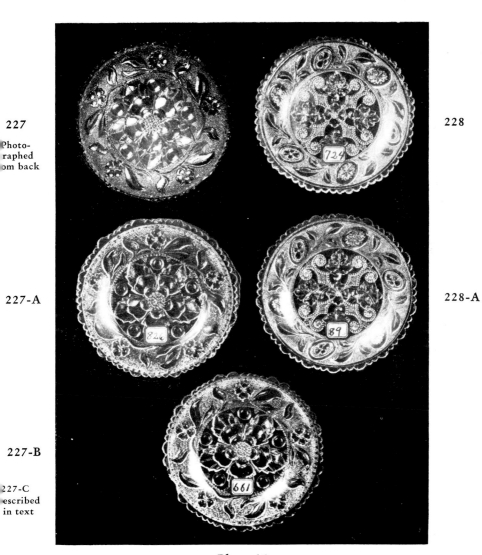

228

228-A

Plate 46

This is the commonest member of the 214 series, but is still not too easy to find. By analogy with the Fort Pitt eagles, blue and even amethyst specimens may eventually turn up.

No. 215	*Diam.*	*Rim*	*Origin*	*Colors*	*Rarity*
	3⅝	60 even scallops	Ft. Pitt Glass Works	Clear	Extremely rare

By false analogy this is commonly associated with No. 379, a late Eastern plate. Nothing could be farther from the truth. This has the same cap-ring as Nos. 211, 212, 214 and 676 and also has the same flat-shoulder surface die. Beyond any doubt, it was made by Curling at his Fort Pitt Works. Condition is usually very bad in this plate. Mr. Marble's beautiful copy is by all odds the best we have seen.

No. 215-A	*Diam.*	*Rim*	*Origin*	*Colors*	*Rarity*
	3⅝	56 even scallops	Ft. Pitt Glass Works	Clear	Unique

Except for serrations, this is exactly like the preceding plates. Others may exist but Dr. Doane's copy is the only one known to us. It was found about twenty-five miles west of Pittsburgh in 1941.

No. 216	*Diam.*	*Rim*	*Origin*	*Colors*	*Rarity*
	3⅝	54 even scallops	Ft. Pitt Glass Works	Clear	Plentiful
				Blue	Extremely rare
				Green tint	Rare

In this series, only the plain rim variety, No. 216-C, uses a cap-ring found on the Ft. Pitt eagles. The flat-shouldered surface die, however, appears throughout.

No. 216-A	*Diam.*	*Rim*	*Origin*	*Colors*	*Rarity*
	3⅝	54 even scallops	Ft. Pitt Glass Works	Clear	Uncertain

The number of serrations and the diameter are both the same as on the preceding plate, but here the shape of the serrations varies. These are less deeply indented or, to put it another way, the scallops are flatter arcs. We can locate only three specimens.

No. 216-B	*Diam.*	*Rim*	*Origin*	*Colors*	*Rarity*
	3⅝	59 even scallops	Ft. Pitt Glass Works	Clear	Plentiful

Proof specimens seem to be unobtainable. The only difference between this and the preceding plates of the series is the number of serrations.

No. 216-C	*Diam.*	*Rim*	*Origin*	*Colors*	*Rarity*
	3⅝	Plain	Ft. Pitt	Clear	Scarce
			Glass Works	Opal	Very rare

The plain rim type is the analogue of the smooth-rim Ft. Pitt eagle and raises the question as to whether or not we may some day find an opalescent eagle. The opal here is a faint, wishy-washy color. This plain rim type is the one used as a base for compotes whose bowls, usually, are in the Roman Rosette pattern. Such compotes are sometimes light green, so No. 216-C may be found in that color eventually.

No. 217	*Diam.*	*Rim*	*Origin*	*Colors*	*Rarity*
	3⅝	60 even	Ft. Pitt	Clear	Plentiful
		scallops	Glass Works		

The center of the plate is stippled in this series. This is the serration counterpart of Nos. 211, 212, 214, 215 and 676.

No. 217-A	*Diam.*	*Rim*	*Origin*	*Colors*	*Rarity*
	3 11/16	20 large	Ft. Pitt	Clear	Plentiful
		scallops	Glass Works		
		with smaller			
		ones between			

The serration pattern is the same as that on Nos. 214-B and 676-B.

Nos. 218 and 219 reserved for new discoveries.

No. 220	*Diam.*	*Rim*	*Origin*	*Colors*	*Rarity*
	3½	Plain rope,	Uncertain	Clear	Rare
		on top only			

This plate was pressed in the early two-piece mold and is usually rather thick. It may antedate the cap-ring period. There is a possibility that it is one of the missing links of Midwestern pressing, dating somewhere between No. 70 and plates like No. 120. Distribution is peculiar and of little help in coming to a decision. Most we have traced have turned up in central or western Pennsylvania but east of the normal distribution area of the Pittsburgh glassfield.

No. 221	Diam.	Rim	Origin	Colors	Rarity
	3½	Rope, top and bottom	Probably Midwest	Clear	Extremely rare

The first of these was found by Mr. J. E. Nevil of Cincinnati; the next by Mr. Earl J. Knittle of Ashland, Ohio; the next find, a set of five or six, was made by Mr. Gailey Wilson near Pittsburgh and the last by Mr. Charles Patrick of Marion, Ohio. Distribution indicates a Western origin, but the evidence hardly warrants any definite attribution.

No. 222	Diam.	Rim	Origin	Colors	Rarity
	3½	Rope, top and bottom	Midwest	Clear	Extremely rare

Of the origin of this plate there can be no doubt. Not only have all the specimens known to us turned up west of the mountains, but the design is a perfect welter of motives typical of Midwestern designing—the cinquefoil, the lunette and the table-rests. A comparative microscope should be used to compare the rope rim of this plate with those on Nos. 221, 223 and 224. If they are identical, the entire group is Midwestern. A sick or frosted specimen is reported.

No. 223	Diam.	Rim	Origin	Colors	Rarity
	3½	Rope, top and bottom	Uncertain	Clear	Plentiful

On the basis of distribution, we have always felt that this plate was of Eastern and probably New England origin, but if its rope ring matches that on the two previous plates, the plate is Midwestern. Distribution is an unsatisfactory guide here, because the plate is plentiful everywhere. Note the fleur de lis in the spandrels of the central plumes. A number of sick specimens are known.

No. 224	Diam.	Rim	Origin	Colors	Rarity
	3½	Rope, top and bottom	Uncertain	Clear	Very rare

The fleur de lis of the previous plate are replaced by rosettes in the spandrels of this one. We have seen only two of these plates, both of which were found in the Midwest. The chances are that others exist misnumbered.

No. 225	Diam.	Rim	Origin	Colors	Rarity
	3⅜	72 even scallops	Philadelphia area, probably Union Glass Works	Clear	Rare

The group of which this series is a part is plainly allied to the Ringgolds and running-vine cabins. These peculiar serration patterns have been very definitely traced to the Philadelphia glassfield, but precise attribution is another matter. The lacier, and hence earlier, members of the group are tentatively assigned to the Union Glass Works, the later members to the newly discovered works across the river at Kaighn's Point. Condition is usually bad and underfilling common, so that immaculate specimens are difficult to find.

No. 225-A	Diam.	Rim	Origin	Colors	Rarity
	3½	12 large scallops with 4 smaller ones between	As above	Clear	Rare

It is to be noted that while in this series, as well as in the Ringgolds and running-vine cabins, no colored examples are as yet known, specimens in various shades of green are found in the following two related series, thus raising the possibility of our eventually finding green plates in this series.

No. 225-B	Diam.	Rim	Origin	Colors	Rarity
	3 7/16	9 pairs of large scallops with 4 smaller ones between	As above	Clear	Rare

Another peculiarity of this factory or factories is that they seem to have made no attempt to match serration patterns in selling plates. We know of five first-hand discoveries of sets in this and related series, and in each case the set was a hodge-podge of serration patterns.

No. 225-C	*Diam.* 3½	*Rim* 18 large scallops with a smaller scallop and 2 points between	*Origin* As above	*Colors* Clear	*Rarity* Rare

No. 226	*Diam.* 3⅜	*Rim* 72 even scallops	*Origin* Philadelphia area	*Colors* Clear Medium green Yellow-green Pink tint	*Rarity* Plentiful Very rare Extremely rare Unique

The pink-tint specimen is indeed a surprise. The only one known to us is in the collection of Mrs. Frederick L. Parker.

No. 226-A	*Diam.* 3½	*Rim* 12 large scallops with 4 smaller ones between	*Origin* As above	*Colors* Clear Medium green Yellow-green	*Rarity* Plentiful Very rare Extremely rare
No. 226-B	*Diam.* 3 7/16	*Rim* 9 pairs of large scallops with 4 small ones between	*Origin* As above	*Colors* Clear	*Rarity* Plentiful

We are convinced that green specimens exist and, in fact, feel sure we have ourselves owned several, but we are unable to locate either our notes to this effect or any actual specimens.

No. 226-C	*Diam.* 3½	*Rim* 18 large scallops with a smaller scallop & 2 points between	*Origin* As above	*Colors* Clear Medium green Yellow-green	*Rarity* Plentiful Very rare Extremely rare

No. 227	Diam.	Rim	Origin	Colors	Rarity
	3⅜	72 even scallops	Philadelphia area, probably Union Glass Works	Deep green	Extremely rare

This is one of a mixed set found in Carlisle, Pa., with a history of having been bought in Philadelphia. The set was the typical mixture of all four serration patterns. We know of no clear specimen. The green is very, very dark.

No. 227-A	Diam.	Rim	Origin	Colors	
	3½	12 large scallops with 4 small ones between	As above	Clear	Extremely rare
				Medium green	Unique
				Deep green	Extremely rare

The first of these to turn up was Mrs. Parker's medium green specimen discovered near Uniontown, Pa. The deep green examples are the very dense color, nearly black in reflected light, and, except for Mr. McGowan's example bought at Wilmington, Del., are from the Carlisle set. Mr. Marble gives 3⅜″ as the diameter of his specimen.

No. 227-B	Diam.	Rim	Origin	Colors	Rarity
	3 7/16	9 pairs of large scallops with 4 smaller ones between	As above	Clear	Extremely rare
				Deep green	Extremely rare

Again, the deep green examples are from the Carlisle discovery.

No. 227-C	Diam.	Rim	Origin	Colors	Rarity
	3½	18 large scallops with a smaller scallop & 2 points between	As above	Deep green	Unique

The only recorded example is Mr. Cannon's deep green one from the Carlisle set. No clear glass specimens are known to date. The serration pattern is that seen on Nos. 225-C and 226-C.

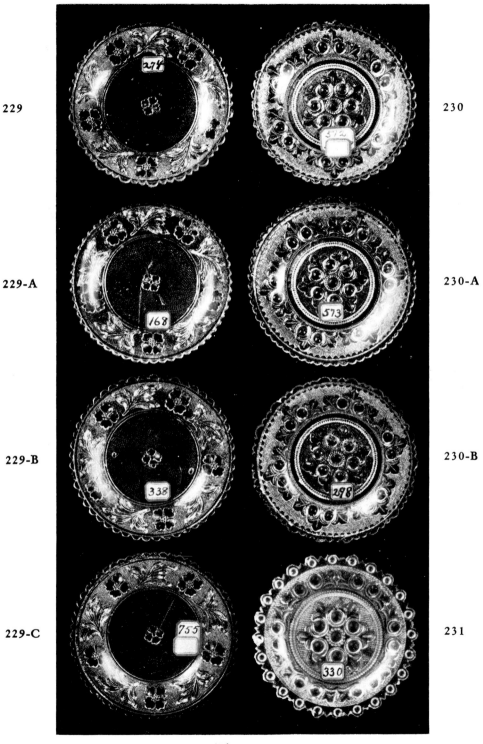

229

230

229-A

230-A

229-B

230-B

229-C

231

Plate 47

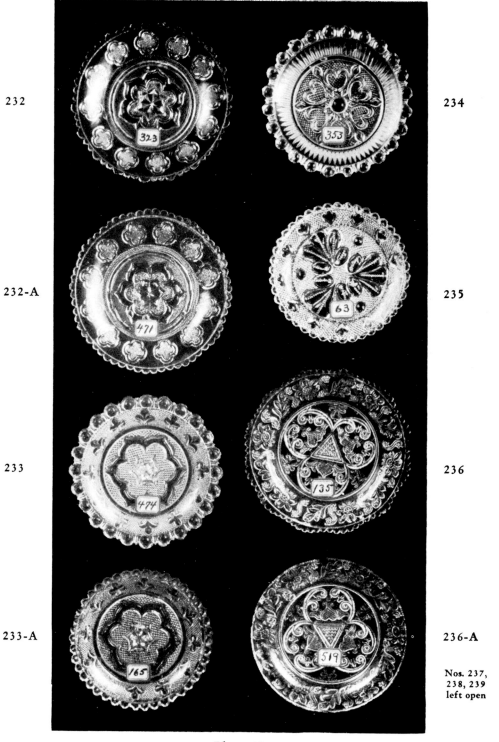

232

234

232-A

235

233

236

233-A

236-A

Nos. 237,
238, 239
left open

Plate 48

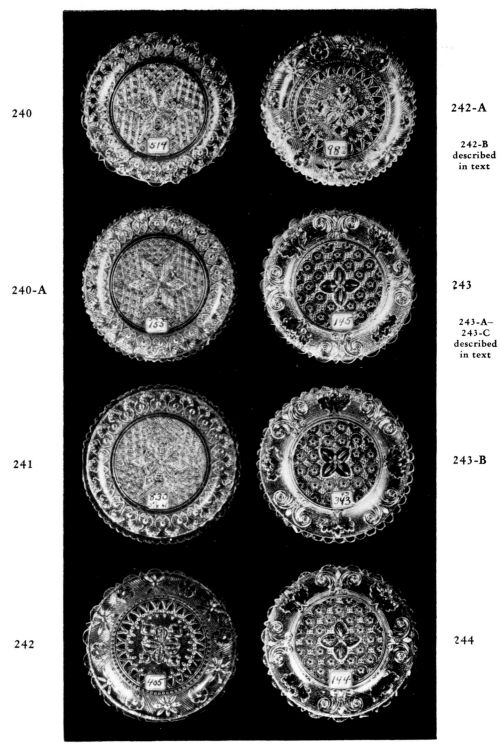

240

242-A

242-B
described
in text

240-A

243

243-A–
243-C
described
in text

241

243-B

242

244

Plate 49

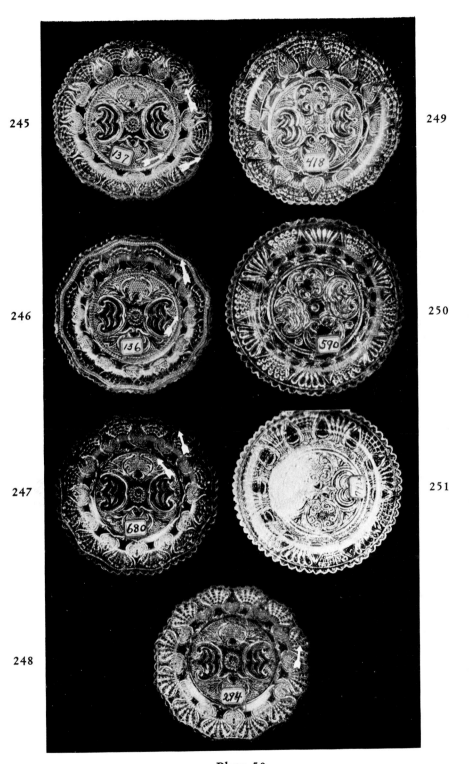

245

246

247

248

249

250

251

Plate 50

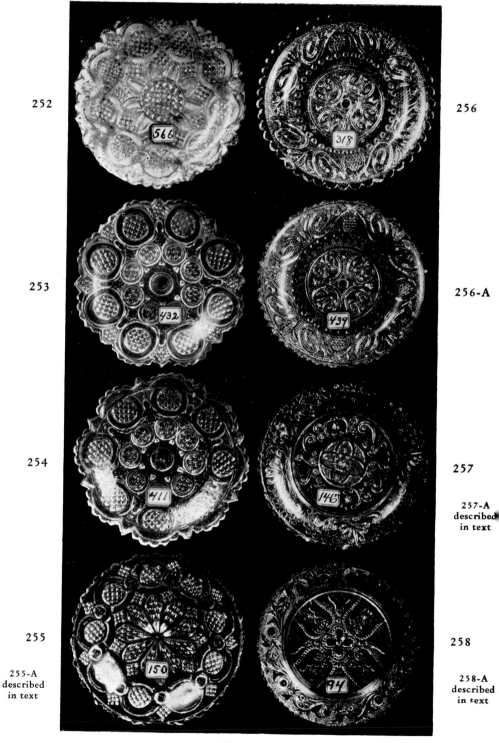

252

256

253

256-A

254

257

257-A
described
in text

255

255-A
described
in text

258

258-A
described
in text

Plate 51

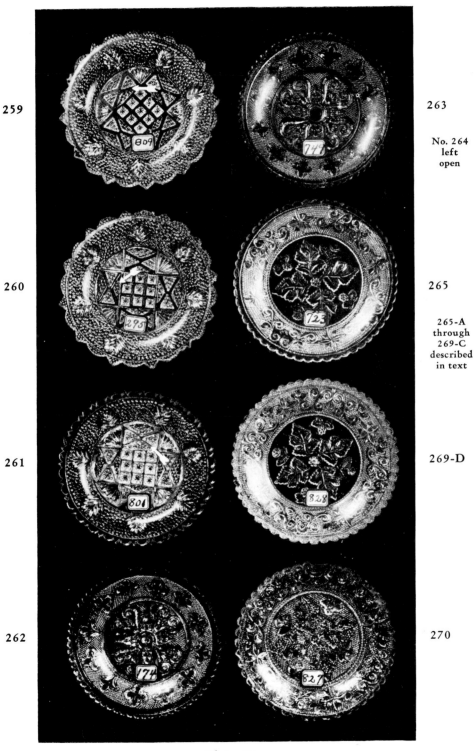

259

260

261

262

263

No. 264
left
open

265

265-A
through
269-C
described
in text

269-D

270

Plate 52

Chapter XI

THE LACY PERIOD

MISCELLANEOUS PLATES, CHIEFLY EASTERN

Nos. 228 through 301

No. 228	*Diam.*	*Rim*	*Origin*	*Colors*	*Rarity*
	3⅜	12-sided and with 60 scallops	Eastern but un- certain	Clear	Extremely rare

In so far as design is concerned, this series seems to us to be related perhaps to the Philadelphia plates of the previous group, but it is also related through its serration patterns to the eagle, No. 666-B, which we have always felt to be of New England origin. One thing is certain, none of these plates is Midwestern.

No. 228-A	*Diam.*	*Rim*	*Origin*	*Colors*	*Rarity*
	3 7/16	18 large scallops with 2 smaller between	Eastern as above	Clear	Rare

It seems likely that serration variants will turn up matching the following series.

No. 229	*Diam.*	*Rim*	*Origin*	*Colors*	*Rarity*
	3⅜	18 large scallops with 2 smaller between	Eastern as above	Clear	Scarce

While this plate is not rare in actual numbers, it *is* rare in proportion to the demand. The so-called "watchcase" stippling, which is simply engine-turning, is very popular.

No. 229-A	*Diam.*	*Rim*	*Origin*	*Colors*	*Rarity*
	3 5/16	56 even scallops	Eastern as above	Clear	Scarce

In our experience, this 56-scallop type is slightly rarer than the large and small scallop type above. It matches the No. 666-A eagle.

No. 229-B	*Diam.*	*Rim*	*Origin*	*Colors*	*Rarity*
	3 7/16	49 even scallops	Eastern as above	Clear	Scarce

This plate, like its matching eagle, is the commonest of the serration variants in the series.

No. 229-C	*Diam.*	*Rim*	*Origin*	*Colors*	*Rarity*
	3½	60 even scallops	Eastern as above	Clear	Uncertain

Possibly this is extremely rare, but we suspect the existence of improperly identified specimens.

No. 230	*Diam.*	*Rim*	*Origin*	*Colors*	*Rarity*
	3⅜	49 even scallops	Eastern as above	Clear	Very rare

Related to the preceding series and to the No. 666 eagles. Since there is a slight difference in diameter between this and its 49-serration mate in the "watchcase" stippling series, the analogy may not be exact. See also No. 177-A, etc.

No. 230-A	*Diam.*	*Rim*	*Origin*	*Colors*	*Rarity*
	3½	60 even scallops	Eastern as above	Clear	Scarce

Note that this, unlike the comparable 60-serration eagle, does not have the vague 12-sided effect. It is well to say here that we have never been able to decide whether or not these seeming resemblances indicate a common source.

No. 230-B	*Diam.*	*Rim*	*Origin*	*Colors*	*Rarity*
	3 7/16	18 large scallops with 2 smaller between	Eastern as above	Clear	Scarce

For some unknown reason, this variety is usually found in better condition than its mates, and is thus the easiest to secure.

No. 231	*Diam.*	*Rim*	*Origin*	*Colors*	*Rarity*
	3 7/16	24 bull's eyes with points between	Midwest	Clear Cloudy	Rare Rare

A Midwestern pirating of the No. 230 design. By analogy with similar Western rims, it seems possible that a 36-bull's-eye rim variant may eventually be discovered. See No. 130 ff. for related plates.

No. 232	*Diam.*	*Rim*	*Origin*	*Colors*	*Rarity*
	3⅜	18 large scallops with 2 smaller between	Eastern but un- certain	Clear	Scarce

The diameter given is that of Mr. Marble's. Theoretically, it and No. 229 should be the same as that of No. 177 (3½"). This, and the following plate, complete our confusion as to the origin of this large group, since these two plates usually turn up in the Philadelphia area and show Philadelphia designers' characteristics in the use of beveled planes. For similar bevelling of Philadelphia origin, see Nos. 225 and 226.

No. 232-A	*Diam.*	*Rim*	*Origin*	*Colors*	*Rarity*
	3 7/16	12-sided with 60 scallops	Eastern as above	Clear	Rare

We feel this serration pattern matches the other faintly 12-sided plates where Mr. Marble records both 3⅜" and 3 7/16" diameters. The variation in size is probably due to warping or, more likely, to clean-ing scale from the surface die, cap-ring assembly.

No. 233	*Diam.*	*Rim*	*Origin*	*Colors*	*Rarity*
	3 3/16	24 large beads with reels be- tween	Probably Midwest	Clear	Rare

The design is patently pirated from the preceding series. The precise origin of the bead and reel rim plates (see Nos. 234, 691, 693 and 694) has not been determined, but what evidence there is seems to favor the Midwest, not only because of distribution, but on account of the coarse stippling typical of some Midwestern die-cutters. All of the plates with bead and reel rims are difficult to find in good condition. It must be noted that Mr. Marble's No. 233 measures $3\frac{1}{4}''$, but it seems certain that all of these plates with this rim were made with the same base-mold assembly.

No. 233-A	Diam.	Rim	Origin	Colors	Rarity
	3	42 even scallops	Probably Midwest	Clear	Plentiful

This 42-serration variety has counterparts in Nos. 691-A and 694-A.

No. 234	Diam.	Rim	Origin	Colors	Rarity
	3 3/16	24 large beads with reels between	Probably Midwest	Clear	Very rare

This is often considered to be one of the heart group. So far, no 42-serration variant has been found.

No. 235	Diam.	Rim	Origin	Colors	Rarity
	3	42 even scallops	Probably Midwestern	Clear	Plentiful

The use of an identical serration pattern with No. 233-A and with the even-serration Lyres and Beehives denotes a common origin. Note that in all these plates, each of the 42 scallops has a tiny dot at its base. As yet, no bead and reel variety of this design has been found.

No. 236	Diam.	Rim	Origin	Colors	Rarity
	$3\frac{1}{2}$	12-sided with 81 scallops	Probably Sandwich	Clear	Plentiful
				Green	Extremely rare
				Pink tint	Very rare

This is not the same serration pattern seen on other 12-sided plates. The attribution rests on distribution only.

No. 236-A	Diam.	Rim	Origin	Colors	Rarity
	$3\frac{1}{4}$	Plain	Probably Sandwich	Clear	See note

This is almost certainly a swindle. The rims of all we have traced are ground and polished. They are half-round in cross section and show no trace of a fin, so that they could not have been made by a mold. It has been suggested that the grinding and polishing was done at the factory when these plates were made. We doubt this but, of course, it is not impossible. What seems more likely is that some unscrupulous dealer had a few imperfect plates ground down. The only reason for listing the plate is to caution collectors and dealers not to buy it. Ground and polished rims show up rather frequently on other plates, and should not be bought. For another example of a polished rim see No. 275-A.

Nos. 237, 238 and 239 are reserved for new discoveries.

No. 240	Diam.	Rim	Origin	Colors	Rarity
	3½	19 large scallops, points between	Eastern, see note	Clear	Rare

A New England, and possibly Sandwich, origin seems indicated on the basis of serration resemblance to the following series. An attribution based on distribution would point to the Philadelphia area, where most of these plates and all the colored specimens (see below) are found. We have never seen, nor have we heard of, a proof or even a good example of this plate.

No. 240-A	Diam.	Rim	Origin	Colors	Rarity
	3½	60 even scallops	Eastern as above	Clear	Rare
				Light blue	Very rare
				Light blue with opal overcast	Extremely rare
				Translucent-blue	Extremely rare

As we said above, all the blues with opal overcast and most of, if not all, the plain light blues have been found in the Philadelphia area. These are so rare that it is not safe to base any conclusions on them.

No. 241	Diam.	Rim	Origin	Colors	Rarity
	3⅝	61 even scallops	Eastern as above	Clear	Unique

The uniqueness of this plate is subject to the usual precautionary statement, noting its resemblance to the preceding one. Mr. Marble says this has more stippling on its shoulder. Note the extra serration.

No. 242	Diam.	Rim	Origin	Colors	Rarity
	3½	19 large scallops, points between	Eastern	Clear	Plentiful

Distribution seems to favor New England with the Philadelphia region as a possibility. We know of no proof example.

No. 242-A	Diam.	Rim	Origin	Colors	Rarity
	3½	60 even scallops	Eastern	Clear	Plentiful
				Amber	Extremely rare
				Blue	Very rare
				Medium blue	Extremely rare
				Black-amethyst	Extremely rare

The black-amethysts seem to be concentrated near Philadelphia.

No. 242-B	Diam.	Rim	Origin	Colors	Rarity
	3 9/16	61 even scallops	Eastern	Clear	Plentiful
				Blue	Very rare

All the blue ones known to us came from eastern Pennsylvania, but we still favor a New England origin. The size given is that of Mr. Marble's, but we feel it matches No. 241.

No. 243	Diam.	Rim	Origin	Colors	Rarity
	3½	19 large scallops, points between	Eastern, see note	Clear	Plentiful
				Opal	Scarce

The central background is machined and this, coupled with the scallop and point serration pattern, indicates a possible relation to the 240 and 242 series. Note that in this variety the leaves in the center have midribs only; they lack diagonal veins. This plate is found throughout the East, and we are unable to say whether it is New England or more southerly pressing.

No. 243-A	Diam.	Rim	Origin	Colors	Rarity
	3½ scant	Similar to above	Eastern as above	Clear Opal	Uncertain Uncertain

The difference between this and the previous plate cannot be photographed or described. There is a very slight difference in the curve of the scallops, so that the surface of No. 243 will not match that of No. 243-A. We realize that it is impossible to identify either variety from this description. Probably this plate is as plentiful as No. 243, since it was discovered by Mr. Cannon, Mr. Carapata and Mr. Wood, each working independently, at about the same time.

No. 243-B	Diam.	Rim	Origin	Colors	Rarity
	3½	43 even scallops	Eastern as above	Clear	Very rare

This is exactly like the preceding plates, except for its serration pattern.

No. 243-C	Diam.	Rim	Origin	Colors	Rarity
	3⅝	46 even scallops	Eastern as above	Clear	Unique

Exactly like the previous plate, except for the slightly larger size and the 3 extra serrations. We can locate only one example, but very likely others exist, misnumbered.

No. 244	Diam.	Rim	Origin	Colors	Rarity
	3½	19 large scallops, points between	Eastern as above	Clear	Uncertain

The four center leaves have diagonal veins, as well as a midrib. It is not impossible that this design variant will be found with both the 43- and 46-scallop rims. In our personal experience this plate is extremely rare, but this is not confirmed by collectors' want lists on which the plate seldom appears. Either we have been unlucky, or the want lists are incomplete or inaccurate.

THE SHELL BORDER PLATES

No. 245	*Diam.*	*Rim*	*Origin*	*Colors*	*Rarity*
	3 7/16	12-sided	New England,	Clear	Plentiful
		with 81	probably	Milky-white	Rare
		scallops	Sandwich	Blue	Very rare
				Opal	Very rare
				Violet-blue	Very rare

The milky-white specimens may be opalescent plates improperly heat-treated.

No. 246	*Diam.*	*Rim*	*Origin*	*Colors*	*Rarity*
	3 7/16	12-sided	New England,	Clear	Plentiful
		with 81	probably	Opal	Unique
		scallops	Sandwich		

This differs from the preceding plate in having a rope band on its shoulder just inside the serrations. While not rare, it is less frequently found than the first of the series. The opal example is in Mr. Marble's collection.

No. 247	*Diam.*	*Rim*	*Origin*	*Colors*	*Rarity*
	3 7/16	12-sided	New England,	Clear	Rare
		with 60	probably	Medium green	Very rare
		scallops	Sandwich	Blue-green	Very rare
				Emerald-green	Very rare

In our experience, clear specimens are harder to find than colored ones. We feel, however, that this is a false rarity due to non-specialists' inability to distinguish between these rare 60-scallop plates and the much commoner 81-scallop type. Any dealer would recognize the importance of the green examples, so perhaps more of these are reported.

No. 248	*Diam.*	*Rim*	*Origin*	*Colors*	*Rarity*
	3⅜	12-sided	New England,	Clear	Very rare
		with 60	probably		
		scallops	Sandwich		

The shells of the border reach to the very rim. It seems to us that the shapes of the shells differ somewhat from those of the previously shown plates. This plate is the rarest of the Eastern shell borders.

No. 249	*Diam.*	*Rim*	*Origin*	*Colors*	*Rarity*
	3⅝	12-sided	Uncertain	Clear	Plentiful
		with 72			
		scallops			

The rope-ring center of the preceding plates becomes a sunburst, and there are further differences in the center scrolls and in the shape of the shells. The origin still may be New England, but there is a possibility that this is a pirating of the Sandwich pattern by another area.

No. 250	Diam.	Rim	Origin	Colors	Rarity
	3¾	63 even scallops	Midwest, see note	Clear	Very rare

A rather crude Western pirating of the Eastern shell border plates. The unusually flat shoulder may indicate Curling's Ft. Pitt Works as the source.

No. 251	Diam.	Rim	Origin	Colors	Rarity
	3¾	63 even scallops	Midwest as above	Clear	Extremely rare

This seems to be a recutting of the design die of No. 250, eliminating the big central dot and substituting a sunburst for it. There are other variations in the recut die and some stippling has been added, probably in an attempt to match the brilliancy of the Eastern version.

THE ROMAN ROSETTE PLATES

No. 252	Diam.	Rim	Origin	Colors	Rarity
	3⅝	9 large serrated scallops, points between	Probably Midwest	Light green Yellow-green	Very rare Extremely rare

No clear specimens are known. Since the metal is, so far as we have observed, very bad, the possibility arises that this is a late, decadent plate. It seems to us more likely that it is a first attempt of a bottle-glass factory to invade the tableware field.

No. 253	Diam.	Rim	Origin	Colors	Rarity
	3 9/16	8 large serrated scallops, points between	Probably Midwest	Clear	Plentiful
				Cloudy	Plentiful
				Bluish-green	Scarce
				Olive-green	Very rare
				Opal tint	Unique
				Light green	Rare

The attribution is not definite. Bluish-green and olive-green speci-mens seem more common in the Philadelphia area and an origin in that glassfield is possible.

No. 254	*Diam.*	*Rim*	*Origin*	*Colors*	*Rarity*
	3 9/16	8 large	Probably	Clear	Scarce
		serrated	Midwest	Cloudy	Scarce
		scallops,		Milky-white	Rare
		points			
		between			

This differs from the preceding plate in having the circles on the shoulder incomplete. Seemingly, this is some sort of makeshift repair job. The large percentage of cloudy plates is a puzzle, unless this is due to too much soda in the mix.

No. 255	*Diam.*	*Rim*	*Origin*	*Colors*	*Rarity*
	3⅝	24 bold	Sandwich	Clear	Common
		scallops		Opal tint	Common
		divided by		Opalescent	Plentiful
		pairs of		Green tint	Scarce
		smaller		Amethyst tint	Plentiful
		ones			

It seems well established that procedure is here reversed, and we have the East stealing a design from the West. This plate has concave, almost sauce-dish shoulders.

No. 255-A	*Diam.*	*Rim*	*Origin*	*Colors*	*Rarity*
	3⅝	As above	Probably	Clear	Scarce
			Sandwich		

This differs from the above only in top shape, having convex shoul-ders like the similar Clays. Colors may exist.

No. 256	*Diam.*	*Rim*	*Origin*	*Colors*	*Rarity*
	3 9/16	46 even	Eastern but	Clear	Rare
		scallops	see note		

This plate and its variant seem to be related to a much earlier series, Nos. 62 and 62-A. The early series reaches its peak of distribution in New England. In the present series, the greatest density of distribution seems to be in Pennsylvania. We do not profess to know the answer. The even-serration type is rarer than the scallop and point variety.

No. 256-A	*Diam.*	*Rim*	*Origin*	*Colors*	*Rarity*
	3 7/16	29 stippled scallops, points between	As above	Clear	Rare

In all cases the trick of stippling serrations points fairly definitely to New England.

No. 257	*Diam.*	*Rim*	*Origin*	*Colors*	*Rarity*
	3½	54 even scallops	New England, probably Sandwich	Clear	Plentiful

The attribution is based on style as well as distribution.

No. 257-A	*Diam.*	*Rim*	*Origin*	*Colors*	*Rarity*
	3½	53 even scallops	As above	Clear	Plentiful

Oddly enough, this relatively late discovery has proved to be more common than the 54-scallop type.

No. 258	*Diam.*	*Rim*	*Origin*	*Colors*	*Rarity*
	3⅜	76 even scallops	Probably Sandwich	Clear	Plentiful
				Opalescent	Rare
				Cloudy	Rare

Here, again, the attribution is based on both style and distribution.

No. 258-A	*Diam.*	*Rim*	*Origin*	*Colors*	*Rarity*
	3½	48 even scallops	Probably Sandwich	Clear	Very rare

The seeming rarity may be due to careless serration counting by collectors and dealers, but we doubt it. Colored specimens may well exist.

No. 259	*Diam.*	*Rim*	*Origin*	*Colors*	*Rarity*
	3 7/16	12 large stippled scallops, points between	Eastern, possibly Sandwich or NEG	Clear	Rare

Note that the straight lines dividing the various elements of the center pattern are *single*. There is a clear relation between this and the eagle, No. 665-A. Thus, variants with plain (not stippled) serrations may turn up as well as specimens in opal.

No. 260	*Diam.*	*Rim*	*Origin*	*Colors*	*Rarity*
	3 7/16	As above	Eastern, possibly Sandwich or NEG	Clear	Scarce

Here *some* of the straight lines in the center are *doubled*. While we say Sandwich, it is, of course, equally possible that these coarsely stippled plates originated at NEG. Note the domed shoulder character-istic of Eastern practice.

No. 261	*Diam.*	*Rim*	*Origin*	*Colors*	*Rarity*
	3⅜	28 scallops, points be-tween and not stippled	As above	Clear	Unique

All the straight lines of the center are *doubled*. We recall no other instance of the use of this serration pattern.

No. 262	*Diam.*	*Rim*	*Origin*	*Colors*	*Rarity*
	3 5/16	66 even scallops	Uncertain	Clear	Common
				Dark blue	Scarce
				Grayish-blue	Rare
				Lavender	Rare
				Amethyst	Rare

There is a dot in the center. This series is so common and so widely distributed that no attribution can be based on find-spots. Nor is style any help. Taking the colors found in both for evidence, the Midwest seems the most likely source. See Nos. 319, 320 and 322 in the late transition period for similar serrations.

No. 263	*Diam.*	*Rim*	*Origin*	*Colors*	*Rarity*
	3 5/16	66 even scallops	As above	Clear	Scarce
				Dark blue	Rare
				Olive-green	Rare

This has no dot in the center.

No. 264 is reserved for a new discovery.

271

271-A
described
in text

272

272-A

273

274

275

275-A

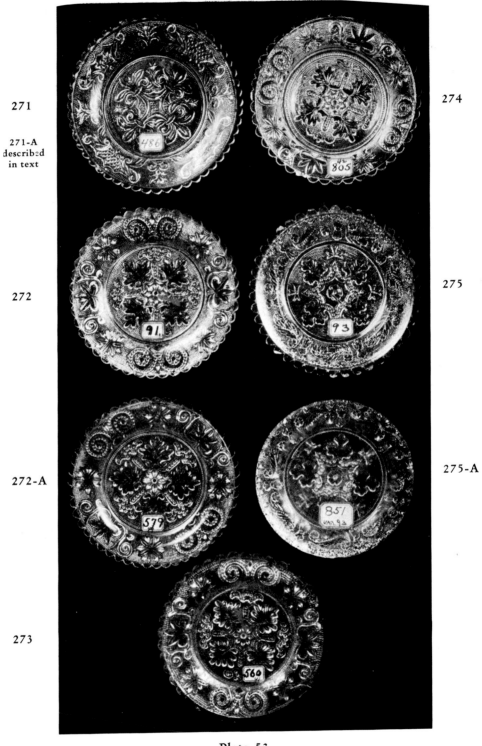

Plate 53

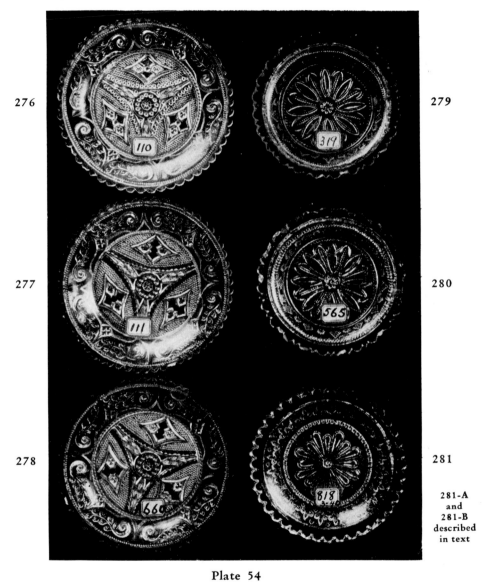

276   279

277   280

278   281

281-A
and
281-B
described
in text

Plate 54

282

284

282-A

285

283

Plate 55

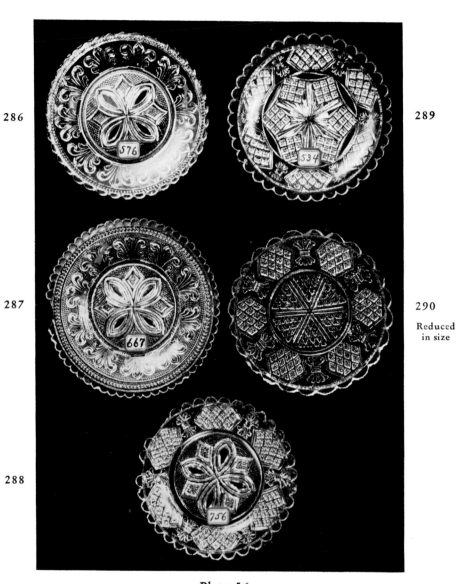

286

289

287

290

Reduced
in size

288

Plate 56

291

294

295
described
in text

292

296

293

296-A

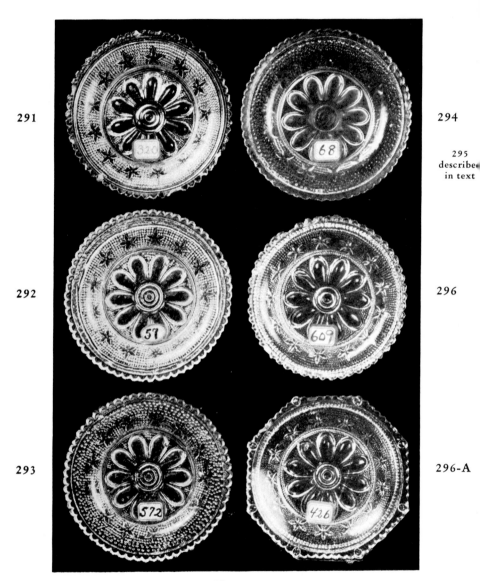

Plate 57

297

300

298

hoto-
aphed
m back

301

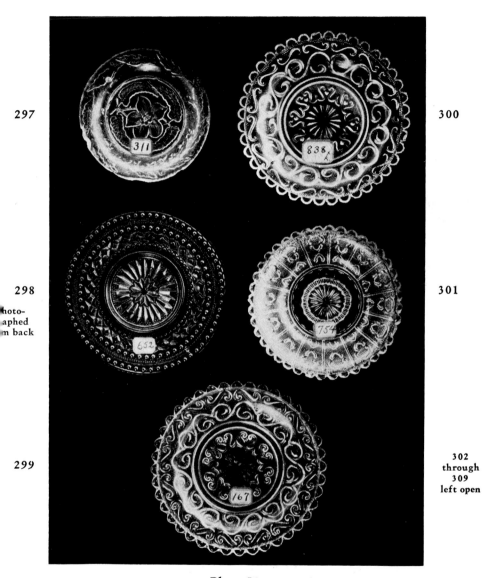

299

302
through
309
left open

Plate 58

Even the specialists have difficulty cataloguing the following series. The basic design was the "best seller" of the lacy period, and many design dies were used to produce it. According to Mr. Marble, the distinguishing characteristics are the presence, or absence, of little rosebuds (they can barely be seen in the photographs) on the shoulder. When these are present, they are located between the rosette and the S-scroll on the shoulder pattern. To complicate matters, these rosebuds not only vary in number, but are of several sizes and shapes. When a number of size, serration and stippling variations are added, the result is chaos. Beyond any doubt, the listings here are incomplete. Someone should specialize in this series. When and if this happens we expect the number of variants will be doubled or even tripled.

No. 265	*Diam.*	*Rim*	*Origin*	*Colors*	*Rarity*
	3½	53 even scallops	New England, probably Sandwich	Clear	Rare

The No. 265 type has no rosebuds on the shoulder. Rarity statements throughout the series are based on want lists. Most collectors are in just as desperate confusion as we are in numbering these plates, and their perplexity is probably reflected in their want lists; consequently, rarity appraisals are at best tentative and should be accepted with caution.

No. 265-A	*Diam.*	*Rim*	*Origin*	*Colors*	*Rarity*
	3½	63 even scallops	As above	Clear	Rare

This is like the preceding plate, except for its 10 extra serrations.

No. 266	*Diam.*	*Rim*	*Origin*	*Colors*	*Rarity*
	3½	63 even scallops	As above	Clear	Rare

This has one distinct pair of large rosebuds on the shoulder, and a second pair so small and indistinct that it can barely be seen. A 53-serration variant will probably be found.

No. 267	*Diam.*	*Rim*	*Origin*	*Colors*	*Rarity*
	3½	53 even scallops	As above	Clear	Scarce

This has 3 rosebuds on the shoulder and the plate, in cross section, is a different shape from the other members of the series. This indicates the use of a different surface die.

No. 268	*Diam.*	*Rim*	*Origin*	*Colors*	*Rarity*
	3½	63 even scallops	As above	Clear	Plentiful
				Opal	Plentiful
				Opaque-white	Rare

This has one pair of large roses, another pair of small roses and a single rose in two of the other four possible locations on the shoulder.

No. 269	*Diam.*	*Rim*	*Origin*	*Colors*	*Rarity*
	3½	53 even scallops	As above	Clear	Plentiful
				Clam broth	Rare

This has four pairs of rosebuds on its shoulder. The clam broth specimen is in Mr. Marble's collection and is possibly unique. A single fragment of this plate was, we believe, the only trace of the series found in the Wynn excavations at Sandwich. One would have thought the place would be littered with them.

No. 269-A	*Diam.*	*Rim*	*Origin*	*Colors*	*Rarity*
	3 9/16	53 even scallops	As above	Clear	Plentiful
				Peacock-blue	Very rare
				Opaque-blue	Unique

The only difference between this and the preceding plate is the size. There is no way to tell, of course, whether the increase in diameter of 1/16″ indicates a new base-mold assembly, or was the result of cleaning scale from the old one. The opaque-blue is a turquoise. An opal example is reported but not reliably confirmed.

No. 269-B	*Diam.*	*Rim*	*Origin*	*Colors*	*Rarity*
	3⅜	63 even scallops	As above	Clear	Plentiful
				Opaque-white	Unique

This has 63 serrations and a much smaller diameter. One would think the diameter would be the same (3½″), as in the other 63-scallop types. The opaque-white example appears in our notes for July, 1940, and is presumably from the Jerome Strauss collection. There is a possibility that we misnumbered it.

No. 269-C	*Diam.*	*Rim*	*Origin*	*Colors*	*Rarity*
	3⅜	48 even scallops	As above	Clear	Plentiful

Like the rest of the 269 series, this has four pairs of rosebuds on its shoulder. Outside No. 270, it is the only one of the design to occur with 48 scallops. It is reasonable to expect the other varieties to turn up in this serration pattern.

No. 269-D	*Diam.*	*Rim*	*Origin*	*Colors*	*Rarity*
	3 9/16	53 even scallops	As above	Clear	Very rare

Again, there are four pairs of rosebuds, but note that the serrations are stippled. This stippling is on a cap-ring which is interchangeable with the other design dies. The original find was made by Sam Laidacker from, we believe, the Coan collection.

No. 270	*Diam.*	*Rim*	*Origin*	*Colors*	*Rarity*
	3 7/16	48 even scallops	As above	Clear	Rare

This has the four pairs of rosebuds on its shoulder, but the center of the plate has been stippled. There is a possibility that the stippled-center type will be found with both 53 and 63 serrations. The original find was also made by Mr. Laidacker and, for a while in the early 1940's, the plate was thought to be unique. Since that time, we have ourselves had four, and two other specimens have been reported. Probably "rare" is too low a category for a plate where we know of only seven copies, but we are afraid to appraise it higher.

No. 271	*Diam.*	*Rim*	*Origin*	*Colors*	*Rarity*
	3½	70 even scallops	Probably Sandwich	Clear	Plentiful

Greenish tints too faint to record are not infrequently found. These are not likely to be traces of a previous green batch but are probably from a batch of glass not properly cleansed of a trace of iron.

No. 271-A	*Diam.*	*Rim*	*Origin*	*Colors*	*Rarity*
	3⅝	52 even scallops	Probably Sandwich	Clear	Plentiful

Like the preceding plate, except for the size and the serrations.

The plates in the following series, seemingly so much alike, differ from each other in many ways. The simplest way of identifying them is by comparing the shapes of the central leaves and even this requires a most precise attention to detail. It is quite likely that serration switches from one design die to another exist that are not recorded here. Collectors should keep a close watch for these.

No. 272	Diam.	Rim	Origin	Colors	Rarity
	3½	42 even scallops	Probably Sandwich	Clear	Plentiful
				Opal tint	Plentiful
				Opal	Plentiful
				Opal-opaque	Rare

The four central leaves are very deeply indented. Attribution is on the basis of distribution, which reaches its greatest density in New England.

No. 272-A	Diam.	Rim	Origin	Colors	Rarity
	3 9/16	49 even scallops	Probably Sandwich	Clear	Plentiful

The design magnified about two diameters seems to us to be the same as that of the previous plate, but we are not completely sure of it. There are some differences but these, we feel, are due to a variation in the quality of the imprint, rather than to the use of a different design die. This is a flatter plate than No. 272. Opal specimens probably exist.

No. 273	Diam.	Rim	Origin	Colors	Rarity
	3½	41 even scallops	Probably Sandwich	Clear	Plentiful

The central leaves are much less deeply indented than in the No. 272 type. The stippling throughout is coarser and less regular. The ram's horn scrolls are filled with blocks that are much closer together than they are in other members of the group. Opal examples will probably be found.

No. 274	Diam.	Rim	Origin	Colors	Rarity
	3½	42 even scallops	Probably Sandwich	Clear	Extremely rare

The bases of the leaves are extended so as to surround the central rosette. The top shape differs. It comes nowhere near coinciding with the design die. The shoulder on the top of the plate extends far inside the table-ring of the design die, so that the well or center which holds the cup is very small. While we know of but two of these plates and have appraised the rarity on this basis, we strongly suspect that other improperly numbered specimens exist.

No. 275	*Diam.*	*Rim*	*Origin*	*Colors*	*Rarity*
	3½	42 even	Probably	Clear	Plentiful
		scallops	Sandwich	Opal	Scarce
				Opal-opaque	Unique

The design closely resembles that seen in Nos. 272, 273 and 274 and here, again, there are 42 serrations and a 3½″ diameter. The shoulder of this series is a most peculiar shape, being slightly concave, "dished" so to speak.

No. 275-A	*Diam.*	*Rim*	*Origin*	*Colors*	*Rarity*
	3¼	Plain	Probably	Clear	Unique
			Sandwich		

This plate has a ground edge. Avoid it. See No. 236-A.

No. 276	*Diam.*	*Rim*	*Origin*	*Colors*	*Rarity*
	3 7/16	55 even	Probably	Clear	Plentiful
		scallops	Sandwich	Blue	Very rare

The arcs of the central quadrants are outlined in heavy dots. The diamond-shaped figures in the center have dots in their centers. The table-ring is a coarse rope. A 58-serration variant should turn up.

No. 277	*Diam.*	*Rim*	*Origin*	*Colors*	*Rarity*
	3⅜	58 even	Probably	Clear	Plentiful
		scallops	Sandwich	Peacock-blue	Very rare
				Green	Unique

The dots that outlined the arcs in the preceding plate are here replaced by sawteeth. The diamond-shaped figures have no dots in their centers. The table-ring is a fine, not a coarse, rope. The only green specimen we have seen is in the collection of Mr. J. R. Gabell.

No. 278	*Diam.*	*Rim*	*Origin*	*Colors*	*Rarity*
	3 7/16	55 even	Probably	Clear	Plentiful
		scallops	Sandwich		

Much like the preceding plate (the center stippling is different) except for the diameter and serrations.

No. 279	*Diam.*	*Rim*	*Origin*	*Colors*	*Rarity*
	2⅞	24 scallops, with points between	Eastern, see note	Clear Milky Light green Lavender	Plentiful Common Plentiful Scarce

This has a rope band on the shoulder which, while narrower and made up of finer lines than that on the following, is rather crudely cut. Distribution seems to favor a New England origin, but not clearly enough to warrant any positive attribution.

No. 280	*Diam.*	*Rim*	*Origin*	*Colors*	*Rarity*
	2⅞	24 scallops, with points between	As above	Clear Milky Light green Lavender	Plentiful Plentiful Scarce Rare

The rope band on the shoulder is heavier and more coarsely, but also more evenly, cut than on the previous plate. In our experience, this plate both in clear and color is less frequently found than its mate.

No. 281	*Diam.*	*Rim*	*Origin*	*Colors*	*Rarity*
	3	40 even scallops	Probably Midwest	Clear	Uncertain

At the moment, this seems to be quite rare, but since the only difference between it and the two following plates is in the number of serrations, and these are very easily miscounted, this is not definite.

No. 281-A	*Diam.*	*Rim*	*Origin*	*Colors*	*Rarity*
	3 1/16	41 even scallops	As above	Clear	Plentiful

The only difference is in the number of serrations and the slightly larger diameter.

No. 281-B	*Diam.*	*Rim*	*Origin*	*Colors*	*Rarity*
	3	42 even scallops	As above	Clear	Plentiful

Again the difference is in the number of serrations. The attribution of these three plates is based not only on distribution, but on stylistic grounds as well. The only other use we recall of this 42-scallop serration is on the late sunburst, No. 533.

No. 282	*Diam.*	*Rim*	*Origin*	*Colors*	*Rarity*
	3½	51 even scallops	Uncertain, see note	Clear	Extremely rare

This should not be mistaken for No. 283, which differs not only as to the number of serrations, but is slightly different in design. Distribution favors an attribution to the East, somewhere a little south of New England.

No. 282-A	*Diam.*	*Rim*	*Origin*	*Colors*	*Rarity*
	3½	10 large points with sets of 3 points between	Uncertain, see above	Clear	Very rare

This is the only use we recall of this curious serration pattern. It was, of course, impossible to center properly the large points of the serration pattern (these were formed by the base-mold assembly) in the shoulder plumes. Probably the mold was an experiment and was soon abandoned. We have probably understated the rarity of this plate.

No. 283	*Diam.*	*Rim*	*Origin*	*Colors*	*Rarity*
	3½	49 even scallops	Uncertain, see above	Clear	Rare

The squarish stippling, if anything so coarse may be called stippling, in both the center and on the shoulder differs slightly from that on the 282 series. This is the variety of this group most frequently found. It is by no means common and it seems to turn up a little farther north than the 282 series.

No. 284	*Diam.*	*Rim*	*Origin*	*Colors*	*Rarity*
	3 3/16	24 large bull's eyes or beads divided by points	Philadelphia area	Clear	Extremely rare

This is one of the most beautifully made of all cup plates. It is very thin, flat and delicate. All specimens known to us have been found in the Philadelphia area.

No. 285	*Diam.*	*Rim*	*Origin*	*Colors*	*Rarity*
	3⅝	12 large scallops, points between	Probably Sandwich	Clear Opal Opal tint	Plentiful Plentiful Plentiful

This was, and still is, one of the most popular patterns ever made. It is likely that minor variations exist but none has been reported so far.

No. 286	*Diam.*	*Rim*	*Origin*	*Colors*	*Rarity*
	3⅝	38 even scallops	Probably Sandwich	Clear	Extremely rare

The attribution is based on distribution and on the similarity of the center pattern to that of the 12- and 13-heart border plates, which are mostly of New England and probably Sandwich origin. In the present variety, the stippling is confined to the center.

No. 287	*Diam.*	*Rim*	*Origin*	*Colors*	*Rarity*
	3⅞	60 even scallops	As above	Clear	Extremely rare

A stippled background has been added on the shoulder.

No. 288	*Diam.*	*Rim*	*Origin*	*Colors*	*Rarity*
	3½	36 even scallops	As above	Clear Blue	Unique Extremely rare

Mr. Marble's clear specimen is the only one known to us. The blue examples are all from one set discovered by Mr. Tilden in 1942.

No. 289	*Diam.*	*Rim*	*Origin*	*Colors*	*Rarity*
	3⅝	38 even scallops	As above	Clear	Extremely rare

It is possible that any of these last four plates may be discovered in the serration patterns of the others.

No. 290	*Diam.*	*Rim*	*Origin*	*Colors*	*Rarity*
	4 3/16	24 even scallops	Unknown	Clear Sage green	Unique Unique

This is a much larger plate. It is also very flat, quite thick and rather crude. The suspicion is inevitable that it is an attempt to pirate the preceding plates. The only clear specimen known to us is Mr. Cannon's. It was discovered in the Philadelphia-Baltimore region in 1944. Due to its size, there is some doubt as to whether or not this is a cup plate. The green example is in the collection of the late Dr. Herman A. Morrill.

No. 291	*Diam.*	*Rim*	*Origin*	*Colors*	*Rarity*
	3	62 even	Uncertain,	Clear	Common
		scallops	see note	Light blue	Scarce
				Medium blue	Rare
				Opaque-white	Scarce
				Milky-white	Scarce
				Light green	Rare
				Amethyst	Very rare

The background of both the center and the shoulder is stippled. The table-ring is plain, not stippled. The shoulder stippling is more regular and even than it is on the following plate. A fragment in "cobalt" (probably our medium blue) was found in the Sandwich excavation. This may indicate Sandwich origin or the fragment may have been cullet or the factory may have had one of a competitor's plates as a sample. No one really knows.

No. 292	*Diam.*	*Rim*	*Origin*	*Colors*	*Rarity*
	3 1/16	62 even	Uncertain,	Clear	Common
		scallops	see above	Blue (?)	Uncertain

This is similar to No. 291 in that both the center and shoulder have stippled backgrounds, although the stippling is less regular and even here. The diameter is 1/16″ larger. The chief difference is that about 3/32″ in from the fin or line formed on the back of the shoulder by the joint between the cap-ring and design die, a wavering line has been cut into the design die. Between this line and the fin line, there is a faint row of stippling. The blue specimen is in Mrs. Parker's collection and was numbered by us. In view of the fact that all other blue specimens are in the 3″ size (No. 291), our numbering may have been in error. Light green examples are reported, but have not been reliably confirmed.

No. 293	*Diam.*	*Rim*	*Origin*	*Colors*	*Rarity*
	3⅛	62 even	Uncertain,	Clear	Scarce
		scallops	see above	Blue	Rare

As in Nos. 291 and 292, both the center and shoulder are stippled and the table-ring is plain. The stippling, however, is very irregular. Note also the larger diameter. The serrations here are deeply indented, unlike those on the following plate. The "scarce" listing is based on want lists and is probably not accurate.

No. 294	*Diam.*	*Rim*	*Origin*	*Colors*	*Rarity*
	3⅛	62 even scallops	Uncertain, see above	Clear	Common

The shoulder is coarsely and unevenly stippled, as though the punch used in adding the stippling was blunt. The center of the plate is plain, not stippled. The serrations are not as deeply indented as they are in No. 293.

No. 295	*Diam.*	*Rim*	*Origin*	*Colors*	*Rarity*
	3⅛	62 even scallops	Uncertain, see above	Green tint	Unique

This is very much like No. 294, except that its center is faintly stippled. It is not impossible that No. 294 is a bad imprint of this plate. The only example we have seen is a faint green tint, but we have no doubt that others exist and, in fact, suspect the plate is actually common.

No. 296	*Diam.*	*Rim*	*Origin*	*Colors*	*Rarity*
	2 15/16	53 even scallops	Probably Midwestern	Clear Lavender tint	Scarce Very rare

Both the center and shoulder are evenly stippled, but there is a rope ring just inside the line of serrations. The table-ring, unlike that on Nos. 291 through 295, is not plain but is a rope ring. The attribution is made on the basis not only of distribution, but on the relation of this serration pattern to that seen on No. 191-E.

No. 296-A	*Diam.*	*Rim*	*Origin*	*Colors*	*Rarity*
	3 across	Octagonal	Probably Midwest	Clear	Common

This is exactly like the preceding plate except for its octagonal cap-ring. The serration pattern again is one found on a series of Midwestern origin, Nos. 193 through 196. While we classify the plate as "common," proof specimens are practically impossible to obtain. If the analogy with the Nos. 193–196 group is valid, light green and olive-green specimens may eventually be found.

No. 297	*Diam.*	*Rim*	*Origin*	*Colors*	*Rarity*
	3	Plain	Eastern	Clear Bluish-purple	Extremely rare Unique

This is one of the rarest, most desirable and most puzzling of all plates. It has no stylistic affinities with any other plate, and the attribution is based on distribution only. Since it was made without a cap-ring, it may be very early. Cloudy and sick examples are the rule. Mr. Marble's colored specimen, the only one known, is blue in some lights and purple in others.

No. 298	*Diam.*	*Rim*	*Origin*	*Colors*	*Rarity*
	3 15/16	Plain	Uncertain	Deep amethyst	Extremely rare
				Emerald-green	Extremely rare

This type with its 68 dots about the rim has not been recorded in clear glass. Of the amethyst specimens, we believe several sets of six have been found in New England. The emerald-green example is reported by Mr. George S. McKearin and may be unique. Another similar plate with 69 dots on the rim (there are other slight variations) occurs in clear and some most peculiar colors, pink, a smoky blue, etc., and does not ring. This 69 dot variety is probably a modern fake. In any event it seems best to avoid either the 68 or 69 dot type if it does not ring.

No. 299	*Diam.*	*Rim*	*Origin*	*Colors*	*Rarity*
	4	40 even scallops	Uncertain	Clear	Common
				Light green	Very rare

Although a 4 1/16″ variant which, like this, has 40 serrations is known (see No. 861) with an inscription "Val St. Lambert Belgique," there is some evidence that Sandwich also made the same pattern. A clear fragment is said to have been dug up there. Distribution of this plate, as well as that of No. 301, seems to reach a peak in French Canada, extending west into Ontario. By all means, avoid specimens of this and the two plates immediately following, if they do not ring.

No. 300	*Diam.*	*Rim*	*Origin*	*Colors*	*Rarity*
	3⅞	40 even scallops	Uncertain, see No. 299	Clear	Probably common

The serrations are half-circles, instead of the flatter arcs of No. 299. The stippling is much finer and the border and center scrolls vary slightly. We have seen only one of these plates, but are convinced they are not rare.

No. 301	*Diam.*	*Rim*	*Origin*	*Colors*	*Rarity*
	3½	40 even scallops	Uncertain	Clear	Common

The character of the design seems to us to be very like that of No. 299, and we suspect a foreign origin. It is possible, nevertheless, that the pattern was made at Sandwich.

Nos. 302 through 309 left open.

Chapter XII

THE SECOND TRANSITION PERIOD

Nos. 310 through 404

The period is marked by technical advance and artistic retreat. Higher working temperatures partly eliminated the scars and unevenness characteristic of earlier production and, consequently, the necessity of concealing such defects by elaborate designs and stippled backgrounds. At the same time, competition increased immeasurably. New factories were built to exploit the now fully developed pressing process, while old firms that had hitherto resisted such innovations now adopted the new method. Furthermore, the vogue for using cup plates had already begun to decline in eastern, urban and more sophisticated centers, so that the new patterns were made to appeal to a less-demanding segment of the population. All these factors combined to produce a general reduction in quality. Nor was this decadence confined to a simplification of design. The glass itself was cheapened by the addition of less and less lead.

Judging on the evidence presented by the historicals, the log cabins and Harrisons for example, stippling was considered dispensable by 1839 or 1840. It must be emphasized that it is altogether likely that dies for lacy, namely stippled, plates were still being cut long after these dates. The transition period and the lacy period tend to overlap, and plates are assigned to one category or the other on the basis of style, not of date. The later limits of these forms cannot be set with accuracy, but 1850 would seem to be a fair guess.

Oddly enough, at this relatively late date we know much less about origins than in the earlier periods. This is due in part to the greatly increased number of factories in operation. Chiefly, though, it is the result of an immense improvement in transportation. New roads were built facilitating wider distribution. Railroads, while still in their infancy, began to be an influence in the dispersal of manufactured goods. As a consequence, find-spots and density of distribution come to mean

310

310-A

310-B

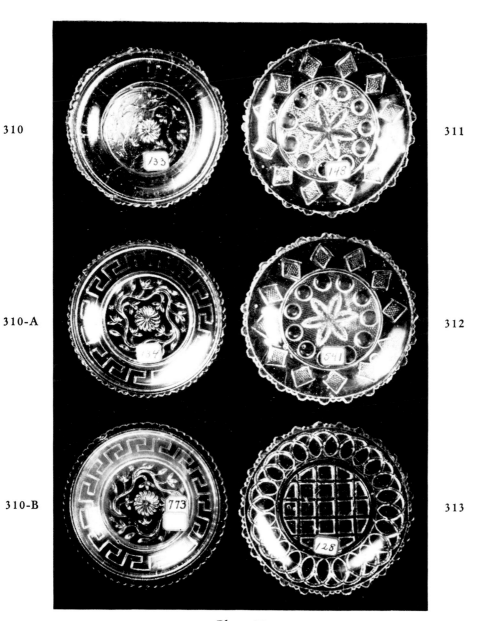

311

312

313

Plate 59

314

315

316

317
described
in text

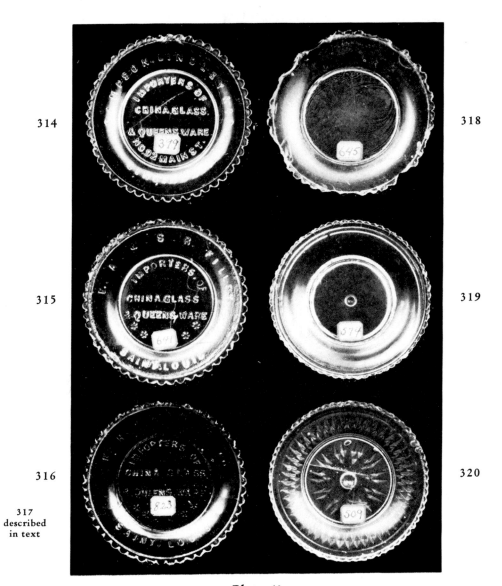

318

319

320

Plate 60

321

324

321-A

326

321
C, D
cribed
text

322

326-A

326-B
described
in text

323

Plate 61

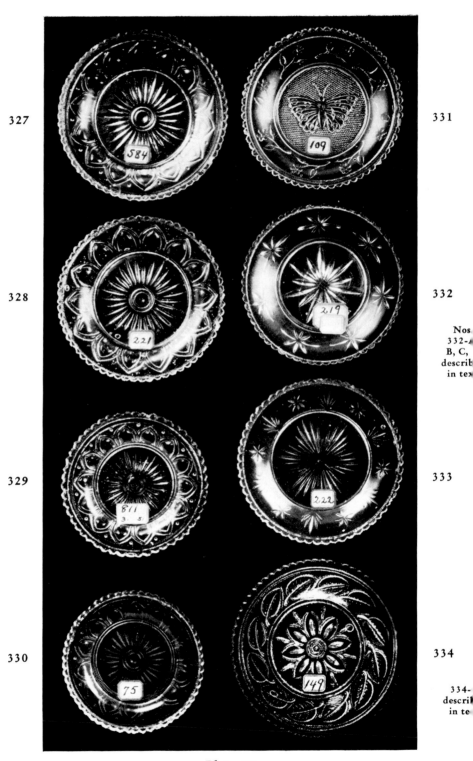

327

328

329

330

331

332

Nos
332-
B, C,
describ
in tex

333

334

334-
descri
in te

Plate 62

335

339

336

340

337

341
Reduced
in size

338

342

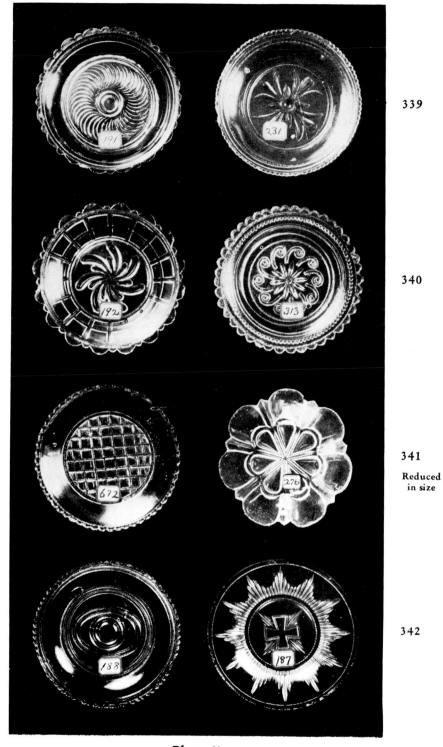

Plate 63

less and less. Only when special conditions prevail are we able to hazard an opinion.

No. 310	*Diam.*	*Rim*	*Origin*	*Colors*	*Rarity*
	3¼	10-sided, see note	Probably Philadelphia area	Clear	Rare

Each of the ten sides has 4 scallops. The corners are larger scallops, flanked by tiny points or prongs. We recall no other use of this curious serration pattern. Superficially, the serration scheme of this series resembles the No. 663 eagles, the watchcase stippling series and so on. Examined closely, they differ markedly and are probably from another source. The attribution is made on the basis of distribution only.

No. 310-A	*Diam.*	*Rim*	*Origin*	*Colors*	*Rarity*
	3¼	63 even scallops	Probably Philadelphia	Clear	Scarce

This plate is not so rare as was once supposed, but is still hard to find outside the Philadelphia region. Opal examples are likely to turn up.

No. 310-B	*Diam.*	*Rim*	*Origin*	*Colors*	*Rarity*
	3 7/16	63 even scallops	Probably Philadelphia	Opal	Extremely rare

Note the much larger diameter. Note, too, that the scallops are much less deeply indented than in the preceding plate. We know of no clear glass specimens.

No. 311	*Diam.*	*Rim*	*Origin*	*Colors*	*Rarity*
	3⅝	23 bold scallops, with pairs of smaller ones between	Probably Sandwich	Clear Opal Light green	Common Scarce Rare

Through its serrations, this series seems related to the so-called Cadmuses, hence the attribution. Both opal and clear fragments were found in the Sandwich excavations.

No. 312	*Diam.*	*Rim*	*Origin*	*Colors*	*Rarity*
	3⅝	As above	As above	Clear Opal Light green	Scarce Rare Very rare

Here the central rosette is outlined in heavy stippling.

No. 313	Diam.	Rim	Origin	Colors	Rarity
	3⅝	25 bold scallops, with pairs of smaller ones between	Probably Sandwich	Clear Opal Amethyst tint	Common Scarce Scarce

Related to the Clays, on which basis the attribution is made. An opal fragment was found at Sandwich.

No. 314	Diam.	Rim	Origin	Colors	Rarity
	3 7/16	50 even scallops	Midwest, possibly Pittsburgh	Clear	Rare

This is a product of one of the "private molds" so often advertised by the early glass factories. It can be rather accurately dated. Mr. Marble says a William Sampson was in business in Cincinnati in 1846; Sampson, Lindley & Co., in 1848–49 and Lindley & Company in 1851. Mr. J. E. Nevil has kindly searched the Cincinnati directories for us and reports the following: the 1843–46 directory lists a Nathan Sampson in business at 227 Main Street; the 1847–49 directory is not available; the 1850 directory lists Sampson, Lindley & Company at 92 Main Street and the 1851–53 directory, a George F. Sampson at 92 Main Street. The only possible conclusion is that the latest possible date for these plates is 1850 since the firm name changed in 1851. The earliest possible date is 1847. It is quite possible that a glass factory located farther west than Pittsburgh made this and the following plates.

No. 315	Diam.	Rim	Origin	Colors	Rarity
	3 7/16	50 even scallops	As above	Clear	Rare

We have no data on E. A. & S. R. Filley, but the dates may be assumed to be about those of the preceding plate.

No. 316	Diam.	Rim	Origin	Colors	Rarity
	3 7/16	50 even scallops	As above	Clear	Extremely rare

According to Mr. Marble, R. H. Miller & Company were successors to N. E. Janney & Company and advertised in a newspaper on June 28, 1852.

No. 317	*Diam.*	*Rim*	*Origin*	*Colors*	*Rarity*
				Clear	Unique

A third Saint Louis advertiser exists. It was sold about ten years ago by a Kansas City dealer to a local collector. We have had no replies to our letters asking for details, and so are unable to be more specific.

No. 318	*Diam.*	*Rim*	*Origin*	*Colors*	*Rarity*
	3 7/16	50 even scallops	As above Midwest, possibly Pittsburgh	Clear	Extremely rare

Not very spectacular, but one of the rarest of plates. It is the uncut and uninscribed plunger die of the advertising plates shown above. We have never seen this plate in good condition.

No. 319	*Diam.*	*Rim*	*Origin*	*Colors*	*Rarity*
	3 5/16	66 even scallops	Uncertain	Clear	Very rare

The diameter and serration pattern would indicate a relation to the lacy Nos. 262–263, which we tentatively assigned to the Midwest. On the other hand, there also seems a connection with the heart, No. 477, which we believe to be of Eastern origin.

No. 320	*Diam.*	*Rim*	*Origin*	*Colors*	*Rarity*
	3 5/16	66 even scallops	Uncertain	Clear Pink tint	Common Rare

Here, again, the same facts are noted as in the previous plate. Nor is distribution any help; the plate is common both east and west of the mountains. See also No. 322 following.

No. 321	*Diam*	*Rim*	*Origin*	*Colors*	*Rarity*
	3⅜ across	10-sided	Uncertain	Clear	Very rare

Specimens in good condition are virtually unknown. Marble's photograph shows the finest condition we have seen in this plate. The plate is probably relatively early and may antedate 1840.

No. 321-A	*Diam.*	*Rim*	*Origin*	*Colors*	*Rarity*
	3¼	27 scallops, points between	Uncertain	Clear	Common

No. 321-B	*Diam.* 3⅛	*Rim* 52 even scallops	*Origin* Uncertain	*Colors* Clear	*Rarity* Common

No. 321-C	*Diam.* 3	*Rim* 50 even scallops	*Origin* Uncertain	*Colors* Amethyst	*Rarity* Very rare

No clear glass specimens have come to our attention. For the sake of the record, all we can trace came from the Midwest. Related to the earlier No. 191-C; eagle, No. 680-A; and sunburst, No. 520.

No. 321-D	*Diam.* 3⅛	*Rim* 34 even scallops	*Origin* Uncertain	*Colors* Clear	*Rarity* Common

This plate is usually, perhaps always, thicker than other members of the series. See related sunbursts, Nos. 525 and 545.

No. 322	*Diam.* 3 5/16	*Rim* 66 even scallops	*Origin* Uncertain	*Colors* Clear	*Rarity* Common

The concentric rings on the shoulders of the preceding members of the group disappear and are replaced by half-sunbursts. This seems to be the latest version of the basic design. Note the serration relationship to Nos. 319 and 320.

No. 323	*Diam.* 3¼	*Rim* 66 even scallops	*Origin* Eastern, probably Sandwich	*Colors* Clear Honey-amber Medium amber Dark amber Opal	*Rarity* Common Plentiful Plentiful Scarce Common

Distribution is nation-wide but reaches its peak in New England. See the note on the following plate.

No. 324	*Diam.* 3¼	*Rim* 66 even scallops	*Origin* Eastern, probably Sandwich	*Colors* Clear Honey-amber Light amethyst Deep amethyst Opal	*Rarity* Common Doubtful Scarce Rare Common

Even veteran collectors find it hard to distinguish this from the preceding plate. Here the central dot is smaller, and the lines forming the central rosette are lighter and more attenuated. Distribution is the same as on No. 323, except for the light and dark amethyst specimens which are concentrated in eastern Pennsylvania, due, probably, to the Pennsylvania Dutch love for color.

No. 325	*Diam.*	*Rim*	*Origin*	*Colors*	*Rarity*
	3 3/16	66 even scallops	Eastern, probably Sandwich	Clear	Probably common

In the only specimen we have seen, the central dot and its radiating lines are heavier than on the preceding plate, but not quite as heavy as on No. 323. Note the size.

No. 326	*Diam.*	*Rim*	*Origin*	*Colors*	*Rarity*
	3 7/16	65 even scallops	Eastern, as above	Clear	Common

Besides the larger diameter and the change in serration count, there is a design change. The central dot is surrounded by a circle, and there are 7 of the shorter rays between the long rays of the shoulder pattern instead of the 8 short rays of the previous group.

No. 326-A	*Diam.*	*Rim*	*Origin*	*Colors*	*Rarity*
	2 15/16	57 even scallops	Eastern, as above	Clear	Common

This is much smaller and has fewer serrations. Perhaps this and the following plate are different design dies and deserve separate numbers.

No. 326-B	*Diam.*	*Rim*	*Origin*	*Colors*	*Rarity*
	3	51 even scallops	Eastern	Clear	Probably common

Like the two preceding plates, except for size and serrations.

No. 327	*Diam.*	*Rim*	*Origin*	*Colors*	*Rarity*
	3½	65 even scallops	Eastern, perhaps Sandwich	Clear	Common

Note the dots between the arches on the shoulder. The center is a double circle but lacks the centering dot of the following plate. This series seems to us to be related to the preceding one through its serrations and diameters but note the different color range.

No. 328	*Diam.*	*Rim*	*Origin*	*Colors*	*Rarity*
	3 7/16	64 even scallops	Eastern as above	Clear	Common
				Blue	Scarce
				Ice-blue tint	Rare
				Pink tint	Scarce

There are no dots between the shoulder arches. There is a dot in the precise center. Count serrations carefully on these plates.

No. 329	*Diam.*	*Rim*	*Origin*	*Colors*	*Rarity*
	3	51 even scallops	Eastern as above	Clear	Common

This has dots between the shoulder arches. The easiest method of determining this whole series is by counting serrations. This is connected to No. 326-B by a common serration pattern.

No. 330	*Diam.*	*Rim*	*Origin*	*Colors*	*Rarity*
	2 15/16	57 even scallops	Eastern as above	Clear	Common
				Cloudy	Common
				Blue	Scarce

There are dots between the shoulder arches. This may be a bad imprint of No. 329, but is more likely to be a different die.

No. 331	*Diam.*	*Rim*	*Origin*	*Colors*	*Rarity*
	3¼	66 even scallops	Eastern, perhaps Sandwich	Clear	Common

Related by surface die and cap-ring to the preceding group. Since its center is stippled, it may be earlier. Beware of colored specimens, especially blue and a pinkish-amber. These are modern reproductions. In old plates, the shoulder flower at the lower right has an extra petal, 7 petals in all, while the other border flowers have 6 petals each. Modern reproductions have flowers with 6 petals throughout.

No. 332	*Diam.*	*Rim*	*Origin*	*Colors*	*Rarity*
	3 5/16	63 even scallops	Sandwich	Clear	Common
				Opal	Unique

This series should rightfully be included in the sunbursts, but it is so often confused with the No. 323 series that we feel it should be considered here to avoid confusion. The only opal specimen known to us is in Mrs. Parker's collection, but it is most likely that others exist.

No. 332-A	*Diam.*	*Rim*	*Origin*	*Colors*	*Rarity*
	3½	63 even scallops	Sandwich	Clear	Common
				Opal	Common
				Blue	Unique
				Yellow	Fragments only

Larger diameter than the previous plate and with its serrations less deeply indented. Numerous fragments were among the finds in the excavations at Sandwich, including clear, opal and the yellow (or canary) pieces noted above. The only blue example we can locate is in the Cannon collection.

No. 332-B	*Diam.*	*Rim*	*Origin*	*Colors*	*Rarity*
	3⅝	63 even scallops	Sandwich	Clear	Common
				Yellow	Scarce

The diameter is still larger, and the indentation of the serrations is so slight that they become little more than a wavy outline. It seems possible that the yellow fragments found at Sandwich may have been this plate, rather than the one noted above.

No. 332-C	*Diam.*	*Rim*	*Origin*	*Colors*	*Rarity*
	3 11/16	63 even scallops	Sandwich	Clear	Undetermined

This plate is noted by Mr. Marble, but is not photographed or numbered by him. We have not seen it and cannot say whether the scallops are of the deeply indented or shallow type, but presume they are the latter. Size is the determining factor.

No. 332-D	*Diam.*	*Rim*	*Origin*	*Colors*	*Rarity*
	3⅜	53 even scallops	Sandwich	Clear	Common

The only one of the group with 53 serrations and hence easily indentified. The scallops are deeply indented. No colors have been reported, but they probably exist.

No. 333	*Diam.*	*Rim*	*Origin*	*Colors*	*Rarity*
	3 7/16	59 even scallops	Probably Sandwich	Clear Soft blue	Common Scarce

Another plate that properly belongs with the sunbursts, but included here because of its similarity to the preceding series. Clear and blue specimens were found in the Sandwich excavations.

No. 334	*Diam.*	*Rim*	*Origin*	*Colors*	*Rarity*
	3 7/16	67 even scallops	Probably Sandwich	Clear Opal	Common Scarce

Clear and opal fragments were found at Sandwich. Related through serrations to the Harrisons.

No. 334-A	*Diam.*	*Rim*	*Origin*	*Colors*	*Rarity*
	3 5/16	67 even scallops	Probably Sandwich	Clear Opal	Common Scarce

The only difference is in the diameter.

No. 335	*Diam.*	*Rim*	*Origin*	*Colors*	*Rarity*
	3 3/16	16 large scallops, smaller ones between	Unknown	Clear	Scarce

No. 336	*Diam.*	*Rim*	*Origin*	*Colors*	*Rarity*
	3⅜	16 large scallops, smaller ones between	Unknown	Clear	Plentiful

No. 337	*Diam.*	*Rim*	*Origin*	*Colors*	*Rarity*
	3 3/16	55 even scallops	Unknown	Clear	Extremely rare

Although very plain, this plate looks and may be much earlier than our classification would indicate. For other waffle centers see Nos. 58 through 63 and 140 through 145.

No. 338	*Diam.*	*Rim*	*Origin*	*Colors*	*Rarity*
	3¼	78 even scallops	Unknown	Clear	Common

No. 339	*Diam.*	*Rim*	*Origin*	*Colors*	*Rarity*
	3⅛	96 even scallops	Unknown	Clear Light blue	Common Extremely rare

It is possible that this is the same serration pattern found on No. 200, in which case either this plate is earlier than we think or No. 200 is later.

No. 340	*Diam.*	*Rim*	*Origin*	*Colors*	*Rarity*
	3¼	42 even scallops	Unknown	Clear	Common
				Light green	Extremely rare

This plate is thicker and heavier than is customary in the late period, and may be earlier than we think. Distribution hints at an origin west of the mountains.

No. 341	*Diam.*	*Rim*	*Origin*	*Colors*	*Rarity*
	3⅜	7 large scallops, points between	Unknown	Clear	Common

To us, no more puzzling plate exists. Its plainness looks late. It is thin and delicately made. On the other hand, it was pressed without a cap-ring; its metal is fine and the center pattern is similar to that cut on the foot of rather early goblets made in the Pittsburgh-Wheeling area. Some years ago, impressed by the quantity of these plates found northeast of Pittsburgh, we suspected an origin in the Midwest. Time has shown that distribution is universal, so that no attribution can be made. There is a possibility, due to the shape of the center, that this plate was not intended to be a cup plate.

No. 342	*Diam.*	*Rim*	*Origin*	*Colors*	*Rarity*
	3 5/16	Plain	Unknown, perhaps Philadelphia	Clear	Common
				Opaque-white	Very rare

The rim pattern and the color range seems to be that seen on No. 388, a somewhat later plate, and there, too, distribution points to an origin somewhere in the Philadelphia area. ·

No. 343	*Diam.*	*Rim*	*Origin*	*Colors*	*Rarity*
	3 7/16	Plain	Philadelphia area	Clear	Unique

This is a recent discovery of Mr. Richard H. Wood's and is now in Mr. Marble's collection. Its rim is not embellished on the under-side, as is the case on the two plates immediately following. We have not seen this plate, but presume it is glassy (fire polished), like its A and B variants.

No. 343-A	Diam.	Rim	Origin	Colors	Rarity
	3 7/16	Plain but stippled below	As above	Clear	Rare

Throughout this series the attribution is based on the density of distribution. This plate has fine stippling cut on its cap-ring. All we have seen were fire polished.

No. 343-B	Diam.	Rim	Origin	Colors	Rarity
	3 7/16	Plain but dotted below	As above	Clear	Scarce

This is the member of the series most often found. As is the case with No. 343-A, it is always in our experience very glassy. The attribution rests heavily on the distribution of this variety, since it is the only one seen frequently enough to permit any conclusions.

No. 344	Diam.	Rim	Origin	Colors	Rarity
	3	28 scallops, points between	Eastern	Clear	Rare
				Clam broth	Extremely rare

This is a deep plate much like a sauce dish or, considering its small size, a so-called honey dish. It may not have been made as a cup plate. Beyond the fact that neither it nor its related plates, which follow, ever turn up west of the mountains, and that such examples of all three as we have bought in shops were from New York or Philadelphia, we have no data on origin. The rarity statement is based on want lists.

No. 345	Diam.	Rim	Origin	Colors	Rarity
	3 1/16	28 scallops, points between	Eastern	Clear	Common

Another deep plate. The measurement is Mr. Marble's, and may be from a distorted or warped plate. It would seem likely that this should be 3″, as are the preceding and following plates. Note that the rays of the sunburst are all of the same length.

No. 346	Diam.	Rim	Origin	Colors	Rarity
	3	28 scallops, points between	Eastern	Clear	Rare

Also a deep plate. The sunburst's rays are alternating long and short. This and the former plate belong with the sunbursts, but are inserted here because of their relationship to the similar plate with target center.

No. 347	Diam.	Rim	Origin	Colors	Rarity
	3¾	65 even scallops	Unknown	Clear	Rare
				Yellow	Very rare

We have found most of these in the stocks of dealers who handle European goods. It is possible that the plates are not American. A 56-scallop variant with the rosette center of No. 348 has been found as we go to press.

No. 348	Diam.	Rim	Origin	Colors	Rarity
	4 3/16	51 even scallops	Unknown	Clear	Rare
				Deep green	Extremely rare

Note that this has a central rosette not present in the preceding plate. It is also much larger and on the verge of our arbitrarily set upper limit of size.

No. 349	Diam.	Rim	Origin	Colors	Rarity
	3 15/16	8 large scallops, blocks of 5 smaller ones between	Unknown	Clear	Scarce

Our estimate of rarity is based solely on want lists. In our experience it is very rare. We recall no other plate with this curious serration pattern, and there is no question but that the Midwest can be eliminated as a possible source. We suspect it is much later than our classification indicates, and feel the pattern is reminiscent of late XIX century cut glass design.

343

343-A

343-B

344

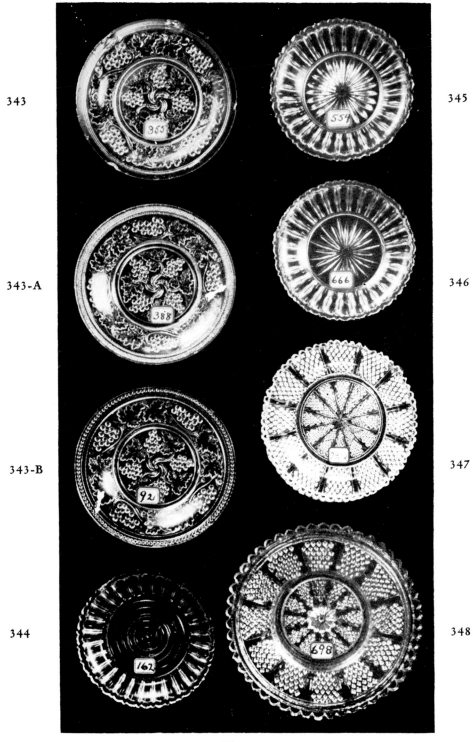

345

346

347

348

Plate 64

349

350

351

352

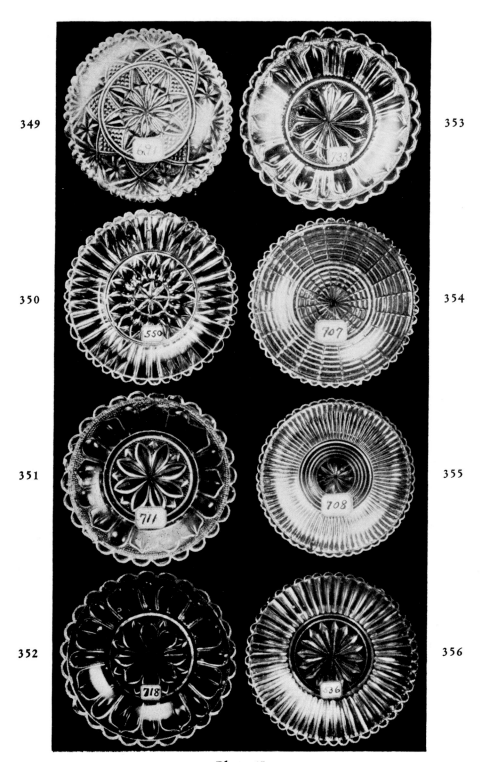

353

354

355

356

Plate 65

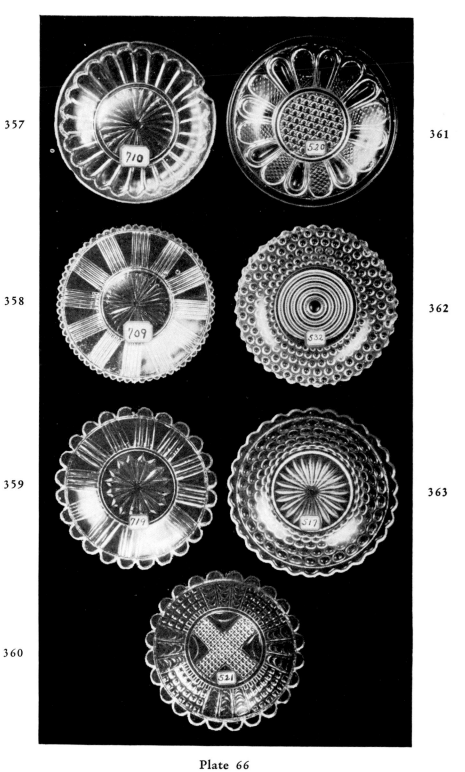

357

361

358

362

359

363

360

Plate 66

364

366

364-A

367

365

Plate 67

368

369

370

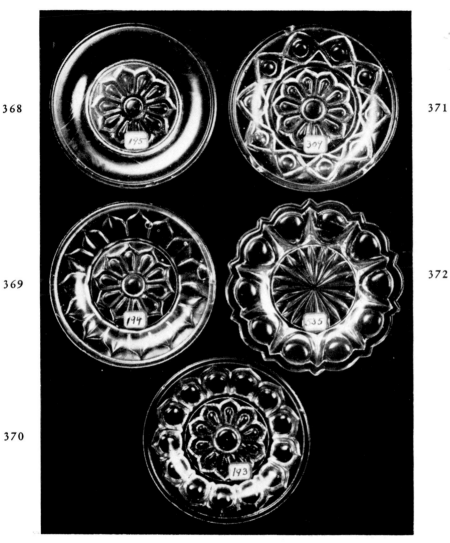

371

372

Plate 68

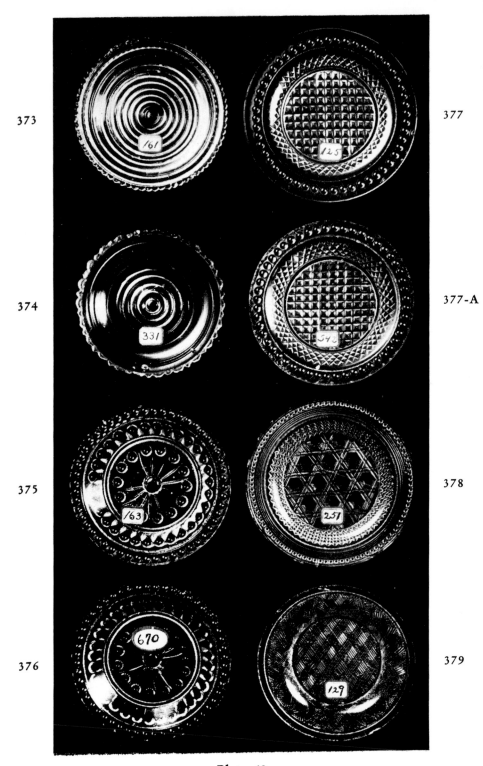

373

374

375

376

377

377-A

378

379

Plate 69

No. 350	*Diam.*	*Rim*	*Origin*	*Colors*	*Rarity*
	4 1/16	42 even scallops	Unknown	Clear	Very rare

Here, again, we feel that there may be an attempt to copy late cut glass. We are not convinced that the large plates now being considered are necessarily cup plates.

No. 351	*Diam.*	*Rim*	*Origin*	*Colors*	*Rarity*
	4 1/16	26 even scallops	Unknown	Clear	Scarce

This displays a very late use of stippling.

No. 352	*Diam.*	*Rim*	*Origin*	*Colors*	*Rarity*
	4 1/16	26 even scallops	Unknown	Clear	Scarce

The shape of the central petals is less attenuated and the loops on the shoulder are longer than in the preceding plate.

No. 353	*Diam.*	*Rim*	*Origin*	*Colors*	*Rarity*
	4⅛	30 even scallops	Unknown	Clear	Scarce

The central rosette resembles that of the first member of the series, but lacks the points between the petals. The shoulder figures are much narrower.

No. 354	*Diam.*	*Rim*	*Origin*	*Colors*	*Rarity*
	3⅞	48 even scallops	Unknown	Clear	Rare

We can say with reasonable certainty that this plate is not Midwestern. The few specimens we have seen have come from the East.

No. 355	*Diam.*	*Rim*	*Origin*	*Colors*	*Rarity*
	3⅝	50 even scallops	Unknown	Clear	Very rare

There is a possibility that the listing should be extremely rare. The only specimen we have seen is Mr. Marble's, but we have heard of several others, all of which originated in the East.

No. 356	*Diam.*	*Rim*	*Origin*	*Colors*	*Rarity*
	4	48 even scallops	Unknown	Clear	Scarce

Possibly this should be classed as common. We have seen few, but this may be due to the dealers' prejudice against what they consider toddies.

No. 357	*Diam*	*Rim*	*Origin*	*Colors*	*Rarity*
	3 15/16	Plain	Unknown	Clear	Extremely rare

The only one we have seen is Mr. Marble's. We have heard of one or two additional specimens, all in the East.

No. 358	*Diam.*	*Rim*	*Origin*	*Colors*	*Rarity*
	3⅞	64 even scallops	Unknown	Clear	Very rare

Again, what little we know about distribution seems to indicate Eastern manufacture.

No. 359	*Diam*	*Rim*	*Origin*	**Colors**	*Rarity*
	4	24 even scallops	Unknown	Clear	Rare

The design is vaguely similar to that of the preceding plate but, since the pattern is so prosaic and unimaginative, this has little significance. Distribution, what there is of it, is Eastern.

No. 360	*Diam.*	*Rim*	*Origin*	*Colors*	*Rarity*
	3⅞	24 even scallops	Unknown	Clear	Common

Measurements of both this and the previous plate are Mr. Marble's. The 24 scallops on both just might indicate use of the same cap-ring or surface die, in which case diameters should agree. It is our impression that this plate is deeper. Those we have seen are of a better quality of glass than one expects to find in this period.

No. 361	*Diam.*	*Rim*	*Origin*	*Colors*	*Rarity*
	4 1/16	Plain	Unknown	Clear	Common

We have a vague recollection of once, years ago, owning a copy of this in color. We think in a deep green. Since we are unable to locate and thus confirm it, we are not listing the color. All we have seen are in an inferior metal, and the distribution is Eastern.

No. 362	*Diam.*	*Rim*	*Origin*	*Colors*	*Rarity*
	3 15/16	36 even scallops	Unknown	Clear	Scarce

We have no data whatsoever on distribution.

No. 363	Diam.	Rim	Origin	Colors	Rarity
	4⅛	30 even scallops	Unknown	Clear	Common

The plate is found in all sections of the country, so that we cannot even guess its source. It is probably too late to have been used as a cup plate.

No. 364	Diam	Rim	Origin	Colors	Rarity
	3 7/16	59 even scallops	Unknown	Clear	Common

This serration pattern is not, it should be noted, the same as that on such plates as No. 619-A. These scallops are less deeply indented. There are 16 rays in the sunburst.

No. 364-A	Diam.	Rim	Origin	Colors	Rarity
	3¼	Plain	Unknown	Clear	Common

Like the preceding, except for the smooth rim and different size.

No. 365	Diam.	Rim	Origin	Colors	Rarity
	3¼	Plain	Unknown	Clear	Common

Superficially like the previous plate, but the border panels are wider, the sunburst has 14 rays and the central porthole is much larger.

No. 366	Diam.	Rim	Origin	Colors	Rarity
	3¼	Plain	Unknown	Clear	Common

The central porthole is more heavily outlined. The sunburst has only 12 rays. The shoulder pattern varies.

No. 367	Diam.	Rim	Origin	Colors	Rarity
	3 15/16	Plain	Unknown	Clear	Common

Much larger than the rest of the group and with 14 rays in its sunburst.

No. 368	Diam.	Rim	Origin	Colors	Rarity
	3⅝	Plain	Unknown	Clear	Common

The quality of the glass throughout this group is poor.

No. 369	Diam.	Rim	Origin	Colors	Rarity
	3⅝	Plain	Unknown	Clear	Common

The shoulder is decorated with a broad but pointed leaf motif. The central petals are more pointed.

No. 370	Diam.	Rim	Origin	Colors	Rarity
	3⅝	Plain	Unknown	Clear	Common

The central porthole is larger. The leaves on the shoulder are outlined in heavy beveling.

No. 371	Diam.	Rim	Origin	Colors	Rarity
	3⅝	Plain	Unknown	Clear	Common

The central porthole is the smaller type, but the shoulder pattern is running, large diamonds enclosing bull's eyes.

No. 372	Diam.	Rim	Origin	Colors	Rarity
	3 13/16	10 large scallops, points between	Unknown	Clear	Common

This group, Nos. 368 through 372, is vaguely related in feeling to the previous group, Nos. 364–367, and is possibly from the same glass factory.

No. 373	Diam.	Rim	Origin	Colors	Rarity
	3⅝	73 even scallops	Eastern	Clear	Common
				Opal	Rare

There appears to be a relationship between this plate and the heart series, No. 447-B. If this is correct, it is probably of Sandwich origin. Note the different color range. A 3 5/16″ specimen is in Dr. Doane's collection.

No. 374	Diam.	Rim	Origin	Colors	Rarity
	3¼	22 scallops, points between	Eastern	Clear	Common
				Green	Scarce
				Sage-green	Very rare
				Amber	Scarce
				Amethyst	Very rare
				Blue	Scarce

We have not discovered any specimens that ring when tapped. The blue examples are in a dirty and cloudy shade. Attribution is based entirely on distribution.

No. 375	*Diam.*	*Rim*	*Origin*	*Colors*	*Rarity*
	3½	Plain	Unknown, probably Eastern	Clear	Common

This is difficult to distinguish from the following. Both have 52 small bull's eyes on the top of the rim, and were probably pressed with an identical surface die. The design dies vary. This has 30 bull's eyes on the shoulder and 14 in the center.

No 376	*Diam.*	*Rim*	*Origin*	*Colors*	*Rarity*
	3½	Plain	As above	Clear	Common

This has 3 more, a total of 33, bull's eyes on the shoulder and 1 more, a total of 15, in the center.

No. 377	*Diam.*	*Rim*	*Origin*	*Colors*	*Rarity*
	3¾	Plain	Unknown, probably Eastern	Clear	Common

Even though diameters are larger, this series seems to us to have the same surface die as the previous one with the 52 bull's eyes on the top of each plate. In this variety, these bull's eyes are farther from the rim than in the following plate.

No. 377-A	*Diam.*	*Rim*	*Origin*	*Colors*	*Rarity*
	3 9/16	Plain	As above	Clear	Common

The diameter is smaller and, as a result, the top bull's eyes are nearer the rim.

No. 378	*Diam.*	*Rim*	*Origin*	*Colors*	*Rarity*
	3¾	Plain	Unknown, probably Eastern	Clear	Common

So far as we know this plate has no variants.

No. 379	*Diam.*	*Rim*	*Origin*	*Colors*	*Rarity*
	3 7/16	Plain	Eastern, probably Sandwich	Clear	Common

This is not, as is frequently assumed, related to the much earlier and infinitely rarer Midwestern series, No. 215.

No. 380	Diam. 3⅜	Rim Plain	Origin Unknown, probably Eastern	Colors Clear Silver stain	Rarity Common Unique

The example flashed in amber is in Mr. Carleton V. Bates' collection. It is a very late use of this technique.

No. 381	Diam. 3⅜	Rim 29 even scallops	Origin Probably Midwestern	Colors Clear Pink tint	Rarity Common Common

All of these we have seen are in poor quality glass and do not ring. Attribution is based on distribution only. See also No. 491.

No. 382	Diam. 3⅞	Rim 40 points	Origin Unknown, probably Eastern	Colors Clear Green	Rarity Rare Extremely rare

This differs from the following plate in that the relatively parallel curved lines forming the shoulder pattern are so arranged that each pair encloses *seven* squares. Judged by its frequent occurrence on collectors' want lists, it is rare. The pointed serrations resemble Belgian practice. See Nos. 853 and 857.

No. 383	Diam. 3⅞	Rim 40 points	Origin Unknown, probably Eastern	Colors Clear	Rarity Unique

The curved shoulder lines here form *six* complete squares. The rarity is almost certainly more apparent than real. It seems likely that many exist misnumbered.

No. 384	Diam. 3 15/16	Rim 40 points	Origin Unknown, probably Eastern	Colors Clear	Rarity Uncertain

The diameter given is that noted by Mr. Marble. We lean to the view that the size is the same as that of the two plates just listed, or 3⅞″. While in our experience this plate is quite rare, we recognize the fact that no one is likely to become excited over finding such a late

380

381

382

383

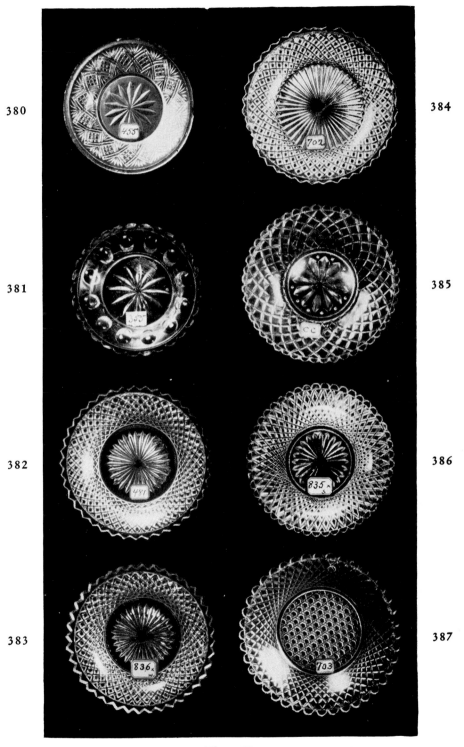

384

385

386

387

Plate 70

388

391

389

392

390

393

390-A

394

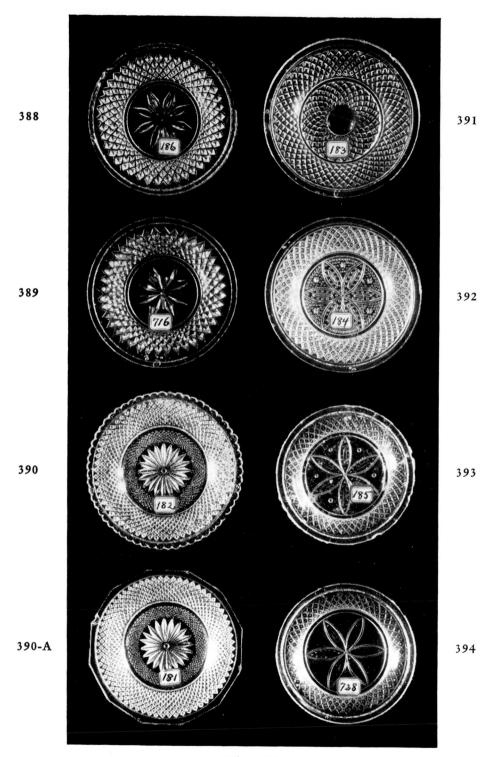

Plate 71

395

398

396

399

397

Plate 72

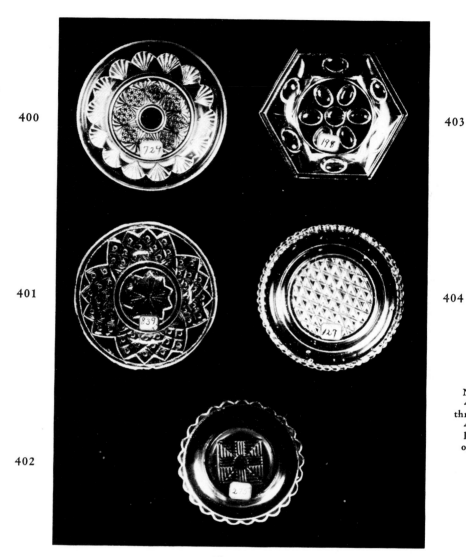

400

403

401

404

Nos
405
throu
409
left
oper

402

Plate 73

plate, so that many finds go unreported. The chances are it is not too rare.

No. 385	Diam.	Rim	Origin	Colors	Rarity
	4	48 even scallops	Unknown, probably Eastern	Clear	Scarce

No. 386	Diam.	Rim	Origin	Colors	Rarity
	3 15/16	48 even scallops	Unknown, probably Eastern	Clear	Unique

This appears to be a bit earlier than the plates just listed. Mrs. Siegrist's specimen is the only one known to us, but here, again, it is possible that the relative unattractiveness of the plate has kept collectors from reporting it.

No. 387	Diam.	Rim	Origin	Colors	Rarity
	4⅛	40 even scallops	Unknown, probably Eastern	Clear	Rare

This, and other plates with similar shoulder patterns, vaguely resemble the Victoria Regina plates of which one variety occurs with a "D" moldmaker's or maker's mark. It has been said that this "D" stands for, variously, Dolflein, a moldmaker, or Dyott, a glass manufacturer, both of Philadelphia. Our experience is that plates of this character do turn up more frequently in the Philadelphia area, so the speculation on the "D" may be correct.

No. 388	Diam.	Rim	Origin	Colors	Rarity
	3 5/16	Plain	Uncertain, possibly Philadelphia area	Clear Opaque-white	Common Common

The lines forming the central star do not meet at the central dot. A doughy-looking impression always. We have met with slightly larger examples, approaching in size the following variant.

No. 389	Diam.	Rim	Origin	Colors	Rarity
	3⅜	Plain	Uncertain, possibly Philadelphia area	Clear Blue	Common Extremely rare

The lines forming the central star meet at the central dot, unlike the preceding. The imprint is sharp. The tentative attribution is based on the fact that all the blue examples known to us have been found around Philadelphia. These colored specimens are very rare, so the assignment is pure speculation.

No. 390	Diam.	Rim	Origin	Colors	Rarity
	3 7/16	59 even scallops	Uncertain, possibly Sandwich	Clear	Common

The serration pattern coincides with that found on several 12- and 13-heart border plates and the attribution is based on this. The probability is that this plate is slightly earlier than those now being discussed.

No. 390-A	Diam.	Rim	Origin	Colors	Rarity
	3⅝	12 plain sides	Uncertain, possibly Sandwich	Clear	Common

Here, again, the rim matches that on a well-known heart.

No. 391	Diam.	Rim	Origin	Colors	Rarity
	3 7/16	Plain	Uncertain, probably Eastern	Clear	Common

No. 392	Diam.	Rim	Origin	Colors	Rarity
	3 7/16	Plain	Uncertain, probably Eastern	Clear	Common

No. 393	Diam	Rim	Origin	Colors	Rarity
	3	Plain	Uncertain	Clear	Common

This seems to be a decadent copy of the plate just shown and, if this be true, this plate is later. Note the dots in the spandrels of the central figure.

No. 394	Diam	Rim	Origin	Colors	Rarity
	3	Plain	Uncertain	Clear	Extremely rare

This would seem to have been the original version of the plate just shown. Not unreasonably dissatisfied with the appearance of this version, the "designer" had a brainstorm and stuck dots in the spandrels. This type without the dot is of the greatest rarity. We have located only two specimens.

No. 395	*Diam.*	*Rim*	*Origin*	*Colors*	*Rarity*
	3¾	44 points	Unknown	Clear	Common

This is a very late and a very glassy plate and perhaps belongs in the next section, "The Final Phase." In fact, it may not even be a cup plate. The quality of the glass is exceedingly poor.

No. 396	*Diam*	*Rim*	*Origin*	*Colors*	*Rarity*
	3¼	Plain	Possibly	Clear	Common
			Sandwich.	Milky-white	Rare
			See note	Opal	Rare
				Blue	Extremely rare
				Amethyst tint	Rare

The stippling, even though it is of the late, irregular type, and the color range, which is unusual in this period, may indicate a date for this plate earlier than its position in the check list implies. The tentative attribution to Sandwich is made on the find of a peacock-blue fragment there in the Wynn excavations. Although no specimen has been reported in this color, one should turn up.

No. 397	*Diam.*	*Rim*	*Origin*	*Colors*	*Rarity*
	3 1/16	44 even scallops	Unknown	Clear	Common

The serration pattern is very much like that found on the Midwestern sunburst, No. 524, but there seems to us to be a very slight difference in the curvature of the individual scallops, so we hesitate to assign No. 397 to the Midwest. If investigation proves the serration patterns to be identical, blue and possibly amethyst specimens should be found.

No. 398	*Diam.*	*Rim*	*Origin*	*Colors*	*Rarity*
	3½ across	Plain, a square plate with cut corners	Unknown	Clear	Unique

Mr. Marble's is the only example known to us of this late but interesting plate. It was originally in the collection of Mr. George W. Bierce, and since a large share of Mr. Bierce's collecting was done in the Midwest, this plate may have been found there. No attribution can be hung on so slender a thread.

No. 399	*Diam.*	*Rim*	*Origin*	*Colors*	*Rarity*
	3 5/16	Plain	Eastern	Clear	Rare

Rarity statements on these late, unattractive plates are necessarily tentative. No matter how rare such plates are, their commercial value is low. The result is that dealers, even the specialists, overlook them.

No. 400	Diam.	Rim	Origin	Colors	Rarity
	3½	Plain	Unknown	Clear	Very rare

This seems to us to be even later than the preceding plate and appears to fall within the pattern glass period. It also seems rarer but again the necessarily tentative nature of such an opinion should be kept in mind.

No. 401	Diam.	Rim	Origin	Colors	Rarity
	3 11/16	Plain	Unknown	Clear	Unique

Dr. Doane's specimen is the only one we have located. This is the only plate known to us where the mold was divided vertically into three parts after the manner of late pressed pieces.

No. 402	Diam.	Rim	Origin	Colors	Rarity
	3	25 even scallops	Unknown	Clear	Common

While the plate is found everywhere, it seems slightly more common in the East. The difference in distribution is too slight to warrant an attribution.

No. 403	Diam.	Rim	Origin	Colors	Rarity
	3 1/16	Plain with 6 sides	Eastern	Clear	Common

This is related to a six-sided sunburst, No. 499.

No. 404	Diam.	Rim	Origin	Colors	Rarity
	3½	56 even scallops	Unknown	Clear Yellow	Common Unique

These serrations are shaped on top, as well as being scalloped. This is a late plate, and probably should be placed in the next period rather than here. The yellow specimen is in Mr. Cannon's collection.

Nos. 405 through 409 are reserved for new discoveries.

Chapter XIII

THE FINAL PHASE OF THE CONVENTIONALS

Nos. 410 through 418

By this time, the use of cup plates was no longer fashionable, and persisted only in backward rural regions or on the frontier, where there was a cultural lag. With such a limited and declining market, a manufacturer could no longer afford to sink capital into either a large variety of or elaborate and costly individual molds. Quality, if it was considered at all, became at best a secondary consideration and cost became all-important, with the depressing result you see here. It is altogether likely that many patterns dating from the late transition period were still being pressed, so that the consumer's choice was not quite as restricted as the smallness of the group seems to indicate.

Distribution is so universal that nothing is known and little can be guessed about the sources of these late plates. The meagre demand may mean that few glassworks any longer made cup plates.

No. 410	*Diam.*	*Rim*	*Origin*	*Colors*	*Rarity*
	3 5/16	Plain	Unknown	Clear	Common

This seems to be the same rim seen on Nos. 342 and 388.

No. 411	*Diam.*	*Rim*	*Origin*	*Colors*	*Rarity*
	3¼	10 sides	Uncertain, possibly Sandwich	Clear	Common

The guess as to origin hinges on distribution, which is denser in the East, and on the incidence of peacock-green (a color we associate with Sandwich) specimens in the following companion plate.

No. 412	*Diam.*	*Rim*	*Origin*	*Colors*	*Rarity*
	3 3/16	10 sides	Uncertain, possibly Sandwich	Clear	Common
				Peacock-green	Rare
				Peacock-blue	Rare

253

Although the diameter given is 1/16 inch smaller, we are convinced that the same surface die was used on both this and the preceding plate. The surfaces of both rims appear to be polished.

No. 413	*Diam.*	*Rim*	*Origin*	*Colors*	*Rarity*
	3 1/16	Plain	Unknown	Clear	Common

No. 414	*Diam.*	*Rim*	*Origin*	*Colors*	*Rarity*
	3 1/16	Plain	Unknown	Clear	Extremely rare

The rarity seems due to the maker's dissatisfaction with the design and his almost immediate effort to "improve" it by adding a row of dots to the shoulder pattern, thereby creating the following plate.

No. 415	*Diam.*	*Rim*	*Origin*	*Colors*	*Rarity*
	3 1/16	Plain	Unknown	Clear	Common

No. 416	*Diam.*	*Rim*	*Origin*	*Colors*	*Rarity*
	3 1/16	Plain	Unknown	Clear	Common

The origin of this is unknown, as we have said, but it was beyond any doubt the same factory that pressed the two preceding plates.

No. 417	*Diam.*	*Rim*	*Origin*	*Colors*	*Rarity*
	3	Plain	Unknown	Clear	Common

This is the so-called "Barberry" and is generally conceded to be the most common and least desirable of all cup plates.

No. 418	*Diam.*	*Rim*	*Origin*	*Colors*	*Rarity*
	3⅛	Plain	Unknown, possibly Midwestern	Clear	Common

This plate has turned up more frequently west of the mountains, hence the tentative attribution. Specimens are known with a slightly different top-shape.

Nos. 419 through 424 are reserved for new discoveries.

410

412

411

4:

Plate 74

414

417

415

418

Nos.
419
throug
424
left
open

416

Plate 75

Chapter XIV

THE HEART GROUP

Nos. 425 through 480

Originally it was our intention to classify hearts in "factory" groups along with other conventionals. On consulting other specialists, we found that most of them objected to this and that they preferred to have us list the hearts separately, their theory being that such a subdivision would facilitate locating plates. Accordingly, we have compromised. Where hearts are the primary feature of any pattern, they are listed here; where the heart motif is secondary, the plate is listed along with other conventionals. See Nos. 78, 79, 80 and 234.

THE SECOND PHASE OF THE EARLIEST PERIOD

This is the initial appearance of the heart as a decorative device. The heart lends itself perfectly to circular patterns and from this time forth continues to be in great favor with the designer and, apparently, with the public. For some unaccountable reason, this preference was Eastern. There are hearts that presumably were made west of the mountains, but easily 90% of the known specimens appear to have originated in the East.

The following early series is justly considered difficult to number, and we have tried to simplify the points used in identification. All these plates were made before the invention of the cap-ring.

No. 425	*Diam*	*Rim*	*Origin*	*Colors*	*Rarity*
	3⅜	9 large scallops, hearts between	Eastern, see note	Clear	Plentiful
				Deep blue	Very rare
				Blue tint	Rare
				Medium amethyst	Unique

We are tempted to credit the whole series to Sandwich or NEG, but the fact that many clear specimens and most of the blue ones have

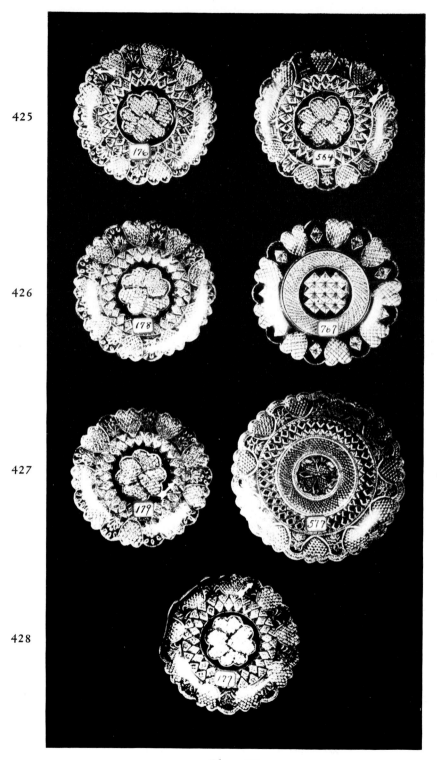

425

429

430
describ
in tex
No. 4
left
open

426

432

427

433

No. 4
left
open

428

Plate 76

435

439

439-A, B, C
described
in text

436

440

440-A
described
in text

436-A

No. 437
left
open

440-B

438

440-C

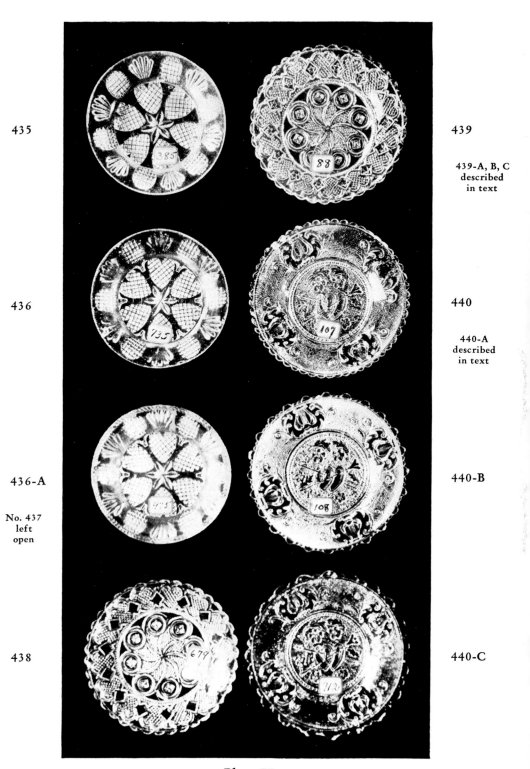

Plate 77

441

443

441-A

444

444-A
describe[d]
in text

442

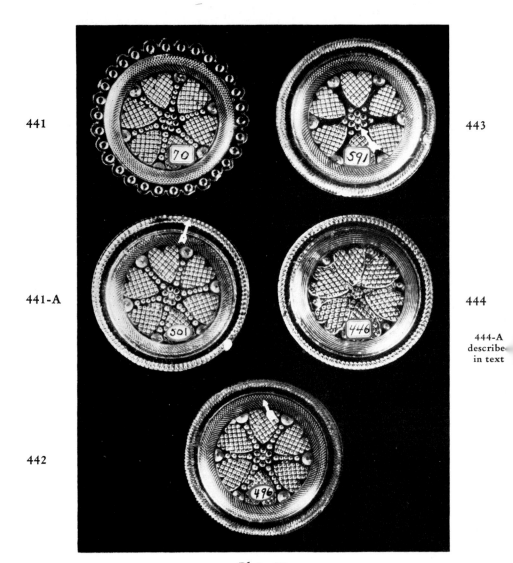

Plate 78

445

448

446

449

Nos. 450
through
454
left open

447

47-A, B
scribed
n text

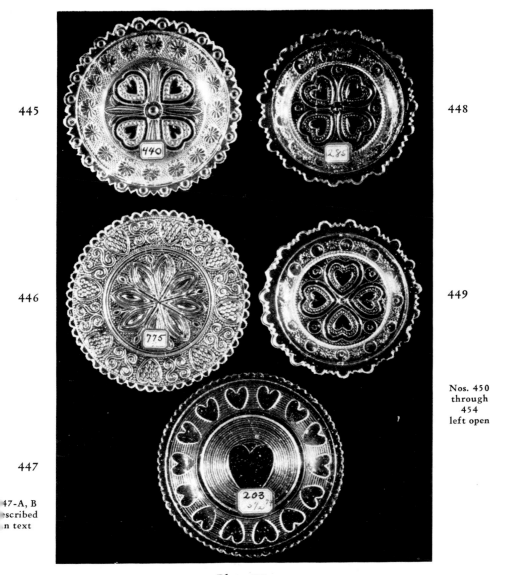

Plate 79

455

455-A
described
in text

455-B

455-C
described
in text

456

456-A, B
described
in text

457

457-A, B
described
in text

458

458-A,
describe
in text

459-C

459
through
459-Q
describe
in text

460
throug
460-B
describe
in text

461
throug
464
left
open

465-I

465-Q

465
throug
465-S
describe
in text

No. 46
left ope

Plate 80

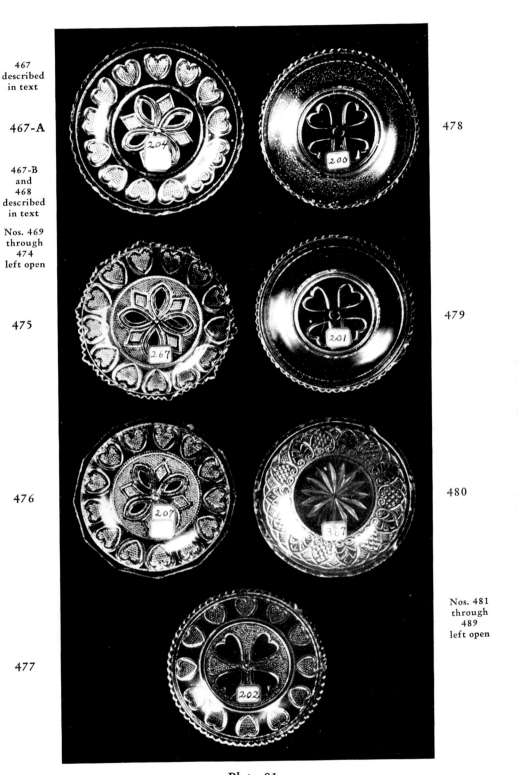

467
described
in text

467-A

467-B
and
468
described
in text

Nos. 469
through
474
left open

475

476

477

478

479

480

Nos. 481
through
489
left open

Plate 81

turned up in eastern Pennsylvania injects an element of doubt. This type has 3 *round* dots in each scallop and the inner border of the band of strawberry diamonds is a circle.

No. 426	Diam.	Rim	Origin	Colors	Rarity
	3⅜	9 large scallops, hearts between	Eastern, as above	Clear Blue tint	Scarce Rare

The 3 dots in the scallops are *elongated,* not round as in the preceding plate, and the inner ring of the band of strawberry diamonds is indented to outline each diamond.

No. 427	Diam.	Rim	Origin	Colors	Rarity
	3⅜	9 large scallops, hearts between	Eastern, as above	Clear	Scarce

Much like the preceding plate but the cutting of the strawberry diamonds differs. In this plate it is coarser and has fewer tiny points in each diamond.

No. 428	Diam.	Rim	Origin	Colors	Rarity
	3⅜	9 large scallops, hearts between	Eastern, as above	Clear Opaque-white	Scarce Very rare

The dots in the scallops are numerous and very small.

No. 429	Diam.	Rim	Origin	Colors	Rarity
	3⅜	9 large scallops, hearts between	Eastern, as above	Clear Opalescent	Plentiful Very rare

This is the easiest to determine in the entire series since it has *no* dots in its scallops.

No. 430	Diam.	Rim	Origin	Colors	Rarity
	3⅜	9 large scallops, hearts between	Eastern, as above	Clear	Unique

The diamond diapering of the shoulder hearts does not extend to the rim. Dr. Doane's specimen is the only one we have seen.

No. 431 is reserved for a new discovery.

No. 432	Diam.	Rim	Origin	Colors	Rarity
	3½	9 large scallops, hearts between	Unknown	Clear	Extremely rare

At first glance, this is startlingly like the series just discussed. The size differs and the central ornament is unique. The temptation is to assign it to New England, but every known specimen has turned up in Pennsylvania or Ohio. Thus the evidence is not clear. We favor an attribution to the Philadelphia area, which at this early date appears to have copied and adapted many New England designs.

No. 433	Diam.	Rim	Origin	Colors	Rarity
	4⅛	11 large scallops, hearts between	Unknown	Clear	Scarce

The plate turns up, not too commonly, everywhere, so any attribution would be based entirely on style and would point toward New England. Due to its large size and especially to the large center, there is room for doubt of its having been made as a cup plate.

No. 434 is reserved for a new discovery.

THE EARLY TRANSITION PERIOD

The hearts shown here were made prior to the invention of, or at least without the benefit of the use of, the cap-ring. For plates carrying the heart motif in a subordinate degree and where the wide, early, experimental cap-ring was used, see Nos. 78, 79 and 80.

No. 435	Diam.	Rim	Origin	Colors	Rarity
	3	Plain	Uncertain, probably Midwestern	Clear	Rare

Distribution is for all practical purposes confined to the Midwest.

Note that if these are of the early period to which we have assigned them, they would be the earliest pressings west of the mountains. They do not appear to us to be that early. There is a very high incidence of frosted or "sick" specimens in the first two members of this series, and they have a strong relationship with the E Pluribus Unum eagle group. Now "sickness" in this proportion is characteristic of early Philadelphia pressing, as is the acorn motif so prominent in the 653–654 eagle series. Stylistically, the attribution would be to Philadelphia. All we can say is that neither these hearts nor the corresponding eagles turn up in that area.

No. 436	Diam.	Rim	Origin	Colors	Rarity
	3	Plain	Uncertain, as above	Clear	Very rare

This differs from the preceding plate in that a crude, two-pronged, fleur-de-lis device has been cut in the spandrels between the center hearts.

No. 436-A	Diam	Rim	Origin	Colors	Rarity
	3	Plain rope on top only	Uncertain, as above	Clear	Scarce

Like its corresponding member of the 653–654 eagle series, this is the most frequently found in this group; and again like the eagle, it is this type that is normally of good quality glass. It would seem that by the time this factory got around to cutting the rope-rim surface die, they had reduced the overload of soda in their mix and so solved the problem of "sickness."

No. 437 is reserved for a new discovery.

The following series is related to the Chancellors, the Franklins and to the two conventional series, Nos. 40 and 276. Not only are there common surface dies and cap-rings but there is also a moldmaker's habit of embellishing blank portions of the design, that appears and reappears. Then too a characteristic color, peacock-blue, shows up in most of these kindred series.

No. 438	Diam.	Rim	Origin	Colors	Rarity
	3⅜	38 even scallops	Probably Sandwich	Clear	Rare

The shoulder squares lack the stars that persist throughout the balance of the series. This "plain square" type should turn up with other serration patterns.

No. 439	Diam. 3⅜	Rim 38 even scallops	Origin Probably Sandwich	Colors Clear	Rarity Plentiful

Exactly like the preceding plate, except that stars have been added to the shoulder squares. This is the member of the series most frequently found.

No. 439-A	Diam. 3⅜	Rim 55 even scallops	Origin Probably Sandwich	Colors Clear	Rarity Rare?

The main variation is in the number of scallops. Note that there is but 1/16″ variation between this and the following plate. We do not doubt that both sizes exist, but we suspect that this is due, not to different dies, but to warping of plates or dies and that thus, by our definition, no true variant exists.

No. 439-B	Diam. 3 7/16	Rim 55 even scallops	Origin Probably Sandwich	Colors Clear	Rarity Rare?

Our doubts as to the comparative rarity of this and the preceding plate are due to the fact that if we are correct, and no valid variation exists, the supply of these plates would be doubled, and neither would be more than scarce.

No. 439-C	Diam. 3½	Rim 57 even scallops	Origin Probably Sandwich	Colors Clear Peacock-blue	Rarity Scarce Rare

At this writing, no other member of the series has been found in color. The chances are they will.

These Valentines are near the peak of laciness. There is, however, a considerable difference in quality. No. 440-B is usually the most brilliant. The Clays with the reversed "N" are related through common surface dies and cap-rings, although the analogy is not complete, since each series has a serration pattern not so far found in the other. Moreover this variety of Clay is not known in color.

No. 440	Diam.	Rim	Origin	Colors	Rarity
	3 7/16	53 even scallops	Probably Sandwich	Clear	Common
				Peacock-blue	Scarce
				Greenish	Scarce

No. 440-A	Diam.	Rim	Origin	Colors	Rarity
	3 9/16	56 even scallops	Probably Sandwich	Clear	Plentiful

In our experience, this is rarely found in good condition.

No. 440-B	Diam.	Rim	Origin	Colors	Rarity
	3½	24 large scallops with 2 smaller between	Probably Sandwich	Clear	Common
				Light blue	Rare
				Gray-blue	Rare
				Deep blue	Scarce
				Opal	Very rare
				Amethyst	Unique
				Pink tint	Uncertain

This type is usually more brilliant than the rest of the series and was the most popular. This may be a different design die.

No. 440-C	Diam.	Rim	Origin	Colors	Rarity
	3⅝	20 large scallops with small ones between	Probably Sandwich	Clear	Rare

We have never seen a proof specimen.

This series is allied to a number of Midwestern groups. See Nos. 124-A, 124-C, 125, 150, 150-B, etc.

No. 441	Diam.	Rim	Origin	Colors	Rarity
	3	30 bull's eyes	Midwest, probably Pittsburgh	Clear	Plentiful

Collectors should be on the lookout for variants with the U-juncture bull's eyes which, by analogy with similar series, should exist.

No. 441-A	Diam.	Rim	Origin	Colors	Rarity
	3	Plain, rope on bottom only	Midwest, probably Pittsburgh	Clear	Common

There are 3 rows of stippling just outside the band of diagonal ribbing on the shoulder.

No. 442	*Diam.*	*Rim*	*Origin*	*Colors*	*Rarity*
	3	Rope on top and bottom	Midwest, probably Pittsburgh	Clear	Scarce

The rarity appraisal includes the normal rough examples. Any collector who insists on proof condition will have difficulty locating anything approximating such condition. This has 4 rows of stippling on its shoulder.

No. 443	*Diam.*	*Rim*	*Origin*	*Colors*	*Rarity*
	3	Rope on top and bottom	Midwest, probably Pittsburgh	Clear	Very rare

This lacks the rows of dots that separate the hearts in the preceding members of the series. It is likely that this was the first version of the design die to be made; that it proved unsatisfactory and was changed almost at once to the dotted type.

No. 444	*Diam.*	*Rim*	*Origin*	*Colors*	*Rarity*
	2 15/16	Plain, rope on bottom only	Midwest, probably Pittsburgh	Clear	Common

The pattern is entirely changed. Not only are the center hearts placed much closer together, so that no rows of dots could be run between them, but the shoulder pattern consists of concentric rings, instead of the diagonal lines bordered by stippling, as in the preceding plates.

No. 444-A	*Diam.*	*Rim*	*Origin*	*Colors*	*Rarity*
	2 15/16	Plain, rope on bottom only	Midwest, probably Pittsburgh	Clear	Uncertain

This questionable variant has a shortened foot so that, from the top the foot looks like a dot in a depressed circle.

No. 445	*Diam.*	*Rim*	*Origin*	*Colors*	*Rarity*
	3 7/16	24 bull's eyes, points between	Midwest, probably Pittsburgh	Clear Cloudy	Very rare Very rare

By analogy with the large bull's-eye and point plates, it seems possible that a blue specimen may eventually be found. A smaller and later heart that, ·for reasons we cannot fathom, has often been considered a variant of this plate will be found in the next period. See No. 448.

No. 446	*Diam.*	*Rim*	*Origin*	*Colors*	*Rarity*
	3½	56 even scallops	Probably Sandwich	Clear	Extremely rare

The cap-ring and surface die seem to be the one used on No. 459-L.

No. 447	*Diam.*	*Rim*	*Origin*	*Colors*	*Rarity*
	3½	74 even scallops	Probably Sandwich	Clear	Plentiful
				Yellow?	Extremely rare
				Green?	Extremely rare
				Peacock-blue	Extremely rare

The colored specimens questioned here were determined from fragments dug up at Sandwich and should, we feel, be credited to the following plate where complete specimens exist. The attribution is based chiefly on the colors which are typical of Sandwich.

No. 447-A	*Diam.*	*Rim*	*Origin*	*Colors*	*Rarity*
	3⅝	73 even scallops	Probably Sandwich	Clear	Plentiful
				Yellow	Extremely rare
				Green	Extremely rare

This variety has one less serration and the diameter differs.

No. 447-B	*Diam.*	*Rim*	*Origin*	*Colors*	*Rarity*
	3 7/16	73 even scallops	Probably Sandwich	Clear	Plentiful

The only difference between this and the preceding plate is the diameter.

No. 448	*Diam.*	*Rim*	*Origin*	*Colors*	*Rarity*
	3 1/16	19 large scallops, two points between	Midwest	Clear	Scarce
				Lavender tint	Rare
				Lavender	Very rare

Note that the center dot is in a depressed circle. This plate is almost always found rough. There is a relation between this and No. 507.

No. 449	*Diam.*	*Rim*	*Origin*	*Color*	*Rarity*
	3 1/16	19 large scallops, two points between	Midwest	Clear	See note

This is a new discovery. It is much like No. 448 except that the points of the hearts come closer together. The center dot is not really a dot at all, but is a tiny circle. There is no depressed ring around this center dot. It is quite possible that some of the colors listed under the preceding plate occur actually in this variety. Rarity is hard to evaluate. Offhand, we think this is rarer than the cotype. Many may exist miscatalogued. The original find was made at Washington, Pa., some thirty miles south of Pittsburgh.

Nos. 450 through 454 are reserved for new discoveries.

THE 12- AND 13-HEART BORDER PLATES

When in our opening remarks on Hearts we said that they were predominantly of Eastern origin we had these in mind. Beyond any doubt these were the most popular cup plate patterns ever made. Pressing of the type seems to have started in the middle of the lacy period, perhaps about 1835, and continued for many years. Late types belonging properly in the late transition period are listed here for collectors' convenience. Unluckily during the several decades of the design's manufacture so many varieties were made that collectors, bewildered at their multiplicity, have tended to avoid them. We believe that no one, not even Mr. Marble or Mrs. Parker, has anything like a complete muster.

The result is that our coverage of the group is far from perfect. It is based on Mr. Marble's collection plus such other varieties as we have owned at one time or another. Unquestionably other variants, probably many of them, exist. But not only is our classification of this group incomplete, it is less than adequate in other respects. For example:

1. No one has examined the group carefully for slight differences in plunger design. Certain types have a square at the intersection of the center scrolls. Others do not. This is obviously an important variation but we have ignored it since no statistics exist at present. Another variation which we have not seen has recently

been called to our attention by Mr. Douglas Carapata. This consists in a reversal of the direction of the rope in the table-rings of some plates. The research necessary to bring order out of this chaos would cost several thousand dollars for photographs and in traveling expenses and would delay publication several years.

2. No one has any idea of the comparative rarity of the clear glass examples. Clearly some of them must be quite rare. Others are equally common. All colors, with the exception of opals, seem to be rare, some of them extremely so. Nor is it at all unlikely that some of the opalescent plates are rare too. So in most cases we have felt it wise to avoid dogmatic statements concerning rarity.

3. Since most cup plates are out-of-round, diameter statistics are not reliable. A plate measured along one axis may be 3 7/16; on the other axis 3½. Thus some of our listings may be duplications.

4. There are reproductions of these plates in both clear and colored glass. While it is true that some old plates do not ring, until the field is explored more thoroughly it is wise for the beginner to avoid any such specimens.

5. A superficial check on tooling shows that a number of cap-rings and surface dies used on these hearts are those found on other plates we believe to be Sandwich. Most of the known colors are also characteristic of that factory. On the other hand it is hard to believe that so popular and successful a design was not pirated by other glassworks. In two instances on the basis of distribution, coarse stippling and color we have guessed a Midwestern origin. Generally speaking, our attributions are at best no more than tentative.

With Twelve Hearts in the Shoulder Pattern

No. 455	*Diam.*	*Rim*	*Origin*	*Colors*	*Rarity*
	3⅞	48 even scallops	Probably Sandwich	Clear Opal	Scarce Rare

Note that there is a pair of faint discs between the shoulder hearts. These discs seem to have some technical significance, some connection with a problem in pressing or moldmaking, that no one, so far, has been able to explain to our satisfaction. We have found similar discs in a much fainter form on other, smaller hearts but, unfortunately, made no record of these. The serrations are stippled.

No. 455-A	*Diam.*	*Rim*	*Origin*	*Colors*	*Rarity*
	3¾	48 even scallops	Probably Sandwich	Clear	Uncertain

The only difference is in the diameter, and there is a chance that this is a mismeasurement of the previous plate.

No. 455-B	*Diam.*	*Rim*	*Origin*	*Colors*	*Rarity*
	3⅞	43 even scallops	Probably Sandwich	Clear Green	Scarce Very rare

As in the two preceding plates, this has the discs between the hearts. The serrations are *not* stippled and are fewer in number.

No. 455-C	*Diam.*	*Rim*	*Origin*	*Colors*	*Rarity*
	3 7/16	56 even scallops	Probably Sandwich	Clear Electric-blue	Scarce Very rare

This has the discs; serrations are *not* stippled and are greater in number. "Electric-blue" is a sort of peacock-blue, but much more brilliant and with much less green than one normally associates with a true peacock color.

No. 456	*Diam.*	*Rim*	*Origin*	*Colors*	*Rarity*
	3⅜	41 even scallops	Probably Sandwich	Clear	Scarce

The discs of the preceding series are replaced by stars. Serrations are plain. The illustration is of the large (**B**) type. No other is available; we use it here since our listing is in an ascending scale of diameters.

No. 456-A	*Diam.*	*Rim*	*Origin*	*Colors*	*Rarity*
	3⅝	41 even scallops	Probably Sandwich	Clear	Uncertain

With stars between the hearts and plain serrations. The only difference is the larger diameter. We have never seen this size and suspect the diameter to be a misprint for 3⅜. If it exists, it is very rare.

No. 456-B	Diam.	Rim	Origin	Colors	Rarity
	3 13/16	43 even scallops	Probably Sandwich	Clear	Rare

In our experience, this is much rarer than the 3⅜ size. It has stars between the hearts and has plain serrations.

No. 457	Diam.	Rim	Origin	Colors	Rarity
	3⅜	43 even scallops	Probably Sandwich	Clear	Plentiful

The center is stippled and so are the serrations.

No. 457-A	Diam.	Rim	Origin	Colors	Rarity
	3 7/16	57 even scallops	Probably Sandwich	Clear	Plentiful

The surface die and cap-ring, except for the stippling, seem to be the same as that used in making one variety of the Benjamin Franklin. As in the previous plate, the center and serrations are stippled.

No. 457-B	Diam.	Rim	Origin	Colors	Rarity
	3 7/16	59 even scallops	Probably Sandwich	Clear Emerald-green	Plentiful Extremely rare

Precisely like the preceding, except for 2 extra serrations. The size and serrations agree with those on two of the Franklins, as well as on such later plates as Nos. 333, 364 and 390.

No. 458	Diam.	Rim	Origin	Colors	Rarity
	3⅜	55 even scallops	Probably Sandwich	Clear	Scarce

There is stippling in the center and in two of the center scrolls as well. The serrations are plain.

No. 458-A	Diam.	Rim	Origin	Colors	Rarity
	3½	55 even scallops	Probably Sandwich	Clear	Scarce

Exactly like the preceding plate, except this is ⅛″ larger. This serration pattern and surface die seem to be the same as that on one variety of Benjamin Franklin.

No. 458-B	Diam.	Rim	Origin	Colors	Rarity
	3⅝	55 even scallops	Probably Sandwich	Clear	Scarce

No. 459	Diam.	Rim	Origin	Colors	Rarity
	3¼	81 even scallops	Probably Sandwich	Clear Opaque-white	Common Rare

Only the center is stippled. In this series, the largest of the 12-heart type, the serrations are always plain and the central scrolls too. The table-ring is shown in the cut as being a rope form. We have been unable to] te this type with a plain table-ring, but suspect it exists.

No. 459-A	Diam.	Rim	Origin	Colors	Rarity
	3 5/16	68 even scallops	Probably Sandwich	Clear Dark blue	Common Rare

The difference is in the size and number of serrations.

No. 459-B	Diam.	Rim	Origin	Colors	Rarity
	3 5/16	76 even scallops	Probably Sandwich	Clear Opal Dark blue	Common Plentiful Rare

The surface die and cap-ring agree with that used on several Bunker Hills.

No. 459-C	Diam.	Rim	Origin	Colors	Rarity
	3⅜	41 even scallops	Probably Sandwich	Clear Opal	Common Scarce

As throughout this series, the only variation is in the diameter and the number of the serrations. This is the plate used to illustrate the series.

No. 459-D	Diam.	Rim	Origin	Colors	Rarity
	3⅜	43 even scallops	Probably Sandwich	Clear Electric-blue Green Peacock-blue Opaque-white	Common Rare Rare Rare Rare

It is possible, in fact probable, that the electric-blue and peacock-blue are the same colors, but of varying thicknesses of glass.

No. 459-E	Diam.	Rim	Origin	Colors	Rarity
	3 7/16	43 even scallops	Probably Sandwich	Clear	Common

This may be mismeasured and so a duplicate of the preceding plate.

No. 459-F	*Diam.*	*Rim*	*Orgiin*	*Colors*	*Rarity*
	3 7/16	55 even	Probably	Clear	Common
		scallops	Sandwich	Clam broth	Rare

Size and serrations appear to agree with Nos. 276, 278 and 439-B.

No. 459-G	*Diam.*	*Rim*	*Origin*	*Colors*	*Rarity*
	3 7/16	56 even	Probably	Clear	Common
		scallops	Sandwich	Silver stain	Extremely
					rare

"Silver stain" is an amber that is "washed" on the finished plate and then fixed with heat. In this country, it is believed this technique was used only at Sandwich. See the Franklins for other examples.

No. 459-H	*Diam.*	*Rim*	*Origin*	*Colors*	*Rarity*
	3 7/16	76 even	Probably	Violet-blue	Very rare
		scallops	Sandwich		

We know of no clear specimen and, in fact, of but the one in color. Nevertheless, we hesitate to list it as unique. The tooling agrees with two Bunker Hills.

No. 459-I	*Diam.*	*Rim*	*Origin*	*Colors*	*Rarity*
	3½	38 even	Probably	Clear	Scarce
		scallops	Sandwich		

The serrations and size agree with Chancellor Livingstons.

No. 459-J	*Diam.*	*Rim*	*Origin*	*Colors*	*Rarity*
	3½	41 even	Probably	Clear	Common
		scallops	Sandwich	Opal	Plentiful

Tooling agrees with No. 273.

No. 459-K	*Diam.*	*Rim*	*Origin*	*Colors*	*Rarity*
	3½	53 even	Probably	Clear	Common
		scallops	Sandwich	Dark blue	Rare

Size and serration pattern seem to be that on Nos. 257-A, 265, 549 and 550.

No. 459-L	*Diam.*	*Rim*	*Origin*	*Colors*	*Rarity*
	3½	56 even	Probably	Clear	Common
		scallops	Sandwich	Dark blue	Rare

This corresponds with No. 446.

No. 459-M	*Diam.*	*Rim*	*Origin*	*Colors*	*Rarity*
	3¾	43 even scallops	Probably Sandwich	Clear Jade-opaque	Common Extremely rare

The jade is a lovely light green often streaked with a darker green. It is, so far as we know, the only use of this color in a cup plate.

No. 459-N	*Diam.*	*Rim*	*Origin*	*Colors*	*Rarity*
	3¾	81 even scallops	Probably Sandwich	Clear	Common

No. 459-O	*Diam.*	*Rim*	*Origin*	*Colors*	*Rarity*
	3 13/16	43 even scallops	Probably Sandwich	Clear Opal	Common Scarce

No. 459-P	*Diam.*	*Rim*	*Origin*	*Colors*	*Rarity*
	3 13/16	52 even scallops	Probably Sandwich	Clear	Common

No. 459-Q	*Diam.*	*Rim*	*Origin*	*Colors*	*Rarity*
	3 13/16	82 even scallops	Probably Sandwich	Opal	Rare

We know of no clear glass examples.

No. 460	*Diam.*	*Rim*	*Origin*	*Colors*	*Rarity*
	3⅜	38 even scallops	Probably Sandwich	Clear	Common

There is *no stippling* in the bottom of the plate, except in the center diamonds. This lack of stippling probably means that the type is later, perhaps as late as the last transition period.

No. 460-A	*Diam.*	*Rim*	*Origin*	*Colors*	*Rarity*
	3 7/16	43 even scallops	Probably Sandwich	Clear	Common

Like the preceding plate, except for a slightly larger diameter and an increase in the number of serrations.

No. 460-B	*Diam.*	*Rim*	*Origin*	*Colors*	*Rarity*
	3 13/16	81 even scallops	Probably Sandwich	Clear Milky	Common Scarce

This also differs in diameter and the number of serrations.

Nos. 461 through 464 are reserved for new discoveries

With Thirteen Hearts in the Shoulder Pattern

No. 465	Diam.	Rim	Origin	Colors	Rarity
	3¼	54 even scallops	Uncertain, see note	Clear	Uncertain

According to Mr. Marble's listings, this is a thick plate. Our own lists make no mention of unusual thickness. This could be an oversight. If all examples are thick, it is unlikely that the plate is of Sandwich manufacture, since at this date their pressings were uniformly rather thin and delicate. All plates in this particular series have stippling in the center and a rope table-ring. They differ only in diameter and the number of serrations. All except Q, R, and S have plain (not stippled) serrations.

No. 465-A	Diam.	Rim	Origin	Colors	Rarity
	3¼	63 even scallops	Probably Sandwich	Clear	Common

No. 465-B	Diam.	Rim	Origin	Colors	Rarity
	3 5/16	54 even scallops	Possibly Midwestern	Clear	Uncertain
				Lavender	Extremely rare
				Olive-yellow	Unique

See the first of this series, the "thick" plate, and note that there is a variation of but 1/16″. We feel this is the same plate. The half-dozen lavender specimens which are all we can locate were found in Ohio in 1932 by Mr. Earl J. Knittle. The olive-yellow example, now in Mrs. Parker's collection, was found in Ohio in 1940 by Mr. Howard Mauch. Considering the fact that these plates seem somewhat crude, that the color range is by no means characteristic of Sandwich (or Eastern) practice, that so far as we know distribution is Western, we feel the attribution may be correct.

No. 465-C	Diam.	Rim	Origin	Colors	Rarity
	3 5/16	56 even scallops	Probably Sandwich	Clear	Common

The tooling appears that of No. 229-A.

No. 465-D	*Diam.*	*Rim*	*Origin*	*Colors*	*Rarity*
	3 5/16	67 even scallops	Probably Sandwich	Clear Dark blue	Common Rare

Seemingly related to No. 334-A, a relatively late plate.

No. 465-E	*Diam.*	*Rim*	*Origin*	*Colors*	*Rarity*
	3⅜	53 even scallops	Probably Sandwich	Clear Opal	Common Scarce

The tooling seems the same found in No. 332-D.

No. 465-F	*Diam.*	*Rim*	*Origin*	*Colors*	*Rarity*
	3⅜	63 even scallops	Probably Sandwich	Clear Opal Blue Violet-blue	Common Scarce Very rare Rare

We have not checked the "blue" example. It may be a duplicate of the "violet-blue." If it exists, it is probably very rare. The tooling agrees with No. 269-B.

No. 465-G	*Diam.*	*Rim*	*Origin*	*Colors*	*Rarity*
	3 7/16	53 even scallops	Probably Sandwich	Clear Opal	Uncertain Uncertain

We suspect this is the 3⅜″ variety mismeasured. The tooling is that of several Valentines.

No. 465-H	*Diam.*	*Rim*	*Origin*	*Colors*	*Rarity*
	3 7/16	59 even scallops	Uncertain	Clear	Uncertain

This plate is a puzzle. Such specimens as have been brought to our attention were found in the Midwest and have coarse stippling typical of that area. On the other hand, the diameter and cap-ring seem the same as on Nos. 333, 364, 465-H, 617 and 619-A.

No. 465-I	*Diam.*	*Rim*	*Origin*	*Colors*	*Rarity*
	3 7/16	61 even scallops	Probably Sandwich	Clear	Common

No. 465-J	Diam.	Rim	Origin	Colors	Rarity
	3½	48 even	Probably	Clear	Common
		scallops	Sandwich	Opal	Scarce
				Opal-	
				opaque	Rare
				Violet-blue	Rare

The serrations and size are the same as Nos. 258-A, 532, 591 and 619.

No. 465-K	Diam.	Rim	Origin	Colors	Rarity
	3½	52 even	Probably	Clear	Common
		scallops	Sandwich	Blue	Rare

No. 465-L	Diam.	Rim	Origin	Colors	Rarity
	3½	53 even	Probably	Clear	Common
		scallops	Sandwich	Opal	Scarce
				Violet-blue	Rare

The surface die and cap-ring are the same as those used on Nos. 267, 269, and 566.

No. 465-M	Diam.	Rim	Origin	Colors	Rarity
	3½	61 even	Probably	Clear	Common
		scallops	Sandwich		

This may be a duplication of the "I" member of the series.

No. 465-N	Diam.	Rim	Origin	Colors	Rarity
	3½	63 even	Probably	Clear	Common
		scallops	Sandwich	Opal	Scarce

The tooling appears to be the same as we find on Nos. 265-A, 268 and 332-A.

No. 465-O	Diam.	Rim	Origin	Colors	Rarity
	3 9/16	48 even	Probably	Clear	Uncertain
		scallops	Sandwich	Opal	Uncertain

This may be a duplication of the "J" type in this series. If not, and the size is correct, the surface die and cap-ring are that used on the Ft. Meigs cabin.

No. 465-P	Diam.	Rim	Origin	Colors	Rarity
	3 13/16	81 even	Probably	Clear	Scarce
		scallops	Sandwich		

No. 465-Q	Diam.	Rim	Origin	Colors	Rarity
	3 7/16	52 even	Probably	Clear	Scarce
		scallops	Sandwich		

The *serrations are stippled,* as well as the center of the plate, in this series.

No. 465-R	*Diam.*	*Rim*	*Origin*	*Colors*	*Rarity*
	3 7/16	53 even scallops	Probably Sandwich	Clear	Scarce

This has one more stippled serration than the preceding plate.

No. 465-S	*Diam.*	*Rim*	*Origin*	*Colors*	*Rarity*
	3½	61 even scallops	Probably Sandwich	Clear	Scarce

The serrations are stippled.

No. 466 is reserved for a new discovery.

No. 467	*Diam.*	*Rim*	*Origin*	*Colors*	*Rarity*
	3½	102 even scallops	Probably Sandwich	Clear	Common

In this series the center of the plate is not stippled, and outside of one member, No. 468, the table-ring is plain. The chances are these plain center hearts are a later development of the design and that they belong in the late transition period.

No. 467-A	*Diam.*	*Rim*	*Origin*	*Colors*	*Rarity*
	3⅝	48 even scallops	Probably Sandwich	Clear Yellow Violet-blue	Common Very rare Rare

This is the plate shown in the cut at the beginning of the series, on Plate 81. It differs from the previous plate only in size and number of serrations.

No. 467-B	*Diam.*	*Rim*	*Origin*	*Colors*	*Rarity*
	3 11/16	48 even scallops	Probably Sandwich	Clear Amethyst	Common Very rare

The only difference between this and the preceding plate is in size. This is 1/16″ larger. It may be a duplication.

No. 468	*Diam.*	*Rim*	*Origin*	*Colors*	*Rarity*
	3 7/16	59 even scallops	Probably Sandwich	Clear	Common

Here the design changes. *The table-ring is a rope.* The center is still plain. Serration and diameter variants should be found.

Nos. 469 through 474 are reserved for new discoveries.

No. 475	Diam.	Rim	Origin	Colors	Rarity
	3 5/16	10-sided	Uncertain	Clear	See note
				Blue tint	

The serration pattern appears the same as that found on No. 321. Both may be Sandwich. The evidence is not sufficient to justify a direct attribution. Proof specimens are almost impossible to find.

For a somewhat similar 13-heart plate with twelve plain sides see No. 476 in the transition period.

HEARTS (THE LATE TRANSITION PERIOD)

No. 476	Diam.	Rim	Origin	Colors	Rarity
	3 5/16	12 plain sides	Uncertain, possibly Sandwich	Clear	Common

This plate superficially resembles No. 475 with which we closed the preceding period, but this has twelve sides against the other's ten and is, we feel, later.

No. 477	Diam.	Rim	Origin	Colors	Rarity
	3 5/16	66 even scallops	Probably Sandwich	Clear	Common
				Opal	Very rare

The stippling of the earlier lacy period is retained, but a glance at the plate will demonstrate its comparative lateness.

No. 478	Diam.	Rim	Origin	Colors	Rarity
	3 5/16	66 even scallops	Probably Sandwich	Clear	Common

The shoulder is covered with the irregular stippling characteristic of late practice.

No. 479	Diam.	Rim	Origin	Colors	Rarity
	See note	66 even scallops	Probably Sandwich	Clear	Common

Mr. Marble gives the diameter as 3¼″. Those we have measured are between this and the 3 5/16″ of the other members of the series. We feel the surface die and cap-ring were the same in all cases; if this is true, diameters should coincide. We are not prepared to say which measurement is the more accurate. Size varies slightly from plate to plate.

No. 480	*Diam.*	*Rim*	*Origin*	*Colors*	*Rarity*
	3⅜	Plain	Unknown	Clear	Common

Nos. 481 through 489 are reserved for new discoveries.

Chapter XV

THE SUNBURST GROUP

Nos. 490 through 550

A designer, faced with the problem of filling a circular space with a pattern, automatically chooses some device in which lines radiate from the center. Accordingly, a high percentage of cup plate patterns are, broadly speaking, sunbursts. Commonly, the term "sunburst" is applied only to the comparatively small group of plates we show here.

For various reasons, little is known concerning the origin, the comparative rarity or the dates of manufacture of the type. Most collectors without regard for the evidence have tended to consider these plates late, common and, hence, uninteresting. Actually, though none of them is stippled, there can be no doubt that some of them were pressed within the lacy period, around, say, 1835–1837. The use of lacy period caprings in their pressing and the very extensive color range in which they occur establishes this. Color, you will notice, is seldom encountered in the late transition period or afterward.

This is not to say that all sunbursts are early. Some of them probably post-date 1850, but most of them seem to have been made before. The truth appears to be that the earlier of these plates were made to satisfy a demand for a cup plate less expensive than the elaborate lacy patterns then in vogue. Sunburst dies required little, if any, hand finishing and, tnus, were much cheaper to make than the more complicated patterns. The sunburst, then, was the Ford of the style. Without a comprehensive group of these plates, a collector can no more understand the true breadth of the field than a mechanical engineer could understand the automotive age, if his study were based solely on the Rolls Royce.

For convenience in locating a particular plate, the group is arranged not in any chronological sequence but in accordance with the number of rays or, if you prefer, points in the sunburst.

490

498

491

Nos.
92–493
ft open

499

494

500

495

501

Nos.
96–497
ft open

502
described
in text

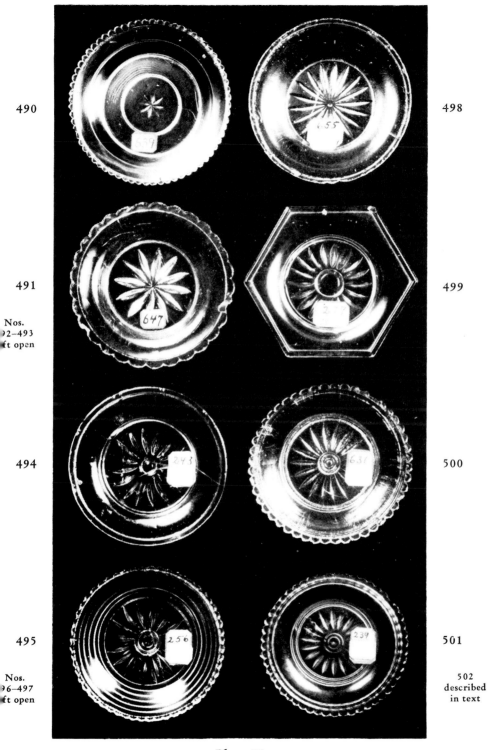

Plate 82

503

504

505

506

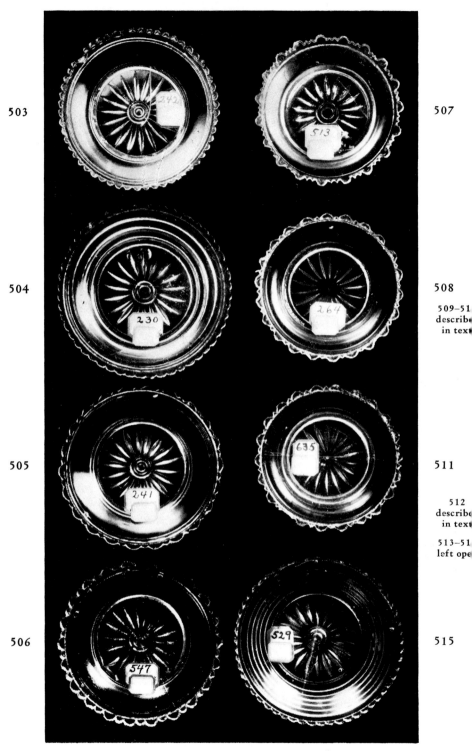

507

508

509–51
describe
in text

511

512
describe
in text

513–51
left ope

515

Plate 83

516

518

517

519

517-A

520

520-A
and
521
described
in text

517-B

522

523
and
523-A
described
in text

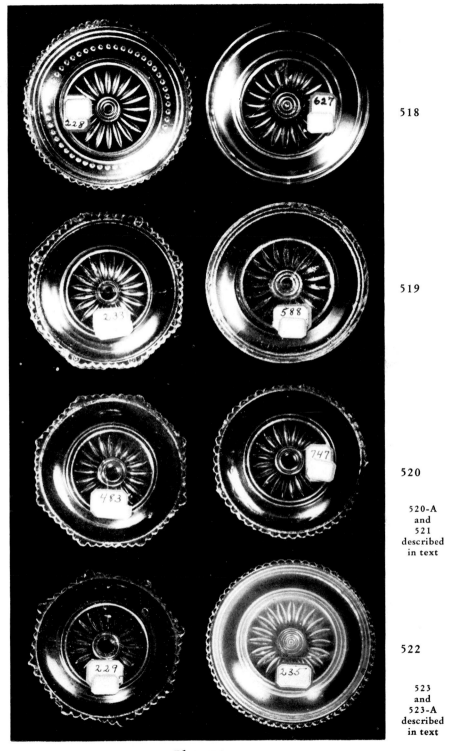

Plate 84

524

525

526

526-A
described
in text

Nos. 527
through
529
left open

530

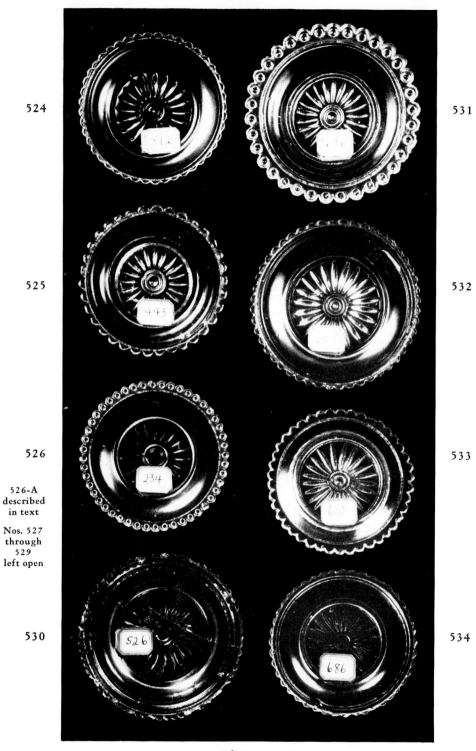

531

532

533

534

Plate 85

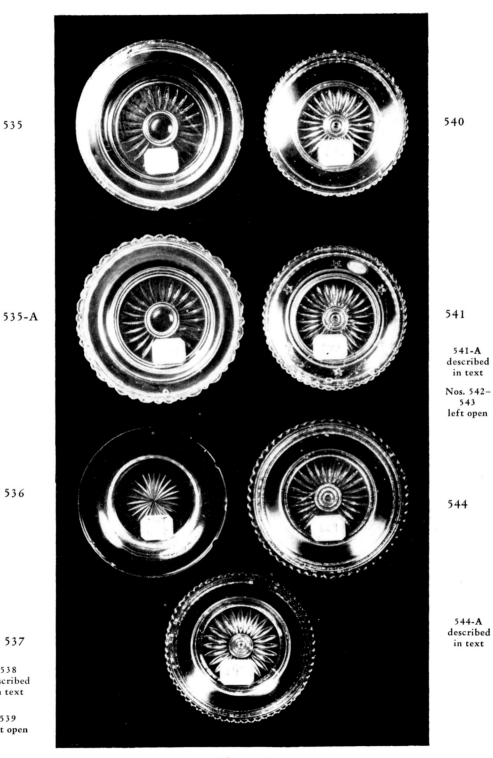

535

535-A

536

537

538
scribed
n text

539
ft open

540

541

541-A
described
in text

Nos. 542–
543
left open

544

544-A
described
in text

Plate 86

545

548

546

549

547

550

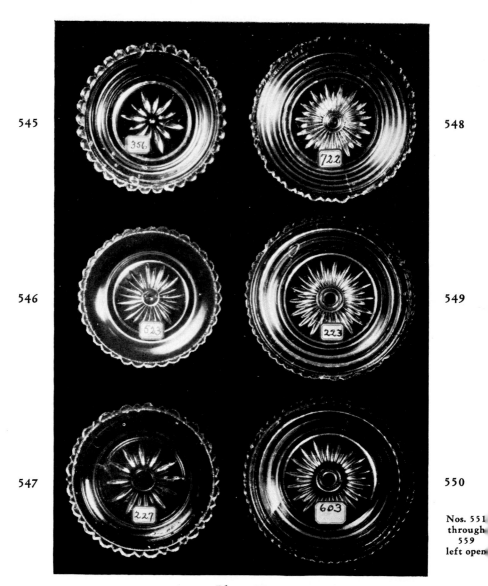

Nos. 551
through
559
left open

Plate 87

With Eight Rays in the Central Sunburst

No. 490	*Diam.*	*Rim*	*Origin*	*Colors*	*Rarity*
	3 5/16	68 even scallops	Unknown	Clear	Extremely rare

This is a much earlier plate than the illustration indicates. For a plate of this character, it is quite thick. We have located but two specimens.

With Twelve Rays in the Central Sunburst

No. 491	*Diam.*	*Rim*	*Origin*	*Colors*	*Rarity*
	3⅜	29 even scallops	Midwestern	Clear Pink tint	Common Scarce

All we have seen are of a very inferior glass that does not ring. The attribution is based on distribution and the plate is related to No. 381, which also has a Western distribution. The chances are that we have underestimated rarity. Dealers and collectors east of the mountains seldom see this plate, so if it were more attractive and in demand it would be quite difficult to acquire. It is a late plate.

Nos. 492 and 493 are reserved for new discoveries.

With Sixteen Rays in the Central Sunburst

No. 494	*Diam.*	*Rim*	*Origin*	*Colors*	*Rarity*
	3¼	Plain	Uncertain, probably Eastern	Clear	Common

The rim is not, as it would appear from the illustration, like that on such plates as No. 388, but is a convex mold. This is a late plate, made after the close of the lacy period.

No. 495	*Diam.*	*Rim*	*Origin*	*Colors*	*Rarity*
	3 3/16	55 even scallops	Unknown	Clear	Common

The center target is composed of 3 rings and a dot and there are 4 rings on the shoulder. Figures on distribution are lacking, but we have a vague suspicion the origin is New England and possibly Sandwich.

Nos. 496 and 497 are reserved for new discoveries.

No. 498	Diam.	Rim	Origin	Colors	Rarity
	3¼	Plain	Unknown	Clear	Extremely rare

It should be noted that all the plain rim sunbursts, with the single exception of the one with 16 rays, are extremely rare. At least they are when judged by collector's want lists.

No. 499	Diam.	Rim	Origin	Colors	Rarity
	3 1/16 across	Plain, hexagonal	Eastern	Clear	Common

The rim is a convex mold, as on No. 494. Remarks on the great rarity of plain rim sunbursts do not, of course, apply to this six-sided, late plate. Related to No. 403.

No. 500	Diam.	Rim	Origin	Colors	Rarity
	3¼	48 even scallops	Unknown	Clear	Extremely rare
				Blue	Unique

The rarity statement is based entirely on collector's want lists and may be exaggerated. The blue specimen is in Dr. Doane's collection. Note that the center target is composed of 3 circles and that the shoulder has 2 rings near the rim and another just outside the table-ring.

No. 501	Diam.	Rim	Origin	Colors	Rarity
	2 15/16	51 even scallops	Uncertain, but not New England	Clear	Common
				Blue	Rare
				Amethyst	Very rare
				Deep green	Extremely rare
				Olive-green	Scarce
				Light green	Unique
				Greenish-yellow	Rare
				Amber	Rare

This plate has a target of 2 circles around a dot and in that respect is like the following one. It has but 1 circle on the shoulder near the rim and another near the table-ring, and in this respect differs from the following, which has these shoulder rings doubled. We are not too sure there is no duplication in the colors assigned to these very similar plates. Distribution is Pennsylvania and Ohio, with the density, it seems to us, increasing near Philadelphia. The quality of the glass here, as in the following plate, is poor and has no ring in such specimens as we have observed. The light green specimen is in Mrs. Parker's collection.

No. 502	*Diam.*	*Rim*	*Origin*	*Colors*	*Rarity*
	3	51 even scallops	Uncertain, see preceding plate	Clear	Common
				Light green	Scarce
				Green	Scarce
				Olive-yellow	Scarce
				Blue	Unique
				Amethyst	Unique

This is exactly like the preceding plate, except that there are two rings near the rim on the shoulder and another pair near the table-ring. As in the previous plate, the glass is of very bad quality. Note that there is 1/16″ difference in diameter. The measurements are Mr. Marble's and we do not doubt their accuracy, but we suspect the same cap-ring and surface die were used on both plates and that the increase in diameter is due to cleaning these parts of the mold. We also feel that some of the colors credited to this plate may be due to misnumbering of the preceding plate, and vice versa.

No. 503	*Diam.*	*Rim*	*Origin*	*Colors*	*Rarity*
	3¼	56 even scallops	Eastern, probably Sandwich	Clear	Common
				Opal	Common

The tentative attribution is based on distribution. The fact that we cannot tie this tooling, this rim, to other plates of better authenticated Sandwich origin means little, since the factory was so busy turning out this common plate that the surface die and cap-ring were not available for use with other plunger dies.

No. 504	*Diam.*	*Rim*	*Origin*	*Colors*	*Rarity*
	3 9/16	53 even scallops	Probably Sandwich	Clear	Scarce

Note the concentric circles on the shoulder. Here our attribution is on somewhat firmer ground, since the cap-ring and surface die seem the same as those we find on a Bunker Mill Monument and on conventionals, such as Nos. 269-A and 269-D, which are pretty certainly Sandwich. If the attribution is correct, opal and possibly other colored specimens should turn up.

No. 505	*Diam.*	*Rim*	*Origin*	*Colors*	*Rarity*
	3 5/16	22 large and 22 small scallops	Uncertain but Eastern	Clear	Scarce

These shallow alternating large and small scallops resemble those on such Eastern plates as the Liberty Cap cabin and the Wedding Day, but are the product of a different mold. Nevertheless, the serration scheme is characteristic of Eastern practice.

No. 506	*Diam.*	*Rim*	*Origin*	*Colors*	*Rarity*
	3⅜	22 large, 22 small	Unknown	Clear	Rare

The serrations are much more deeply indented and this is typical of Midwestern practice, so the plate may be a Western pirating of the preceding Eastern plate.

No. 507	*Diam.*	*Rim*	*Origin*	*Colors*	*Rarity*
	3	19 scallops with 2 points between	Probably Midwestern	Clear	Common

The serration pattern appears the same as that on the little Western heart, No. 448. The rim is so typical of Midwestern practice that we feel no doubt as to the origin, although we lack figures on distribution.

No. 508	*Diam.*	*Rim*	*Origin*	*Colors*	*Rarity*
	3	22 scallops, points between	Probably Eastern, possibly Sandwich	Clear	Common
				Blue	Plentiful
				Peacock-blue	Rare
				Amethyst	Scarce

This has no dot in the center. The rays of the sunburst are narrow and attenuated.

No. 509	*Diam.*	*Rim*	*Origin*	*Colors*	*Rarity*
	3	As on the previous plate	As above	Clear	Common
				Blue	Scarce

This has the narrow rays of the previous plate but has a tiny dot, no larger than stippling, in its center.

No. 510	*Diam.*	*Rim*	*Origin*	*Colors*	*Rarity*
	3	As on the previous plate	As above	Blue	Rare

With the thin rays of the two previous plates, but with a larger and heavier central dot as in *coarse* stippling. These two or even these three plates may be nothing more than good or bad pressing from the same plunger. In this particular variety we have seen only blue examples.

No. 511	*Diam.*	*Rim*	*Origin*	*Colors*	*Rarity*
	3	As on the previous plates	As above	Clear	Common
				Blue	Plentiful
				Peacock-blue	Rare
				Green	Very rare
				Peacock-green	Very rare
				Amethyst	Rare
				Lavender	Scarce

The rays on this plate are thicker and heavier than on the three just listed, and the central dot is larger, about 1/16″ in diameter. The color range is, as you see, much the same as in No. 508, but these plates are extraordinarily difficult to catalogue correctly. Part of the similarity may be due to misnumbering. The guess at a Sandwich origin throughout these plates is based mostly on characteristic colors.

No. 512	*Diam.*	*Rim*	*Origin*	*Colors*	*Rarity*
	3	As on the previous plates	As above	Clear	Unique

Exactly like the plate immediately preceding, but here the central dot is of truly gigantic size, measuring about 3/16″ in diameter. There is a possibility that this is not a dot produced by the die but is simply a blob of glass that in some accidental fashion stuck to the exact center of the plate. We have seen but the one example and that was clear glass.

Nos. 513 and 514 are reserved for new discoveries.

With Nineteen Rays in the Central Sunburst

No. 515	Diam.	Rim	Origin	Colors	Rarity
	3 7/16	56 even scallops	Possibly Sandwich	Clear	Scarce

This is the only sunburst with 19 rays that has come to our attention. The tooling is not the same as we find on the 18-ray, 56-scallop sunburst which is 3/16″ smaller. Distribution seems limited to New England; we feel this is also possibly a Sandwich pressing and that there is an excellent chance of its turning up in opal.

With Twenty Rays in the Central Sunburst

No. 516	Diam.	Rim	Origin	Colors	Rarity
	3¼	66 even scallops	Probably Sandwich	Clear Amethyst	Common Unique

The serration pattern appears to be the same as that found on the No. 594 cabin and on the butterfly, which are definitely of New England and probably Sandwich origin. An element of doubt is thrown on this attribution by the colors in which these plates occur. The cabin turns up in amber and, very rarely, in opal. The butterfly is unknown in color. We have an amethyst specimen reported from Mrs. Parker's collection.

No. 517	Diam.	Rim	Origin	Colors	Rarity
	3 across	Octagonal	Probably Midwestern	Clear Ice-blue	Common Very rare

This plate has 7 scallops on each side between the corner scallops and has an egg in each corner. It thus agrees with the conventional, No. 193. If the analogy is correct, light green examples may eventually be found. Really proof examples are scarce.

No. 517-A	Diam.	Rim	Origin	Colors	Rarity
	3 across	Octagonal	Probably Midwestern	Clear	Common

This has 6 scallops on each side between the corner scallops which here lack the egg and are larger so that they project a bit beyond a true octagonal contour. The plate is related to the eagle, No. 680-D, and to the conventional No. 192, neither of which has been found in color.

No. 517-B	Diam.	Rim	Origin	Colors	Rarity
	2 15/16 across	Octagonal	Probably Midwestern	Clear Lavender	Common Rare

This has 5 scallops on each side between corner scallops of larger size and greater extent, hence, is related to the No. 680-E eagle and to No. 192-A conventional. The eagle relationship may mean that blue examples will be found.

No. 518	Diam.	Rim	Origin	Colors	Rarity
	3⅛	Plain	Unknown	Clear	Extremely rare
				Amethyst	Unique

This plate is difficult to distinguish from the following one. In this, the center target is made up of 3 circles around a dot. The shoulder has 1 ring near the rim and 2 rings just outside the table-ring. The amethyst specimen is in Mr. Cannon's collection.

No. 519	Diam.	Rim	Origin	Colors	Rarity
	3⅛	Plain	Unknown	Clear	Extremely rare

Here the target is composed of 3 circles but lacks the central dot of the preceding plate. The shoulder rings are reversed from the previous plate with 1 at the table-ring and 2 near the rim.

No. 520	Diam.	Rim	Origin	Colors	Rarity
	3	50 even scallops	Unknown	Clear	Scarce

The rarity statement is probably an underestimate. The target is made up of 2 circles with no center dot. The shoulder is plain.

No. 520-A	Diam.	Rim	Origin	Colors	Rarity
	3	44 even scallops	Unknown	Clear	Common
				Blue	Scarce

This is much like the preceding plate and the serrations are the chief difference. Two shades of blue are encountered in this plate, one of them much like the rather dull shade typical of some Midwestern factory, but we are unable to properly name these colors or to distinguish between them in rarity.

No. 521	Diam.	Rim	Origin	Colors	Rarity
	3	52 even scallops	Unknown	Clear	Common
				Light green	Unique

The target is composed of 2 rings around a very tiny dot. There is a ring on the shoulder just inside the line of serrations. The light green example has just been found and is in very bad condition.

No. 522	Diam.	Rim	Origin	Colors	Rarity
	3 5/16	66 even scallops	Probably Sandwich	Clear	Common
				Light amethyst	Scarce
				Amethyst	Rare
				Opal	Common
				Opaque-white	Rare
				Red-amber	Rare
				Deep red-amber	Very rare

The target is composed of 3 circles surrounding a dot. The shoulder has 2 circles near the rim and 2 more just outside the table-ring. Although this seems to be a variation of 1/16″ in diameter we believe this plate, like the 20-ray sunburst with dotted shoulder, is related to the No. 594 cabin and the butterfly.

No. 523	Diam.	Rim.	Origin	Colors	Rarity
	3 1/16	61 even scallops	Uncertain	Clear	Common
				Light amethyst	Scarce
				Amethyst	Rare
				Medium blue	Rare
				Blue	Scarce
				Olive-green	Scarce
				Yellow-green	Rare

The target differs from that in the previous plate in having only 2 circles around the central dot. The shoulder circles are the same, 2 near the rim, 2 near the table-ring. The easiest identification is by size and serration count. If the olive-green and yellow-green, neither by any means typical of Sandwich, did not exist, we would attribute the plate to Jarves' factory. Related to No. 590.

No. 523-A	*Diam.*	*Rim*	*Origin*	*Colors*	*Rarity*
	3	62 even scallops	Uncertain	Olive-green	Very rare

This variant was discovered in 1946 by Richard H. Wood. It is 1/16″ smaller than the preceding plate and has 1 more serration. No clear specimens have been brought to our attention, but it seems likely they exist. It is also probable that the rarity is not so great as it seems. Note: As this goes to press a clear specimen is reported by Mr. Carapata.

No. 524	*Diam.*	*Rim*	*Origin*	*Colors*	*Rarity*
	3 1/16	44 even scallops	Midwestern, probably Pittsburgh	Clear Blue Amethyst	Scarce Rare Unique

The target is made up of 2 circles around a central dot. There are 2 faint rings on the shoulder near the rim. The attribution is based entirely on distribution, every specimen known to us having turned up in the Pittsburgh area. The amethyst example is in Mrs. Parker's collection.

No. 525	*Diam.*	*Rim*	*Origin*	*Colors*	*Rarity*
	3⅛	34 even scallops	Unknown	Clear	Scarce

The target is composed of 2 rings around the central dot. The shoulder pattern is evenly spaced concentric rings. The serrations match those on No. 545 and seem vaguely Midwestern, but the evidence is not sufficient to warrant an attribution.

No. 526	*Diam.*	*Rim*	*Origin*	*Colors*	*Rarity*
	3⅛	48 bull's-eye scallops	Midwestern	Clear	Plentiful

The target is made up of 2 rings with no central dot. The shoulder is plain. The cap-ring and surface die are those used on eagle, No. 680-B, and on No. 191-A. The rarity appraisal applies to the average battered specimen. Proof examples are extremely difficult to find.

No. 526-A	*Diam.*	*Rim*	*Origin*	*Colors*	*Rarity*
	3 3/16	45 bull's-eye scallops	Midwestern	Clear	Plentiful

This appears to be the same plate with a different number of bull's eyes and, of course, a different diameter. As above, proof specimens are hard to find. The rim agrees with the eagle, No. 680-C, and with No. 191.

Nos. 527 through 529 are reserved for new discoveries.

With Twenty-One Rays in the Central Sunburst

No. 530	Diam.	Rim	Origin	Colors	Rarity
	3½	65 even scallops	Uncertain	Clear	Common
				Light blue	Rare
				Dark blue	Scarce
				Light green	Rare
				Olive-green	Rare
				Light amethyst	Rare
				Olive-yellow	Rare

The target is 3 circles around a small central dot. There are 2 rings just inside the serration ring and another just outside the table-ring. The serrations agree with those on the so-called Sandwich Star, No. 326, and on No. 327, both of which are most likely Sandwich, but the olive-green examples cast a doubt on such an attribution.

With Twenty-Two Rays in the Central Sunburst

No. 531	Diam.	Rim	Origin	Colors	Rarity
	3⅝	34 bull's-eye scallops	Midwestern	Clear	Plentiful
				Light green	Scarce
				Yellow-green	Rare
				Lavender	Very rare

The target is composed of 2 rings and a dot. The shoulder has a ring just inside the serration ring, giving the effect of 2 rings, and the table-ring is a double ring with a faint ring *inside* it. This mold is not the same as that used in making the 34-bull's-eye plates like Nos. 172 and 176. It is slightly larger and the scallops are not so deeply indented.

No. 532	Diam.	Rim	Origin	Colors	Rarity
	3½	48 even scallops	Eastern, probably Sandwich	Clear	Common

The target is 3 rings and a dot. There are 2 rings just inside the serration line and another just outside the table-ring, which is a curious ledge with a depressed ring inside it. The serrations agree with those found on the rare cabin, No. 591, which is undoubtedly of New England and probably Sandwich origin. This would date this sunburst as about 1840.

No. 533	Diam.	Rim	Origin	Colors	Rarity
	3	42 even scallops	Probably Midwestern	Clear	Scarce

The deeply indented serrations have a Midwestern look about them and seem to agree with those found in No. 281-B. The attribution is made on this evidence. We have no data on distribution. The target is 2 circles around a dot. Working from a photograph we cannot be sure of the arrangement of the shoulder circles.

No. 534	Diam.	Rim	Origin	Colors	Rarity
	3 1/16	44 even scallops	Probably Midwestern	Clear Amethyst	Rare Unique

The target is 2 circles around a small dot. Judging from the photograph, there are 2 rings on the shoulder just inside the serration ring and no rings near the table-ring. The 22 rays, coupled with the size and the 44 serrations, should be sufficient to determine the number. These serrations seem to be the same as those encountered on No. 524, and the attribution is made on that basis. This is apparently a much rarer plate and we know nothing about its distribution.

With Twenty-Four Rays in the Central Sunburst

No. 535	Diam.	Rim	Origin	Colors	Rarity
	3 11/16	Plain	Probably Curling's Ft. Pitt Works	Clear Green	Extremely rare Unique

The target is a large bull's eye or porthole, surrounded by 2 rings. There are 2 rings, we think, near the rim (there may be more) and one each inside and outside the table-ring. For a discussion of origin, see the following plate.

No. 535-A	*Diam.*	*Rim*	*Origin*	*Colors*	*Rarity*
	3 11/16	20 large scallops with small ones between	Probably Curling's Ft. Pitt Works	Clear	Plentiful

The serrations coincide with those on the Fort Pitt eagle, No. 676-B, and with others of Curling's pressings, Nos. 214-B and 217-A. The shape is the same also, with the characteristic very flat shoulder. The plain rim of the preceding plate also has its analogies with Fort Pitt eagles and conventionals. This may mean that in these two plates we have just about the earliest of the true sunbursts. It may also mean that blue and amethyst examples will turn up and, possibly, a variant with even serrations.

No. 536	*Diam.*	*Rim*	*Origin*	*Colors*	*Rarity*
	3¼	Plain	Unknown	Clear	Extremely rare

This seems to us to be a very late plate. It is cut glass. There is no denying its great rarity, though. We know of but one other specimen besides Mr. Marble's.

No. 537	*Diam.*	*Rim*	*Origin*	*Colors*	*Rarity*
	3¼	66 even scallops	Probably Sandwich	Clear Opal	Common Common

The target has 3 rings around a dot. There are 2 rings near the rim and 2 near the table-ring on the shoulder. The serrations agree with such probable Sandwich products as Nos. 323, 324 and 594, and the attribution is based on this as well as on distribution.

No. 538	*Diam.*	*Rim*	*Origin*	*Colors*	*Rarity*
	3¼	66 even scallops	Probably Sandwich	Clear	Common

Precisely like the preceding, except that here the target is 2 rings around a dot instead of 3. Opal examples should turn up.

No. 539 is reserved for a new discovery.

With Twenty-Six Rays in the Central Sunburst

No. 540	*Diam.*	*Rim*	*Origin*	*Colors*	*Rarity*
	3⅛	60 even scallops	Probably Midwestern	Clear	Scarce

The surface die and cap-ring appear to be the same as those found on such Midwestern eagles as Nos. 673, 674 and 675, and this analogy is reinforced by the 6-star variant listed below.

No. 541	*Diam.*	*Rim*	*Origin*	*Colors*	*Rarity*
	3⅛	60 even scallops	Probably Midwestern	Clear	Very rare

This is related to the same Midwestern eagles as the preceding plate. We are at a loss to account for its rarity, since the eagles with 6 stars on their shoulders are by no means rare.

No. 541-A	*Diam.*	*Rim*	*Origin*	*Colors*	*Rarity*
	3½	54 even scallops	Probably Midwestern	Clear	Extremely rare

We are unable to locate any exactly similar serration patterns on other plates; but, since this seems to be pressed with the same design die as the preceding plate with the 6 stars on the shoulder, the only change being the serrations and, of course, the diameter, the natural conclusion is that it is from the same unknown Midwestern glasshouse. We can locate only two specimens, Dr. Doane's and Mr. Marble's.

Nos. 542 and 543 are reserved for new discoveries.

With Twenty-Seven Rays in the Central Sunburst

No. 544	*Diam.*	*Rim*	*Origin*	*Colors*	*Rarity*
	3 7/16	54 even scallops	Unknown	Clear Blue	Common Rare

The serrations are shallow, unlike those in the following plate. Note this carefully, since it is the easiest way to distinguish between them. The 1/16″ difference in diameter may vary some from plate to plate and is not a reliable guide.

No. 544-A	*Diam.*	*Rim*	*Origin*	*Colors*	*Rarity*
	3⅜	54 even scallops	Unknown	Clear	Rare

These serrations are more deeply indented than those on the preceding plate. Both types of serrations have Eastern and Western counterparts and, lacking figures on distribution, we have no idea where these sunbursts were made.

Sunbursts with Alternating Long and Short Rays

No. 545	*Diam.*	*Rim*	*Origin*	*Colors*	*Rarity*
	3⅛	34 even scallops	Unknown	Clear	Common

The sunburst is made up of 6 long and 6 short rays which lack any central target and center in a simple dot. The serrations match those on No. 525 and appear to follow Midwestern practice.

No. 546	*Diam.*	*Rim*	*Origin*	*Colors*	*Rarity*
	3	36 even scallops	Unknown	Clear	Common
				Blue	Rare

The sunburst has 12 long and 12 short rays. The target is a circle around a dot. The shoulder is plain.

No. 547	*Diam.*	*Rim*	*Origin*	*Colors*	*Rarity*
	3¼	20 scallops with points between	Unknown	Clear	Common
				Green tint	Rare

The sunburst has 12 long and 12 short rays centering in a large bull's eye or porthole. The shoulder has concentric rings. We know of no other plate with these same serrations. This is a crude and probably fairly late plate of a poor quality of glass, although it rings.

No. 548	*Diam.*	*Rim*	*Origin*	*Colors*	*Rarity*
	3 7/16	18 scallops with pairs of smaller ones be-tween	Unknown	Clear	Very rare

The sunburst is composed of 15 long and 15 short rays centering in a target of 2 circles around a dot. The shoulder has 4 rings. The serrations match nothing known to us, so we cannot hazard a guess on origin.

No. 549	*Diam.*	*Rim*	*Origin*	*Colors*	*Rarity*
	3½	53 even scallops	Unknown	Clear	Scarce

The sunburst has 18 long and 18 short rays which are narrower than those on the following plate. The target is 2 rings around a bull's eye. The shoulder has 3 rings.

No. 550	*Diam.*	*Rim*	*Origin*	*Colors*	*Rarity*
	3½	53 even scallops	Unknown	Clear	Rare

Precisely like the preceding plate, except that the rays in the sunburst are thicker and heavier and, in such examples as we have seen, do not quite reach the outer circle of the target. This seems much the rarer of the two.

Nos. 551 through 559 are reserved for new discoveries.

Chapter XVI

HISTORICAL BUSTS

Nos. 560 through 586-B

No. 560	*Diam.*	*Rim*	*Origin*	*Colors*	*Rarity*
	3 7/16	24 bull's-eyes with points between	Midwest, probably Pittsburgh	Clear	Extremely rare

This plate is obviously related to such conventionals as Nos. 130, 131, 133, 134 and 135, and to such historicals as Nos. 604, 612 and 671, some of which are known in blue or opal but never, so far, in both colors. Consequently, there is a possibility that some day a blue or, more likely, an opal example of this plate will be found. As similar conventionals also have 36- and 40-bull's-eye rim variants, it is not impossible that such variations will be found. The most likely variation is in the design die, where a plate with rays behind the bust of Washington, as in the following entry, could be found in conjunction with this bull's-eye and point ring. Since the background of this plate is plain, it must antedate the rayed and stippled type which follows. This round Washington is the most desirable of all cup plates. Only two specimens exist. They were found near Scio, Ohio, but had been brought there from Blairsville, Pennsylvania, just east of Pittsburgh.

No. 561	*Diam.*	*Rim*	*Origin*	*Colors*	*Rarity*
	3½ across	Octagonal, 7 scallops each side	Midwest, probably Pittsburgh	Clear	Very rare

Note that the design die has been changed by adding rays behind the head and by covering the rest of the center with a coarse stippling, so coarse that pebbling would be a better term. The relation of this to other plates and also the range of possible variations in rims and in colors is the same as in the previous plate. These octagonal cap-rings have not as yet been fully investigated. Mr. Cannon has definitely

560

562

561

562-A

561-A

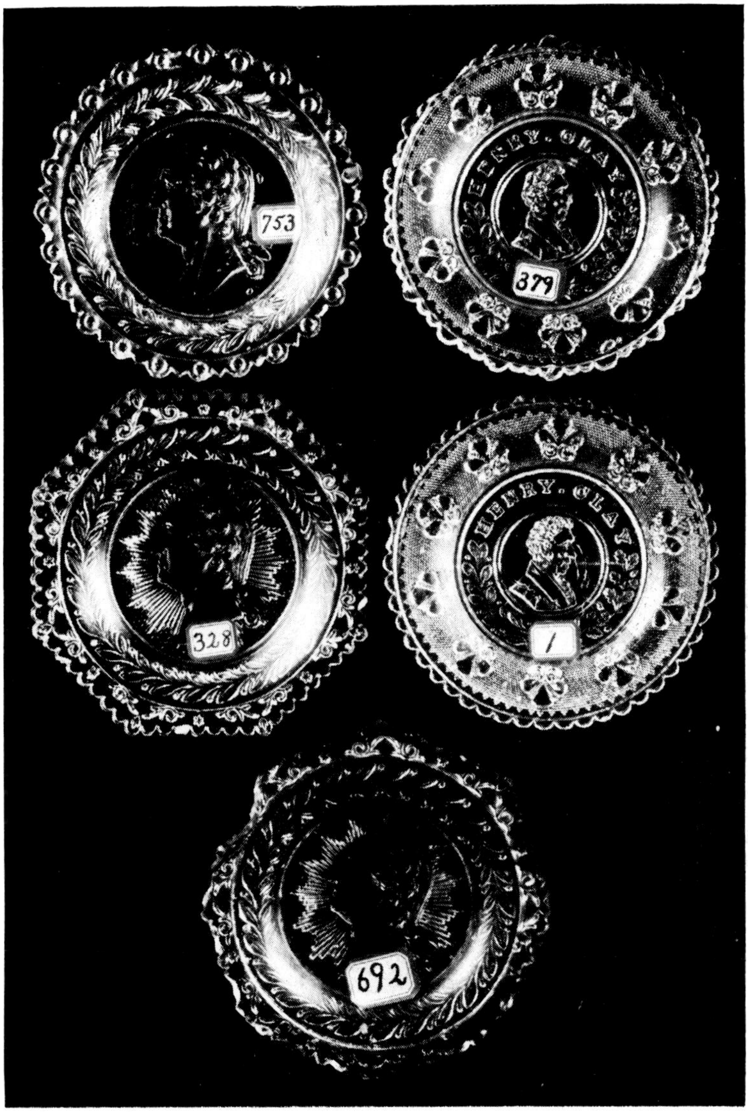

Plate 88

563

565-B

564

566

565

566-A

565-A

566-B

No. 56
left ope

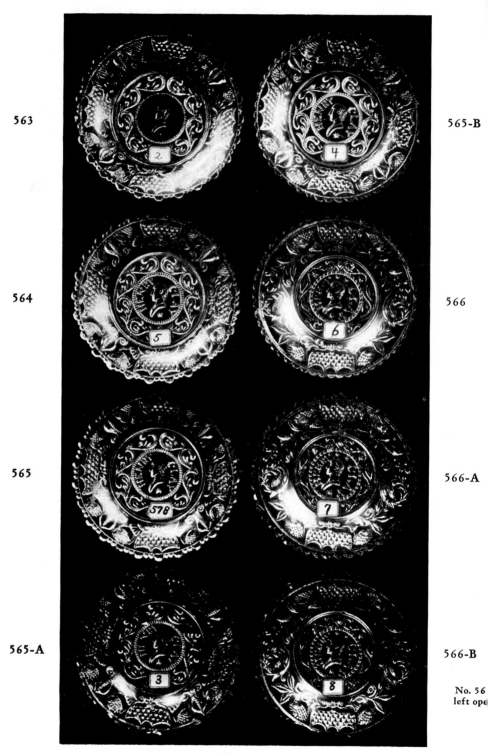

Plate 89

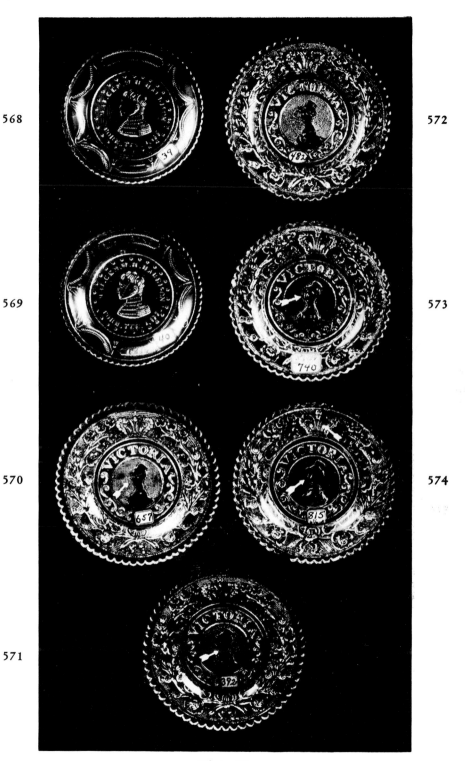

568

572

569

573

570

574

571

Plate 90

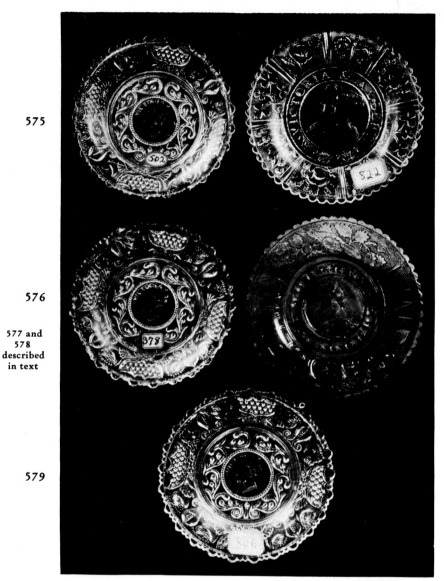

575

580

580-A
and
580-B
described
in text

No. 581
left open

576

582

577 and
578
described
in text

Nos. 583
and 584
left open

579

Plate 91

585

586

585-A

586-A

585-B

586-B

Nos. 587
through
589
left open

585-C

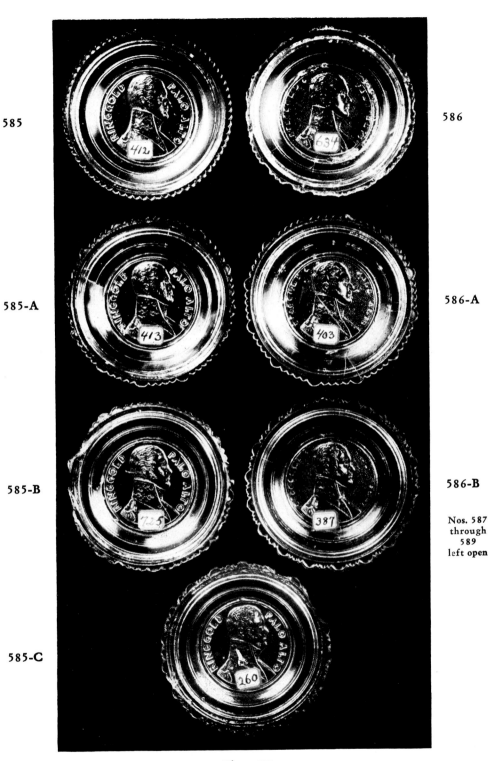

Plate 92

established the existence of 2 such rings as used on the Constitutions, where the variation consists in minute differences in the corner scrolls. Mr. Marble notes two sizes for the rings, the other being 3 7/16″. The attribution is made on the basis of tooling, or in other words, on the related plates. Distribution does not agree, since most octagonal Washingtons and octagonal Constitutions have been found near Philadelphia.

No. 561-A	Diam.	Rim	Origin	Colors	Rarity
	3 7/16 across	Octagonal as above	Midwest, probably Pittsburgh	Clear	Extremely rare

This is simply a shift, a slight rotating of the design die within the cap-ring and is not, by our definition, a true variant. The maker seems to have exercised much better position control on these Washingtons than on the octagonal Constitutions and so-called Fultons, so that tilted-head Washingtons are difficult to find. The easiest way to determine these tilts is to relate the star in the center of each side to one of the long rays behind the bust. As in all octagonal plates, really proof specimens are practically impossible to obtain.

No. 562	Diam.	Rim	Origin	Colors	Rarity
	3 7/16	18 large scallops with 2 smaller ones between	Eastern, probably Sandwich	Clear	Very rare

There may be a relationship between these lacy Clays and the Eastern conventional series, No. 230, although the large scallops on the Clays seem bolder than they do on the conventionals.

No. 562-A	Diam.	Rim	Origin	Colors	Rarity
	3⅜	49 even scallops	Eastern, probably Sandwich	Clear	Very rare

Again there is a relationship with the 230 series, this time with the first member of the series. If this analogy is correct, a 60-serration variant may some day be found. This even-serration Clay is not so rare as No. 562, but proof examples are very hard to find.

No. 563	Diam.	Rim	Origin	Colors	Rarity
	3⅝	25 large scallops with 2 smaller ones between	Probably Sandwich	Clear	Plentiful
				Green tint	Plentiful
				Yellow-green tint	Plentiful

This is the so-called "No Name" Clay. Through its serrations, it is related to the Clay-type Victorias but not as is commonly thought, to the so-called Cadmuses. The similar Cadmus has only 23 large scallops. While both colored and clear specimens are frequently seen, really proof examples are not too easy to find.

No. 564	Diam.	Rim	Origin	Colors	Rarity
	3⅝	25 large scallops with 2 smaller ones between	Probably Sandwich	Clear	Plentiful
				Dark blue	Plentiful
				Medium blue	Scarce
				Purple-blue	Rare
				Peacock-blue	Scarce
				Lavender	Extremely rare
				Opal	Very rare

This is related to the "No Name" Clay and, as in that plate, the cornucopias at the lower left have the elongated fruit, generally called a pomegranate, arranged right and left or, in other words, symmetrically.

No. 565	Diam.	Rim	Origin	Colors	Rarity
	3⅝	25 large scallops with 2 smaller ones between	Probably Sandwich	Clear	Plentiful
				Blue	Very rare
				Peacock-blue	Very rare
				Green tint	Scarce

The so-called pomegranates in the cornucopias at the lower left are arranged differently than in Nos. 563 and 564. Here, the upper cornucopia has its pomegranate at the top near the shield. In the lower cornucopia the pomegranate is also at the top, so that the two pomegranates are not symmetrically arranged.

No. 565-A	Diam.	Rim	Origin	Colors	Rarity
	3 9/16	25 flat scallops, points between	Probably Sandwich	Clear	Plentiful

As in No. 565, the pomegranates in the cornucopias at the lower left are unsymmetrically arranged. This plate is related through its serration pattern to the No. 610-B so-called Cadmus. The lack of colored specimens is puzzling, and it seems not unlikely that the various blues and perhaps even an opalescent example will eventually be found.

No. 565-B	*Diam.*	*Rim*	*Origin*	*Colors*	*Rarity*
	3 9/16	51 even scallops	Probably Sandwich	Clear	Plentiful
				Blue	Scarce
				Peacock-blue	Scarce
				Green tint	Scarce

This too is related to a pseudo Cadmus, No. 610. It has the unsymmetrically placed pomegranates of the rest of the 565 series in its lower-left cornucopias.

No. 566	*Diam.*	*Rim*	*Origin*	*Colors*	*Rarity*
	3½	53 even scallops	Probably Sandwich	Clear	Rare

While the preceding Clay series has 4 shields on the shoulder, this series has but 2, one at the top, the other at the bottom. The side-shields are replaced by leafy branches. Here the "N" in "Henry" is reversed and this is the easiest way to distinguish these plates. Through the use of two common surface dies, these Clays are related to certain members of the Valentine series. We believe that the Valentines are somewhat earlier and that we are here encountering a re-use of the surface die. Since both the Valentines and the regular Clays turn up not infrequently in color, we are at a loss to understand why these reversed "N" Clays are found in clear glass only.

No. 566-A	*Diam.*	*Rim*	*Origin*	*Colors*	*Rarity*
	3 9/16	23 scallops, points between	Probably Sandwich	Clear	Scarce

This plate differs from the preceding one only in its serration pattern, a pattern used, we believe, only on this plate. Of the three plates in the series, this is the easiest to find.

No. 566-B	*Diam.*	*Rim*	*Origin*	*Colors*	*Rarity*
	3⅝	20 large scallops with smaller ones between	Probably Sandwich	Clear	Rare

Like the similar Valentine this plate is almost impossible to find in good condition. In fact, even ragged specimens are not easy to get. No. 567 is reserved for a new discovery.

No. 568	*Diam.*	*Rim*	*Origin*	*Colors*	*Rarity*
	3 7/16	67 even scallops	Probably Sandwich	Clear	Scarce

In this variety the lozenges are blank. These two plates have the same serration pattern as the conventional No. 334, and we understand that fragments were found at Sandwich. It seems strange that such a factory as Sandwich would make so crude a plate. The Clays made at the same time were far better quality.

No. 569	*Diam.*	*Rim*	*Origin*	*Colors*	*Rarity*
	3 7/16	67 even scallops	Probably Sandwich	Clear Opal	Plentiful Very rare

Exactly like the preceding plate, except that here the upper lozenge is filled in with "President" and the lower one with "1841." This is a recutting and reissue after Harrison's election.

No. 570	*Diam.*	*Rim*	*Origin*	*Colors*	*Rarity*
	4	65 even scallops	Uncertain	Clear	Rare

The V-device centering the border crown is not stippled. The bust has practically no details. The most noticeable feature of the face is the beadiness of the eyes. As in all these lacy Victorias, the shoulder pattern is slightly different from other members of the series. Mr. Marble lists a 65-scallop variant only 3¾″ in diameter which we have not seen.

No. 571	*Diam.*	*Rim*	*Origin*	*Colors*	*Rarity*
	3⅞	59 even scallops	Uncertain	Clear	Rare

This is rarer than the preceding plate and differs from it not only in size and number of serrations but in minor details of the shoulder pattern. Here, the mouth and nose show, the neckline of the dress is higher and a necklace or, possibly, the edge of a collar appears. The V-device is not stippled, and the three lobes of the cross atop the crown are plainly delineated as in the previous plate.

No. 572	*Diam.*	*Rim*	*Origin*	*Colors*	*Rarity*
	3 15/16	60 even scallops	Uncertain	Clear	Rare

This is still rarer than either of the preceding plates. The Maltese cross atop the crown is smaller. The hair is arranged in a softer way. The necklace and neckline of the gown is much the same, but the front of the bodice is made up of more prominent diagonal lines. Again the V-device in the crown is not stippled.

No. 573	*Diam.*	*Rim*	*Origin*	*Colors*	*Rarity*
	3⅞	58 even scallops	Uncertain	Clear	Very rare

Details of the face and bust are almost completely lacking, much as in No. 570, but the beady-eyed effect of that plate is missing. The V-device is stippled. The gown is the off-the-shoulder type and no collar can be seen. There is a distinct part in her hair.

No. 574	*Diam.*	*Rim*	*Origin*	*Colors*	*Rarity*
	3⅞	58 even scallops	Uncertain	Clear	Extremely rare

The V-device in the crown is stippled. The face and details of the gown (the high-necked type) are much clearer than in the preceding plate and there seems to be a collar above the bodice. Border details differ considerably.

No. 575	*Diam.*	*Rim*	*Origin*	*Colors*	*Rarity*
	3½ scant	25 large scallops with 2 smaller ones between	Probably Sandwich	Clear	Scarce

All specimens we have seen were fire-polished.

No. 576	*Diam.*	*Rim*	*Origin*	*Colors*	*Rarity*
	3 9/16	25 large scallops with 2 smaller ones between	Probably Sandwich	Clear Dark blue Medium blue Amethyst	Scarce Extremely rare Unique Unique

We cannot be sure that this is a true variant. The slightly larger diameter could be due to a little less heat in fire-polishing. The medium blue and amethyst specimens are in the collection of the late Dr. H. A. Morrill.

No. 577	*Diam.*	*Rim*	*Origin*	*Colors*	*Rarity*
	3 9/16	25 large scallops with 2 smaller ones between	Probably Sandwich	Clear Dark blue	Extremely rare Unique

The shoulder of this type is concave. In other words, the shape is rather like a sauce dish. The blue example is in Mr. Cannon's collection.

No. 578	*Diam.*	*Rim*	*Origin*	*Colors*	*Rarity*
	3⅝	25 large scallops with 2 smaller ones between	Probably Sandwich	Amber	Extremely rare

This also has the concave shoulder. No clear specimens are known. One amber one is in Mrs. Parker's collection and the other is in the Morrill collection.

No. 579	*Diam.*	*Rim*	*Origin*	*Colors*	*Rarity*
	3 15/16	25 large scallops with 2 smaller ones between	Probably Sandwich	Clear	Very rare

No. 580	*Diam.*	*Rim*	*Origin*	*Colors*	*Rarity*
	3¾	56 even scallops	English	Clear	Extremely rare

Although there is, so far, no analogous serration pattern, we feel that these Victoria and Albert plates were most likely made in the same factory that pressed the lacy Victorias. The location and type of the inscription is similar and the treatment of the elongated rosebud is, we think, characteristic.

No. 580-A	Diam.	Rim	Origin	Colors	Rarity
	3¾	57 even scallops	English	Clear	Extremely rare

Figures are lacking as to whether or not there is a measurable difference in rarity between the three variants of this plate. It is possible that the 57- and 58-scallop types are the rarer.

No. 580-B	Diam.	Rim	Origin	Colors	Rarity
	3¾	58 even scallops	English	Clear	Extremely rare

As in the preceding plate, the only variation is in the number of serrations. For larger, toddy size, Victoria and Alberts see No. 826.

No. 581 is reserved for a new discovery.

No. 582	Diam.	Rim	Origin	Colors	Rarity
	3¾	56 even scallops	English	Blue?	Uncertain

The serrations, judged from a photograph, seem to match those on the 56-scallop Victoria and Albert. On this plate the serrations are lightly flashed. No clear examples have been reported and the only colored one known is in the Hutchins Estate. We have not seen this plate, whose color is described as both green and blue.

Nos. 583 and 584 are reserved for new discoveries.

No. 585	Diam.	Rim	Origin	Colors	Rarity
	3⅜	72 even scallops	Philadelphia area, possibly Union Glass Works	Clear	Very rare

All Ringgolds have the serration patterns of the conventional series, Nos. 225, 226 and 227, and the cabin series, Nos. 600 and 601, but are eight years later than the cabins and probably ten or fifteen years later than the earliest of the conventional groups. This type, with the larger lettering and without stippling behind the bust, is found, as a type, more frequently than the stippled-ground variety, although even here all varieties are so rare that the difference is negligible. No collector can afford to wait for proof examples of any of these plates. The usual specimen is badly battered.

No. 585-A	*Diam.*	*Rim*	*Origin*	*Colors*	*Rarity*
	3 7/16	12 large scallops with 4 smaller ones between	As above	Clear	Extremely rare

This is much rarer than the even-serration type. Since colored examples (green) are known in two of the conventional series, there is a bare possibility of their turning up here, but this is unlikely since the conventionals antedate this series by a decade.

No. 585-B	*Diam.*	*Rim*	*Origin*	*Colors*	*Rarity*
	3⅜	9 pairs of large scallops with 4 smaller ones between	As above	Clear	Extremely rare

We have never seen a proof or even a good specimen of this plate. As in the conventional series, when a set of Ringgolds turns up it is likely to contain an assortment of serration varieties. Apparently, this factory made no attempt to match serrations. It should be noted that the diameter of Mr. Marble's plate is 1/16″ smaller than that of the conventionals.

No. 585-C	*Diam.*	*Rim*	*Origin*	*Colors*	*Rarity*
	3 7/16	18 large scallops with a smaller scallop and 2 points between	As above	Clear	Very rare

This is the Ringgold most often found but it is, nevertheless, very rare. Again, Mr. Marble's dimensions given above are small, and this may indicate a different die than that used on the similar conventionals.

No. 586	Diam.	Rim	Origin	Colors	Rarity
	3⅜	72 even scallops	As above	Clear	Extremely rare

This series has much smaller lettering in the inscription, has a grotesquely large period after "Ringgold" and has the background stippled. It should be noted that this stippling is of the uneven, pebbly type characteristic of late practice. Stippled-type Ringgolds are, in general, even rarer than the variety with plain background. Proof specimens are virtually unobtainable.

No. 586-A	Diam.	Rim	Origin	Colors	Rarity
	3 7/16	12 large scallops with 4 smaller ones between	As above	Clear	Extremely rare

Of the stippled type this is the variety most often found, although "often" used in connection with so rare a plate verges on absurdity. The "small lettering" Ringgold with serrations like those on No. 585-B has not yet been discovered.

No. 586-B	Diam.	Rim	Origin	Colors	Rarity
	3 7/16	18 large scallops with a smaller scallop and 2 points between	As above	Clear	Extremely rare

This plate is much rarer than its plain-background companion with similar serrations. It should be noticed that the attribution to the Union Glass works is tentative. There is a possibility that The Excelsior Glass Works of Kaighn's Point, South Camden, N. J., made the Ringgolds, using surface dies and cap-rings from the Union Glass Works.

Nos. 587 and 589 are reserved for new discoveries.

Chapter XVII

THE LOG CABIN GROUP

Nos. 590 through 601-C

No. 590	Diam.	Rim	Origin	Colors	Rarity
	3 1/16	61 even scallops	Uncertain	Clear	Plentiful

The serrations seem to match those on the sunburst, No. 523, which occurs in many colors, so there is a possibility of our some day finding this little cabin in color. Note that the door has no latchstring.

No. 591	Diam.	Rim	Origin	Colors	Rarity
	3½	48 even scallops	Eastern, probably Sandwich	Clear	Very rare

Again, the serrations match those on a sunburst, No. 532. This cabin superficially resembles the preceding one, but is much larger and has a number of differences in design, the chief of which is that here we have a latchstring on the door. Distribution is almost entirely confined to New England.

No. 592	Diam.	Rim	Origin	Colors	Rarity
	3 7/16	21 large scallops with smaller ones between	Uncertain but Eastern	Clear	Extremely rare
				Green tint	Unique

The serrations match those on the so-called Wedding Day, No. 697. The average specimen usually lacks a serration or two. We have not seen the example in a green tint, but it has been reported by a reliable source and its existence could have been predicted, since the Wedding Day occurs frequently in both green and pink tints. The distribution is entirely Eastern but is not confined to New England.

No. 593	*Diam.*	*Rim*	*Origin*	*Colors*	*Rarity*
	3 5/16	10-scallop rope, top & bottom	Midwestern	Clear	Scarce

Curiously enough, this is the only cabin that can be definitely assigned to the Midwest. Clay was a Western candidate and one would think the Western factories would have capitalized on his local popularity. While by analogy with similar plates there is a possibility of bull's-eye and plain rope-rim varieties turning up, this is unlikely. This use of the rim is relatively late, and the chances are the dies for the other rims had long since been scrapped.

No. 594	*Diam.*	*Rim*	*Origin*	*Colors*	*Rarity*
	3¼	66 even scallops	Probably Sandwich	Clear Amber Opal	Plentiful Rare Extremely rare

The serrations are the same as those found on such plates as the Butterfly, some of the so-called Sandwich stars and several sunbursts. Two shades of amber are found, one a bit darker than the other, but no specific name can be assigned to differentiate between them, nor do they differ in rarity. The door has faint vertical planking.

No. 595	*Diam.*	*Rim*	*Origin*	*Colors*	*Rarity*
	3¼	66 even scallops	As above	Clear	Scarce

Because this plate is easily confused with the preceding one, we are in doubt as to its rarity. The door has no planking.

No. 596	*Diam.*	*Rim*	*Origin*	*Colors*	*Rarity*
	3 9/16	48 even scallops	Uncertain	Clear	Plentiful

We have found no plates with identical serrations. Distribution is universal, and there is no real guide to origin. To us, the style and serrations look Eastern, but good judges consider it Midwestern. Note, particularly, that the door has a latchstring. We are informed that in the fragments dug up at Sandwich by Mr. Wynn there was one with no latchstring. When a reasonably complete specimen of this latchstringless variety is found, it will be numbered 597.

Nos. 597 through 599 are reserved for new discoveries.

590

594

591

595

592

596

Nos. 597,
598, 599
left open

593

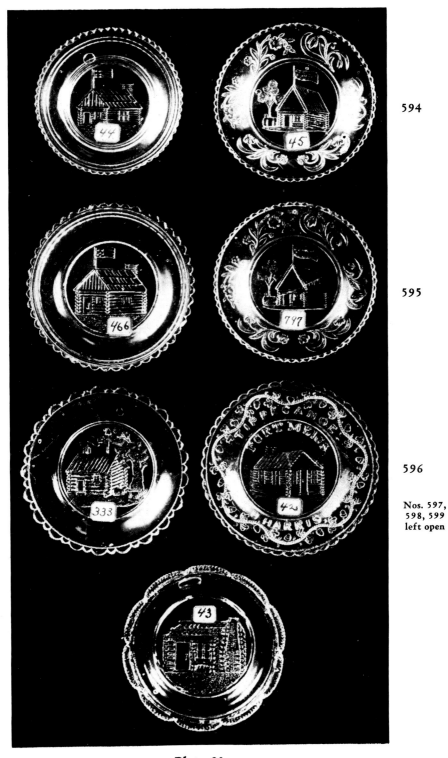

Plate 93

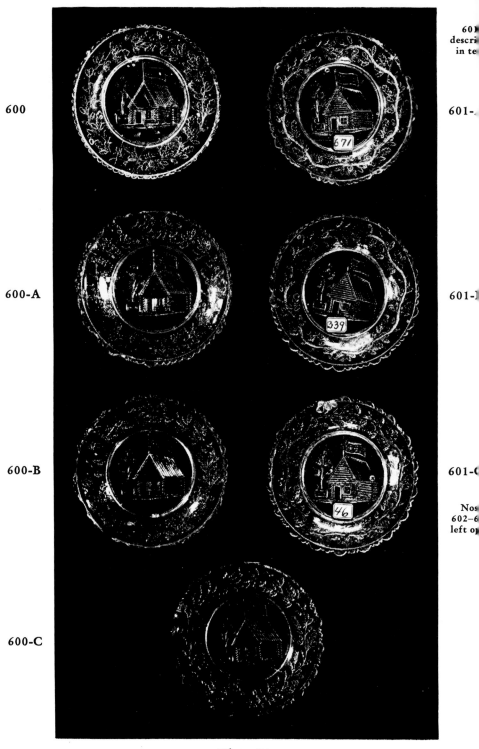

600

601
descri
in te

601-

600-A

601-

600-B

601-C

Nos
602-6
left o

600-C

Plate 94

No. 600	Diam.	Rim	Origin	Colors	Rarity
	3⅜	72 even scallops	Philadelphia area, probably Union Glass Works	Clear	Extremely rare

The four varieties in this series have a plain (not stippled) vine on the shoulder. They are not listed by Mr. Marble and seem even rarer than the type with stippled vine. The specimen illustrated is from Mr. Carapata's collection.

No. 600-A	Diam.	Rim	Origin	Colors	Rarity
	3 7/16	12 large scallops with 4 smaller ones between	As above	Clear	Extremely rare

We have been able to locate but two specimens of this plate. The one illustrated is in Mr. Cannon's collection, the other in Dr. Doane's. Both came from the Baltimore-Philadelphia area.

No. 600-B	Diam.	Rim	Origin	Colors	Rarity
	3⅜	9 pairs of large scallops with 4 smaller ones between	As above	Clear	Extremely rare

Again, we can locate but two copies. The cut shows Mr. Cannon's plate. There is another in the collection of Mr. Paul Carson. Naturally this series, as well as the one immediately following, is related to the Ringgolds and to the conventionals, Nos. 225, 226 and 227.

No. 600-C	Diam.	Rim	Origin	Colors	Rarity
	3 7/16	18 large scallops with a smaller one and 2 points between	As above	Clear	Unique

We credit these plates to the Union Glass Works since that factory's temporary closing and the possible dispersal of its molds did not occur until 1844, and these cabins seem to have been pressed for the campaign of 1840. The only example known to us is in the collection of Mr. Paul Carson.

No. 601	Diam.	Rim	Origin	Colors	Rarity
	3⅜	72 even scallops	As above	Clear	Unique

These cabins are simply the previous group with the running vine stippled. The only even-serration specimen of the stippled-vine type known to us is the one in Mrs. Palmer Graham's collection.

No. 601-A	Diam.	Rim	Origin	Colors	Rarity
	3 7/16	12 large scallops with 4 smaller ones between	As above	Clear	Extremely rare

This is slightly more common than its prototype with the plain vine. We have been able to locate about six examples and one of these may be a duplicate. The relation between these cabins and the Ringgolds and with the three conventional series having the same serration patterns is self-evident.

No. 601-B	Diam.	Rim	Origin	Colors	Rarity
	3⅜	9 pairs of large scallops with 4 smaller ones between	As above	Clear	Extremely rare

Again the stippled-vine type is a shade more often found than its plain-vine counterpart. All of these cabins, both stippled and plain, are practically never found proof, in which respect they resemble the fragile Ringgolds and the other plates from this factory.

No. 601-C	Diam.	Rim	Origin	Colors	Rarity
	3 7/16	18 large scallops with a smaller one and 2 points between	As above	Clear	Extremely rare

Sets of these plates, when and if they appear (we know of two finds, each consisting of two plates), are likely to turn up in a mixture of the various serration types. As in all plates from this factory, it is possible that green examples may be found.

Nos. 602 and 603 are reserved for new discoveries.

Chapter XVIII

THE SHIP GROUP

Nos. 604 through 632-A

No. 604	Diam.	Rim	Origin	Colors	Rarity
	3 7/16	24 bull's eyes with points between	Midwest, probably Pittsburgh	Clear	Extremely rare

In this variety the rigging ropes are not stippled. This plain-rope type is rarer than the varieties with the rigging partly stippled. Through its serrations the plate is related to the Plows, the 612 steamboat series, the Washingtons and to the 24 bull's-eye and point conventionals.

No. 604-A	Diam.	Rim	Origin	Colors	Rarity
	3½ across	Octagonal	Midwest, probably Pittsburgh	Clear	Rare

As on No. 604, the rigging is plain. There is conflicting evidence as to origin of the octagonal Constitutions. As is the case with the Washingtons, the octagonal types turn up most frequently in the Philadelphia area, but the octagonal cap-ring is almost certainly Midwestern. The most plausible explanation is that these plates sold better in the East than in the West.

No. 605	Diam.	Rim	Origin	Colors	Rarity
	3 7/16	24 bull's eyes with points between	Midwest, probably Pittsburgh	Clear	Extremely rare

This resembles No. 604, except that here the rigging is a combination of plain and stippled ropes. At the present time the mixed-rigging type is the one more often found, but since the difference is one of not more than six or eight specimens, it cannot be translated into a different rarity

328

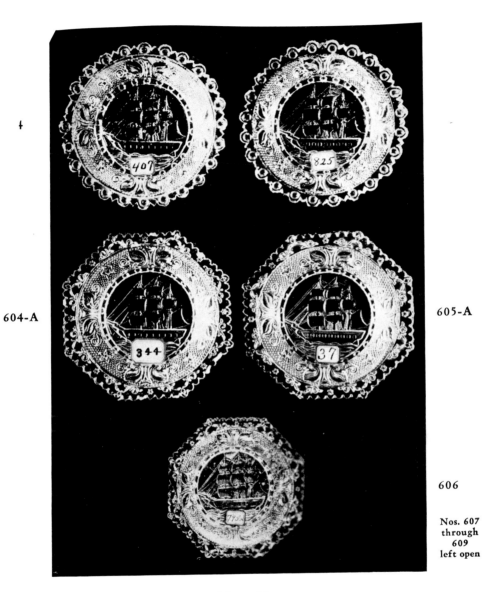

604-A

605-A

606

Nos. 607
through
609
left open

Plate 95

Plate in bottom row reduced in size.

610

610-A

610-B

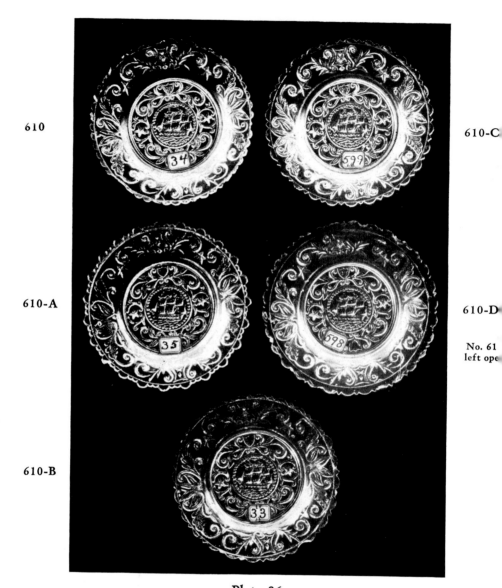

610-C

610-D

No. 61
left ope

Plate 96

2

615

612-A

615-A

No. 613
ft open

No. 616
left open

614

Plate 97

617

619-A

619-B
describe
in text

618

620

Nos. 62
throug
623
left ope

619

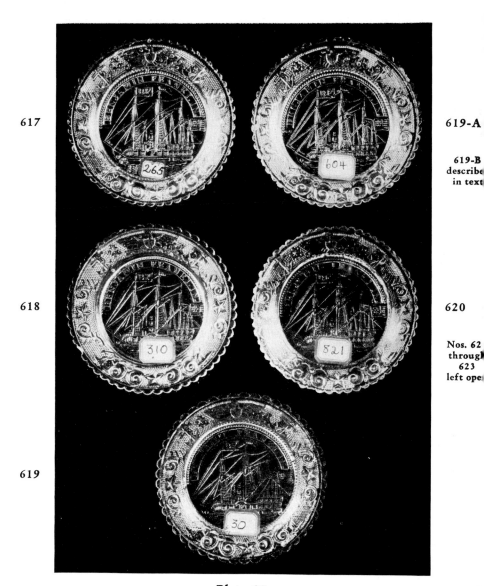

Plate 98

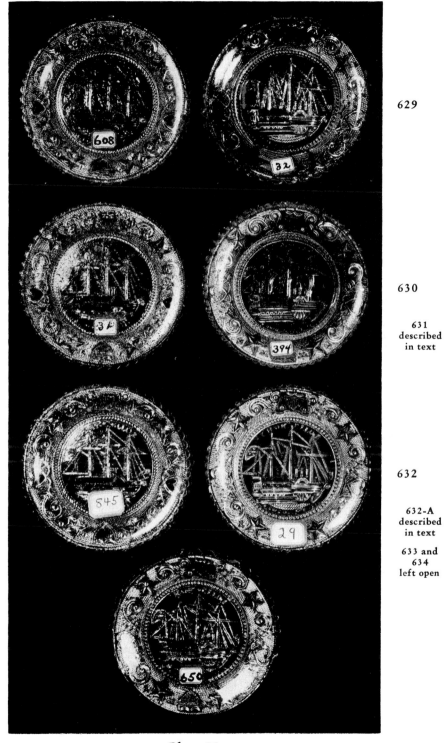

624

24-A
scribed
n text

625

25-A
scribed
n text

626

627
t open

628

629

630

631
described
in text

632

632-A
described
in text

633 and
634
left open

Plate 99

statement. All examples of both types of round Constitutions we can trace were found west of the mountains.

No. 605-A	Diam.	Rim	Origin	Colors	Rarity
	3½ across	Octagonal	Midwest, probably Pittsburgh	Clear Light opal	Scarce Extremely rare

The rigging is a combination of stippled and plain ropes as in No. 605. This is the variety most often found, but proof specimens are very hard to find. The light opal examples, of which we can locate only one set of six, have the mainmast tilted slightly to the left of center.

No. 606	Diam.	Rim	Origin	Colors	Rarity
	3½ across	Octagonal	Midwest, probably Pittsburgh	Clear	Uncertain

Of the ropes running up from the bowsprit, only the foreskysail stay (the front rope to landlubbers) is stippled. We are not sure this is a distinct variant. It is possible that the lack of stippling on other standing rigging results from a poor impression, rather than from a change in the mold. If the variety can be established, it is rare.

Nos. 607 through 609 are reserved for new discoveries.

No. 610	Diam.	Rim	Origin	Colors	Rarity
	3 9/16	51 even scallops	Probably Sandwich	Clear	Plentiful

Serrations seem to agree with those found on the No. 565-B Clay. Occasionally, the top-shape seems to differ. If it can be established that this is the result of different dies and is not due to warping or careless handling, another variety exists. Proof examples are hard to obtain.

No. 610-A	Diam.	Rim	Origin	Colors	Rarity
	3⅝	23 bold scallops with 2 smaller ones between	Probably Sandwich	Clear	Common
				Green tint	Scarce
				Yellow-green tint	Scarce
				Blue	Scarce
				Peacock-blue	Scarce
				Opal	Rare

This serration pattern resembles superficially that found on the

Clays, Nos. 563 and 565, and the No. 575 type Victoria. It should be noted that here we have only 23 of the large scallops, while the Clays and Victoria have 25. The design die of this variety seems to differ in contour with the ship raised slightly above the table-ring, so that the plate has a tendency to rock. Proof specimens are more easily found than in the other varieties of these so-called Cadmuses.

No. 610-B	*Diam.*	*Rim*	*Origin*	*Colors*	*Rarity*
	3 9/16	25 flat	Probably	Clear	Common
		scallops,	Sandwich	Green tint	Scarce
		points		Blue	Scarce
		between		Peacock-blue	Scarce

The serrations match those found on the No. 565-A Clay. Here, again, immaculate specimens are hard to find.

No. 610-C	*Diam.*	*Rim*	*Origin*	*Colors*	*Rarity*
	3⅝	26 flat	Probably	Clear	Plentiful
		scallops,	Sandwich		
		points			
		between			

Note that this plate has one more large scallop and one more point than the preceding plate. In our experience this is the hardest to find of the series. No colors have been reported but they may exist improperly numbered.

No. 610-D	*Diam.*	*Rim*	*Origin*	*Colors*	*Rarity*
	3¾	30 flat	Probably	Clear	Plentiful
		scallops,	Sandwich		
		points			
		between			

This is a larger plate and its scallops do not extend to the inner rim of the cap-ring. Perfect specimens are practically impossible to find.

No. 611 is reserved for a new discovery.

No. 612	*Diam.*	*Rim*	*Origin*	*Colors*	*Rarity*
	3 7/16	24 bull's	Midwest,	Clear	Extremely
		eyes with	probably		rare
		points	Pittsburgh		
		between			

These are closely allied to the Constitutions, Washingtons, Plows, the No. 670-A eagles and the corresponding conventionals with 24-bull's-eye and point rims. The crook in the flagstaff of Mr. Marble's plate is peculiar to that one specimen and is accidental. So far as we know, there are but seventeen of the circular variety known and these represent three Ohio finds of the late 1920's. None has been found since.

No. 612-A	*Diam.*	*Rim*	*Origin*	*Colors*	*Rarity*
	3½ or 3 7/16 across	Octagonal, 7 scallops each side between corners	As above	Clear	Rare

The tooling, as in the previous plate, is the same as that of the Washingtons, Plows, etc. Mr. Marble gives 3 7/16″ as the diameter of this octagonal type, but those we have measured are all 3½″. He also lists several "tilts" which, by our definition, are not true variants. In general these octagonal Steamboats are rarer than the corresponding Constitutions.

No. 613 is reserved for a new discovery.

No. 614	*Diam.*	*Rim*	*Origin*	*Colors*	*Rarity*
	3½ across	Octagonal, 6 scallops each side between corners	Pittsburgh, probably Parke, Campbell and Hanna	Clear Blue tint	Extremely rare Unique

No other use of exactly the same serrations is known, but there is a resemblance to the octagonal eagles, No. 677-E, with "egg" serrations and to the corresponding conventionals, Nos. 197 and 197-A. In this plate, however, the "eggs" are in coffin form. The most curious feature is that each of the octagonal sides is numbered, from one to eight, on the shoulder. The plate is dated 1836 and is inscribed "Union Glass Works Pittsburgh." The angle of the ship is simply a tilt (no level specimen is known), so the ship is not, as early writers thought, sinking. The blue tint is faint and is in Mrs. Parker's collection.

No. 615	*Diam.*	*Rim*	*Origin*	*Colors*	*Rarity*
	3 9/16	41 even scallops	Uncertain	Clear	Extremely rare

Not only is this one of the rarest plates known (we can locate but four copies), but no proof specimen exists. Three of the known copies can be traced to Ohio. No other plate has precisely this serration pattern, although No. 273 differs by but 1/16″. For further discussion of origin see the following variant.

No. 615-A	*Diam.*	*Rim*	*Origin*	*Colors*	*Rarity*
	3⅜	25 scallops, points between	As above	Clear Pink tint	Very rare Unique

Again, there is no identical serration pattern on any other plate, unless it be that on No. 96, which by our measurements is 1/16″ larger. Thus, the only basis for attribution is distribution. This is Ohio, stretching east as far as York, Pennsylvania. Our conclusion is that on the present evidence no attribution can be made. This scallop and point type is much more often found than its even-serration companion. The pink tint mentioned is very faint and is in the collection of Mrs. Frederick L. Parker.

No. 616 is reserved for a new discovery.

No. 617	*Diam.*	*Rim*	*Origin*	*Colors*	*Rarity*
	3 7/16	59 even scallops	Probably Sandwich	Clear	Scarce

This variety with the plain (not stippled) rigging and with a rope table-ring seems to be scarce, judged by its frequent appearance on want lists. There should be a variant with a plain table-ring and plain rigging, but it has not been reported as yet.

No. 618	*Diam.*	*Rim*	*Origin*	*Colors*	*Rarity*
	3½	55 even scallops	Probably Sandwich	Clear	Plentiful

Here, the rigging is stippled and the table-ring is plain. In other words, we have here a reversal of the features found in the preceding plate. These Franklins, in general, are related through serrations to such plates as the No. 591 cabin, to conventionals, like No. 278, and to some of the 12- and 13-heart border plates.

No. 619	*Diam.*	*Rim*	*Origin*	*Colors*	*Rarity*
	3½	48 even scallops	Probably Sandwich	Clear Blue Violet-blue Opal	Plentiful Rare Extremely rare Rare

This has both stippled rigging and a rope table-ring. The 48-serration type is being reproduced. The modern version has sans serif letters in the inscription and lacks the walking beam over the paddlewheel. These reproductions should fool no one, but until you are familiar with them better avoid clear and blue specimens that do not ring. As this goes to press, a blue example, an old one, has turned up that seems to have a trace of opal pigment in the mix giving it a peculiar bloom. It is in Mrs. L. C. Wells' collection.

No. 619-A	*Diam.*	*Rim*	*Origin*	*Colors*	*Rarity*
	3 7/16	59 even scallops	Probably Sandwich	Clear Silver stain	Plentiful Extremely rare

The plate has stippled rigging and a rope table-ring. The variation is in the serrations. The silver stain (amber) covers only the center of the plate. The shoulder is clear. Only two of these colored examples are known. They were found in Maine in 1946 by Mrs. Whichelow and are now in Mr. Marble's and Dr. Ruff's collections.

No. 619-B	*Diam.*	*Rim*	*Origin*	*Colors*	*Rarity*
	3 7/16	57 even scallops	Probably Sandwich	Clear Silver stain	Plentiful Extremely rare

Again, the rigging is stippled and the table-ring is a rope. The difference is in the serrations. Silver-stained specimens occur two ways: one has the color covering all of the plate, except the serrations, and is the type ordinarily found. The other has just the raised portions of the design in the amber stain and is extremely rare. We can locate but two of these. They were found in Maine about 1936 by the late Clifford Nutting.

No. 620	*Diam.*	*Rim*	*Origin*	*Colors*	*Rarity*
	3⅜	59 even scallops	Probably Sandwich	Clear	Unique

Statistically, this resembles No. 619-A, having the stippled rigging, the rope ring and even the same number of serrations although it is 1/16″ smaller. The startling difference is in the shape. This plate is deep like a small sauce dish. It is possible that this shape is the result of hand manipulation after pressing, but such a technique would be difficult and would probably produce distortion so the chances are it is from a different mold. Mr. Marble's is the only specimen we have seen.

Nos. 621 through 623 are reserved for new discoveries.

Chancellor Livingstons with Plain (not stippled) Hearts

No. 624	Diam.	Rim	Origin	Colors	Rarity
	3 7/16	54 even scallops	Probably Sandwich	Clear	Scarce

In this plate the rigging is plain, not stippled. These "plain heart" Chancellors are considerably rarer than the stippled heart type. So far, they have not been recorded in any color.

No. 624-A	Diam.	Rim	Origin	Colors	Rarity
	3½	53 even scallops	Probably Sandwich	Clear	Scarce

Like the preceding plate, this has plain rigging. The difference is in the size and the number of serrations. The serrations apear to be the same as those found on a Valentine No. 440 and such conventionals as Nos. 257-A and 267.

No. 625	Diam.	Rim	Origin	Colors	Rarity
	3 7/16	54 even scallops	Probably Sandwich	Clear	Scarce

On this plate, the rigging is partly plain and partly stippled.

No. 625-A	Diam.	Rim	Origin	Colors	Rarity
	3½	54 even scallops	Probably Sandwich	Clear	Rare

Here, again, the rigging is partly plain, partly stippled. Normally, with a 3½" diameter, one would expect 53 instead of 54 serrations. Eventually, this mixed-rigging type should be found with 53 serrations.

No. 626	Diam.	Rim	Origin	Colors	Rarity
	3½	53 even scallops	Probably Sandwich	Clear	Rare

Here, all the rigging is stippled. A variant with 54 serrations and measuring 3 7/16" should be found.

No. 627 is reserved for a new discovery.

Chancellor Livingstons with the Border Hearts Stippled

No. 628	Diam.	Rim	Origin	Colors	Rarity
	3½	38 even scallops	Probably Sandwich	Clear	Scarce
				Strong blue tint	Extremely rare
				Medium blue	Very rare
				Peacock-blue	Very rare
				Light bluish-green	Very rare
				Cloudy-green	Very rare
				Medium green	Extremely rare

The rigging is plain, not stippled. The table-ring is made up of a rope ring with stippled and plain rings just inside it. Note that this plate has a boom and rigging (a spanker) at the stern.

No. 629	Diam.	Rim	Origin	Colors	Rarity
	3½	38 even scallops	Probably Sandwich	Clear	Scarce
				Medium blue	Very rare

This is like the preceding plate, except that it lacks the spanker boom and accompanying rigging that overhangs the stern in the previous plate. In color, this is the rarer plate; in clear glass it seems a shade the more common.

No. 630	Diam.	Rim	Origin	Colors	Rarity
	3 7/16	63 even scallops	Probably Sandwich	Clear	Plentiful

This has the spanker boom at the stern and the rigging throughout is plain. The table-ring makeup varies in that this has two stippled rings just inside the rope ring.

No. 631	Diam.	Rim	Origin	Colors	Rarity
	3 7/16	63 even scallops	Probably Sandwich	Clear	Plentiful
				Emerald-green	Extremely rare

This is like the preceding plate, except that its rigging is stippled.

No. 632	Diam.	Rim	Origin	Colors	Rarity
	3 7/16	63 even scallops	Probably Sandwich	Clear	Plentiful

The rigging is stippled. The rope table-ring has stippled and plain rings just inside it.

No. 632-A	*Diam.*	*Rim*	*Origin*	*Colors*	*Rarity*
	3½	38 even scallops	Probably Sandwich	Clear	Plentiful

As in the preceding plate, the rigging is stippled and the table-ring has stippled and plain rings just inside it. The difference is in the diameter and number of serrations. Mr. Carapata has a specimen measuring only 3 7/16″. This may or may not be a true variant.

Nos. 633 and 634 are reserved for new discoveries.

Chapter XIX

MAID OF THE MIST. BUNKER HILL MONUMENTS

Nos. 635 through 646

No. 635	Diam.	Rim	Origin	Colors	Rarity
	3 7/16	Plain	Probably Midwestern	Light green	Extremely rare
				Yellow-green	Extremely rare
				Deep olive-green	Extremely rare

This type has no dot in the center of the large circles on its shoulder. It is the rarest of the three. No clear glass specimen is known to date.

No. 636	Diam.	Rim	Origin	Colors	Rarity
	3 7/16	Plain	Probably Midwestern	Clear	Plentiful
				Light green	Scarce
				Yellow-green	Rare

The large circles on the shoulder have dots in their centers. The waves run to the edge of the center within precipitous banks.

No. 637	Diam.	Rim	Origin	Colors	Rarity
	3 7/16 plus	Plain	Probably Midwestern	Clear	Very rare

The shoulder circles have dots. The most prominent feature of the design is the two arcs of stars. This seems to be a recutting of the design die of the previous plate, with stone masonry in the bridge towers and abutments added, and with the steep banks of the preceding design removed, although a trace of these still shows. Until a few years ago, this was one of the rarest of plates, but four sets of six turned up in Pennsylvania, another set in Maryland and a sixth set in Ohio, greatly diminishing its former rarity. No colored specimens have been reported as yet.

Nos. 638 and 639 are reserved for new discoveries.

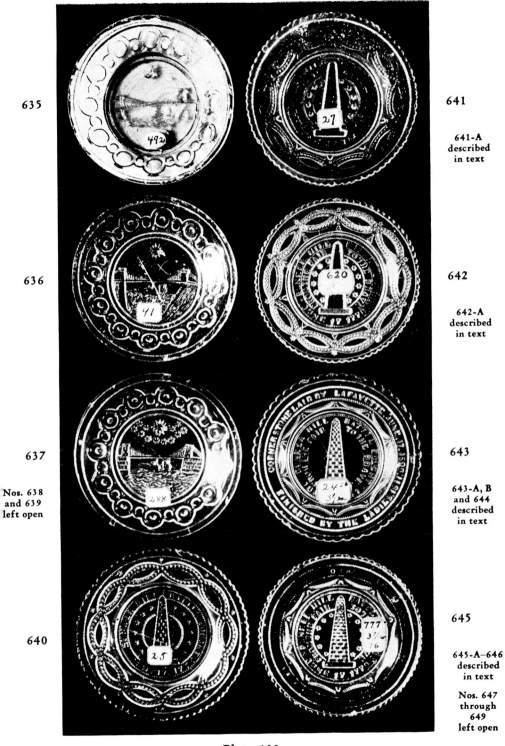

635

636

637

Nos. 638
and 639
left open

640

641

641-A
described
in text

642

642-A
described
in text

643

643-A, B
and 644
described
in text

645

645-A–646
described
in text

Nos. 647
through
649
left open

Plate 100

Monuments with a Chain Pattern on Their Shoulders

No. 640	*Diam.*	*Rim*	*Origin*	*Colors*	*Rarity*
	3⅝	76 even scallops	Probably Sandwich	Clear Yellow	Common See note

In this plate there are no tassels at the junctures of the links of the chain on the shoulder. It is, so far, the only one of the type showing masonry in the monument. There is but one line of inscription, inside which are 12 stars enclosed in stippled circles. There is a star over the tip of the monument. So far as we know, no yellow specimen is extant but two fragments in this color were found in the Wynn excavations at Sandwich.

No. 641	*Diam.*	*Rim*	*Origin*	*Colors*	*Rarity*
	3 9/16	76 even scallops	Probably Sandwich	Clear Yellow Peacock-blue	Common Very rare Unique

This has tassels between the links of the chain. The monument has a plain (not stippled) outline and no masonry is shown. There are two lines of inscription inside of which are 12 stars. There is no star over the monument. So far as we have observed, the impression is always bad. The peacock-blue example is in the collection of the late Dr. H. A. Morrill.

No. 641-A	*Diam.*	*Rim*	*Origin*	*Colors*	*Rarity*
	3⅝	76 even scallops	Probably Sandwich	Clear	Common

This is similar to the preceding plate in every way except the diameter, which is 1/16″ larger. Here, too, the imprint is always bad.

No. 642	*Diam.*	*Rim*	*Origin*	*Colors*	*Rarity*
	3 7/16	76 even scallops	Probably Sandwich	Clear Yellow Amethyst	Common See note See note

The monument is outlined by stippling. Statistically, except for this stippling and the smaller diameter, it is like the preceding plate, but the imprint is fine and clear and there is little danger of confusing the two. No colored specimens have been reported, but one yellow and two amethyst fragments are among those dug up by Mr. Wynn.

No. 642-A	*Diam.*	*Rim*	*Origin*	*Colors*	*Rarity*
	3½	76 even scallops	Probably Sandwich	Clear	Common

Similar to the preceding plate, but 1/16″ larger. No colors are reported even as fragments, but since the difference between this and the previous plate is in size only, we think it possible that the fragments mentioned above may be this plate.

Monuments with the Drape Pattern on Their Shoulders

No. 643	*Diam.*	*Rim*	*Origin*	*Colors*	*Rarity*
	3 9/16	53 even scallops	Probably Sandwich	Clear Opal	Common Rare

The variety has three lines of inscription, one on the shoulder, two in the center. On this particular plate the shoulder inscription is enclosed by stippled lines, the center inscription by one stippled and two plain lines. Tassels hang from the drapes. There are no stars in the center.

No. 643-A	*Diam.*	*Rim*	*Origin*	*Colors*	*Rarity*
	3⅝	53 even scallops	Probably Sandwich	Clear	Common

Like the preceding plate, but 1/16″ larger.

No. 643-B	*Diam.*	*Rim*	*Origin*	*Colors*	*Rarity*
	3 11/16	53 even scallops	Probably Sandwich	Clear	Uncertain

The diameter is again increased by 1/16″. These larger plates may be true variants or their increase in size may be due to cleaning scale from the base-mold assembly. We lack data on rarity.

No. 644	*Diam.*	*Rim*	*Origin*	*Colors*	*Rarity*
	3⅝	53 even scallops	Probably Sandwich	Clear	Uncertain

According to Mr. Marble, the drapes on this plate are heavier and more prominent than they are on the 643 series. Such a variation is impossible to detect, unless both plates are at hand for direct comparison so, while this plate often appears on want lists and *may* be rare, the chances are that many exist misnumbered.

No. 645	*Diam.*	*Rim*	*Origin*	*Colors*	*Rarity*
	3 7/16	76 even scallops	Probably Sandwich	Clear	Uncertain

Twelve stars have been added in the center. Note, too, the much smaller size and the increase in the number of serrations. Judging by want lists this plate is rare.

No. 645-A	*Diam.*	*Rim*	*Origin*	*Colors*	*Rarity*
	3¾	53 even scallops	Probably Sandwich	Clear	Common
				Emerald-green	Extremely rare
				Amethyst	See note
				Blue	See note

Like No. 645, except for size and serrations. The amethyst and blue specimens exist as fragments only, found in the Wynn excavations at Sandwich.

No. 646	*Diam.*	*Rim*	*Origin*	*Colors*	*Rarity*
	3 11/16	53 even scallops	Probably Sandwich	Clear	Unique

Like No. 645-A, but with no tassels hanging from the drapes. We have not seen this plate, which is reported by Mr. Carapata from a specimen in his collection.

Nos. 647 through 649 are reserved for new discoveries.

Chapter XX

THE EAGLE GROUP

Nos. 650 through 680-E

No. 650	Diam.	Rim	Origin	Colors	Rarity
	3 11/16	Rope, top & bottom	New England, possibly NEG	Opal	Extremely rare
				Pale blue	Extremely rare

Either this plate, or one of the two immediately following, was the first eagle design made and also the first historical. Discussions of precedence are futile, and boil down to whether New England or the Philadelphia area made the first eagle. All available evidence seems to show that pressing in New England, both at NEG and Sandwich, antedated the first pressing in the Philadelphia area, but a good share of this "evidence" is of a sentimental nature. However, the odds are even, and it is quite likely that this particular eagle was the first of its tribe to be made. The attribution is based on strong similarities to such plates as Nos. 77, 78, 79 and 80, and on distribution. The pale blue specimens are accidental colors; they are opals gone wrong. The design of this plate is on top. The back pattern is simply concentric rings. The plate was pressed without a cap-ring, possibly before its invention.

No. 651	Diam.	Rim	Origin	Colors	Rarity
	3¼	Plain	Eastern, Philadelphia area	Clear	Unique

As we have said above, this may be the first of the eagles. But one specimen, Mr. Marble's, is known. It was found in Philadelphia just a few years ago by the late Mrs. N. W. Corson. The attribution is made on the basis of the distribution of this and the following variant, and on their obvious relation to the 99–100 series. This, too, is made without cap-ring.

No. 651-A	*Diam.*	*Rim*	*Origin*	*Colors*	*Rarity*
	3¼	Plain	Eastern, Philadelphia area	Clear	Extremely rare
				Apple-green	Unique

This is the back die of the preceding plate, combined with a top die bearing a so-called hopvine shoulder pattern. Again, the analogy with the 99–100 series is plainly evident. As before, no cap-ring was used. The "apple-green" specimen is in the collection of Mr. Henry F. duPont. We have not seen it and the color description comes to us from Mr. N. C. Gest. Probably this is the light green found in No. 99. The green and all the clear examples we have been able to trace were found in the Philadelphia area.

No. 652 is reserved for a new discovery.

No. 653	*Diam.*	*Rim*	*Origin*	*Colors*	*Rarity*
	3	Plain	Uncertain, probably Midwestern	Clear	Very rare

Note the plain band just outside the laurel wreath surrounding the eagle. The few specimens of this plate we have seen have been cloudy and sick. This brings up the question of attribution, which is discussed under the 435–436 heart series. As is the case with the hearts, distribution is entirely Midwestern, but no plate looks more Philadelphian. The acorn and the high incidence of sickness are typical of early Philadelphia pressings. In this dilemma all we can do is guess.

No. 654	*Diam.*	*Rim*	*Origin*	*Colors*	*Rarity*
	3	Plain	Uncertain, probably Midwestern	Clear	Extremely rare

The plain band found in the previous plate has been filled in here with cross-hatching. All of these E Pluribus Unum eagles were made without a cap-ring. They may antedate its invention, but this is doubtful. This type is not, we believe, usually sick.

No. 654-A	*Diam.*	*Rim*	*Origin*	*Colors*	*Rarity*
	3	Plain, rope on top only	Uncertain, probably Midwestern	Clear Red and green slag	Rare Unique

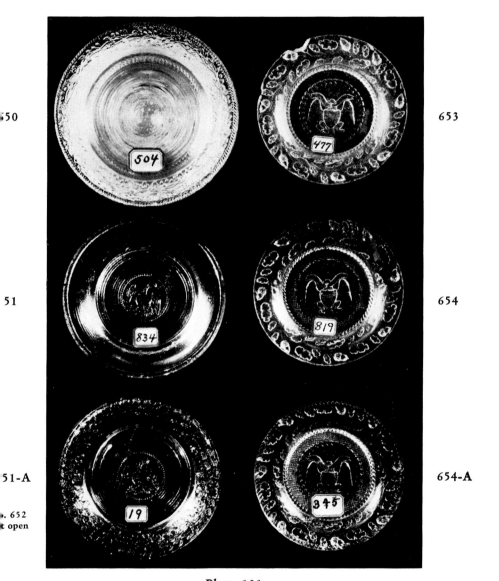

650   653

651   654

651-A   654-A

. 652
t open

Plate 101

655

656-

656

656-

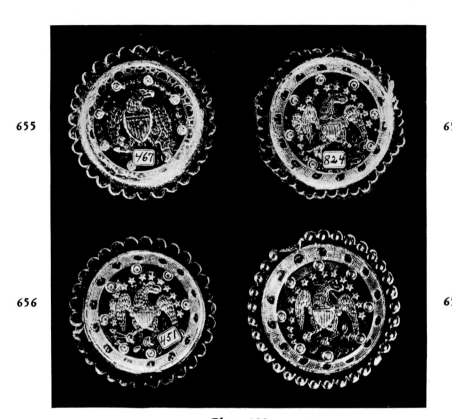

Plate 102

657

658

659

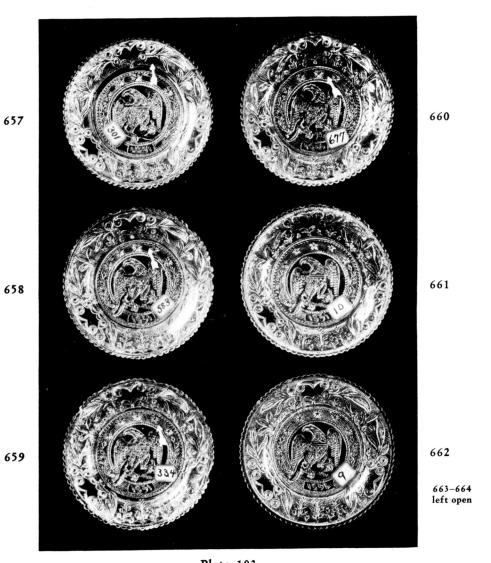

660

661

662

663–664
left open

Plate 103

665

665-A

667

667-A
described
in text

666

666-A

666-B

668

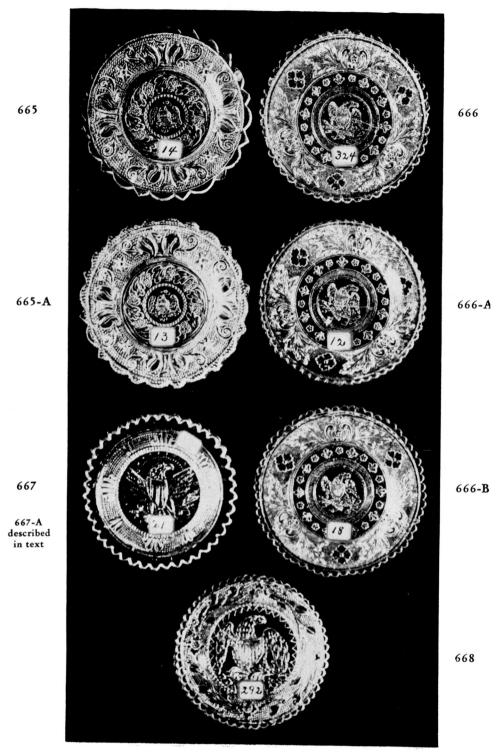

Plate 104

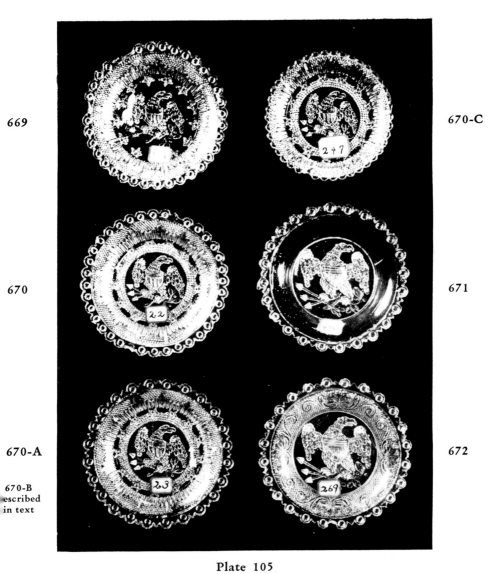

669

670-C

670

671

670-A

670-B
escribed
in text

672

Plate 105

673

676

676-A
described
in text

674

676-B

675

676-C

675-A, B, C
described
in text

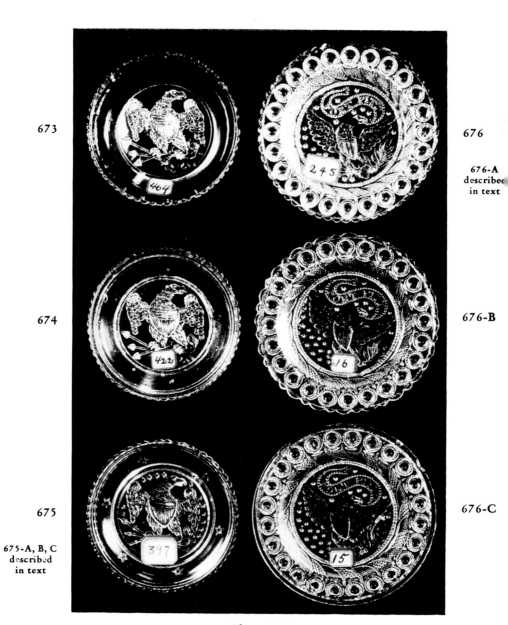

Plate 106

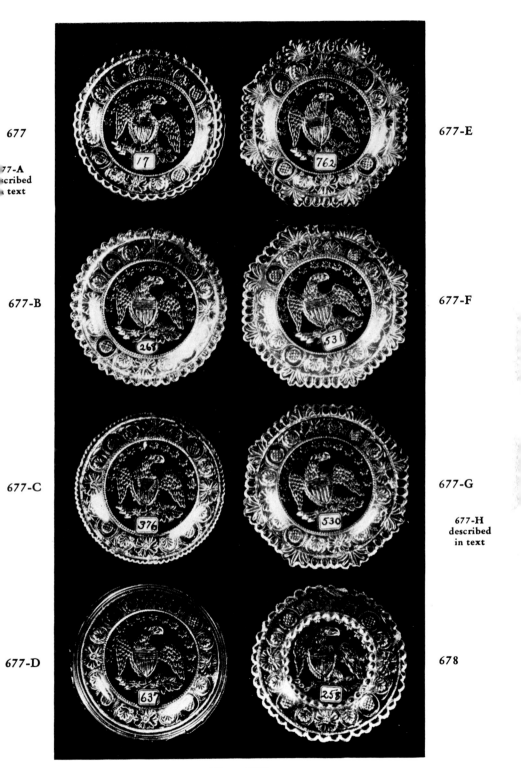

677

677-A
described
in text

677-B

677-C

677-D

677-E

677-F

677-G

677-H
described
in text

678

Plate 107

679

680-D

680

680-A
described
in text

680-E

Nos. 6
throu
684
left o

680-B

680-C
described
in text

Plate 108

Here, again, the band is cross-hatched, as in the preceding plate, but a rope rim has been added to the surface die. This is the variety of this eagle usually found. We have seen no sick specimens and, presumably, this means it is of a slightly later date when the factory had improved its mix. The red and green color description requires clarification. In reflected light the plate is a dull, streaky brown and is hideous to behold. In transmitted light it is a beautiful clear green streaked with ruby-red. Mr. Marble's is the only specimen known. The history of the finding of this plate is interesting. One of the writers remembers, bitterly, the importunities of a central Ohio picker who, for several years, kept telling him of a "red and green" eagle cup plate she knew of "out in the country." Even more bitterly, he now recalls his refusal to go with the picker to see the plate. Subsequently, it was purchased by the Cluffs who sold it to Mr. Harry Garber who, in turn, sold it to the writer who sold it to Mr. Marble.

No. 655	*Diam.*	*Rim*	*Origin*	*Colors*	*Rarity*
	3 1/16	30 even scallops	Midwestern, probably Pittsburgh	Clear	Rare

The shoulder pattern is large portholes separated by pairs of smaller portholes. The plate also has the pimple or lathe center in the exact center of the top. The 15 stars are arranged in an arc following the edge of the center. This plate is obviously from the same factory that made Nos. 120, 121 and 122, and is the Midwest's first attempt at an eagle or, for that matter, at any historical. It was made with a cap-ring and probably dates from about 1830 or a bit earlier.

No. 656	*Diam.*	*Rim*	*Origin*	*Colors*	*Rarity*
	3 1/16	30 even scallops	Midwestern, probably Pittsburgh	Clear	Very rare

Here the shoulder pattern is portholes on a stippled band. There is no turning pimple on top of the plate. The stars are arranged in an arc midway between the eagle and the edge of the center. This is a much more finished design and is a later plate. Whether it was made in the same factory as the preceding plate, we do not know. It is undoubtedly Midwestern.

No. 656-A	*Diam.*	*Rim*	*Origin*	*Colors*	*Rarity*
	2⅞ across	Octagonal	Midwestern, probably Pittsburgh	Clear	Extremely rare

This is like the preceding plate, except for its shape. Only six of these plates are known at this writing. These were a set and were found south of Pittsburgh in 1941 by Mr. Gailey B. Wilson and Mr. H. L. Richardson. Compare with Nos. 122-B and 123-A.

No. 656-B	*Diam.*	*Rim*	*Origin*	*Colors*	*Rarity*
	3	33 bull's eyes	Midwestern, probably Pittsburgh	Clear	Extremely rare

This differs from the preceding plates only in its bull's-eye serration pattern which is the same curious type found on the conventional, No. 190, and on the lyre, No. 690-A. We know of but three specimens of this great rarity, Mr. Douglas Carapata's, which is shown here, Mr. Maurice Mandelbaum's, and Mrs. Palmer Graham's.

No. 657	*Diam.*	*Rim*	*Origin*	*Colors*	*Rarity*
	3½	78 even scallops	Probably Sandwich	Clear	Scarce

The shoulder background and the band around the eagle are both made up of concentric rings. The shoulder directly above the eagle's head is plain, i.e., it has no tiny, leafy sprigs. The date is 1831. Proof examples are hard to find.

No. 658	*Diam.*	*Rim*	*Origin*	*Colors*	*Rarity*
	3½	78 even scallops	Probably Sandwich	Clear Emerald-green	Scarce Extremely rare

The shoulder background and the band around the eagle are still plain concentric rings, but two relatively large tree-like sprigs, flanked by tiny sprigs, have been added at the top just below and at either side of the top blank medallion. Other large and small sprigs have been added to the shoulder pattern at each side, directly above the side medallions. Battered specimens are not hard to find. Proof examples are quite rare.

No. 659	Diam.	Rim	Origin	Colors	Rarity
	3½	78 even scallops	Probably Sandwich	Clear	Rare

A few more sprigs have been added around the inner edge of the shoulder. The band in the center around the eagle has been changed from plain rings to cross-hatching, and the shoulder background at the, so to speak, southeast and southwest has also been changed to cross-hatching.

No. 660	Diam.	Rim	Origin	Colors	Rarity
	3½	78 even scallops	Probably Sandwich	Clear	Scarce

Much like the previous plate, but the cross-hatching on the left shoulder has been carried up beyond the medallion as far as the fleur-de-lis device at the northwest. Proof examples are hard to find.

No. 661	Diam.	Rim	Origin	Colors	Rarity
	3½	79 even scallops	Probably Sandwich	Clear Opal	Plentiful Very rare

The entire shoulder background is now cross-hatched, as is the band around the eagle. This is the variety most often found. Note that this and the following have 1 more serration than the rest of the series.

No. 662	Diam.	Rim	Origin	Colors	Rarity
	3½	79 even scallops	Probably Sandwich	Clear Opal Violet-blue	Plentiful Very rare Very rare

Similar to the preceding plate, but with the date changed to 1832 by the addition of a diagonal line at the base of the "1."

Nos. 663 and 664 are reserved for new discoveries.

No. 665	Diam.	Rim	Origin	Colors	Rarity
	3 7/16	12 large scallops, points between	Eastern, possibly Sandwich or NEG	Clear	Rare

While this and the following plate are related to the 259–260 series (the cap-ring and the domed-shoulder surface die are seemingly identical, and both series have characteristic coarse stippling), this particular type antedates the others, since the stippling has not yet been added to the cap-ring. Mr. Marble lists a pontil-marked specimen under his No. M-833.

No. 665-A	*Diam.*	*Rim*	*Origin*	*Colors*	*Rarity*
	3 7/16	As above, but the scallops have been stippled	Eastern, possibly Sandwich or NEG	Clear Opal	Plentiful Very rare

Differing from the preceding plate only in that its serrations are stippled. See also a larger size, No. 807.

No. 666	*Diam.*	*Rim*	*Origin*	*Colors*	*Rarity*
	3⅜	49 even scallops	Eastern but uncertain	Clear	Plentiful

These eagles are related through a common serration pattern to the 177, 229 and 230 series. For an inconclusive discussion of origin see those series. This 49-serration type is the most frequently found of this eagle group.

No. 666-A	*Diam.*	*Rim*	*Origin*	*Colors*	*Rarity*
	3 5/16	56 even scallops	As above	Clear	Scarce

Similar to the preceding plate, except in diameter and number of serrations.

No. 666-B	*Diam.*	*Rim*	*Origin*	*Colors*	*Rarity*
	3 7/16	12-sided and with 60 scallops	As above	Clear	Scarce

This 12-sided type seems to be the hardest to find of the series and in this respect corresponds to the relative rarities in the analogous conventionals, although the eagles are far more frequently encountered than the conventionals.

No. 667	*Diam.*	*Rim*	*Origin*	*Colors*	*Rarity*
	3⅛	41 even scallops	Probably Midwestern	Clear	Plentiful

These two eagles seem to have the same serrations as those met with on the 281 series and on the sunburst, No. 533, but the shape of the scallops seems to vary slightly and the analogy may not be correct.

No. 667-A	Diam.	Rim	Origin	Colors	Rarity
	3	42 even scallops	Probably Midwestern	Clear	Plentiful

The only difference is in the diameter and the number of serrations. Most specimens of both of these plates are rather cloudy. The glass is not sick but neither is it clear and brilliant.

No. 668	Diam.	Rim	Origin	Colors	Rarity
	3 1/16	56 even scallops	Probably Midwestern	Clear Strong pink tint	Rare Extremely rare

The attribution is made on the basis of distribution which is entirely Midwestern, and on the peculiar pink tint which we have found only on No. 677-A and 159-B, both indubitably of Midwestern origin. On the other hand, the plate has some Eastern characteristics in the crude version of the Eastern so-called nectarine and the sawtooth pattern in the center. Although these two features are unquestionably Eastern in their more refined versions, they are so coarsely interpreted here that we feel they are simply piratings by some unscrupulous Western designer. Apparently, no other plate has this same serration pattern.

No. 669	Diam.	Rim	Origin	Colors	Rarity
	3⅜	36 bull's eyes	Midwestern, probably Pittsburgh	Clear	Extremely rare

Note that, unlike the rest of the series, this has no band of stippling back of the stars. It is extremely rare (we know of but about five specimens) and all examples we have seen are in very bad condition. The series is related to such conventionals as Nos. 134-A, 136-A, etc.

No. 670	Diam.	Rim	Origin	Colors	Rarity
	3 7/16 scant	36 bull's eyes	Midwestern, probably Pittsburgh	Clear	Scarce

A band of stippling has been added as a background to the stars.

Specimens we have measured range from 3⅜″ to 3 7/16″. It is possible that two serration rings were in use and if this can be definitely established, there are two varieties of this plate.

No. 670-A	Diam.	Rim	Origin	Colors	Rarity
	3 7/16	24 bull's eyes with points between	Midwestern, probably Pittsburgh	Clear Blue Medium blue	Plentiful Rare Extremely rare

Like the preceding plate, except for the serration pattern.

No. 670-B	Diam.	Rim	Origin	Colors	Rarity
	3 7/16	24 bull's eyes with points between	Midwestern, probably Pittsburgh	Clear	Uncertain

Like the preceding plate, except that the little domes that form the bull's eyes are larger. This may be due to cleaning and polishing the cap-ring, or it may mean a new cap-ring, there is no way of telling. With so slight a variation, it is impossible to be positive about comparative rarity. At the moment it seems rare.

No. 670-C	Diam.	Rim	Origin	Colors	Rarity
	3	42 even scallops	Midwestern, probably Pittsburgh	Clear	Rare

This has a different type serration and is much smaller than the other members of the series. We have never seen a proof specimen and most of them are badly battered.

No. 671	Diam.	Rim	Origin	Colors	Rarity
	3½	24 bull's eyes with points between	Midwestern, see note	Clear Opal tint Opal Opal opaque Café-au-lait	Very rare Rare Rare Unique Unique

While this bull's eye and point rim closely resembles the serration pattern of the preceding group, it is slightly larger. It may be that this increase in size is due to the cleaning and polishing of accumulated scale from the cap-ring used on the rayed eagles and their companion plates. On the other hand, this and the following eagle are not infrequently found in shades of opal, a color not found in the plates with the smaller cap-ring, and these two eagles reach their greatest density of distribution south of Pittsburgh near Wheeling and extending from there west into central Ohio. Thus, it seems not unlikely that the origin of these two eagles may be Wheeling or, possibly, some unidentified source south of Pittsburgh on the Monongahela River. The opalopaque specimen came from near Barnesville, Ohio, while the badly damaged café-au-lait example came from Mr. J. E. Nevil of Cincinnati, although its exact find-spot is unknown. The café-au-lait is a curious color. It is a semi-opaque brown and is undoubtedly an opal improperly mixed or improperly heat-treated. It is in Mrs. Parker's collection.

No. 672	Diam.	Rim	Origin	Colors	Rarity
	3½	24 bull's eyes with points between	As above	Clear Opal tint Opal	Scarce Rare Rare

Similar to the preceding plate, but with an anthemion and scroll pattern on a stippled ground added to the shoulder. Note the strong resemblance of this shoulder pattern to that on No. 203 and on the large round and octagonal plates shown on Plates 169 and 170 in Lee, *Sandwich Glass,* Northborough, Mass., 1947. This similarity poses a problem, since these other pieces seem to be of Pittsburgh origin. The only solution that occurs to us is that the one pattern is a copy of the other or, more likely, that all are the work of a single independent moldmaker and not from a specific factory.

No. 673	Diam.	Rim	Origin	Colors	Rarity
	3⅛	60 even scallops	As above	Clear	Very rare

This seems to be the same eagle design die with a different serration pattern, minus the shoulder pattern.

No. 674	Diam.	Rim	Origin	Colors	Rarity
	3⅛	60 even scallops	As above	Clear	Scarce

Like the previous plate, but with two rings added to the shoulder just inside the line of serrations. Years ago a blue specimen was rumored but no reliable observer has seen one.

No. 675	*Diam.*	*Rim*	*Origin*	*Colors*	*Rarity*
	3⅛	60 even scallops	As above	Clear	Plentiful

Similar to the preceding plate, but 6 large stars have been added to the shoulder and 13 small stars to the center in an arc over the eagle. Whether or not this is a recutting of the eagle die cannot be determined. Unquestionably, there are slight variations in the eagle's wings, but this does not necessarily denote a new die; it can just as easily result from cleaning and touching up the earlier die.

No. 675-A	*Diam.*	*Rim*	*Origin*	*Colors*	*Rarity*
	3 3/16	60 even scallops	As above	Clear	Plentiful

Like the above plate, but 1/16″ larger.

No. 675-B	*Diam.*	*Rim*	*Origin*	*Colors*	*Rarity*
	3¼	60 even scallops	As above	Clear	Plentiful

The diameter is again increased 1/16″.

No. 675-C	*Diam.*	*Rim*	*Origin*	*Colors*	*Rarity*
	3 5/16	60 even scallops	As above	Clear	Plentiful

This is still another 1/16″ larger.

No. 676	*Diam.*	*Rim*	*Origin*	*Colors*	*Rarity*
	3 11/16	60 even scallops	Curling's Ft. Pitt Glass Works	Clear	Plentiful

Not only do these eagles have the serration patterns of such conventionals as 211, 212, 214, etc., series, but they also have the characteristic flat shoulder of Curling's known plates.

No. 676-A	*Diam.*	*Rim*	*Origin*	*Colors*	*Rarity*
	3⅝	60 even scallops	As above	Clear	Uncertain

This varies from the previous plate in diameter only. We have not seen it, but it has been reported by Mr. Douglas Carapata. There is no way of telling whether it is a true variant or not. It may be slightly out of shape, or it may be due to a cleaning of the mold.

No. 676-B	*Diam.*	*Rim*	*Origin*	*Colors*	*Rarity*
	3 11/16	20 large and 20 small scallops	As above	Clear Blue Amethyst Lavender tint	Plentiful Very rare Unique Scarce

The only difference is in the type of serration. Mr. Marble's amethyst specimen is the only one known. It came, we understand, from Mr. J. E. Nevil who found it in Michigan.

No. 676-C	*Diam.*	*Rim*	*Origin*	*Colors*	*Rarity*
	3 11/16	Plain	As above	Clear	Scarce

Here, the difference is the plain rim without serrations.

No. 677	*Diam.*	*Rim*	*Origin*	*Colors*	*Rarity*
	3⅛	46 even scallops	Midwestern	Clear	Plentiful

The resemblance to the 197 conventional series is evident, although here in the 32-table-rest eagle and the plain rim type we meet two rim varieties so far unknown in the conventional prototypes. In our experience, No. 677 is usually a cleaner and better imprint than its 44-serration variant, No. 677-A, which follows.

No. 677-A	*Diam.*	*Rim*	*Origin*	*Colors*	*Rarity*
	3 3/16 plus	44 even scallops	Midwestern	Clear Blue Strong pink tint	Plentiful Rare Extremely rare

This is a larger plate, nearer to 3¼" in diameter than to 3 3/16" which is the measurement of Mr. Marble's copy, with 2 less serrations. The imprint of the shoulder pattern is usually, if not always, indistinct. We know of but two specimens in the strong pink tint. This peculiar color is much the same as that seen in the so-called Torch, No. 159-B, and in the sawtooth eagle, No. 668.

No. 677-B	*Diam.*	*Rim*	*Origin*	*Colors*	*Rarity*
	3¼	48 egg and dart scallops	Midwestern	Clear	Scarce

This is like the first two members of the series, except for its size and serration pattern. The imprint is usually fairly good. A "milky-white" example has been reported, but has not been seen by any reliable observer. It may or may not exist.

No. 677-C	Diam.	Rim	Origin	Colors	Rarity
	3⅛	98 sawtooth scallops	Midwestern	Clear	Scarce

These tiny serrations (compare with Nos. 197-E and 198) are very vulnerable and proof specimens simply do not exist. The imprint is usually good.

No. 677-D	Diam.	Rim	Origin	Colors	Rarity
	3¼	Plain	Midwestern	Clear	Extremely rare

We can locate only ten specimens of this plate, but undoubtedly others exist in collections unknown to us. This has no counterpart in the 197 conventional series, or at least none has been reported so far.

No. 677-E	Diam.	Rim	Origin	Colors	Rarity
	3 7/16 across	Octagonal	Midwestern	Clear	Extremely rare

Note that each of the eight sides has 4 eggs in its serrations. Not only is this plate of extraordinary rarity but, as in all octagonal plates, proof specimens are nearly unobtainable.

No. 677-F	Diam.	Rim	Origin	Colors	Rarity
	3 7/16 across	Octagonal	Midwestern	Clear	Very rare

Six of the eight sides have 4 eggs in their serrations, but the other two sides, those at the north and northwest, have only 3 eggs. As always in octagonal plates, proof examples are hard to find.

No. 677-G	Diam.	Rim	Origin	Colors	Rarity
	3 7/16 across	Octagonal	Midwestern	Clear	Very rare

Here, the two sides with but 3 eggs each have shifted to the south and southeast. By our definition, this is not a true variant, being no more than a shift of the cap-ring in relation to the design die. It is included to demonstrate that some measure of control was attempted over the relative positions of the various parts of the mold assembly. In other words, the 3-egg sides never appear at the east or west positions. Mr. Marble's example of this plate measures 3⅜″, but those we have checked are 1/16″ larger.

No. 677-H	*Diam.*	*Rim*	*Origin*	*Colors*	*Rarity*
	3⅜ across	Octagonal	Midwestern	Clear	Extremely rare

Like the preceding plate with its 3-egg sides at the south and southeast, but with a different top shape. This is a deeper plate and must be directly compared with the other octagonal plates in this series to be properly identified. Mr. Marble's is the only one we have seen, but others probably exist misnumbered. Specimens should be found with the 3-egg sides at the north-northwest position.

No. 678	*Diam.*	*Rim*	*Origin*	*Colors*	*Rarity*
	3¼	42 even scallops	Midwestern	Clear Cloudy	Very rare See note

Thirty-two feet or table-rests have been cut in the design die around the edge of the center. This plate is, in our experience, always crude and of an inferior metal. Sick, cloudy and even pitted surfaces are the rule. We have never seen a proof example. The cloudiness varies in degree, sometimes approaching a faint pinkish tint. Any collector who holds out for a proof specimen in a brilliant quality of metal is doomed to disappointment. Even badly battered examples are not common.

No. 679	*Diam.*	*Rim*	*Origin*	*Colors*	*Rarity*
	3 7/16	Plain	Uncertain but Eastern	Clear	Plentiful

Here we have the latest of the lacy eagles. Most, if not all, specimens are glassy from flashing, but the rim must have been protected by a kind of muffle, since its edges are always sharp.

No. 680	*Diam.*	*Rim*	*Origin*	*Colors*	*Rarity*
	3	44 even scallops	Probably Midwestern	Clear Blue Bluish-amethyst	Plentiful Very rare Very rare

This, along with its companion plates, is the latest of the eagle designs and probably does not date before the late 1840's. There is a close resemblance to the 191–192 series throughout; thus, it is not impossible that variants with 52 and 53 even serrations will be found. The colors listed above are reasonably deep in tone and should not be confused with the faint blue tints frequently found. The imprint is faint more often than not.

No. 680-A	*Diam.*	*Rim*	*Origin*	*Colors*	*Rarity*
	3	50 even scallops	Probably Midwestern	Clear	Uncertain

Similar to the preceding plate, but with 6 more serrations. This little plate seems scarce or even rare, but it is possible that much of this seeming rarity is due to improper numbering. Unlike the previous plate, the imprint here is usually fairly good.

No. 680-B	*Diam.*	*Rim*	*Origin*	*Colors*	*Rarity*
	3⅛	48 bull's eyes	Probably Midwestern	Clear	Plentiful

Like the preceding plates, except for the 48 bull's-eye serrations.

No. 680-C	*Diam.*	*Rim*	*Origin*	*Colors*	*Rarity*
	3¼	45 bull's eyes	Probably Midwestern	Clear	See note

Mr. Marble's is the only specimen of this plate we can locate, and this extraordinary rarity is partly confirmed by the appearance of this number on the want list of every major collector we have on file. Nevertheless, since this plate is so much like the preceding one (they differ only in the number of bull's eyes), we hesitate to list it as unique.

No. 680-D	*Diam.*	*Rim*	*Origin*	*Colors*	*Rarity*
	3 across	Octagonal	Probably Midwestern	Clear	Plentiful

Note that each of the eight sides has 6 scallops between the slightly larger corner scallops. Blue examples have been reported but have not been seen by any competent observer. They are probably the following plate. While we list this plate as plentiful, proof specimens are hard to find.

No. 680-E	*Diam.*	*Rim*	*Origin*	*Colors*	*Rarity*
	2⅞ across	Octagonal	Probably Midwestern	Clear	Plentiful
				Blue	Rare
				Lavender	Very rare
				Amethyst	Very rare

Here, there are but 5 scallops on each side between the somewhat larger corner scallops. Again, proof or even fair examples are difficult to find, and in the colored specimens extraordinarily so.

Nos. 681 through 684 are reserved for new discoveries.

Chapter XXI

MISCELLANEOUS SEMI-HISTORICAL PLATES

Nos. 685 through 699

No. 685	*Diam.*	*Rim*	*Origin*	*Colors*	*Rarity*
	3⅝	Plain rope	Possibly Midwestern	Clear	Extremely rare

There is a great deal of controversy as to whether or not this is a cup plate. It is deep and has concave shoulders much like a small sauce dish. On the other hand, we know of a family in southeastern Ohio who used a set of these as cup plates. Such use, of course, does not prove that the manufacturer intended them to be cup plates. Whether they are cup plates or not is an open question. The attribution is made on the basis of distribution. The few specimens we can trace have been found in Ohio. The inscription reads "New Patent Steam Coach."

No. 686	*Diam.*	*Rim*	*Origin*	*Colors*	*Rarity*
	3 7/16	24 bull's eyes with points between	Midwestern, probably Pittsburgh	Clear Blue	Rare Extremely rare

The relationship with the Plows, Constitutions, rayed eagles and the many conventionals with similar serration pattern is obvious.

No. 687	*Diam.*	*Rim*	*Origin*	*Colors*	*Rarity*
	3 7/16	24 bull's eyes with points between	Midwestern, probably Pittsburgh	Clear	Extremely rare

Note that this variety has no crossbar between the plow handles; that the single tree is shown in outline or, if by lines, these are very faint and that the foliage in the center above and below the plow is

685

689

686

689-A

687

688
escribed
in text

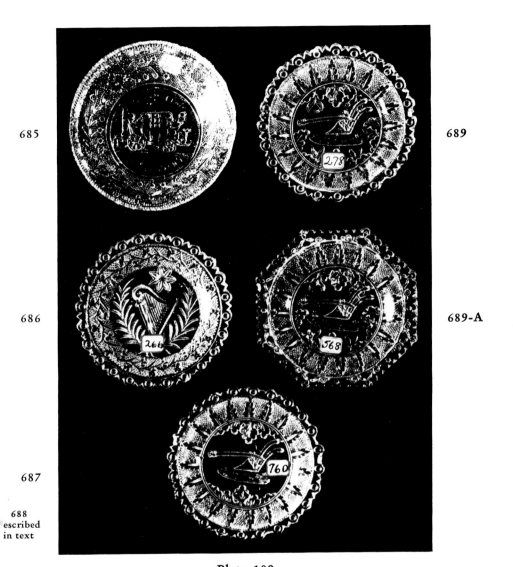

Plate 109

690

690-A
described
in text

691

691-A

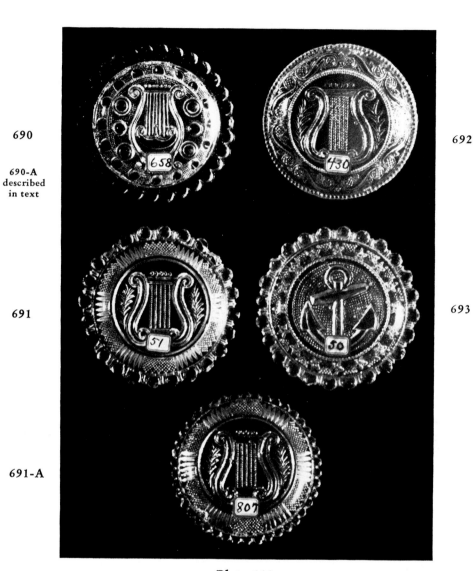

692

693

Plate 110

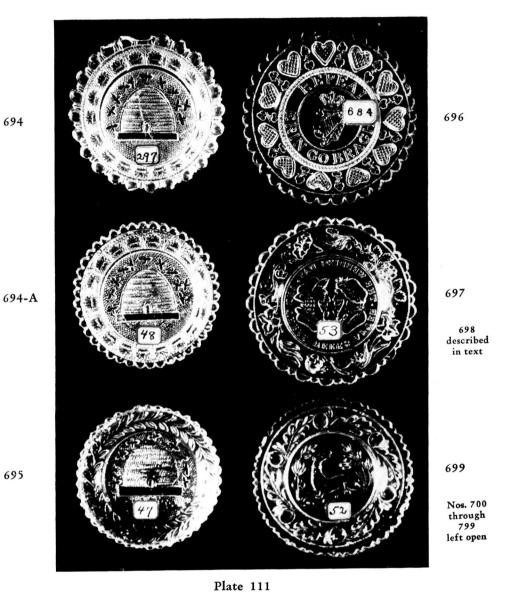

694

694-A

695

696

697

698
described
in text

699

Nos. 700
through
799
left open

Plate 111

composed of rounded-end acanthus leaves. We can locate but three specimens of this great rarity. One of those is badly damaged.

No. 688	*Diam.*	*Rim*	*Origin*	*Colors*	*Rarity*
	3 7/16	24 bull's eyes with points between	Midwestern, probably Pittsburgh	Clear	Unique

We have not seen this variant which is reported by Dr. Grace O. Doane. It is exactly like the previous plate, except that the single tree has lines in it as in the following variety. The chances are that the lines in the single trees of both plates are the same and the apparent difference is only a matter of good or bad imprints.

No. 689	*Diam.*	*Rim*	*Origin*	*Colors*	*Rarity*
	3 7/16	24 bull's eyes with points between	Midwestern, probably Pittsburgh	Clear	Very rare

This is unlike the two previous plates in that there is a crossbar between the plow handles; pointed-leaf foliage has been added to the former acanthus leaves above and below the plow and other leafy forms have been added in front and in back of the plow. This, while distinctly rare, is the variety usually found. We list no colors and none has been confirmed, but years ago, about 1927, a rumor of a blue Plow swept Ohio. Since several of the kindred plates occur in blue, such a thing is possible.

No. 689-A	*Diam.*	*Rim*	*Origin*	*Colors*	*Rarity*
	3½ across	Octagonal	Midwestern, probably Pittsburgh	Clear	Extremely rare

This is like the previous plate, except for its shape. Only six specimens are known. These were from one set divided among two sisters living near Mansfield, Ohio, and were bought in the mid-1920's by Mr. Neil C. Gest and Mr. Joseph Yeager. According to Mr. E. J. Wessen, an ancestor of the owners was at one time superintendent of the Bakewell factory. Such ownership is by no means conclusive evidence of origin, but is worth mentioning in case other information turns up pointing to a Bakewell origin.

| No. 690 | *Diam.*
3 1/16 | *Rim*
30 even
scallops | *Origin*
Midwestern,
probably
Pittsburgh | *Colors*
Clear | *Rarity*
Extremely
rare |

The relationship to the footed eagles and to such conventionals as Nos. 120, 121, etc., is evident. We can locate only eight or nine of these plates, and believe one of these is recorded twice.

| No. 690-A | *Diam.*
3 | *Rim*
33 bull's
eye scallops | *Origin*
Midwestern,
probably
Pittsburgh | *Colors*
Clear | *Rarity*
Unique |

This is exactly like the preceding plate, except that it has the peculiar experimental bull's-eye serrations found only on Nos. 190 and 656-B. We recall only one of these great rarities, the one in Mrs. Palmer Graham's collection, but believe another exists, although we have no idea where it is.

| No. 691 | *Diam.*
3 3/16 | *Rim*
24 large
beads with
reels
between | *Origin*
Probably
Midwestern | *Colors*
Clear | *Rarity*
Scarce |

The relationship with such conventional groups as Nos. 233 and 234, as well as with the anchor and 11-bee beehives which follow, is evident. Really proof examples are almost impossible to find. The average example is about like the illustration.

| No. 691-A | *Diam.*
3 | *Rim*
42 even
scallops | *Origin*
Probably
Midwestern | *Colors*
Clear | *Rarity*
Extremely
rare |

This differs from the preceding plate only in the serration pattern. We can trace but ten of these plates, of which six were in a set that turned up nearly ten years ago in Tennessee. However, beyond any doubt others exist whose importance is not recognized.

| No. 692 | *Diam.*
3 | *Rim*
Plain with
108 dots
on bottom | *Origin*
Probably
Midwestern | *Colors*
Clear | *Rarity*
Scarce |

This is not a variant of the two preceding plates, but is an entirely different and, we think, somewhat later design. The plate is subject to spalling and most of those found are rather rough. Note the relationship to Nos. 155 and 199.

No. 693	*Diam.*	*Rim*	*Origin*	*Colors*	*Rarity*
	3 3/16	24 large beads with reels between	Probably Midwestern	Clear	Scarce

As is the case with all bead and reel rim plates, proof examples are practically impossible to obtain. By analogy with similar series, a 3″, 42 even-scallop variant may be found.

No. 694	*Diam.*	*Rim*	*Origin*	*Colors*	*Rarity*
	3 3/16	24 large beads with reels between	As above	Clear	Rare

This is the rarest of the beehives and the hardest to find in even fair condition.

No. 694-A	*Diam.*	*Rim*	*Origin*	*Colors*	*Rarity*
	3	42 even scallops	Probably Midwestern	Clear	Scarce

The only difference between this and the preceding plate is the serrations. Most examples are found in rather ragged condition.

No. 695	*Diam.*	*Rim*	*Origin*	*Colors*	*Rarity*
	3	42 even scallops	Probably Midwestern	Clear	Plentiful

This is not the same design as the two preceding plates. Here, there are only 9 bees as against the 11 found in the other series, and the shoulder pattern is entirely different. This shoulder pattern, incidentally, is much like that found on the Washingtons. The rarity statement applies only to average specimens; proof examples are hard to find, although this is the most common of the beehives.

No. 696	*Diam.*	*Rim*	*Origin*	*Colors*	*Rarity*
	3½	38 even scallops	Possibly Sandwich	Clear	Extremely rare

The origin of this great rarity is in dispute. Statistically, the serration pattern seems the same as that found on the No. 628 Chancellor Livingston, but these scallops seem to be deeper. If the serrations are the same or even a recutting or polishing of the Chancellor type, the plate was probably made at Sandwich for the Irish market. Another school of thought has it that the plate was pressed in England. In any event it is very rare (we know of but eight or nine examples) and desirable.

No. 697	*Diam.*	*Rim*	*Origin*	*Colors*	*Rarity*
	3 7/16	21 large scallops with small ones between	Probably Sandwich	Clear Green tint Pink tint	Scarce Scarce Scarce

Note that the periods between the two inscriptions are, in this variety, dots or beads. Examples in good condition are difficult to find.

No. 698	*Diam.*	*Rim*	*Origin*	*Colors*	*Rarity*
	3 7/16	21 large scallops with small ones between	As above	Clear	Uncertain

This is similar, but the dots between the inscriptions have tiny rays added to them. This is a new discovery and its rarity cannot now be estimated.

No. 699	*Diam.*	*Rim*	*Origin*	*Colors*	*Rarity*
	3¼	27 scallops, points between	Unknown	Clear Pink tint Yellow	Rare Very rare Unique

There are no clues to the origin of this plate. While it is rare, it seems to turn up in about the same proportion in New England, Pennsylvania and Ohio. Proof specimens are probably not to be found. The only yellow example we know of is in the collection of Mr. Maurice Mandelbaum.

Nos. 700 through 799 are reserved for new discoveries.

Chapter XXII

PONTIL-MARKED PLATES

Plate 112

Once in a great while you will chance upon a plate with a pontil mark on its top. These were not blown, as so many beginners think. They were pressed exactly like their unscarred counterparts, but were then stuck onto a punty rod, preparatory to being attached to the stem of a lamp, candlestick or compote where they served as a foot. And, indeed, all we have seen have been so attached at some time, since they invariably have a spall or fracture on their backs on the opposite side from the pontil mark. Such spalls are due to a part of the plate's adhering to the stem of the lamp or candlestick when it is broken off. Their presence indicates that actual attachment had taken place. The problem then is why and how they were separated.

A few cynics are convinced that dealers stay up nights prying such bases off lamps and sticks. Since a piece with a cup plate base is worth more in today's market than a pontil-marked cup plate, the people who hold this theory must also go on to assume that dealers are feeble-minded, a wholly unwarranted assumption. Occasionally, the base may be pried off a badly damaged lamp, but this cannot happen often enough to account for more than a few of the known plates having pontils.

Now and then, but by no means frequently, a lamp or stick will turn up with its foot so insecurely attached that it snaps off in washing or drying. This accounts for a few more such plates.

In all probability, most such separations took place at the time of manufacture. The technique of exactly centering such a foot, while relatively simple, is not foolproof; when bad centering occurred the logical thing to have done was to crack off the bad base and apply a new foot. The old foot, the old cup plate, could not be re-used because of the spall broken out of its back in removing it. Such doubly scarred plates were not, it seems, used as cullet but were saved and sold, probably as seconds. At least, we can think of no other explanation for such plates turning up in sets.

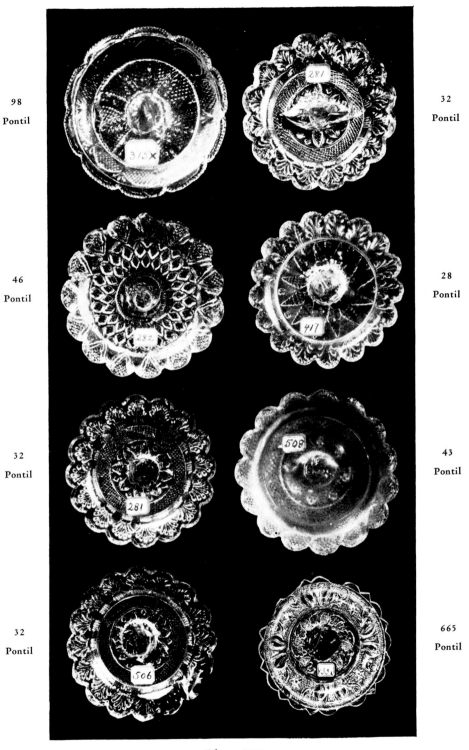

98
Pontil

32
Pontil

46
Pontil

28
Pontil

32
Pontil

43
Pontil

32
Pontil

665
Pontil

Plate 112

One other theory to account for pontil-marked plates deserves mention. Mr. W. D. Quattlebaum suggests that a punty may have been used sometimes to remove a plate that stuck in a mold. This, of course, is quite possible, but it does not account for scars on both surfaces. If, on the other hand, plates exist with a pontil on one side and no scar on the other, it does not necessarily follow that Mr. Quattlebaum's theory is confirmed. In many cases the lamps or candlesticks to which these feet were attached were blown, and blowing and shaping pieces of this nature is a slower operation than pressing the feet. In effect, we have here two production lines, one faster than the other. At the end of a day's run, more cup plate feet could have been made than the various objects to which they were to be attached. If a few such embryo feet had already been attached to punty rods, there would be no lamps or sticks to which to attach them. The result would be plates with pontil marks but no scar on their other sides.

It will be observed that all the plates shown on Plate 112 are of Eastern origin and, with one possible exception, No. 98 pontil, from the New England glassfield. This does not mean that the Midwest did not use cup plates as bases or feet for larger pieces. The Fort Pitt Glass Works made a number of lamps and compotes using one of the 216 series as a foot, but so far no such Midwestern plate has been reported separated from its top. Whether this means that Curling had developed a more secure method of attachment, or was less fussy about centering, no one knows. The former is more likely, since these Midwestern pieces are probably about six to ten years later in date, giving, in this period of rapid technological advance, plenty of time to devise superior methods.

Most of the recorded pontil-marked plates are shown on Plate 112. The notable exceptions are No. 13-C, of which there is a pontil-marked specimen in the collection of Mr. George C. Cannon; No. 16, which usually has a pontil, and No. 50, of which but one unscarred example, that in the Essex Institute, is known. Since any early cup plate with a reasonably flat shoulder could have been used as a foot for other objects, it is almost certain that additional pontil-marked designs will be found.

The question arises as to just which factory in New England made these plates. We know from the Mayhew papers now deposited at the Enoch Pratt Free Library in Baltimore that the New England Glass Company billed their Baltimore agent before 1830 for pieces with cup plate bases. Since the early, heavy plates with both sheaf of wheat and fan shoulder patterns have always been quite generally attributed to The New England Glass Company it is not impossible that this factory made all such plates. Still, it is difficult to believe that they were not also produced at Sandwich.

All pontil-marked plates are rare. Two of those shown on Plate 112 are, so far as we know, unique: Nos. 98-pontil and 665-pontil. No. 43 pontil is the only pontil-marked plate in color that has been brought to our attention. We have not seen this plate but, according to Mr. Marble in whose collection it is, it is "brownish." Blown lamps and candlesticks are rare. It is unlikely that many colored bases for such pieces will be found, although there is a possibility of an occasional use of a foot in a contrasting color which, in this early period, would be likely to be blue or opal or opal-opaque.

Since these plates were pressed in the regular cup plate molds, further details are not necessary. It is well to note that usually a pontil-marked plate is a bit larger than its unscarred prototype, because the plate has been slightly flattened in order to further adapt it to its use as a foot. Having been made in the same molds, such plates, by our rather arbitrary definition, are not variants, but every good collection should have as many of them as possible. Since they are not variants, they are not separately numbered. In correspondence, they should be referred to by their check list number, plus "pontil" or "pontil-marked" or some similar device—thus, "665 pontil."

Chapter XXIII

TODDY PLATES

Nos. 800 through 841

The diameters of Nos. 800 through 804 on Plate 113 are 4¼″ or more, and so fall outside the arbitrarily set limits of cup plates in this book. While they are universally called toddy plates, there is an excellent chance that they were made for and used as cup plates. The argument is that these larger plates provided a receptacle for a spoon and, in fact, the problem of what was done with a spoon when the smaller plates were used has always puzzled us. Left in the cup, it would have invited disaster; put on the tablecloth, it would have left a stain. Even if the bowl of a teaspoon were put onto one of the smaller plates, its handle would have slanted in such a way that drops of whatever beverage was being used might have drained onto the cloth. These larger plates may very well be an attempt to solve this problem. They exist in great variety and should be investigated, classified and recorded. Here we have not even made a beginning.

Of those shown, No. 800 with its bull's-eye rim is extremely rare, but Nos. 800-A through 804 are readily found. The only ones of the group to be found in color are No. 800-A, which turns up occasionally in a reddish puce, and No. 802 which is recorded in both blue and opal. A 77 even-serration variant (with the stippled center) of No. 802 is listed by Mr. Marble under his number, M-846. As a matter of fact, it is not at all unlikely that other variations of all these plates exist.

Nos. 800, 800-A, 801 and 802 are of Midwestern origin, according to distribution as well as style. No definite attribution can be made in the case of either No. 803 or No. 804. These are widely distributed and their peacock-feather shoulder pattern was used both in the West (Curling's Fort Pitt Glass Works) and in the East at Sandwich.

No. 805 has been reserved for a new discovery.

The plates shown on Plate 114 all exceed 4¼″ in diameter and, consequently, are universally considered toddy plates although, as we have

800

800-A

801

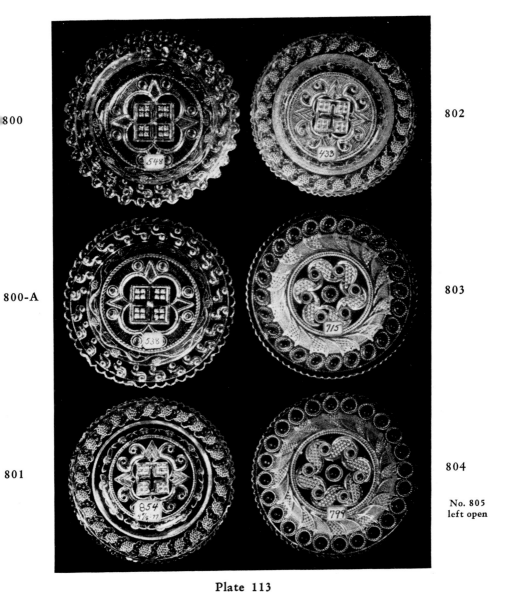

802

803

804

No. 805
left open

Plate 113

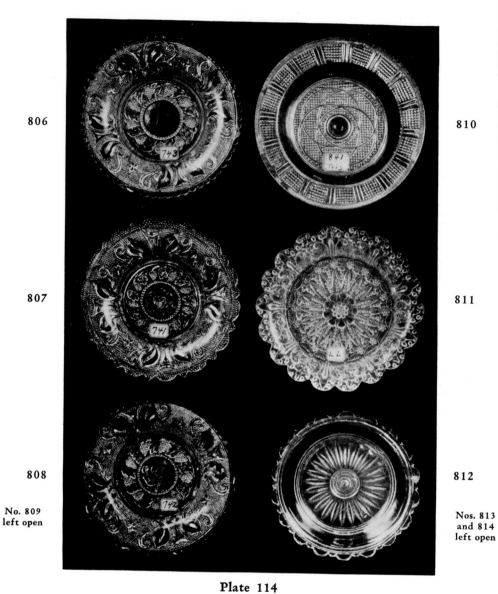

806

810

807

811

808

810

No. 809
left open

811

812

Nos. 813
and 814
left open

Plate 114

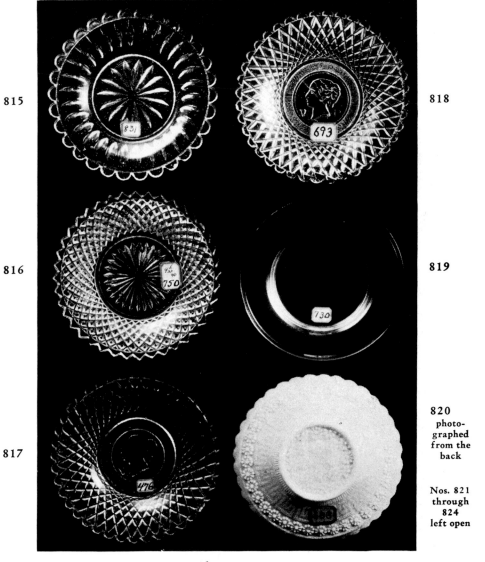

815

818

816

819

817

820
photo-
graphed
from the
back

Nos. 821
through
824
left open

Plate 115

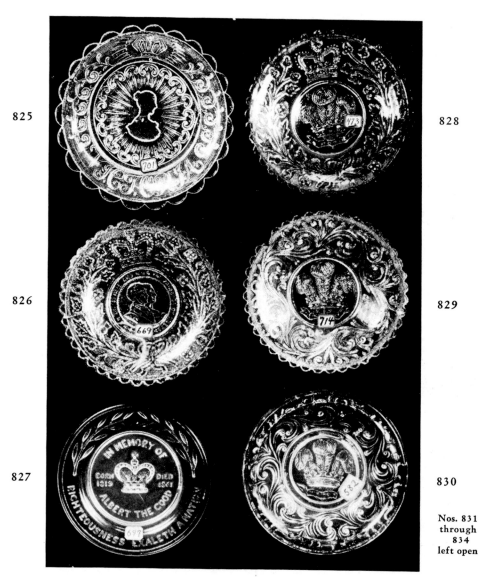

825

828

826

829

827

830

Nos. 831
through
834
left open

Plate 116

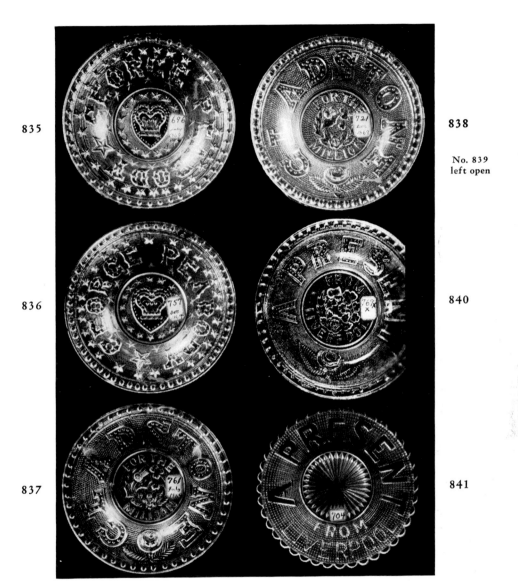

835

836

837

838

No. 839
left open

840

841

Plate 117

said earlier, they may have been manufactured as cup plates for a more exacting clientele, the carriage trade, so to speak. Nos. 806, 807 and 808 are of Eastern, probably New England, origin, in spite of the fact that their shoulder pattern is remarkably like that on the Midwestern Constitution cup plates. Everything—characteristic color range, typical stippling of serrations as well as density of distribution—indicates this.

Of the three, No. 806 is the rarest and No. 808 the commonest. No. 807 is found, very rarely, in a deep blue, while No. 808 occurs not only in this same deep blue but in a curious soft, light blue and, rarely, in a brilliant peacock-blue.

No. 809 has been reserved for a new discovery.

The peculiar No. 810 is a thick, early pressing. It is found, in our experience, mostly in central Pennsylvania, but the plate is so rare that distribution is meaningless so far as attribution is concerned.

No. 811 is equally rare; it turns up a little farther east in the normal distribution range of the early Philadelphia glasshouses, like its matching cup plate, No. 69, and there can be little doubt that it was made somewhere in that area.

No. 812 is no more than a sample of a type of which there are a legion of variants. Some of these are probably quite rare, but the majority are most likely to be common.

Nos. 813 and 814 are reserved for new discoveries.

Plate 115 shows another group of large plates. No. 815 has the initial "D" between two rays of its sunburst. The possible significance of this mark is discussed under No. 818. As with other plates similarly marked, distribution is centered around Philadelphia. No. 815 seems to be quite rare and all those we have seen are underfilled.

Although New England is the distribution range of No. 816, as it is in the case of the related cup plates, Nos. 382 and 383, a foreign origin is not impossible. The pointed serrations have a Belgian look about them. At this relatively late date, however, some New England glass factory, probably Sandwich, may very well have adopted a number of European practices. Blue specimens of No. 816 are known, but are extremely rare.

To the casual glance Nos. 817 and 818 are identical, but closer inspection will show that the profiles are different. Moreover, No. 818, which is much the rarer of the two, has the initial "D" in one of its shoulder diamonds. This is supposed to stand for either Dolflein, a

Philadelphia moldmaker of the mid-XIX century, or Dr. Dyott, the famous Philadelphia glassmaker. While these Victoria Regina toddies are occasionally found as far north as New England, most of them turn up in the Philadelphia-New York region. Proof specimens of either are hard to find.

No. 819 is a blown, clear glass plate with a red rim and is neither a cup plate nor a toddy plate. According to Mr. L. W. Wheelock, a set of six of these with matching bowls in the form of hats turned up in New England a few years ago, but were quickly divorced and the plates and hats were sold separately. They may be European.

No. 820 belongs in the pattern glass period and is, therefore, too late to have been a cup plate, regardless of its size. No clear glass specimens have been reported, but opaque-white and opaque-turquoise-blue examples are not uncommon. Clear, not opaque, medium blue and light amethyst specimens are much rarer.

Nos. 821 through 824 are reserved for new discoveries.

Nos. 825 through 830 on Plate 116 appear to be English pressings, although it is not impossible that the Prince of Wales feather plates were made at Sandwich. The Victoria and Albert toddy is seemingly very rare, as is the No. 825 Victoria. Both plates, nevertheless, may be much more common in England, so that it would be unwise to pay high prices for either.

The amusing misspellings in No. 827 add a great deal to the demand for this plate, which is late and otherwise unattractive. Without these errors, it would be practically worthless; with them, it is a favorite of many collectors.

Of the three Prince of Wales plume plates, No. 828 is the one most often seen and No. 829 the rarest. No. 830 has a curious variant, not shown here, in which there seems to have been some repair to the cap-ring. Mr. Richard H. Wood discovered this variant, the only one we can locate, which is now in the collection of Dr. Grace O. Doane.

No. 828 is the only one of the group of which we have record in color. It occurs, very rarely, in a lovely deep blue.

Nos. 831 through 834 are reserved for new discoveries.

The six large plates shown on Plate 117 are all of English origin and were made at too late a date to be of interest to serious collectors. Many of them have English registry marks on their top surfaces, usually either July or December, 1869. The George Peabody plates are readily available in this country and must be common in England. The Gladstone plates are not seen as frequently here, but the chances are that England is full of them. There is an interesting and rather American-looking variant of these "For the Million" plates with lyres and thistles on its shoulder (not illustrated), but this, too, is late and relatively common.

No. 839 has been reserved for a new discovery.

Chapter XXIV

CAMEO SULPHIDE BUSTS

Plate 118

The cameo busts or "glassed in pastes" shown on Plate 118 were probably never used as cup plates. All we have seen have had holes drilled through the shoulders so that they could be hung on the wall as plaques. For some reason not now clear, this drilling was a difficult operation. The hole was bored from the back of the plate and, as the drill neared the surface, spalls were knocked off the top. When these spalls were small, a shallow channel cut across the surface of the shoulder served to remove them. More often, the spalling was extensive and the whole surface of the plate had to be ground and polished.

The manufacture of these plates must have been a complicated and relatively expensive process. The silvery-white busts were made of a ceramic material having the same coefficient of expansion as glass. Otherwise, unequal expansion or contraction would have cracked either the glass casing or the bust. How the busts were centered in the plates is a puzzle; although, as you see in the illustration, some latitude was permissible in this respect.

The prevailing opinion based on subject matter and distribution is that all of these plates are French, but this does not account for the fact that the No. 842 type appears to have been made in the same mold that was used in pressing No. 54. Uncut specimens of No. 842 carry a row of dots on the top of the shoulder that is remarkably like that on No. 54. If precision methods show that both of these plates were pressed in the same mold, the theory of a French origin for all the cameo plates will be considerably weakened, but not necessarily invalidated. In anticipation of such proof, it has been suggested that a French moldmaker pirated a New England design or, conversely, that a New England moldmaker stole the pattern from the French. Neither seems very likely. France had competent designers and they would hardly have been tempted to copy so crude a plate as No. 54. As No. 54 seems to have been made in New England before 1830, it antedates any period we can

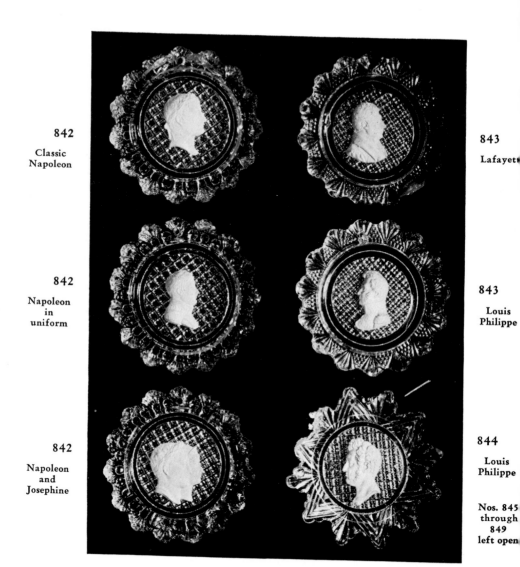

842

Classic
Napoleon

843

Lafayett

842

Napoleon
in
uniform

843

Louis
Philippe

842

Napoleon
and
Josephine

844

Louis
Philippe

Nos. 845
through
849
left open

Plate 118

assign to No. 842 on historical grounds. Those with Napoleon or Napoleon and Josephine could have been made at any time after the invention of pressing, but the Lafayette centers were probably brought out at the time of his death in 1834. Louis Philippe is shown as both a young and an old man. The more youthful version seems likely to have been made about 1830 when he was proclaimed "The Citizen King," while the elderly bust seems to have been pressed at about the time he abdicated in 1848. Thus, 1830 seems to be the earliest possible date for the cameos, while all the evidence is that No. 54 was made in New England several years earlier than this.

If the comparison microscope shows that both plates were made in the same mold, all this discussion is beside the point. In that event, only two explanations fit the case: the No. 842 type was pressed in New England for the French market or some French glass manufacturer bought the No. 54 mold and took it back to France. The second of these seems to fit the evidence better.

Nos. 843 and 844 have no American counterparts, so there is no doubt of their foreign origin. It is almost certain that one or perhaps all of the three basic pressings will be found some day encasing busts of Washington and Franklin. Of the busts known at present, Lafayette is considered the most desirable because of his connection with American history and Louis Philippe the least desirable, due to American indifference to the European political scene.

Since these plates are not cup plates, they do not, strictly speaking, belong in a cup plate collection. Their great beauty, however, appeals to most collectors, and they are the most desirable of foreign pressings. In correspondence, they should be listed by the number of the casing followed by the name of the subject—thus, No. 842 Lafayette or No. 843 Louis Philippe.

Nos. 845 to 850 are reserved for new discoveries.

Chapter XXV

EUROPEAN PLATES

Nos. 850 through 882

Plate 119 shows a group of European pressings. They are of cup plate size, and the earlier examples may have been so used. In fact, judging by the frequency with which the rinceau shoulder type turns up in this country, they may have been made for the American market. Until very recently, these were generally attributed to France (Baccarat) or Belgium (Val St. Lambert), but there is inconclusive evidence that Sandwich may have pirated the engine-turned center and the rinceau shoulder pattern. Fragments of No. 853 were dug up at Sandwich by Mr. Francis Wynn. Fragments found on a factory site are not an infallible guide to origin. Every progressive factory, then as now, had on hand samples of competitors' wares and every factory bought cullet. Moreover, no authenticated American plate has the curious serration pattern seen on No. 857. Checking the serration patterns of Nos. 850, 851, 852 and 853, we find only one other plate with a similar serration pattern. This turns out to be No. 347, which is itself under suspicion of being foreign. So, while it is not impossible that Sandwich made this pattern, no one can say just which of the many serration variants is American.

It has been established by Mildred Pike, writing in the January, 1939 issue of *The Magazine Antiques* that identical as well as related designs appear in the Val Saint Lambert catalogue as early as 1829 and continue as late as the 1913 catalogue. For all we know, these plates and their variants are still being made in Belgium. To avoid these recently manufactured examples, collectors should limit their purchases to specimens that ring, and should avoid glassy-looking, fire-polished examples. This is not an infallible method of determining relative antiquity but it will serve, since the prices of these plates are low and mistakes are not too painful.

Keeping these restrictions in mind, every collector should have a few

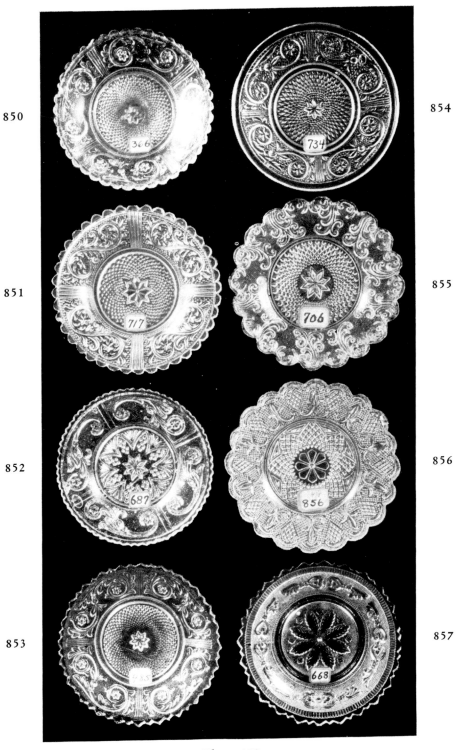

850

854

851

855

852

856

853

857

Plate 119

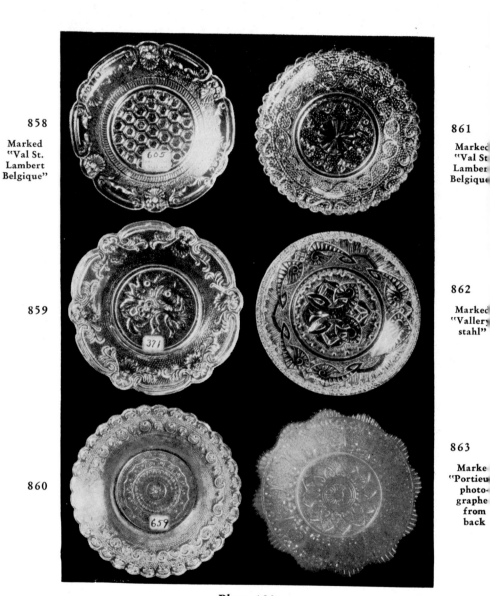

858

Marked
"Val St.
Lambert
Belgique"

859

860

861

Marked
"Val St
Lamber
Belgique

862

Marked
"Vallery
stahl"

863

Marke
"Portieu
photo-
graphe
from
back

Plate 120

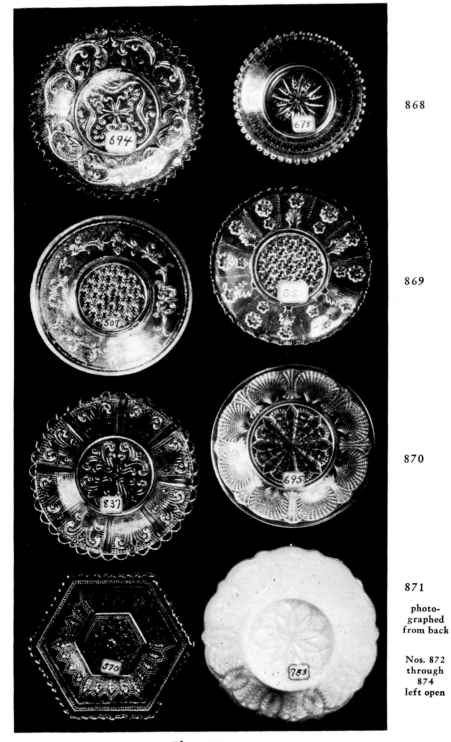

864

868

865

869

866

870

867

871

photo-
graphed
from back

Nos. 872
through
874
left open

Plate 121

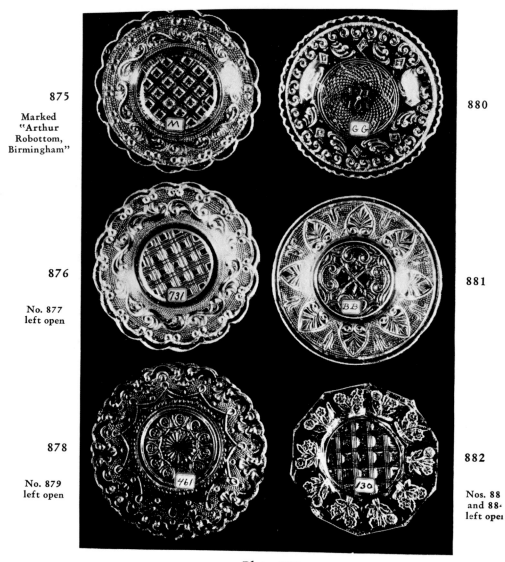

875

Marked
"Arthur
Robottom,
Birmingham"

876

No. 877
left open

878

No. 879
left open

880

881

882

Nos. 88
and 88.
left ope:

Plate 122

representative examples of these plates for study and for comparison with American designs and techniques.

Another group of European plates is shown on Plate 120. Nos. 858 and 861 are marked "Val St. Lambert Belgique" on their top centers. For similar unmarked variants of No. 861, see Nos. 299 and 300 in the check list. These may be Sandwich piratings of the European patterns, but they are far more likely to be European variants pressed with a top die lacking the inscription. Nor was Val Saint Lambert the only European factory to mark its cup plates. Others illustrated here are marked "Portieux" (No. 863) and "Vallerystahl" (No. 862). We do not know the location of the Portieux factory but assume it was in either France or Belgium. Vallerystahl was a glassworks in the Vosges Mountains.

The chief reason for having a few of these European plates in a collection is to become familiar with their characteristics, so that the collector will not become unduly excited when he comes across an unlisted design from one of these sources. An American plate in an unrecorded pattern is a great prize, but a European plate whose comparative rarity cannot be guessed is another matter. We have no objection to collecting foreign plates. In fact, we feel a specialized collection of them would be interesting and most informative. However, until England and the Continent have been thoroughly combed and until valid standards of comparative desirability and rarity are demonstrated, great care should be exercised in buying such plates.

Plate 121 shows more plates of European origin. No. 864 was found in Pittsburgh about fifteen years ago by Mr. John Ramsay and is the only specimen of this particular plate that has come to our attention. It has a very glassy surface and, judging by the rather pointed serrations, may be Belgian.

No. 865 turns up most frequently in French Canada, but is by no means uncommon south of the border. Blue, as well as yellow-green, examples are known but seem to be quite rare. The exact origin is unknown but may be England, France or Belgium.

No. 866 is another plate that is usually found in Canada. It seems to be rarer than No. 865 and is recorded only in clear glass. The serration pattern is a curious one, with blocks of 4 large scallops separated by a single small serration. This is the exact reverse of American practice. Nothing is known concerning the origin of this plate.

Mr. Marble's copy of No. 867 is the only one of which we have any record. Its hexagonal center may indicate that it was never used as a cup plate. Neither design nor technique gives any clue to its origin.

No. 868 is a small, late plate, found not infrequently in shops that handle European goods. We have seen it in blue, as well as in a peculiar milky-opal. There is a similar plate, not shown here, with a bull's-eye rim that looks, and may be, of identical origin. This variant is usually found in blue.

No. 869's distribution is densest in Canada. It closely resembles No. 865 and was probably made in the same factory. Several rim varieties are known. No colored examples have been recorded, but they probably exist.

No. 870 which is in Mr. Marble's collection may be unique. It is a very late plate and is unlikely to have been made as a cup plate.

We know nothing whatsoever about No. 871, which is also in Mr. Marble's collection. It is decidedly not American in appearance but, on the other hand, neither does it have stylistic affinities with any European plate with which we are familiar.

Nos. 872 through 874 are reserved for new discoveries.

The waffle center and scroll border plates on Plate 122 are English. One of them, No. 875 is inscribed "Arthur Rowbottom, Birmingham" on its table-ring. It is not known whether Rowbottom was a glass manufacturer or simply a dealer.

The other waffle-center plate, No. 882, is the subject of some controversy. According to Mr. Marble, it is of Scandinavian origin. Others insist it is English. Mr. Marble lists a larger variety, 4 3/16″ in diameter, which is quite common, but the 3 9/16″ type shown here is, in our experience, very rare. Both sizes are usually highly fire-polished and very glassy looking. Most of those we have traced have come in from Canada.

The rest of the plates on Plate 121 are probably French or Belgian, except for No. 881 about which nothing is known beyond the fact that it is late and unimportant. It is sometimes seen in a soft, medium blue.

Nos. 877, 879, 883 and 884 are reserved for new discoveries.

Chapter XXVI

MISCELLANEOUS LATE PLATES

Nos. 885 through 898

With the possible exception of Nos. 886 and 888, the plates shown on Plate 123 are American—but are not cup plates. No. 885 was made for use as a sauce dish, as is the case with No. 887. No. 889 is the saucer for a cup. Cups, of course, are more easily broken than saucers so that usually only the base is found. Nos. 890, 891 and 892 are, in our opinion, too late to have been intended for use as cup plates, but they may have been used as such by those who persisted in drinking from their saucers long after glass manufacturers had discontinued making cup plates. No. 890 occurs in 3½″ and 4½″ sizes and in a wide range of blues, ambers and opaque-whites. No. 891 is usually found in clear glass, but a puce specimen is known. This is the "Loop and Dart with round ornament" known to collectors of American pattern glass. It is illustrated in Mrs. Lee's *Early American Pressed Glass*. The design was made in complete sets of tableware by the Portland Glass Company, who were in business from 1863 to 1873. This plate was very likely intended as a butter chip. The same holds true for No. 892. It is also shown in Mrs. Lee's book. While the pattern was produced in several items in tableware, it was not carried on into complete sets. No. 892 belongs to the Pittsburgh area.

Both Nos. 886 and 888 have a vaguely European look about them, but it is not impossible that they are American. In any event they are not cup plates.

Nos. 893 and 894 are still later and are so-called "butter chips" or "butter pats." No. 895 and a closely similar variant which we do not illustrate are the bases to covered butter dishes from toy sets. No. 896 is also a child's toy. It has several variants and is often found in the bright colors of late pressed glass. No. 897 also seems to be a toy and is probably Bohemian glass of the mid- or late XIXth century. It is clear glass flashed with ruby. Mr. Marble's specimen is the only one we have seen. No. 898 is the stand for a mustard pot. All we have seen are either opaque-white or opaque light blue.

401

885

886

887

888

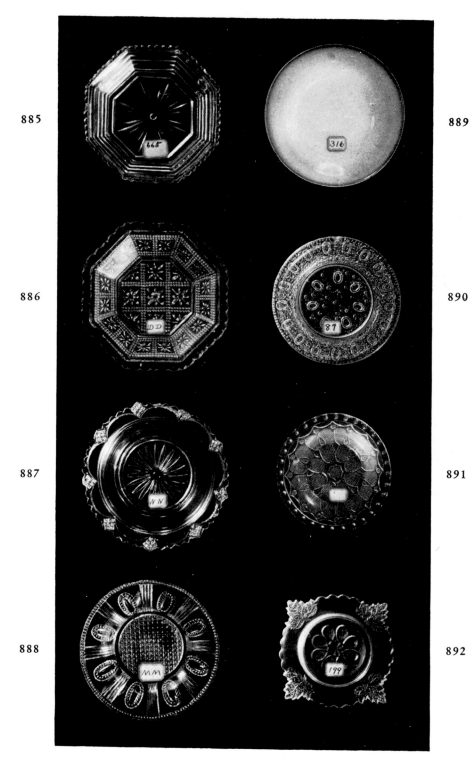

889

890

891

892

Plate 123

893

896

894

897

895

898

Plate 124

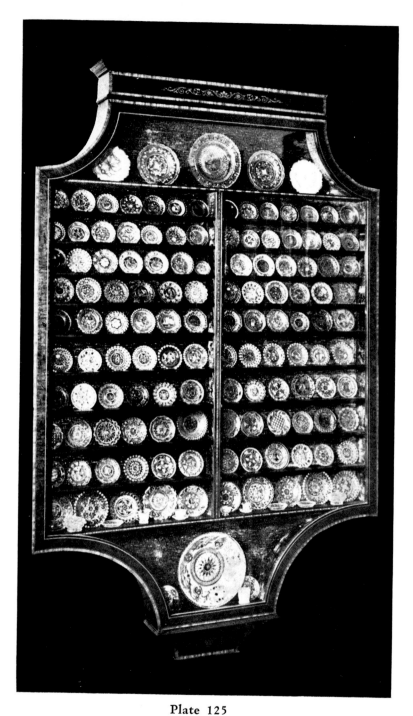

Plate 125

Interesting manner of displaying a part of his collection in a wall
case was devised by Mr. Paul Carson, the owner.

Chapter XXVII

CURIOSITIES

Plate 126

Every now and again, collectors or dealers may come across a curiosity, in the form of a cup plate, made in either iron or pottery. When found in iron, the quick conclusion on the part of a few has been that it is an original mold. Nothing could be further from the truth, since not a single old mold for a cup plate is known to exist. More direct testimony to this fact is given in the concluding paragraphs in the chapter dealing with reproductions. The iron Log Cabin cup plate shown on Plate 126 is purely a curiosity, and bears not the slightest resemblance to a mold used for pressing these little plates.

The iron Log Cabin plate has the pattern on the back only. What apparently happened was that a foundryman took a cup plate of his wife's, or perhaps his great-grandmother's, to his foundry and made a sand mold. The authors are not too confident about details of pottery technique, but in casting iron plates the sand mold was essential. The result was iron plates which are scarce enough today to be highly valued by collectors, even though there is apparently not one iota of information available as to their age. The iron Log Cabin plate is owned by Mr. Marble. Mr. George C. Cannon has an iron so-called Cadmus (Constitution) which is one of a set found some years ago. The latter plate carries the design *both* on the front and back. Whoever made it went to extraordinary pains.

Also illustrated is a dated 1831 eagle cup plate in pottery. It was made from yellow clay with a brown glaze, possibly of the so-called Rockingham type, on the top. The back was left unglazed. Instead of a sand mold, it is not inconceivable in this case that the plate itself was used, without need of an intervening mold. Suffice to say the pottery examples are interesting and an addition to any collection.

Besides the iron and the pottery cup plates, a peacock-feather bowl, copied from a lacy Sandwich design, has been found and is now owned

Plate 126

Curiosity in form of log cabin cup plate made from iron, pattern
appearing on back only. Enlarged for detail. Lacy Peacock
Feather dish is pottery. 1831 Eagle cup plate is also pottery.

by Mr. Cannon. It is of red clay with a Rockingham glaze all over, front and back.

These curiosities were not confined to cup plates and a lacy dish, for in Mrs. Lee's collection is a pottery salt copied from the early New England Glass Company's well-known rectangular salt, having the basket of flowers on the side panels and a single flower on each end. This salt is in a combination of gray and blue glaze, glazed inside and out.

Collectors would do well to add these interesting pieces to their collections, when it is possible to find them.

Chapter XXVIII

REPRODUCTION AND SOUVENIR PLATES

Plates 127, 128, 129, 130 and 131

Reproductions in cup plates cannot be considered a serious threat to collectors today, because there are so few of them. Exactly ten have been produced in this country up to 1948. It is a simple enough matter to detect the new ones, because there is no ring to the glass. Of course one must know how to go about testing them. By holding the cup plates securely in the center with the thumb on one side and the fore-finger on the other, with no other part of the hand touching the glass, it is easy to tap it with a pencil or any metallic object and listen for the telltale sound. In the case of most old plates, there is a clear resounding ring. From the new plates, one hears a flat, deadened thud. While there are some old cup plates that were made from window or bottle glass and therefore do not have a bell tone, it so happens that any of the plates which have been copied so far *do* ring in the originals. The great harm reproductions do to new collectors is to make them suspicious of every plate. Many good pieces are rejected which really are authentic, thereby nipping in the bud more than one promising collector.

The first fake to come on the market was the Henry Clay facing to the left with a star under the bust. It appeared along about 1922 or 1923. Aside from the fact it does not ring, there are minor differences in the design. The lettering is smaller with plain ends of letters. The scrolls in the center and all border designs are lighter and skimpy. The lettering of "Henry" is too small and the "Clay" large. This plate was a copy of our No. 565-B. It was made in blue, as well as clear glass.

The next reproduction of a Henry Clay appeared in recent years and attempts to copy our No. 564. The chief differences are in the plain ends of the letters, which are bereft of serifs. The bust is that of a boy with a receding chin, small nose and high rounding forehead. This plate appeared in pink and in clear glass.

For some strange reason, the Henry Clay was again chosen as a plate

408

Plate 127

Four reproduction cup plates. Enlarged for detail.

Plate 128

Four reproduction cup plates. Enlarged for detail.

Plate 129

Three reproduction cup plates. Enlarged for detail.

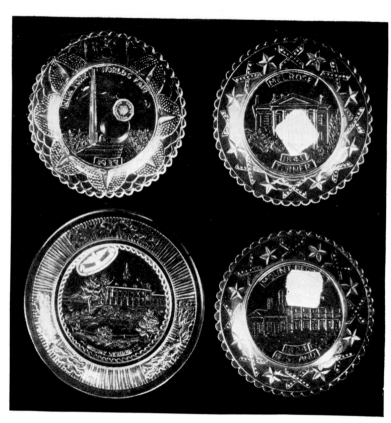

Plate 130

Four modern souvenir cup plates.

Plate 131

Two modern Washington souvenir cup plates. Open-edge dish at left is modern and not a true cup plate. Odd plate at lower right is old but has serrated edge ground off.

to copy in France, apparently for export to this country. One may be seen in Plate 127 with the paper label "Made in France" prominently displayed. It was produced in several colors, including light blue, pink and a deep salmon shade. Should the paper label be removed, this plate is still easy to detect aside from its non-ringing quality. There are many discrepancies in the design. The head is shaped differently from that in any of our old ones, having a more prominent forehead. The lettering is smaller, the star under the bust is smaller and the dots surrounding the bust are very light. The shields in the border are noticeably much too shallow. The serrations on the edge are large and even. Old serrations are never absolutely even. The same serration error may also be noted in the copy of No. 565-B on Plate 127.

Along about 1923 the first reproduction of the ship Benjamin Franklin appeared. It was made at this time in sapphire blue and in clear glass. There are a number of discrepancies in the design but, even so, the workmanship is better than in the more recent copies.

The older fraud (Plate 128) shows slight waves under the boat, whereas they are heavy on the original plate. The bell is entirely different in the new, and the cable cord surrounding the center is heavier. There are minor discrepancies in the design, such as: the plain ends of the letters, that is, no serif; and no walking beam over the paddle wheel. Some of the details in the old are missing in the new.

Some seven or eight years later, another copy of the ship Benjamin Franklin was produced by the Westmoreland Glass Company. Their product may also be seen on Plate 128, adorned with their company paper label. In the old plate the stippling has a silvery sheen, while there is no lustre to the new. The rope rigging appears to be rope in the original, but is hardly more than a rippled line on the new. The same evenness of the scalloped edge is apparent. As stated before, these are never exactly even on the old. The lettering is better on the Westmoreland copy than in the earlier (1923) version.

The first of the epidemic of new cup plates made during the early 1930's was a copy of the Butterfly, pictured on Plate 128. It was made by a Midwestern factory on order for a private party in central New York State, who paid fifty dollars for the mold. The whole country was flooded with them in clear glass and in colors. Many were sold in gift shops for thirty-five to fifty cents each.

We are not certain that the next series of six plates was made to special order. It is more likely that the factory, seeing how quickly the Butterflies flew into antique shops, decided to make a few other varieties on their own. At any rate, the Bunker Hill, Thirteen Hearts, the Henry Clay with star under the bust, dated 1831 Eagle, and the Before and After Marriage, as well as the Benjamin Franklin previously described, all appeared in rapid succession. A Butterfly plate in a toddy size, which was never made originally, appeared in gift shops at this period.

The Butterfly reproduction has the usual discrepancies in workmanship. In the new, the stems of the two leaves on each sprig are almost directly opposite each other and each flower has 6 petals. On the old, the stems of the leaves are at least $\frac{1}{8}''$ apart and one flower has 7 petals. The stippling in the background is too coarse and mechanical. Arrows point to errors in the design on Plate 128.

The copy of the Thirteen Hearts plate is the most obviously new of any of the reproductions. The smaller, more pointed hearts in the border are so widely separated as to resemble the 12-heart cup plate. It rests on a plain rim instead of a rope rim. Apparently two molds have been made because the stippling in the earlier one is finer. One is shown on Plate 128.

Of all the fakes, the dated 1831 Eagle, shown on Plate 129, is by far the best. The non-ringing quality of the glass is a quick, sure test of the reproduction. The old dated Eagles have 78 or 79 serrations. The new has 79. There are noticeable small differences in minor details of the border. Also, in the new the upper portion of the Eagle's legs appear in heavier outline and they are slightly larger. The chief difference between the old and the new dated Eagle plate is in the clarity of the design. The old one was done by a moldmaker whose work shows more care and precision. The result was a finished product showing sharpness of detail. So far the copies have appeared only in clear glass.

Copies of the Bunker Hill cup plate have been widely distributed via gift shops and department stores. The arrows on the illustration of the copy point to numerous means of identifying the fake. The serrations on the border are too even. They are never so exactly regular in the originals. The tassels at the ends of each drape are missing. The lettering is plain, without serifs, and is noticeably much too large. The monument adorning the center of the plate is much taller and bigger in the new and the bricks in the monument are larger. So far this reproduction has only appeared in clear glass. It is shown on Plate 129.

The Before and After Marriage cup plate is an amusing subject so the manufacturers of the copy undoubtedly figured it would have a wide sale. Collectors of cup plates who take their hobby seriously develop a practiced eye for small details, so when the new plates appear in antique shops, they are not easily deceived. The old plate is 3½" in diameter, while the new is 3⅜". The fake has dots in between the lettering, while the old has dots or stars. (Plate 129.) This reproduction is a copy of our No. 698.

In the case of the old Valentine cup plate, the stippling is heavier and more evenly distributed than on the new. The original is heavier and, of course, has a good, clear ring when tapped. The new Valentine has a thinner stippling, which is thicker and heavier in some spots than in others. The design does not have the same depth or brilliance. Then, too, the old plate is a trifle smaller than the new. The reproduction is shown on Plate 127.

Confusing to new collectors is a series of commemorative plates which has historical significance but is strictly modern. Four of these plates are shown on Plate 130 and two others on Plate 131.

In the upper left on Plate 130 is a "New York World's Fair" souvenir which is so marked and dated 1939. The center design in the base pictures the sphere and trylon, familiar to all those who attended the Fair. Probably all this series of plates was planned to serve a double purpose—a souvenir to take home which was readily adaptable to use as an ash tray.

The cup plate in the upper right of Plate 130 is marked and dated, "Melrose—1845—Turner." It has been said that these were souvenirs sold at a Garden Festival in Natchez, Miss.

Beneath the plate just described, in the lower right-hand corner, is a similar one showing a building in the center and marked "Mount Repose —1824—Bisland."

At the lower left is a modern plate which may be another from a World's Fair series. It carries a paper label inscribed, "Historical America." In the center is a view of Mount Vernon, marked accordingly. The border is ribbed and carries a design of acorns and oak leaves.

Not illustrated is another souvenir plate of the Golden Gate World's Fair in California.

Confusing to new collectors are two Washington cup plates which are not reproductions but purely commemorative pieces. These are both shown on Plate 131. It will be noted that one is marked "G. Washington, 1732–1799" and the other is marked "G. Washington, 1732–1932." Obviously, one carries the dates of his birth and death, and the other honors the two-hundredth anniversary of the birth of the Father of Our Country. It is thought that these were also a World's Fair souvenir.

In the lower row of Plate 131 at the right is a cup plate with the scalloped edge ground smooth. Some unsuspecting collector might well come across such a plate, always found with a serrated edge, and feel he had found an unknown variant. It is always well to scrutinize such an oddity with care.

In the lower left of Plate 131 is a little, open chain-bordered 3¼″ item which is not a true cup plate, though some have been added to collections as such. It is not a reproduction of an old piece because it is modern. It is simply not a cup plate.

Some of the fakes often have artificial age marks added, such as the chip on the Henry Clay on Plate 127. Besides the many distinguishing characteristics of old and new, as noted, remember that the quality of the glass tells the story. At least it does on the ten copied to date in this country, for any of the originals should have an unmistakable ring to the glass.

In particular, collectors and dealers should not be discouraged by reading advertisements stating that cup plates are being made from original molds. The following appeared in *The Boston Herald* one bright morning in 1947, accompanied by a photograph of reproductions of seven old cup plates plus a modern Washington souvenir plate, pictured on our Plate 131. The quotation is exact:

"Lacy Sandwich Glass. Precious Little Cup Plates (measurements 3¼″ in diameter). You'll find every one of these listed in the antique glass books. They are currently produced from old molds—even an expert has trouble telling the old ones from these of modern day. Left to right—top row by names: Benjamin Franklin, Bunker Hill, Henry Clay, Butterfly. Bottom row—The Wedding Day and Three Weeks Later, Hearts and Darts, Washington, 1831 Eagle. 8 Assorted to set. $2.50 set."

The "Hearts and Darts" refers to the Valentine. All the reproductions are pictured in this chapter.

A letter to the Better Business Bureau in Boston protesting the statements that these cup plates were made from old molds and that even an expert would have difficulty telling them from the old brought an equally prompt reply from the Bureau stating an investigation had been made and that the writer was correct. The letter stated further that the store under whose name the advertising appeared had acted on information given them by the agent selling them the cup plates and that the glass would not be advertised again in the same manner. A great deal of damage was done, but at least it was stopped quickly. Collectors and dealers alike would be doing an infinite amount of good by reporting to their local Chamber of Commerce or Better Business Bureaus, any similar misstatements.

A Table showing major ingredients, specific gravities, ultraviolet reactions and temperature range of some key cup plates. The working temperatures given represent the ideal and were unobtainable when wood was the fuel.

	R-564-B	R-610-A	R-242	R-670	R-120	R-184-B	R-694	R-585-A
Silica	52.01%	51.69%	50.04%	55.46%	52.60%	57.72%	57.64%	56.68%
Lead Oxide	35.66%	35.40%	35.75%	29.75%	35.14%	28.60%	24.81%	31.64%
Potassium Oxide	9.88%	10.75%	12.52%	11.48%	9.74%	9.64%	11.46%	8.48%
Sodium Oxide	0.91%	0.97%	0.79%	1.60%	1.21%	1.62%	1.62%	1.89%
Major Constituents	98.46%	98.81%	99.1%	98.29%	98.69%	97.58%	98.52%	98.69%
Minor Constituents ...	1.28%	1.19%	0.90%	1.51%	1.31%	2.42%	1.28%	1.47%
Totals	99.74%	100.00%	100.00%	99.80%	100.00%	100.00%	99.80%	100.16%
Specific Gravity	3.1105	3.2267	3.2556	3.0775	3.2222	2.9826	2.9478	3.1172
Ultraviolet Light	(Bluish)	(Bluish)	(Bluish)	(Yellowish Green)	(Bluish) Sl. Purple	(Yellow-green)	(Yellowish Green)	(Bluish)
Softening Point	1970°F.	1820°F.	1845°F.	1725°F.	1925°F.	1860°F.	1665°F.	1695°F.
Working Temp.	2460°F.	2415°F.	2430°F.	2415°F.	2530°F.	2515°F.	2415°F.	2415°F.
Fluid Point	2545°F.	2530°F.	2570°F.	2595°F.	2665°F.	2645°F.	2525°F.	2500°F.

A CROSS INDEX OF MARBLE AND ROSE NUMBERS

In this index Marble numbers are in sequence. Rose numbers are in rotation in the check list. Where a Marble number is followed by asterisks, an explanation will be found at the end of the cross index. In dealers' lists or in correspondence, the system of numbering being used should be indicated by prefixing either "M" or "R," as the case may be, to the number. Thus, the "No Name Clay" can be either M-2 or R-563. See page 424 for explanation of asterisks.

M	R	M	R	M	R	M	R
1	562-A	29	632	56	133	84	225-C
2	563	30	619	57	292	85	225-A
3	565-A	31	625	58	158-B	86	177
4	565-B	32	629	59	162-B	87	890
5	564	33	610-B	60	121	88	439
6	566	34	610	61	151	89	228-A
7	566-A	35	610-A	62	146	90	269
8	566-B	36	***	63	235	91	272
9	662	37	605-A	64	172-B	92	343-B
10	661	38	612-A	65	193	93	275
11	679	39	568	66	124-A	94	258
12	666-A	40	569	67	208	95	46
13	665-A	41	636	68	294	96	45
14	665	42	596	69	171-A	97	44
15	676-C	43	593	70	441	98	242-A
16	676-B	44	590	71	145-C	99	95
17	677	45	594	72	281-B	100	43
18	666-B	46	601-C	73	150	101	32
19	651-A	47	695	74	197-C	102	37
20	680	48	694-A	75	330	103	36
21	667	49	896	76	69	104	33
22	670	50	693	77	155	105	40
23	670-A	51	691	78	154-B	106	41
24	643	52	699	79	65	107	440
25	640	53	697	80	226-A	108	440-B
26	645-A	54	149	81	226-C	109	331
27	641	55	148	82	79	110	276
28	632-A			83	78	111	277

M	R	M	R	M	R	M	R
112	27	156	214-B	200	478	244	520-A
113	28	157	410	201	479	245	676
114	30	158	12	202	477	246	680-B
115	26	159	15	203	447	247	670-C
116	29	160	13-C	204	467*	248	680-E
117	25	161	373	205	465*	249	147
118	22	162	344	206	465-Q	250	130
119	97	163	375	207	476	251	378
120	54	164	48	208	455	252	178-B
121	56	165	233-A	209	455-B	253	412
122	53	166	52	210	456	254	417
123	61	167	299	211	458	255	397
124	20	168	229-A	212	459*	256	495
125	377	169	109	213	457	257	532
126	285	170	107-A	214	***	258	678
127	404	171	216	215	***	259	675-C
128	313	172	416	216	332-A	260	585-C
129	379	173	157	217	323	261	147-C
130	882	174	262	218	324	262	223
131	57	175	415	219	332	263	***
132	62-A	176	425	220	396	264	508
133	310	177	428	221	328	265	617
134	310-A	178	426	222	333	266	686
135	236	179	427	223	549	267	475
136	246	180	80	224	366	268	677-B
137	245	181	390-A	225	364	269	672
138	271-A	182	390	226	365	270	619-B
139	105	183	391	227	547	271	148-B
140	104	184	392	228	516	272	159-A
141	100	185	393	229	517-B	273	202
142	106	186	388	230	504	274	229
143	107	187	342	231	339	275	402
144	244	188	338	232	395	276	341
145	243	189	411	233	517	277	499
146	257	190	76	234	526	278	689
147	47	191	335	235	522	279	129
148	311	192	336	236	531	280	177-A
149	334	193	370	237	538	281	***
150	255	194	369	238	523	282	***
151	179	195	368	239	501	283	162-A
152	174	196	321-B	240	537	284	134-A
153	71	197	322	241	505	285	448
154	66	198	403	242	503	286	191-C
155	240-A	199	892	243	494	287	364-A

M	R	M	R	M	R	M	R
288	637	332	187	376	677-C	420	195
289	135-A	333	592	377	1	421	226
290	49	334	659	378	576	422	674
291	101	335	164-A	379	562	423	142
292	668	336	226-B	380	204	424	159-B
293	50	337	216-C	381	181-A	425	439-C
294	248	338	229-B	382	58	426	296-A
295	260	339	601-B	383	169-A	427	140-A
296	103	340	196	384	89	428	187-A
297	694	341	209	385	435	429	148-C
298	230-B	342	31	386	100-A	430	692
299	127	343	243-B	387	586-B	431	151-A
300	200-A	344	604-A	388	343-A	432	253
301	657	345	654-A	389	10	433	802
302	24	346	179-A	390	680-D	434	156-B
303	136-A	347	42	391	75-A	435	156-A
304	580-A	348	176-A	392	571	436	615-A
305	332-B	349	197	393	631	437	321-A
306	225-B	350	123-A	394	630	438	166-A
307	38	351	122	395	106-A	439	256-A
308	39	352	184-B	396	132	440	445
309	371	353	234	397	675	441	225
310	618	354	160-A	398	541	442	135
311	297	355	381	399	314	443	525
312	418	356	545	400	267	444	677-H
313	340	357	198	401	197-B	445	203
314	502	358	178-A	402	88	446	444
315	98	359	171	403	586-A	447	160-B
316	889	360	158-A	404	92	448	321-D
317	62	361	176-B	405	242	449	154
318	256	362	172-A	406	675-A	450	164-B
319	279	363	154-A	407	604	451	656
320	291	364	191	408	671	452	183
321	162	365	326	409	192	453	188
322	217	366	850	410	145	454	124-C
323	232	367	480	411	254	455	380
324	666	368	141	412	585	456	126
325	217-A	369	284	413	585-A	457	157-A
326	35	370	128	414	180-A	458	125
327	199	371	859	415	677-A	459	169-B
328	561	372	***	416	127-A	460	641-A
329	***	373	206	417	***	461	878
330	231	374	166	418	249	462	67
331	374	375	165	419	120	463	90

M	R	M	R	M	R	M	R
464	673	508	***	552	99	596	269-B
465	126-A	509	320	553	11	597	269-C
466	591	510	175	554	345	598	610-D
467	655	511	667-A	555	215	599	610-C
468	77	512	230	556	614	600	447-A
469	184	513	507	557	158	601	447-B
470	157-B	514	240	558	156	602	191-B
471	232-A	515	160	559	163	603	550
472	136	516	894	560	273	604	619-A
473	828	517	363	561	439-B	605	858
474	233	518	893	562	222	606	123
475	436-A	519	236-A	563	23	607	212
476	817	520	361	564	429	608	624
477	653	521	360	565	280	609	296
478	201	522	172	566	252	610	533
479	167-A	523	546	567	189	611	178
480	210	524	122-B	568	689-A	612	177-B
481	382	525	521	569	108	613	148-A
482	572	526	530	570	867	614	194
483	517-A	527	612	571	70	615	283
484	184-A	528	168-A	572	293	616	216-B
485	853	529	515	573	230-A	617	22-A
486	271	530	677-G	574	319	618	182-A
487	134	531	677-F	575	190	619	643-A
488	***	532	362	576	286	620	642
489	182	533	180	577	433	621	642-A
490	96	534	289	578	565	622	164
491	680-C	535	372	579	272-A	623	***
492	635	536	356	580	21	624	536
493	159	537	535-A	581	22-B	625	321
494	13-B	538	800-A	582	830	626	535
495	220	539	895	583	658	627	518
496	442	540	197-A	584	327	628	526-A
497	140	541	312	585	399	629	544
498	169	542	377-A	586	40-A	630	192-A
499	207	543	898	587	197-D	631	500
500	197-E	544	176	588	519	632	540
501	441-A	545	82	589	214	633	334-A
502	575	546	127-Б	590	250	634	586
503	147-B	547	506	591	443	635	511
504	650	548	800	592	145-B	636	675-B
505	***	549	413	593	124	637	677-D
506	***	550	350	594	183-B	638	147-A
507	865	551	161-A	595	268	639	490

M	R	M	R	M	R	M	R
640	258-A	684	696	728	394	772	145-A
641	315	685	644	729	400	773	310-B
642	136-B	686	534	730	819	774	224
643	242-B	687	852	731	876	775	446
644	211	688	820	732	167	776	439-A
645	318	689	131	733	353	777	645
646	282-A	690	85	734	854	778	***
647	491	691	349	735	436	779	181
648	***	692	561-A	736	167-B	780	863
649	13	693	818	737	624-A	781	51
650	628	694	864	738	440-A	782	87
651	615	695	870	739	580-B	783	871
652	298	696	835	740	573	784	200
653	***	697	827	741	807	785	68
654	191-D	698	348	742	808	786	7
655	498	699	173	743	806	787	185
656	***	700	***	744	205	788	16
657	570	701	825	745	191-E	789	398
658	690	702	384	746	544-A	790	321-C
659	860	703	387	747	520	791	***
660	278	704	841	748	124-B	792	251
661	227-B	705	897	749	263	793	347
662	183-A	706	855	750	816	794	***
663	269-A	707	354	751	221	795	606
664	332-D	708	355	752	170	796	60
665	885	709	358	753	560	797	595
666	346	710	357	754	301	798	34
667	287	711	351	755	229-C	799	804
668	857	712	440-C	756	288	800	105-A
669	826	713	150-A	757	836	801	261
670	376	714	829	758	257-A	802	163-A
671	601-A	715	803	759	72	803	86
672	337	716	389	760	688	804	282
673	150-B	717	851	761	837	805	274
674	669	718	352	762	677-E	806	579
675	107-B	719	359	763	670-B	807	691-A
676	***	720	326-A	764	243-C	808	216-A
677	660	721	838	765	106-B	809	259
678	868	722	548	766	***	810	122-A
679	438	723	265	767	432	811	329
680	247	724	228	768	367	812	524
681	75	725	585-B	769	840	813	265-A
682	281-A	726	166-B	770	168	814	59
683	680-A	727	414	771	41-A	815	574

M	R	M	R	M	R	M	R
816	102	827	270	838	300	849	643-B
817	55	828	269-D	839	401	850	***
818	281	829	213	840	***	851	275-A
819	654	830	241	841	810	852	***
820	625-A	831	815	842	214-A	853	326-B
821	620	832	161	843	191-A	854	801
822	580	833	***	844	227	855	343
823	316	834	651	845	626	856	856
824	656-A	835	386	846	***	857	***
825	605	836	383	847	137	858	84
826	227-A	837	866	848	541-A		

EXPLANATION OF ASTERISKS

M-36   is an octagonal Constitution much like No. 605-A (the rigging is a combination of stippled and plain ropes), but with its masts tilted to the right of center. By our arbitrary definition, tilts are not variants and are not listed.

M-214   is not included in Mr. Marble's second set of photographs. See note on M-215.

M-215   is not included in Mr. Marble's second set of photographs. In the first set of photographs both of these plates were heart-border plates.

M-263   is not included in Mr. Marble's second set of photographs. See notes on M-215.

M-281   is pontil-marked version of No. 32. It should be noted that most plates with pontil marks are slightly larger than their prototypes, due to distortion from the pressure used in applying them to the stem of a stick or lamp. Not infrequently, there is also a lateral distortion of the design. This usually takes the form of swirling. The result is that it is sometimes difficult to number these plates properly. By our definition, pontil marks are not variants.

M-282   is a pontil-marked version of No. 46.

M-329   is an octagonal steamboat much like No. 612-A, with the ship tilted slightly to the right of the horizontal position. See also M-794 below.

M-372   is a 4 3/16″ version of the foreign plate No. 882.

M-417   is a pontil-marked version of No. 28, but see the remarks under M-281.

M-488   is an octagonal Constitution like No. 605-A, tilted to the left of center. The rigging is a combination of stippled and plain ropes.

M-505   is the same as M-402, No. 88, but was listed twice by Mr. Marble to show a difference in color.

M-506   is a pontil-marked version of No. 32.

M-508   is a pontil-marked version of No. 43.

M-623 is an octagonal Constitution much like No. 604-A (the rigging is plain, not stippled), but with its masts tilted very slightly to the right of their position on No. 604-A.

M-648 is a blown glass plate very much like No. 1, but smaller. Its diameter is 3⅜″. The range of sizes in blown cup plates is great.

M-653 is a foreign plate not illustrated.

M-656 is an octagonal Constitution much like No. 605-A (the rigging is a combination of stippled and plain ropes), but with its masts tilted slightly to the left of center.

M-676 is a reproduction. See Plate 127.

M-700 is a large, late commemorative plate. It is a Victorian Jubilee plate and is dated 1887, being thus too late to be of interest to cup plate collectors.

M-766 is a foreign plate. No specimen available to photograph.

M-778 is a variant of the foreign plate, No. 850. It has 50 scallops and measures 3⅞″.

M-791 is a tilted version of the No. 564 Clay.

M-794 is an octagonal Steamboat like No. 612-A, with the boat tilted to the extreme right.

M-833 is a pontil-marked version of the grape eagle, No. 665.

M-840 is a blown glass plate with its pontil-mark ground out and polished.

M-846 is a variant of No. 802 with 77 even scallops and measuring 4 5/16″.

M-850 is an octagonal Constitution similar to No. 604-A (the rigging is plain, not stippled), with its masts tilted to the left of center.

M-852 is a variant of the English plate, No. 876. It has the 16 scallops of No. 876 but there are slight variations in the shoulder pattern.

M-857 is a cut glass plate of too late a vintage to have been used as a cup plate.

INDEX

427